MW00638140

Religious Lessons

Religious Lessons

*Catholic Sisters and the Captured
Schools Crisis in New Mexico*

KATHLEEN HOLSCHER

OXFORD
UNIVERSITY PRESS

OXFORD
UNIVERSITY PRESS

Oxford University Press, Inc., publishes works that further
Oxford University's objective of excellence
in research, scholarship, and education.

Oxford   New York
Auckland   Cape Town   Dar es Salaam   Hong Kong   Karachi
Kuala Lumpur   Madrid   Melbourne   Mexico City   Nairobi
New Delhi   Shanghai   Taipei   Toronto

With offices in
Argentina   Austria   Brazil   Chile   Czech Republic   France   Greece
Guatemala   Hungary   Italy   Japan   Poland   Portugal   Singapore
South Korea   Switzerland   Thailand   Turkey   Ukraine   Vietnam

Published by Oxford University Press, Inc.
198 Madison Avenue, New York, New York 10016

www.oup.com

Oxford is a registered trademark of Oxford University Press

Library of Congress Cataloging-in-Publication Data
Holscher, Kathleen A., 1979–
Religious lessons : Catholic sisters and the captured schools crisis in
New Mexico / Kathleen Holscher.
p.   cm.
Based on doctoral dissertation "Habits in the classroom: A court case
regarding Catholic sisters in New Mexico", Princeton (2008).
Includes bibliographical references (p.   ) and index.
ISBN 978-0-19-978173-7 (hardback : alk. paper) 1. Zellers,
Lydia—Trials, litigation, etc. 2. Huff, Raymond—Trials, litigation, etc.
3. New Mexico. State Board of Education—Trials, litigation, etc.
4. Religion in the public schools—Law and legislation—United States.
5. Church and state—United States. 6. Religion in the public schools—New
Mexico—Dixon—History—20th century. 7. Catholic schools—New
Mexico—Dixon—History—20th century. I. Holscher, Kathleen A., 1979–.
Habits in the classroom. II. Title.
KF228.Z45H65   2012
344.73'07—dc23   2011042915

1 3 5 7 9 8 6 4 2

Printed in the United States of America
on acid-free paper

For my parents

TABLE OF CONTENTS

ACKNOWLEDGMENTS

I learned about the Dixon case nearly a decade ago, and I've been thinking about how to tell its story ever since. Doing history is always collaborative, and the account I offer here is a product of all the people I've talked with, shown my work to, and received support and guidance from along the way. The religion department at Princeton University was this project's first home. I am especially grateful for the help of my advisor there, Leigh Schmidt, who helped me to believe early on that an obscure court case like *Zellers v. Huff* could be the subject of more than just a passable dissertation. Leigh has always had the uncanny ability to understand my thought process when I research and write. His creativity, enthusiastic and disciplined curiosity, and respectful attention to the lives of his subjects have all inspired my work. I also thank Marie Griffith, who read several early versions of this story and who offered me, the historian, her sage advice as an ethnographer when it came to working with living sources. In addition, I'm grateful to Albert Raboteau, Eddie Glaude, and Judith Weisenfeld, all of whom read and commented on early versions of the project. While still in graduate school, I was fortunate to receive a Mellon /ACLS Dissertation Completion Fellowship, which let me dedicate a full year to writing and allowed me to spend chunks of time in Santa Fe closer to my source material. I also received support and stimulating feedback on early chapter drafts during my participation in the Religion and Culture Workshop at Princeton's Center for the Study of Religion.

I have gained a great deal in other academic settings as well. A conference on race and ethnicity in the American West, sponsored by Arizona State University in 2006, helped me develop my ideas about New Mexico's Hispano population. The triennial Conference on the History of Women Religious, at the University of Notre Dame in 2007, gave me the opportunity to start thinking about the Catholic sisters at the heart of my project. I am also grateful to the Cushwa Center for the Study of American Catholicism at the University of Notre Dame for inviting me to present my research there in 2008, and especially to Timothy Matovina, Kathleen Sprows Cummings, and Linda Przybyszewski, who gave me their feedback on different parts of the book, but especially on the captive schools discussion that turned into its fourth chapter. I also had the privilege along the way of presenting portions of this project at the annual meeting of the Popular Culture and American Culture Associations, at the American Catholic Historical Society, and at the Fray Angélico Chávez History Library; as well as to faculty at the history department of the University of Michigan, the religious studies department at the University of Texas, and the history department, religious studies program, and American studies program at the University of New Mexico. The conversations that happened as part of those experiences made this project into something richer.

Over the past several years my academic home has been the Department of Theology and Religious Studies at Villanova University. I've benefited in all sort of ways from the support of my department and from the advice of colleagues there. I'm particularly indebted to Bernard Prusak, Tim Brunk, Bill Werpehowski, Rodger Van Allen, and Gustavo Benevides for their input into this book and their support during the writing process. I'm grateful to Peter Spitaler for inviting me to present my work during 2010 as part of our department's graduate colloquium, and to the graduate students who have given me their feedback, both directly as part of the colloquium and indirectly during my coursework with them. Many colleagues outside of my home institution have also supported this project. I am especially grateful for the generous feedback I've received from Tisa Wenger and Joshua Dubler, and for the formative conversations I've had with Andrea Sun-Mee Jones, Christopher Garces, Lisa Cerami, Laura Bennett, Heather White, Devon Powers, and Shreena Gandhi. Sarah Barringer Gordon has played a remarkably important role in my research and writing. I first encountered the Dixon case while reading Paul Blanshard's *American Freedom and Catholic Power* at Sally's recommendation. She's been an enthusiastic advocate for this project from day one, and has demonstrated her generous nature over and over again. Above all, she's offered me guidance on how to be a competent religion scholar in a legal scholar's world (and I hope I've managed to heed it). I was also the beneficiary of both her professional connections and her personal company one spring day when we drove south in search of a dusty old film reel.

I'd like to acknowledge Adam Sarapa of Americans United for Separation of Church and State, who gamely helped us locate that reel; Daniel Linke at Princeton's Mudd Library, who just as gamely oversaw its conversion onto DVD; and Amanda Pike and the media services staff at Princeton University, who provided me with photographic stills from it. I have also been the beneficiary of other displays of archival generosity. I was received graciously by staff at the archives of the Archdiocese of Santa Fe, Catholic University of America, the Menaul School, and—time and time again—the clerk's office and law library at the Supreme Court of New Mexico. It's especially important that I acknowledge the assistance of Tomas Jaehn at the Fray Angélico Chávez History Library, whom I met by accident one afternoon in Santa Fe, and who went above and beyond the demands of scholarly courtesy when he offered me his translation of Peter Küppers' unpublished memoir (written originally in German), as well as personal photographs of the priest. Tomas is a fine historian, and I'm lucky to rely on his work as source material. I also owe a special measure of thanks to the Dominican sisters of Grand Rapids, Michigan, who graciously hosted me at their Marywood convent in 2006 and made me feel at home with their stories about New Mexico. Most of all I am grateful to the community's archivist, Sister Michael Ellen Carling, who has continued to show me her generosity, most recently by providing me with photographs of the women who taught in New Mexico in the 1940s.

I have had dozens of conversations, formal and informal, with people in New Mexico about their memories of the *Zellers* case. This book would be impossible without the generosity of residents of Dixon and Peñasco, New Mexico, many of whom invited me into their homes and talked with me about their experiences as children. I am especially grateful to Lucy Rendon of the Dixon/Rio Arriba County Senior Center, who coordinated my visit there in the summer of 2010; to Viela Gonzales, who made sure I was always well fed during my days of research; and to the members of the center, who gave me good company and a lesson or two in competitive bingo. I'm thankful also to the members of the Embudo Presbyterian Church for inviting me to talk with them. Most of all, I'm grateful for the warm hospitality of Kathy and Tiffin Zellers. Kathy in particular has helped me to accurately present the hard work of her mother-in-law, Lydia, in this book's pages.

I reworked several chapters of this book into an article (Kathleen Holscher, "Contesting the Veil in America: Catholic Habits and the Controversy Over Religious Clothing in the United States," *Journal of Church and State* 54, no. 1 (Winter 2012): 57–81)." In the work of producing the book itself, I'm especially thankful to my editor Theo Calderara at Oxford University Press. He took an interest in the project while several different parts of it were still in pieces, and he's always been charitable with deadline extensions, and prompt, wise, and good natured in answering my questions, as I've worked to make it whole. More recently, Lisbeth Redfield and Pamela Hanley have offered me equally sound guidance through the book's copy editing and production process.

I owe the most gratitude of all to my family. Fernando Indacochea and Rossana Broggi have opened their home in West Virginia as a haven whenever I've needed a change of scenery to clear my head. My brother Nate has always shared my interest in both religion and the American Southwest, and he's given me valuable perspective in conversations about locating one's profession and art in the channels of one's life. In recent months, he and Emily Heintzelman have welcomed me at their new home in Albuquerque. My parents, Marilyn and Rory Holscher, have helped me through every stage of this project. My mother flew down to Santa Fe with me years ago, just because I was curious about the Dixon case and wanted to find out if the transcript to the *Zellers* trial still existed (it did). As I was madly finishing revisions on this book, she flew out to Philadelphia to provide emotional support and a week's worth of home-cooked meals. My father has offered me his ear and his exceptional insight during long talks and on long runs. His talents for close reading, and for identifying unexpected qualities in ordinary things, have shaped my understanding of many parts of this history. I'm incredibly fortunate to have family who are both my support system and my best conversation partners. Finally, I'm so grateful to my husband, Alonso Indacochea. Alonso has done a thousand different things over the past decade, in Philadelphia and New Mexico, to help this book enter the world. He has watched me wrestle this story, and stood reassuringly in my corner on days I'd feared I'd lost, and on days I'd felt I'd won. The promise of a walk with Alonso and our dogs has always helped me to keep my head up, and find my way through the writing process. This book wouldn't exist without him.

Religious Lessons

Introduction

Victoria Johnson sat in a crowded courtroom. It was late September and to alleviate stuffiness the room's windows had been thrown open to cooler air and the smell of the chile harvest roasting across Santa Fe. Inside Victoria was answering questions put to her by an attorney named Harry Bigbee. As the courtroom's audience listened closely Bigbee pressed the young Presbyterian mother to recall details about her family's life in the New Mexican village of Dixon. He asked her to remember the sorts of things her children had learned while attending public school there. "Did they bring any literature home [from school] with them?" he wondered at one point.

"Yes, my son did," Victoria recollected. "He had a sister for a teacher at the time, and he brought home . . . several different pamphlets, and also a—" here she paused, fumbling for the correct word—"something they hang around their necks with a cross around that they have to wear it continually. I had him take it back," she added.

> "Did they recite any prayers they learned in school?" Bigbee asked.
> "Yes. . . . The Hail Mary was one I can distinctly remember."
> "Did you ever talk to any of the Sisters about this?"

"Yes," again was Victoria's emphatic reply. Her words tumbled now. "My son came home one evening, and was very upset. Sister Dorothy, I believe it was, had taken my son by the arm and ushered him into the Catholic Church . . . and told him he was going to Confession, otherwise he would be punished. He was very upset about it. So the next morning I made it a point to see Sister Seferina, the principal at that time, and I spoke to her and she said there would be something done about it. That was all—that was all she said."[1]

Victoria Johnson made these allegations about public education in her hometown during a nine-day trial in a case called *Zellers v. Huff*. The *Zellers* litigation began in the spring of 1948 when some of Johnson's neighbors in Dixon filed a complaint with the district court in Santa Fe. Like Johnson, the men and women who brought the lawsuit worried about the influence of Roman Catholicism on their children. They hoped they could convince the court to break up an alarming pattern of cooperation between public educators and the Catholic Church in their state. Above all they aimed to get rid of dozens of New Mexico's hybrid "public–parochial" schools. These schools were funded by tax money but they were administered and

taught by Catholic religious. For decades public–parochial institutions had provided education to students throughout many of the state's poorest counties. As a
result, *Zellers* was a massive piece of litigation. The complaint cited schools in more
than two dozen districts in New Mexico and its list of two hundred and thirty-five
defendants was a Who's Who of state politicos, from county school board members
all the way up to the governor himself. These public officials were outnumbered in
the complaint, however, by Catholic religious. The *Zellers* suit implicated two priests
and thirteen religious brothers. It also implicated one hundred and thirty-one Catholic sisters who worked as public teachers in New Mexico.[2]

While New Mexico was remarkable at mid-century for the extent of Catholic
involvement in its schools, the public–parochial institutions in the state were not
unique. The teachers named in the *Zellers* lawsuit in 1948 were part of a nationwide
body of Catholic religious professionals participating in American public education. While arrangements that put Catholic priests, brothers, and especially sisters
in public classrooms had antecedents stretching back to the nineteenth century,
they were never more common than during the 1940s and 1950s. Between 1945
and 1960 some two thousand Catholic sisters, along with a small handful of clergy
and male religious, were employed as public teachers in the United States.[3] Running
classrooms from Kentucky to Colorado, these individuals caught the attention of a
segment of the American public that was deeply troubled by both the legal and
moral implications of an educational system left directly in the hands (so it seemed)
of the Catholic Church. These concerns were expressed by people like Victoria Jackson, who lived in the school districts where religious taught, but they were amplified
and organized into a national movement by a Washington-based advocacy group
called Protestants and Other Americans United for Separation of Church and State
(POAU). Through the late 1940s and 1950s POAU's leadership set its sights upon
sister-led institutions like the ones in New Mexico. Denouncing them as evidence of
a national crisis of "captive schools," the organization made it its mission to expose
and fix these collaborative arrangements where it could find them.

The "Dixon case"—as *Zellers* was popularly named—was the largest of dozens of
litigation efforts that POAU sponsored in its drive to eliminate Catholic women religious from American public education. The group wasn't alone in its brand of advocacy work; the middle decades of the twentieth century were filled with all kinds of
activity devoted to church–state questions. Most of this activity was bent on figuring
what support, if any, the government should be giving to religion. At no time since
the nation's founding was the First Amendment's Establishment Clause studied so
carefully by the American courts and by the American people. This scrupulous environment was inspired and exemplified by a pair of U.S. Supreme Court decisions, in
Everson v. Board of Education in 1947 and *McCollum v. Board of Education* in 1948.
The Supreme Court stipulated in *Everson* and then demonstrated in *McCollum* that
the Establishment Clause required no less than a "wall of separation" to keep apart
church and state. By incorporating Thomas Jefferson's architectural metaphor into

First Amendment jurisprudence, the Court's decisions inaugurated a generation of earnest if sometimes fixated legal conversations about the place of religion in American public life. More than a half-century later, the controversies it considered in *Everson* and *McCollum*—over the use of public funds for busing parochial students and over the release of students from public classrooms so they might receive religious instruction in their schools—are the episodes that define that era's stormy church–state contests. In contrast, POAU's captive schools and the women who taught in them have fallen by the historical wayside—this in spite of the fact litigation that challenged sister-taught schooling was more common than either busing or released time lawsuits during the 1940s and 1950s.[4]

Sister-taught schooling cases are unfamiliar because they never left the state courts. In New Mexico, the *Zellers* lawsuit had consequences. After listening to the evidence presented by Victoria Jackson and other witnesses, the judge presiding at trial concluded that any "reasonable person" who visited schools named in the complaint would concede that church–state separation in New Mexico was "a mirage."[5] As a result he barred most of the implicated religious from future employment in the state. Reviewing the case two years later, New Mexico's supreme court issued a broader indictment of sister-led public education. "In short," the court wrote, "New Mexico has a Roman Catholic school system supported by public funds within its public school system."[6] The high court used *Zellers* as an opportunity to comment on the legality of *all* Catholic religious who worked as public employees. No matter how carefully a sister conducted her classroom, its panel of justices concluded, her very appearance—the visual impression that she made—was a breach of the state and federal constitutions. Citing Catholic influence embedded in the distinctive cloth habits sisters wore, the court banned any teacher dressed in "religious garb" from work in the state's schools.[7] Despite this provocative assertion about what church–state separation demanded, however, *Zellers v. Huff* never left New Mexico's courts, and so its anti-garb pronouncement was never binding beyond the state. Courts who heard captive school suits in other states during the same period handed down decisions that like *Zellers* weighed the constitutionality of teaching sisters' costumes. But those cases never reached the U.S. Supreme Court either. The captive school era came and went without a federal court commenting on the presence of sisters or their clothing in public classrooms. The frequency of these lawsuits during the 1940s and 1950s, coupled with their absence from federal case law, prompted one prominent political scholar to describe sister-taught public schools as the "major 'nonissue' in the constitutional law of church-state relations."[8]

This book is the story of the best-known fight over Catholic sisters teaching publicly. Even though *Zellers v. Huff* was a constitutional "nonissue," its litigation and the hubbub that attended it said every bit as much about the church–state relationship within the lives and imaginations of Americans as did precedent-setting cases of the period. The details of the Dixon case were familiar to hundreds of thousands of people who read about them in magazines and newspapers and heard them discussed in church on Sunday mornings. The startling and vivid scenario of Catholic nuns in habits teaching children like Victoria Johnson's son provoked a feeling of urgency in its audience that bus transportation and released time disputes could not.[9] The Dixon case caught the attention of both Catholics and non-Catholics, and it drew reactions from experts in constitutional law as well as citizens who otherwise had little interest in constitutional debates. For many Americans at mid-century, New Mexico's schools and the women who taught in them—rather than the dry discourse of the Supreme Court—embodied the high stakes of church–state conflicts. Because the litigation touched so many people, inside and outside of New Mexico, and because it touched a nerve with many whom it involved, the Dixon case is an opportunity for surveying the dispositions and predilections—often formed by religious experience—that motivated public participation in mid-century church–state disputes. The following chapters recount conversations and activities that oriented Americans in their thinking about the relationship of the Catholic Church to children's schooling, and that intersected during the *Zellers* lawsuit in 1948. Taken together these accounts demonstrate the energy that people of different backgrounds, from Washington attorneys to Catholic sisters to Spanish-speaking residents in New Mexico, exerted to work out the proper role of the church vis-à-vis the state. They also disclose what Clifford Geertz called the forms of "local knowledge," many of them rooted in religion, which informed these men, women, and children in their legal work.[10]

Two arguments frame the book. First, sister-taught schooling disputes like New Mexico's represent a transitional moment in the Protestant–Catholic conflicts that make up so much of American church–state history. For this reason, they complicate the oppositional framework that religious and legal historians tend to use when they describe those conflicts. The Dixon case *did* pit Catholics against Protestants—diametrically so. The Protestant and Catholic advocacy groups who battled one another in *Zellers* and similar episodes, however, also had something important in common. Advocates on either side insisted on evaluating the rightness or wrongness of sister-taught schools using religious dictates as their points of reference. Their shared adamancy that these religious viewpoints had a place within judicial contests over the Establishment Clause was noteworthy at a moment when many in the American legal community—including its high court—appeared, to the chagrin of devout Protestants as well as Catholics, to be moving toward the conclusion that secularism was the only constitutional future for public education in the United States.[11] In this sense, captive school conflicts happened along multiple fronts at once. They pitted Protestants against Catholics, but they also saw Protestants and Catholics similarly pitted against—and articulating legal ideas in opposition to—the specter of a non-religious public sphere. Although this similarity went unrecognized at the time, it presaged the open alliance between conservative Protestants and Catholics that would rock the nation's political landscape during the "culture wars" of the second half of the twentieth century.[12]

My second argument is methodological. Disputes like the one I describe here are inscrutable from a historical perspective that limits itself to the ideas of legal experts. To make sense of sister-taught schools requires a sufficiently catholic model of legal discourse—of the types of people who participate in it and the sorts of motivations that drive it. Likewise it requires a movement beyond ideas themselves as a starting place for studying the separation of church and state. The Dixon case enacted the Supreme Court's interpretation of the Establishment Clause upon tens of thousands of Americans. Unlike advocacy groups who argued systematically about separation's meaning at mid-century, many of these people didn't hold fixed convictions about the correct position of the church when it came to functions of the state. They did, however, hold a stake in the debates happening around them. For Catholics especially, the church–state relationship was often embedded within, and enacted through, activities and experiences—everything from the lessons they learned as children to the friendships and occupations they pursued as adults. Though these Americans never thought much about separation *in principle*, the things they did in their lives made them interested parties in its negotiation. Developing an account of mid-century church–state litigation that is inclusive enough to consider the population it affected requires us to look past forms of legal knowledge that privilege belief to also consider the practices—the habits—that made the church–state relationship real and relevant for many people. This movement from belief to practice is already familiar territory in the study of religion; here it's relevant to the study of law as well. The thousands of people who, in one way or another, became involved in litigation in New Mexico in 1948 were just a fraction of the millions of Americans for whom the law was less about judicial doctrine than it was about social practice.

The story of the Dixon case begins in New Mexico. The desert in the north-central part of that state is broken by high, rugged terrain. Two ranges—the western Jemez Mountains and the taller Sangre de Cristos to the east—mottle the landscape into ridges that parallel one another and then turn to converge as they wear down near Santa Fe. Between them is a swath of lowland in the rough shape of an arrow and narrowest at its southern end. This area, a part of the Upper Rio Grande Basin, is a unique topographic district, and through the twentieth century scholars of the region claimed it as a distinct ethno-cultural district as well.[13] As the Rio Grande runs south through the Basin's main valley it's joined by spring and mountain run-off-fed tributaries. This water has nourished the succession of peoples who have called the Basin home. Ancestors of the Pueblo Indians settled in the Rio Grande valley some two millennia ago; today their descendents live in the linguistically heterogeneous pueblos that extend to the north and west of Albuquerque and Santa Fe. The Spaniards and *criollos* who began arriving in the region in the sixteenth century established their own institutions along the river, and their descendents still occupy land granted to their families by the governments of Spain and later Mexico.[14] Around the turn of the twentieth century, a small but visible population of Anglos—missionaries, artists, and fortune hunters—took up residence in the Basin as well.

The most visible Anglos in the Basin during the first half of the twentieth century were Catholic sisters. Unmistakable even at a distance in their voluminous black, brown, or white habits, the women religious were everyday sights in northern New Mexico. Their veiled faces were especially familiar to children. Nuns taught publicly in twenty-six different New Mexican communities in the 1940s.[15] They worked as far away as Tucumcari to the east and Carrizozo to the distant south, but in the northern part of the state they were a critical mass. In the 1940s at least sixteen villages scattered across the Basin and its surrounding mountains had public schools run by sisters. Eight of these communities were contained within just two counties—Rio Arriba and Taos. In the village of Chama in Rio Arriba County, Franciscan sisters arrived from St. Louis in 1942 to teach in the local school. In Parkview (now Los Ojos) and Tierra Amarilla, a group of Indiana Franciscans had been employed since 1918 and 1923 respectively.[16] In the villages of San Juan, Abiquí, Peñasco, and Ranchos de Taos, Dominican sisters originally from Grand Rapids, Michigan, had a reputation for outstanding public teaching. And in Dixon, which was nestled on a river junction at the Basin's heart, a third community of Franciscans was the most recent cadre of teaching religious to set up shop in the region.

Like other people who lived in the rural villages of northern New Mexico, most of Dixon's residents spoke Spanish as their first language. When it came to religion, however, similarities between Dixon and Catholic enclaves elsewhere in the Basin ended. Only half of Dixon's residents identified as Catholic, while the other half were Protestants—the legacy of turn-of-the-century Presbyterian missions in the region. Competition between Catholics and Protestants surfaced all the time in Dixon, especially when its residents broached the topic of schools. In 1941 an intractable priest named of Peter Küppers persuaded the Rio Arriba County school board to close Dixon's public school and send its students to a nearby parochial one. The county agreed to recognize St. Joseph's Catholic school as Dixon's new—and only—public institution, and it began to pay the Franciscans who were already teaching in it for their services. Protestant parents were furious at the arrangement and before long several of the village's prominent residents, led by a young mother named Lydia Cordova Zellers, organized as the Dixon Free Schools Committee. In the spring of 1948 the committee formalized its grievances with Küppers and the county board with the complaint it filed in Santa Fe.

While the Franciscans' work with Protestant youth in Dixon was the immediate reason for the Free School Committee's action, its lawsuit made bigger allegations about church–state collusion. Its statewide scope and its long list of defendants were possible because of support that came to the committee from outside New Mexico. In the wake of the *Everson* decision, national organizations that promoted

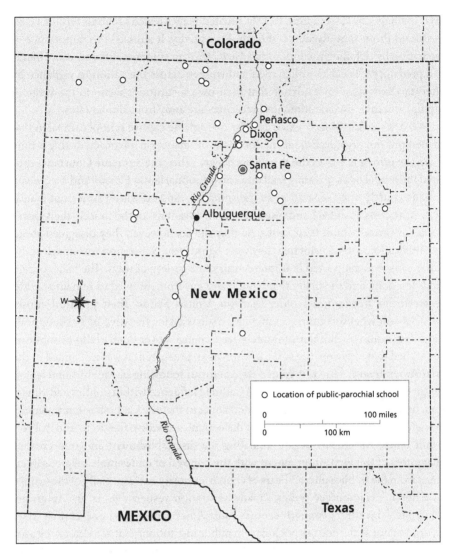

Figure I.1 Religious-taught public schools in New Mexico c. 1948.

church–state separation were looking for opportunities to clear the residue of sectarian influence from public education. POAU was the newest player in this game and its work had a singular target. Its leadership—a coalition of nationally recognized Protestant ministers—vowed to defend against "a powerful church . . . committed in authoritative declarations and by positive acts to a policy plainly subversive of religious liberty as guaranteed by the Constitution."[17] Within weeks of its founding, the organization made the Dixon lawsuit its flagship project and a *cause célèbre*. POAU sent lawyers to New Mexico and promoted the controversy there to an enormous network of supporters across the country. In books and magazine articles,

mass mailings, and later a film, POAU situated New Mexico's schools within a centuries-old Protestant discourse of Catholic captivity. It stressed the importance of
separation by detailing the indignities New Mexican students suffered at the hands
of a predatory Church. It called men and women across the nation to vigilance by
offering Dixon as grim evidence that their own institutions were on the verge of
capture and their own children just a teacher-hire away from similar fates.

POAU's work in New Mexico and the nationwide captive school campaign that
ensued put the organization at the forefront of separation advocacy during a time
when the principle was in the throes of change. When the Supreme Court incorporated the model of a separating wall into constitutional law in *Everson* and *McCollum*,
it made church–state separation an indisputable standard within American education. Advocates at POAU and elsewhere took advantage of the muscle the Court's
decisions threw behind their cause. As they did so, however, they disagreed about
the implications of the principle they were fighting for. Separation was imagined by
Americans who supported it at mid-century in a variety of ways. The value of religious freedom, and the belief that church and government need to remain apart to
preserve this freedom, are older than the United States. Their practical consequences—or what sort of arrangement a person is asking for when he or she appeals
for the exclusion of church from state—have changed over time. Philip Hamburger
has argued that, early on, the value of church–state separation was not linked to the
First Amendment; rather, it gained its American following in the mid-nineteenth
century as a reaction to the prospect of Catholic influence within politics and education. In the face of Irish immigration, and concern that the Catholicism immigrants
brought with them might destroy both the nation's individual freedoms and its Protestant ethos, Americans began conflating the disestablishment and free exercise
guarantees of the First Amendment with the removal of undesirable religious influences from the public sphere. "Fears of church authority and especially of the Catholic Church," Hamburger writes, "made separation respectable as an 'American'
principle."[18] Into the twentieth century most Americans understood church–state
separation not as the erasure of God from public institutions, but as a defense against
forms of religion that could pervert the Christian morals those institutions were
expected to promote. In these imaginings, mainstream Protestantism remained
exempt from scrutiny. Religion, insofar as it was a problem, translated to sectarianism. In most places sectarianism was code for Catholicism.

Though still popular in the 1940s and 1950s, this Protestant reading of separation was being challenged in a way it hadn't been before. Over the first decades
of the century, more and more American liberals—Protestants, Jews, and nonreligious citizens—had begun to argue that church–state separation demanded
not only nonsectarian but non-*religious* public spaces. Although these liberal
separationists remained a minority, *Everson* and especially *McCollum* buoyed
their cause. When the Court made separation a guiding value in First Amendment jurisprudence, it introduced a robust constitutional standard, one this group

rightly anticipated might extend to all organized religious activity in public classrooms. In the first decade after *Everson* and *McCollum*, prayer and Bible reading remained a part of state-sponsored education. By the early 1960s, however, the Court would revisit its decisions, and use them as precedent to remove the vestiges of Christian worship from the nation's schools.[19] In the interim between *Everson* and the Supreme Court's rulings on prayer and Bible reading, liberal and conservative separationists went back and forth about the implications of the Court's wall. The former insisted it required an across-the-board exclusion of religion from public classrooms. The latter hung onto a Protestant-friendly view of separation; these advocates denounced calls for anything stronger as promoting what they described as anti-religious secularism. Both groups held out hope they could define the limits of the new wall accordingly.

While several of POAU's founders fell into the liberal separationist camp, much of its early membership remained committed to a Protestant-centric reading of the principle. Disputes like Dixon helped its leadership find the common ground between these views. Extending his thesis to the twentieth century, Hamburger situates the separation impulses that drove the *Everson* era as late examples in the long and vaguely nativistic push against Catholicism.[20] The rhetoric POAU used during captive school episodes seems to support this claim. Despite conflicting ideas among its members, POAU presented a unified front against sister-taught public schools. The captivity stories its supporters told about these institutions placed the organization and its work in a well-known tradition of Protestant objections to the Catholic Church. At the same time, POAU's captive schools crusade was more than the last hurrah in a long Protestant campaign against Catholicism in the American public sphere. It was also an indicator that many Catholics and Protestants were beginning to share interests within the negotiation of church and state. POAU found its main opponent in an organization called the National Catholic Welfare Conference (NCWC). Even as POAU battled the NCWC over New Mexican schools, the groups had things in common in how they fought. Captive schools conflicts became occasions for both POAU and the NCWC to employ, and publicly promote, traditionally religious modes of evaluating church–state relations in a period marked by formidable secular alternatives. Sister-taught institutions made powerful impressions—as right or wrong, wholesome or corrupt—on the men and women who encountered them. Those impressions had roots in a person's underlying sensibilities about things like the purpose of schooling and the function of the state. For a range of Americans at mid-century, those sensibilities were still cultivated by and within the religious traditions to which they belonged. When POAU and the NCWC made their arguments for and against publicly teaching sisters in 1948, they tested the legal relevance of such sensibilities against one another *and* against the Supreme Court's recent reading of the Establishment Clause.

For the mixed membership of POAU, sister-taught institutions offered a navigable bridge between a Protestant past and a more secular future. The organization promoted the Dixon case so enthusiastically because its details spoke to the multiple constituencies within POAU's own ranks—to religiously oriented separationists, to secularly oriented separationists, and to those who hesitated somewhere in between. Its litigation held the differences between these impulses at bay and offered the Protestant-minded advocates who formed the organization's base a last-minute opportunity to shape the public conversation about church and state in the years after *Everson* and *McCollum*. By promoting captive schools, POAU kept both the public's and the judiciary's attention trained on Catholic assaults upon the separation principle. Paradoxically, the Protestant worldview embedded in the publicity that surrounded these schools helped to prevent—or at least delay—scrutiny of the lingering Protestantism within American education. The dilatory effect of captive schools was neither tactical nor even fully recognized by POAU's own membership. In distracting its audiences from questions about Protestantism within American public life, the organization did an even better job of distracting itself. Serious concerns about Catholic power motivated POAU's campaign. It just so happened that those concerns displaced its members' occasional uneasiness about the principle they were fighting for.

On the Catholic side *Zellers* was an occasion for equally earnest reflection on the mutual relationship of church and state. Responsibility for managing the sisters' defense in New Mexico fell to the Washington-based NCWC. The NCWC was at mid-century the institutional clearinghouse for social policy and engagement within the American Church, and its legal department had the hefty job of advising dioceses across the country troubled by church–state matters. Its attorneys poured their energy into developing a Catholic position in the Establishment Clause debates. Unlike their counterparts at POAU, these NCWC personnel were explicit that their fight to preserve Catholic participation within public education was part and parcel of a struggle against secularism. In their efforts to defend sister-taught schools they asserted readings of the First Amendment that, had they managed to sway the nation's judiciary, would have preserved a place not only for Catholicism but for religion generally within public classrooms. While the religious rhetoric POAU employed during captive school conflicts helped it to avoid directly engaging a secular separation model, the legal minds at the NCWC hoped they could apply a Catholic framework as a means to engage that same model. Insofar as its attorneys represented the Church's official interests, however, their bid at crafting a position on the First Amendment was handicapped from the start. For the Catholic hierarchy the religion clauses of the U.S. Constitution represented both a logistical and a theological headache. Between 1940 and 1960 the Catholic population in the United States doubled.[21] Baby boom children represented most of this growth, and they placed unprecedented demand on Catholic schools as they grew up. Given the circumstances, Catholic leaders all over the country, from local school officials to powerful cardinals, were agitating for funding and other forms of public support to bolster Catholic education. The Church tolerated collaborative arrangements even when they were legally problematic; unlike the American government, the Catholic Church at mid-century didn't recognize any inherent value in either religious liberty or church–state separation. The absence of these principles from Catholic doctrine stymied the NCWC's legal department as it tried to defend teaching sisters. Its attorneys found it impossible to develop a position within the era's First Amendment debates that was both constitutionally compelling and consistently Catholic.

Despite the best efforts of the NCWC and POAU to frame sister-taught schooling conflicts using religious points of reference, in the end their participation in *Zellers* and the suits that followed helped make a secular model of separation reality for both organizations. For the NCWC, the insufficiency of Catholic assertions about church and state within the American judiciary was evident when it failed to exculpate its clients in *Zellers*. The organization acknowledged as much by coaching American sisters who were teaching elsewhere to withdraw from public employment—even in states where their legal status was still an open question. For POAU, capitulation to a secular model of church and state happened a decade later, when the arguments for separation it had helped to promote in its fight against captive schools appeared in litigation that sought to abolish prayer and Bible reading from public education. True to its separationist mission, the organization eventually threw its support behind the suits that took aim at Christian practices. As historian Sarah Barringer Gordon recently put it:

> POAU said again and again [that church–state separation] meant that religious influences within public schools violated the establishment clause. Their own work contributed to the erosion of legal standards that had silently yet effectively screened the kind of religious education that most POAU members thought should be supported by public funds.[22]

In this way, captive schooling disputes signaled a gradual transition for advocacy organizations on both sides of the issue toward recognition—in practice if not always in principle—of a constitutional model of separation that mandated non-religious public classrooms.

Interest in *Zellers* extended beyond advocacy groups. With its massive scope, and following as closely as it did after *Everson* and *McCollum*, the case introduced the Supreme Court's language of a separating wall to thousands of Americans. It required Catholics in some parts of the country to assess for the first time the function and value of separation in their lives. Through the first half of the twentieth century, the American public regarded the principle with a mixture of enthusiasm, skepticism, and indifference. For a generation of Protestants, separating church from state was an imperative that had never been dearer; never more a part of the nation's moral fabric, never more realizable, and never more threatened. As

Hamburger describes this period: "an ever wider range of Americans both agitated for separation and self-consciously attempted to live in accord with this principle. As a result, growing numbers . . . became aware of the tensions raised by separation and thought about them in detailed, concrete ways."[23] Most Catholics in the United States had a different experience. For many of them the impulse to keep church and state apart was unpalatable. For some it was flat-out incomprehensible. For every American during the first part of the century who offered up detailed and concrete reflections on the principle—on its significance to the nation and what behaviors it should (and should not) govern—there were others for whom church–state separation had little or no intrinsic value. These men and women, if they thought about it at all, disregarded it as a remote concept with only marginal relevance to their daily lives.

For many Catholics, separation became relevant only after the *Everson* and *McCollum* decisions. *Everson* did more than create a constitutional mandate for separation; it also stipulated for the first time that the Establishment Clause applied to state education laws.[24] Although most states already had language prohibiting sectarianism in their constitutions and school codes, with *Everson* they became subject both to the First Amendment's religion clauses and to the high court's standard for what those clauses demanded. This development forced lots of Catholic communities to face the prospect of introducing separation into their schools. While most Catholic families in the United States had been required to choose between parochial and public education for decades, tens of thousands of parents and students who relied on Catholic religious in their public schools did not.[25] By pressing states on their obligation to uphold the Supreme Court's wall in the years after *Everson*, captive schooling lawsuits brought separation to these Catholics across the country and made them aware of its weight and consequences. The Dixon case effected church–state separation in the lives of more of them than any other. For its New Mexican participants, *Zellers* didn't start as a symposium on a legal principle. It was first and foremost a troubling episode in the local culture—a commentary on religious differences that had fractured historically Catholic villages since the arrival of Protestant missions in the nineteenth century, on ethnically rooted disagreements that destabilized the state's civic and ecclesiastic institutions, and on the poverty of Spanish-speaking residents and their reactions to it in the absence of innate loyalty to either American common schooling models or constitutional law. For New Mexico's sisters the lawsuit was also a commentary on the challenges of behaving in ways that satisfied both the demands of their religious vows and the expectations of their employers. In New Mexico—which had become a state only in 1912—debates over separation were spread across the front pages of newspapers. They were argued hotly by all sides. But the people who lived there got invested in those debates for fundamentally different reasons than the advocacy groups who intervened in *Zellers*.

During the first half of the twentieth century, people who lived as Spanish Americans and people who lived as Native Americans usually had different schooling experiences. In New Mexico as elsewhere, American Indian education was governed by the federal rather than the state government. For this reason, Native American children rarely attended New Mexico's sister-taught public schools.[26] Nearly all the New Mexicans who had a personal stake in the contested schools were Spanish American. Most Hispanos supported the presence of women religious in their local institutions.[27] From the nineteenth century through the 1940s, these native-born residents demonstrated general disregard for the principle of church–state separation whenever it showed up in the laws of their territory and later their state. This disregard didn't mean New Mexico's inhabitants were cavalier when it came to education—especially in rural areas, parents sometimes went to extraordinary lengths to make sure their sons and daughters attended school. Nor did it imply a simple allegiance between Hispano New Mexicans and the Catholic Church. Though religious loyalties were important in the Rio Grande Basin, the interests of the mainly Catholic people who lived there were a world away from those of the Church's hierarchy and the NCWC's attorneys. New Mexico's Hispano population had a history of butting heads with the Archbishop of Santa Fe over schooling. For adults and especially for children, Catholic sisters inhabited a complicated psychological space, which in turn guided local opinion on their place in the schools. The women inspired a respect among their pupils that was heartfelt and that also carried with it unpleasant feelings like confusion, fear, or shame. Even in the context of these charged relationships, however, most parents and students approved of their teachers. Collective skepticism about Anglo biases in the state's public system paired with the predominant faith to make sister-taught classrooms desirable arrangements in more than two dozen Hispano communities. The obvious exception was Dixon, where in the 1940s a group of Spanish-speaking Protestants tapped a different sort ethnic–religious alliance to develop arguments in favor of separation, and to agitate for the expulsion of sisters from their schools.

The Catholic women religious who worked in New Mexico also negotiated separation differently than the Church personnel advocating on their behalf. For sisters, public teaching was a necessary part of educating Catholics in the postwar era, even as the rules of Catholic religious life during those years made public work difficult. As the postwar baby boom stretched the capacity of Catholic schools, it created unprecedented demand for religious to teach in them. This demand extended to parochial and public institutions alike, and it was answered by a generation of energetic female vocations. Never before (or since) were women religious so ubiquitous in the lives of Catholic children or such widely recognized symbols of Catholic life in the United States generally.[28] Their flourishing as educators, however, happened within the deeply conservative climate that characterized institutional Catholicism during the first half of the twentieth century. In 1917, the Vatican issued a Code of Canon Law that placed tight restrictions upon women's religious communities. The

Code included new rules governing sisters' dress and their behavior outside convent walls, and it secured the authority of American bishops to regulate the activities of women religious in their dioceses. Relatively high levels of public activity and community self-determination that had existed among Catholic sisters in the nineteenth century were checked with the 1917 Code and didn't reappear until the Sister Formation movement of the 1950s and Vatican II.[29]

The religious who taught publicly at mid-century did so in the shadow of the 1917 Code. As a result, they were subject to all types of rules intended to limit their interactions with the non-religious sphere. In New Mexico sisters experienced firsthand the difficulties that could arise when these rules clashed with the requirements of state employment. While sisters found joy in their work, they also took to heart, and often shared, the conservative views of their superiors. As they taught, the women struggled to reconcile the public character of what they were doing with their ideas of an appropriately pious life. The hybrid schooling arrangements that infuriated the Dixon committee and POAU were their attempts to solve this puzzle. Although the sisters who taught publicly in New Mexico in the 1940s were reticent to discuss church–state separation with anyone, their work spoke volumes about their stake in the debate. In their classrooms, women religious acted out a perspective on church and state relations built from religious commitments as well as from civil expectations. During the school day, as they organized lesson plans and designed visual aids, these sisters made hundreds of decisions about the parts Catholic teaching and government curricula should each play in their students' learning. These piecemeal, pedagogic assertions paralleled the macrocosmic deliberations ongoing over the proper relationship between religious and civil influences in children's education.

During the *Zellers* litigation, people who otherwise would never have spent time together met one another and exchanged information. Protestant members of the Dixon Free Schools Committee walked into Catholic sisters' classrooms and watched them work. Nationally prominent figures—people like Frank Mead, former editor-in-chief of the *Christian Herald* magazine, and Charles Fahy, the former U.S. Solicitor General—traveled to New Mexico and talked with people living there. Texts from the U.S. Supreme Court circulated among clergy in the Archdiocese of Santa Fe, and information traveled the other direction as well, as sisters' accounts of their work in New Mexico gathered on the desks of attorneys in Washington. With all this traffic of people and ideas, the Dixon case is poised at the intersection of cultural and legal history. It's tempting to think about sisters' classrooms as the stuff of lived religion—the province of women and children, the ordinary or the everyday—while relegating the courtroom to the pages of intellectual history, as a space for men, public debate, and the creation of governing ideas. To talk about classrooms and courtrooms separately, however, is to conceal similarities between both venues as well as the influence the activities of each have brought to bear on the other. The bustling back-and-forth activity of the Dixon case demonstrates how misleading the distinction between "lived" history and "intellectual" history can be.[30] Among other things, this book is an attempt to recover the potency of a lived approach to studying religious history. It doesn't privilege popular forms of religiosity to the exclusion of governing discourses; rather, it explores the long and eventful border region between the two. Lived religion happens all over the place, but it's easiest to provide a full accounting of it in settings that connect individuals in immediate, and more-or-less transparent, ways to the structures that govern them. Classrooms and courtrooms are two such settings. Because it took place in these sorts of spaces, the Dixon case is a study of the interplay between ordinary people and activities on the one hand, and legal discourse and other formal modes for talking about religion on the other.

Everyone who gathered in the *Zellers* courtroom, whether they were Catholic sisters, New Mexican residents, or Washington legal experts, weighed in—in some shape or form—on the prospect of separation in children's schools. When it came to how church and state were imagined by people in New Mexico, sisters' lessons and the impressions they left on children and parents were every bit as important as the legal arguments POAU and the NCWC brought with them to Santa Fe. Alongside formal debates over separation, those religious lessons steered the course of litigation. Legal discourse made up only the articulated tip of American sensibilities about the part religion should play in education. For most people, presumptions about the correct relationship between one's church and one's child's school were more informed by routine behaviors peculiar to the place one lived in, the job one did, and the people one lived among. Together these activities might enact the importance of strong separation between church and state or—as was the case among so many Catholics—they might suggest a different view.[31] This practical experience of church and state was especially true for individuals untrained in the law, like many residents in northern New Mexico. It was also true for people brought into litigation through no choice of their own, like the Catholic sisters who taught there.

While this story is about a constitutional principle, it is also about Americans who felt that principle's consequences. For this reason I consider lesson plans alongside judicial opinion, customs along with disquisitions, to account for how people implicated in church–state litigation naturalized, transformed, or repudiated separation as a value in their lives. Just as religion scholars reared by a post-Protestant academy still privilege belief over practice when they talk about how their subjects "do" religion, so scholars of the First Amendment also privilege belief when they talk about how their subjects negotiate its religion clauses.[32] The religious lives of people aren't always oriented around fixed convictions, however, and the civic lives of people don't necessarily include fixed convictions about the laws they have a duty to obey. This story is about the meanings people assigned to the principle of church–state separation at mid-century, but it is also about the practices that informed and sometimes destabilized those meanings. These activities were the stuff of day-to-day

life, from exchanges between Spanish-speaking residents and English-speaking officials, to Sunday sermons exclaiming the benefits of American-style education, to
the small victories and defeats that made up a child's school year. While most of
these behaviors were never intended to shape the law, taken together they explain
the investment of people in the legal processes that grew to include them. This was
true for Catholics who supported sister-taught schools and for Protestants who
objected to Catholic sisters teaching their children. It was especially true for sisters
themselves. The women who ended up as defendants in the Dixon case didn't disregard the impetus to keep church and state separate, but whatever significance they
gave the principle stayed implicit in their teaching. When those sisters did eventually stop to reflect, it was only in self-defense and under duress. During the trial,
their efforts to translate the practices of their classrooms into the constitutional discourse privileged by the court were a resounding failure—one welcomed by the
Free Schools Committee and its attorneys.

Of course the conflict at the heart of *Zellers* was not over an activity but an
object. For sisters teaching publicly across the United States, the heavy folds of their
costumes decided their professional fates. For students who studied with sisters,
the Catholic habit was a powerful visual cue, a loaded symbol that (for better or
worse) dominated impressions they formed of their teachers. A woman who
attended public school in New Mexico in the 1940s acknowledged as much when
she described to me how she felt after the sisters left her village. "I missed the habit,"
she emphasized. "It wasn't around anymore, and it meant something. It meant
Catholic, it meant faith."[33] For adults who fought over it, the habit's visibility rendered it dangerous or valuable in equal parts. Everyone knew that its ability to catch
even the smallest child's eye made the costume a high-stakes test of how far the wall
of separation should extend. For the women who actually wore it, the habit was a
material marker of their own wall of separation from the non-Catholic world. Even
as courts and legislatures across the country were deciding that religious needed to
remove their Catholic garb to teach, sisters who were instructed to alter their clothing balked or were prohibited in doing so by their superiors. In New Mexico and
elsewhere, a few pieces of woolen cloth came to stand between two ultimately
incompatible visions of education. Their coarse materiality embodied the mutual
limitation of each.

Today, Catholic habits are unusual sights in the United States. Disputes over
religious garb have continued, however, and laws designed to prohibit the Catholic
sister's tunic and veil now apply to teachers wearing other styles of dress. In the
twenty-first century, clothing remains one of the most recognizable and most
contested markers of religious commitment within civil society. Debates over
the Islamic veil in Europe and to a lesser extent the United States carry echoes of
the captive school era. Like their mid-century predecessors, these episodes are
marked by the particular fury that is sparked when clothing—a medium of
expression so intimate that it is adjacent to the human body itself—is isolated,

reflected upon, and found to be either unduly aggressive or unduly threatened. No one notices sisters' absence from these latest debates. Grounded as they are in the preoccupations of our post-9/11 era, clothing conflicts today offer little indication that a half-century ago Catholic women religious were the targets of their own flurry of publicity, legislation, and judicial decisions, all directed toward settling the place of religious garb within American public institutions.

The following six chapters are organized by both chronology and theme. Together they relate the story of the Dixon case—from the circumstances that precipitated the Free Schools Committee's lawsuit through its early litigation and trial in district court. Each chapter also examines the work of publicly teaching sisters, the legal principle of church–state separation, and the relationship between them from the vantage point of the groups who demonstrated interest in *Zellers*. The book's first two chapters are set in New Mexico. Both explore how people who lived there came by their assumptions about the right relationship of church and state. Chapter One begins in the nineteenth century, and explains how sister-taught public schools became part of New Mexico's culture and why they received support from its Hispano population. I use a comparative framework here—even as Catholic leaders elsewhere in the United States were struggling with the prohibitively Protestant character of "nonsectarian" common schools, the Archdiocese of Santa Fe maintained a working relationship with New Mexico's developing education system. By the time a formal school code and funding structure appeared near the turn of the century, however, that system had begun to resemble its American counterparts in many ways. Its Anglo-Protestant character succeeded in alienating both the Church hierarchy and many local residents. In New Mexico's overlooked rural communities, clergy and laity began to cooperate. Despite their own history of disagreement, a Hispano population disadvantaged by curricular and funding policies found common ground with a Church now preoccupied with the loss of parochial students to the public system.

Chapter Two delves deeper into the local approval for public–parochial schooling by taking a close look at Dixon and its neighboring community of Peñasco. Here my focus is on the relationships between Catholic sisters, nearly all of whom were Anglo transplants to New Mexico, and their Hispano students. When residents today recollect the sisters who taught them during the 1940s, any reflections on the legality of their employment take a back seat to descriptions of the respect those women inspired within the community. Here I examine the respect that students felt for their teachers. I explore the sentiment in light of the childhood happenings, both positive and negative, that formed it. Through their demeanor and their appearance, sisters made complicated and lasting impressions upon children in Spanish-speaking villages. My purpose is to take students' word about these encounters, while also learning something of the psychology of New Mexican support for American religious and their schools. The

second chapter finishes its survey of the "local knowledge" of church–state relations by charting the emergence of a Hispano-Protestant minority in northern
New Mexico during the early twentieth century, and considering the separation
platform its members first articulated in Dixon during the 1940s.

In Chapter Three I move from New Mexico's students to its teachers, to
think about how the Catholic religious at the center of captive schooling litigation themselves engaged the separation ethic. My focus here is the stuff of their
classrooms—the objects and activities that became fodder for the *Zellers* suit. I
consider these as tactical products that enabled Catholic sisters to survive pro-
fessionally, at least for at time, in between public and parochial schooling models. Each day, sisters made unscripted decisions aimed at bringing their
classrooms and their persons into compliance with the state's curricular expectations and the religious mandates enforced by the 1917 Code. Although they
never talked at length about the challenges their work entailed, many things
about the way they taught—from the textbooks they distributed, to the way
they scheduled their class time, to the images they hung on their walls—were
geared toward achieving a sustainable balance between religious and civil influences in their classrooms. I argue that, rather than demonstrating disregard for
church–state separation, the sisters who taught publicly were caught trying to
juggle competing Catholic and civil impulses to keep the church and state apart
from one another in their work.

Chapters Four and Five head east to Washington D.C. to consider the involvement of legal advocacy groups in *Zellers* and the captive schooling litigation that
followed it through the 1950s. Together they demonstrate that both Protestant
and Catholic legal experts relied on recognizably religious arguments about church
and state to secure a stake in the public conversation about the Establishment
Clause and its wall of separation at mid-century. The fourth chapter interrogates
POAU and the captive schools campaign it created and promoted in response to
sister-taught public education. New Mexico's schools and others like them became
mediums for deferring differences among the organization's broad coalition of
Protestants. The captivity rhetoric the group employed when it got involved in
Dixon was both a flexible entrée into litigation and a rallying cry meant to remind
its members and the American public of the foundational relationship between
Protestantism and the First Amendment. In Chapter Five I travel to the other side
of the era's church–state debates to look at the work of the NCWC. I pay attention
here to the sight of religious garb within public classrooms, as it became a pressing
issue among the American public and the American judicial system in the context
of sister-taught schooling litigation. I explore the difficulties the NCWC's legal
department faced as it tried to find a cogent defense of the right of Catholic sisters
to teach publicly in that garb. While POAU was adamant about preserving the distinctive relationship between the Protestant tradition and the First Amendment's
religion clauses, Catholic legal experts struggled to find a theologically sound basis

for asserting a similar type of relationship. Their failure to do so on behalf of sisters, in New Mexico and elsewhere, eventually left the NCWC's attorneys little choice but to advise those women to remove their habits or retreat from public employment altogether. In its policy of avoiding litigation at all costs, the NCWC reluctantly found itself guiding Catholic dioceses and religious orders into compliance with a *de facto* model of separation that was stronger even than many courts of the era demanded.

The book's last chapter returns to New Mexico to recount the *Zellers* trial. For a nine-day stretch in 1948, the courtroom in Santa Fe was the setting for a contest that pitted the parties explored in this book directly against one another. Attorneys from Washington came face to face with New Mexico's residents—most visibly with dozens of Catholic sisters who took the witness stand and spoke about their teaching. This chapter's emphasis is on the dispiriting test sisters faced as they tried to translate their work into legally defensible categories. Just as the NCWC was ill prepared to offer a sustained defense of publicly employed sisters, the women themselves were unable to conform either in principle or in practice to the separation standard demanded by both the plaintiffs and the court. Embarrassed on behalf of sisters who suffered public humiliation at trial, and unwilling to allow them to teach in secular classrooms, the superiors of most of the communities involved in New Mexico recalled their members from public work in the state. Not long after, the state's supreme court made their departure law on the grounds of the clothing they wore. The book concludes with an epilogue that recounts the appeal of *Zellers* to New Mexico's high court. I also take the opportunity in this final section to reflect on the legacy of sister-taught schooling litigation. I end with some thoughts about what these fights over the Catholic habit add to our understanding of controversies surrounding the Islamic veil in twenty-first-century public spaces.

Because this study happens at the intersection of legal and popular understandings of the church–state relationship, the source material I employ throughout it is diverse. Legal treatises, school texts and curricula, judicial opinions, court transcripts, and popular forms of media all play important parts in this book. During research on the project I also conducted interviews, both with former students who attended sister-taught public schools in New Mexico and with women who taught in them. At their request, I have assigned pseudonyms to some of these sources. Others chose to use their true identities. I am grateful for the time and effort all of these people put into recounting events that happened more than a half-century ago. I have done my best to treat their memories with care.

A final note that is methodological and also personal: Although Catholic sisters who taught publicly were aware that special challenges came with their civil employment, they always—so far as I can tell—approached their work educating children as a natural extension of their religious vocation. This is why they agreed to it. The "public" nature of that work was first treated as something different, and strange and problematic, by separation advocates, including those who took these women to court. As the latest party to isolate their work's public quality, I do it because I believe it tells us things about religious life that the closely guarded, parochial endeavors of the era cannot. That said, my interest in the public dimension of sisters' work is one the women themselves didn't share. Clifford Geertz once wrote that, just as legal knowledge situates what happens in one's world within a local structure of "what is lawful," so knowledge produced by the anthropologist should situate what happens in her subjects' world within a local structure of "what is grammatical."[34] My decision to dwell here on publicly employed sisters over their parochial counterparts might (if I were lucky enough to catch his attention at all!) have caused Geertz to wag a finger in my direction. Sister-taught public education is a phenomenon that resonates against my *own* cultural framework for what is grammatical—or oddly ungrammatical—about these women's lives, and why.

Even so, I hope the tension that results—between the perspectives of my subjects and the value-laden outlook I bring with me to this historical encounter—is a productive one. My own cultural framework upon which this narration hangs is assembled of mismatched pieces. It's informed by fond memories of attending a Catholic high school in Indiana and by my current employment at a Catholic institution outside of Philadelphia. It's also informed by my sympathies with feminism, pluralism, and church–state separation—the product of a generally liberal upbringing, reinforced by training at liberal institutions with Quaker and Presbyterian roots. New Mexico's Catholic sisters first attracted me because they confused my allegiances and left me unsure about what sorts of judgments I would make about the Dixon affair were I asked ever to lay them down. The discord between the value of church–state separation and the worth of sisters' work remains alive throughout this history because it's alive in my own mind. I hope this tension gives the book a polyvocal quality. I don't see any need to force its resolution.

This is a story about the search for common meaning, and also about its limits. I entered the study with my own ideas—about the value of church–state separation and about the value of sisters' work in education and the public sphere—but well aware of their cultural peculiarity, their fragility, and their fallibility. The following pages tell a history of public work, but I've tried to allow my subjects and their critics to talk back in word and in practice, rebuffing whatever undue suggestions I make about what public visibility implies. An anthropologist friend recently reminded me that as scholars we come to know things through dialogue with the people we study. This is even true of historians. The same subjects who help build our knowledge of the past remain capable of unsettling that knowledge at every turn. Here the incompatibilities between legal vernaculars—between those notions of separation debated in mid-century legal circles, those enacted through the teaching of Catholic sisters, and also those I bring with me—run like fissures that destabilize my retelling of the Dixon case. My hope is that, rather than compromising the end result, those fissures will relieve some of the artificial pressure produced by history making.

1

Educating in the Vernacular

The Foundations of Sister-Taught Public Schools

On an autumn day in 1912 a Roman Catholic priest named Peter Küppers arrived in Santa Fe. The train trip west had left him tired and frazzled. Unable to communicate with either the English-speaking conductor or his fellow passengers, the German native had found himself questioning once or twice along the way whether he ever would reach New Mexico in safety. Küppers disembarked on the platform still shaken from his most recent misadventure; his attempt to change locomotives at a junction earlier in the day had ended with him confronting a pack of charging dogs, armed only with his umbrella. The "rattling and shaking of the little train" as it crawled on toward Santa Fe afterwards did nothing to calm his nerves.[1] The twenty-seven-year-old priest missed the comforts of his seminary in Switzerland, and he wondered whether he had made the right decision when he accepted the invitation to come to New Mexico from Archbishop John Baptist Pitaval of Santa Fe. As Küppers made his way from the train station toward the cathedral he felt ill prepared for the work he had agreed to, sight unseen, in this remote corner of the United States. The mud-plastered homes he walked past on that first day were astonishing to him, and the people he called "Mexicans" spoke a language that to his ears sounded like Greek. The heat from local chiles made tears roll down his cheeks when the famished priest finally sat down to a meal. Bookish, bespectacled, and prone to illness even at his young age, it never crossed Peter Küppers' mind he might stay to live out his days in these unaccommodating environs.[2]

But he did stay. By the time of his death in 1957, Father Küppers had grown into a larger-than-life figure in his adopted home. Even during his lifetime his reputation assumed near-mythic proportions. Küppers was both well loved and much resented by the people who knew him. To some of the state's residents, he was nothing short of heroic—a twentieth-century successor to the legendary Padre Martínez, who built schools in communities that had none and who fought tooth and nail for the interests of the people he worked among, even when those interests conflicted with the government or the archdiocese itself. Like the *padre* a century before him,

Küppers was arguably the most influential New Mexican priest of his generation. To other New Mexicans, Küppers was difficult and cunning, manipulative and even immoral. He drank liquor and smoked his cigars unapologetically. He had a quick temper that often showed itself during his interactions with superiors—four successive archbishops of Santa Fe. As an old man he chose to live in provocative comfort, with a pair of female housekeepers and quartet of Great Danes, on a lush private orchard he called *Obscurana*. One local reporter who met the priest's gigantic pets quipped, "They have only two dislikes: people carrying shovels and people carrying anything out of Father Küppers' ranch."[3] For years rumors circulated about the priest's personal life, and sometimes those rumors had merit. In 1934 then Archbishop Rudolph Gerken removed Küppers from active service in the archdiocese following accusations of embezzlement and general immorality.[4] Even this censorship did little to curb the priest's influence within New Mexico.

Peter Küppers built his reputation—his accolades as well as his infamy—through his life-long efforts to erect and maintain schools in the parishes he served. If his dream of making education "bloom in the desert" was uncontroversial on its surface, the priest's tactics for building and running those schools contributed more than any other behavior from his long and varied career to his Jekyll and Hyde reputation in the state.[5] Like any ambitious educator in a cash-strapped economy, Küppers found his best-laid plans for children's schooling assaulted by the realities of the impoverished communities where he worked. Rather than scale back his vision for want of money, the priest was driven by these challenges to look for creative solutions to fund local schools. Many times those solutions led him into the political life

Figure 1.1 Father Peter Küppers at work with a group of Dominican sisters. Courtesy of Tomas Jaehn.

of a community, and often they required him to disregard all boundaries between things of his church and things of the state.

The priest discovered his acumen for building schools during his first assignment in New Mexico. Chaperito was a parish with six hundred families and fifteen missions, scattered across San Miguel County in the eastern part of the state.[6] When Küppers took over clerical responsibilities in Chaperito in 1913 he was upset to learn his new parish lacked a school, and especially dismayed to discover its Catholic children were attending a nearby Presbyterian institution. The young priest made education in Chaperito his priority. Küppers began by appealing to the archdiocese and anyone else he thought might be willing to bankroll a new Catholic school. Within a short time, however, he realized his most promising educational allies—and those with the deepest pocketbooks—were sitting in the local government. He revised his strategy in Chaperito accordingly. With support from several Catholic politicians, Küppers drafted a proposal to redraw the educational map of San Miguel County. Adding new school districts to the county would require new public schools to be opened—including one in the vicinity of the parish.[7] Once his redistricting proposal was on the books, Küppers took responsibility for building Chaperito's first public school. He dynamited rock in a local quarry himself, and paid residents to transport the loose stones back to the building site.[8] He oversaw every detail of the construction. The enterprising priest also found teachers to staff the school. Before the start of the academic year Küppers invited a community of Catholic religious in exile from Mexico to come to Chaperito. The sisters soon began work as public teachers, and the county school board agreed to pay their salaries.[9]

The Chaperito school was the first of many public ventures Peter Küppers had a hand in during his career in northern New Mexico. It was also a portent of things stirring across the region. New Mexico had become a state a year earlier, and statehood brought with it the obligation for an expansive—and an adequately staffed—public education system. Schools taught by Catholic sisters began to open across New Mexico during the 1910s to meet the demands of this developing system. In addition to Chaperito, sisters began to teach in public institutions in San Miguel in 1914, Villanueva and Cuba in 1916, and Parkview in 1918.[10] New Mexican statehood precipitated the largest-ever influx of sister-teachers to the region; while three religious communities had received public funds to teach in the nineteenth century, between 1900 and 1947 women from more than a dozen different congregations accepted employment in the state's schools. By the 1940s Catholic sisters had relocated to the Southwest from places like Denver, St. Louis, Milwaukee, and Oldenburg, Indiana. More than one hundred thirty of them taught publicly in the state, and together they were responsible for the education of thousands of students. Both the public and the Catholic education systems in New Mexico counted these sisters' schools as their own.

If statehood provided the impetus for large numbers of sisters to teach publicly in New Mexico, the long-term success of their schools turned upon the will of the state's Hispano residents. Spanish-speaking people represented a strong majority in every New Mexican community where sisters taught publicly, and their endorsement of sister-directed public education allowed it to flourish across multiple generations. When sisters arrived in New Mexico to teach, they received warm receptions from local clergy, politicos, and residents alike. According to one survey taken in the 1940s, more than four out of five residents approved of the sisters in their public schools.[11] The support of Hispanos for women religious derived in part from their religious loyalties; the austere presence of Catholic nuns robed in black, brown, or white habits inspired respect, even veneration, among these mainly Catholic people. The women relished the goodwill of locals who volunteered their time and scarce resources to help build their convents and maintain their school buildings. At the same time, this enthusiasm for sisters masked complicated sentiments embedded in the relationship of Hispanos to their schools. Educational history in New Mexico reveals a fraught backstory to the Hispano-Catholic alliance that made sister-taught public schools possible in the first part of the twentieth century. It suggests that motivations other than just religious affinity made church–state separation undesirable—or at least irrelevant—to the New Mexicans who supported those schools. Religious loyalty was important in New Mexico, but that loyalty was always qualified, contingent, and entangled with other interests.

A Hispano-Catholic educational alliance took time to develop in New Mexico. Native-born residents' early interactions with both public *and* Catholic schools in the territory had been lukewarm at best. A pattern of clerical–popular cooperation eventually cohered from this rough beginning, but it was based more upon the challenges of a changing educational landscape than upon some natural affinity. In the late nineteenth century and the early twentieth century, Anglo-American transplants to New Mexico introduced a series of proposals for public education in the territory and later the state. Most of these people were Protestants, and although their ideas about schooling varied with one another and changed over time, there were persistent qualities about them that bothered both Catholic officials and Hispano residents. From the Catholic leadership's perspective, the prevailing nineteenth-century model of American education was itself offensively Protestant, despite advocates' avowals of nonsectarianism and religious liberty. Even as the Church in New Mexico was beneficiary of the territory's first education funds, elsewhere in the country Catholic leaders battled school officials who insisted on promoting Bible reading and other Protestant devotions while excluding Catholic equivalents from their classrooms. As New Mexico moved toward statehood, Church leaders there worried about an educational system that appeared be going the way of public schooling elsewhere in the United States. Meanwhile, Hispano residents in the region also balked, reacting both to Americanizing impulses within the system and to a funding apparatus that diverted educational resources away from their communities. Living predominantly in rural villages isolated from the decision-making processes in Santa Fe, these people had little preexisting sympathy for either the structure or the content of the system put into place around them.

The sister-taught public schools that multiplied after statehood were practical arrangements struck between Anglo-Catholic clergy and religious and Hispano-Catholic residents. These groups still had distinct interests and imperfectly aligned educational visions, but in the first decades of the twentieth century they coexisted on the margins of an emergent state school system. Their cooperation had roots in a shared Catholic faith and a common desire to instill that faith in children, but it was made secure and tenable by something else—a shared ambivalence over the design and purpose of this expanding system. Their uneasiness gave Hispano residents and the Catholic leaders in their communities a common incentive to piece together other schooling models along the borders of the existing public infrastructure. While New Mexico's educational system was still in its early stages, it preserved a space along its borders for just this sort of improvisational work. New state laws governing schooling contrasted sharply with the isolation of rural districts and the autonomy those districts retained in decisions about facilities and faculty. The schools that residents, clergy, and local officials constructed took into account the state's imperatives, but they were also vernacular products, which modified those imperatives to reflect the interests of the participants and the needs of the community. When litigation threatened sister-taught schools in the 1940s, the incomplete affinity between Hispanos and the Catholic Church revealed itself in other ways. Some Hispanos ended up on the side of separation. While most Catholic residents objected to the lawsuit that tried to close their schools, and dismissed the church–state principle that undergirded it, their reasons for doing so were distinct from those of teaching religious and of the Archdiocese of Santa Fe.

Historians and other people who are interested in New Mexico's territorial days often make two assumptions about education. The first is that education in New Mexico began with the Anglos who moved to the region in the mid-nineteenth century. The second is that an uncomplicated, or even natural, affinity has always existed between the Catholic Church and the region's Hispano residents when it comes to children and schools.[12] Neither assumption is correct. Nineteenth-century New Mexico was a place where both Hispano and Native American residents with their own educational traditions encountered Anglo-American newcomers, who brought with them different ideas about how the territory's children should be schooled. While the number of schools in the new territory did increase significantly after the arrival of Anglos to the region, Hispano inhabitants had been experimenting with their own schools for more than two centuries under both Spanish and Mexican rule. Although the first Anglo educators in New Mexico professed the same Catholic faith as the region's Spanish-speaking population, they brought disruptive educational ideas with them. Residents were generally reluctant subscribers to the pedagogical vision imported by the new Catholic leadership who arrived in the territory in the middle of the nineteenth century.

New Mexico's remote location, its rugged landscape, and its struggling economy made a centralized system of schools no more than a far-off hope under Spanish and Mexican rule, but the province was not without its own educational models and innovators. Formal schooling had been a continual, if uneven and idiosyncratic, presence in the region since the Franciscan missions of the seventeenth century.[13] When those missions secularized and political control of the region transferred from New Spain to Mexico in the early nineteenth century, responsibility for education in New Mexico dispersed, and a loose group of diocesan clergy and citizens struggled to open schools in answer to mandates sent by a distant and distracted Mexico City. During the first half of the century New Mexico was home to between six and eight publicly funded schools, and the first U.S. census of the territory counted eighteen public school teachers already at work.[14] The most ambitious educational project managed under Mexican rule was the school founded in 1826 by Padre Antonio José Martínez, a Catholic priest in Taos. Martínez was a native of the Upper Rio Grande Basin, and after attending seminary in Durango he returned home with strong ideas about both the educational and the political needs of his people. For over forty years the priest oversaw a school of remarkable proportions in Taos; he educated both boys and girls, offered seminary and legal training, and printed his own series of textbooks and catechisms for students' use. He also became one of the region's most prominent political figures, first by advocating for Mexican resistance to American encroachment and eventually by realigning himself with the United States, to act as president of the first Provincial Territorial Assembly. With Martínez's dual interests in education and public life, it is little surprise Peter Küppers drew favorable comparisons to the priest a century later.[15]

Martínez was far and away the most influential native-born member of the Catholic clergy during his generation, but the *padre's* work did not signal an enduring alliance between Hispano communities and Catholic educators in northern New Mexico.[16] During Martínez's own lifetime the prevailing model of Catholic education in the region changed dramatically. In 1848, Mexico conceded its northernmost territory to the United States in the Treaty of Guadalupe Hidalgo. Among the earliest and most tangible consequences of this annexation was the transfer of religious governance over the region. Under Mexican rule, New Mexico's Catholics had been a part of the diocese of Durango with an administrative center several hundred miles away. When political control of the territory shifted to the United States, the Vatican saw fit to reassign ecclesiastical jurisdiction as well and it created the new Diocese of Santa Fe in 1853. In a storied decision Pope Pius IX assigned a French priest named Jean Baptiste Lamy to act as the diocese's first bishop.

In its early years, the relationship between Lamy and New Mexico's residents was anything but amicable. Although the Church already counted the majority of people living there as Catholics in the mid-nineteenth century, Catholicism in the territory was a far cry from anything either Lamy or the United States hierarchy considered orthodox.[17] After the Franciscans' departure from New Mexico the centralized structure of diocesan authority had failed in the remote region, and religious authority had redistributed to a few native priests and a growing number of laymen—members of a mutual aid and penance society called La Fraternidad Piadosa de Nuestro Padre Jesús Nazareno, or *los penitentes*. Lamy later claimed that upon his arrival in Santa Fe he found only nine priests in all of New Mexico.[18] What the bishop did find was a Catholic population he worried was "almost too primitive"—with a rural culture that had subsisted for decades on the fringes of diocesan hierarchy, a clergy who publicly defied their vows (particularly those of poverty and celibacy), and residents who were as likely to gather in *penitente* meeting houses or *moradas* as in the local churches.[19]

Upon settling in Santa Fe Lamy began to correct what he understood as the failings of his diocese. His efforts to "civilize" the population—to bring its unrefined religiosity up to the standards set by Church doctrine and tradition, and its culture to the standards of both his native Europe and his adopted nation—would characterize his tenure as prelate. He issued prohibitive new rules for the territory's *penitentes*, including instructions that restricted their displays of penance and made clear their deferential position beneath the hierarchy.[20] The bishop circumscribed the activities of native-born clerics by suspending several New Mexican clergy from their duties entirely and reassigning others to outlying missions and Indian pueblos.[21] Lamy notoriously excommunicated the venerable Padre Martínez after the aging priest rejected the bishop's choice of a non-native successor for him, and continued to officiate—first in disobedience and later in open schism—from his private Taos residence.[22] The bishop's attempts to rein in both lay and clerical Catholic activity during his first decade in Santa Fe put him at odds with many of the residents for whom his ministry was intended. New Mexicans expressed their dismay at Lamy in several formats. In 1853, members of one parish indirectly challenged the bishop by publicly accusing his closest colleague of indiscretions that included violating the seal of confession and comparing locals to "all kinds of savage animals." Three years later the Hispano-dominated legislative assembly took their grievances with the prelate an audacious step further when they wrote directly to Pius IX to request the Vatican remove Lamy from his office in Santa Fe.[23] The Vatican ignored the petition.

The bishop's distress over New Mexico's situation was acute when it came to the territory's educational resources. As Lamy traveled across his diocese he observed that under Mexican rule, "every vestige of school had vanished, churches and school houses were in a crumbling state and ignorance reigned in the land."[24] To combat this ignorance he began work on the territory's first parochial school system, and he invited the first Catholic women religious to New Mexico to help him with the project. Acting on his belief that both civilizing and re-Catholicizing the Hispano people required educators from points east, in 1852 Lamy traveled to central Kentucky to

personally solicit help at the motherhouse of the Sisters of Loretto. Six Lorettine religious came to Santa Fe the same autumn, and they opened a privately funded girls'
school in the city the following year.[25] Our Lady of Light Academy—nicknamed *la
casa Americana* by locals because of the gabled architecture that distinguished its
building from the flat-roofed adobes of Santa Fe—offered a European-style education to students who could afford the $300 annual tuition, as well as to select day
school students who were admitted at a reduced rate.[26] Girls of varying ages received
instruction in the skills and disciplines sisters deemed proper for young Catholic
women. The academy's offerings were celebrated in the local press at its opening:

> The Sisters . . . gave their elementary pupils instruction in orthography,
> reading, writing, grammar, arithmetic, geography, and history. The more
> advanced pupils studied 'Astronomy with the use of globes, Natural Phi-
> losophy, Botany, etc., etc.' They also gave instruction in needle work, bor-
> dering, drawing, painting, music on the piano and guitar, vocal music,
> and French. . . . Two weeks later the school was offering additional sub-
> jects. . . . Among these were bookkeeping, algebra, geometry, mensura-
> tion, surveying, logic, Latin, and Greek. It was stated that 'the English
> language is taught in the college with care.' . . . 'Scholars are required to
> speak it even during the hours of recreation.'[27]

The Catholic religious offered an expansive education the likes of which New
Mexicans had never seen. Studying with the sisters was not easy, even for girls
whose parents paid dearly to send them to the academy. One former student
remarked years later, "I have never forgotten how the sisters tried to instill into our
hearts a little bit of culture, and the hard time they had doing it."[28]

Our Lady of Light Academy represented the arrival of Catholic women religious
within New Mexico's educational world. Over the next decade the Sisters of Loretto
expanded their mission to the territory north, opening a school in Taos in an effort
to win its Catholics from the renegade Martínez and local *penitentes*.[29] During the
same period the sisters also opened schools in the village of Mora to the northeast
of Santa Fe, and in the cities of Albuquerque and Las Vegas. In 1873, Annunciation
Academy in Mora became the first sister-run school in New Mexico to receive public funds for its support.[30] Bishop Lamy soon invited other Catholic religious communities to the territory to join the Sisters of Loretto in their educational work.
These included the French Christian Brothers, who began to open boys' schools in
New Mexico in 1859, Italian Jesuits in 1867, the Cincinnati-based Sisters of Charity
in 1865, and the Irish Sisters of Mercy in 1880. Together these five congregations
staffed all of territorial New Mexico's Catholic schools.[31]

The early interactions between New Mexico's Catholic clergy and religious and its
Hispano residents were marred by difference and occasionally by open conflict.

Although the parochial schools built during Lamy's prelateship offered a Catholic education to Catholic children, they also pressured students and parents to change their minds about what that Catholicism and that learning should entail. As the century wore on, however, these early disputes became less important. Another set of schooling models began to gain traction in the territory, and their precepts proved challenging for Catholic leaders and Hispano residents alike. This third perspective on New Mexican education was imported by Anglo Protestants and built around the common goal of a public school system. With the exception of Lamy and the religious he invited to come and work with him, transplants to the New Mexican territory were nearly all Protestants who hailed from the Eastern and Midwestern United States. The first of these residents arrived as part of the military conquest and political transfer of the region, and those pioneers were joined through the second half of the nineteenth century by an assortment of bold personalities—ranchers who expanded their ranges west from Texas, home missionaries (many of them women), and industrial entrepreneurs and laborers who arrived with the railroads in 1879. By the turn of the century these men and women were also joined by artists and tourists, many of whom visited and settled on the Spanish and Native American land grants in and around the Rio Grande Basin.[32] In 1850, ninety-five percent of New Mexico's population was native born, either Hispano or Native American. By 1910 that number had shrunk to just over half. This inundation of first-generation inhabitants was made up almost entirely of Protestant Americans.[33] As New Mexico's population grew over the nineteenth century, these Anglos became a visible presence in the region's public institutions, and they eventually gained a controlling voice in the territory's political leadership.

Most Anglo Protestants agreed with Bishop Lamy that New Mexico's residents were ignorant and unrefined. Their theories on the origins of this ignorance differed. Early accounts penned by Protestants in the territory suggest that, while some suspected the discouraging qualities of the Hispano people were innate, a product of mingling Spanish and Indian blood, others attributed their backwardness directly to the Catholic Church's influence.[34] They blamed education as the medium for that influence. Observers in the region wrote of Catholic priests contriving to "entangle the mind [sic] of their pupils in the meshes of superstition and bigotry" and teaching "dogma and spiritual terrors" as a means of conditioning children for the "final mental slavery to which they are destined."[35] Motivated by these concerns, Protestants matched Catholics in touting correct education as the centerpiece of the new territory's development. The first territorial governor, James Calhoun, stressed the importance of education in his inaugural message to the legislature, writing that "nothing will more surely contribute to the mental and moral force of a people, than a well devised system of common schools."[36] In light of their suspicion that the Church was the source of New Mexico's problems, Protestants' calls for education also took on a distinctive tone. Public schooling was required to properly educate the Hispano people and to break the crippling influence of the Church upon their culture. If those schools were to imitate their counterparts elsewhere in the nation—and arrivals to the territory hoped they would—then teachers would accomplish these goals with help from a curriculum that was both American and Protestant.

Most Anglo Protestants in New Mexico relocated from places where public education was well established. By the mid-nineteenth century public or common schools were staples in urban centers throughout the eastern half of the United States, where they existed to educate the poor and working classes unable to afford private study. As the first wave of Catholic immigration reached the nation's shores in the 1830s and 1840s, common schools assumed responsibility for assimilating that population to an American way of life. It was widely agreed that their Protestant character was key to this work. As Irish newcomers settled in the nation's cities in large numbers, many in the country feared their foreign customs and especially their religious loyalties would overwhelm a still-young American culture and government.[37] Similar concern extended to the nation's expanding western perimeter, where some Americans worried that Catholic settlement in sparsely populated areas might tip the political scales against democracy. These apprehensions were rooted in beliefs that the Church opposed values like liberty and individualism, which democracy rested upon, and that its agenda in the United States was political as well as pastoral. Although he wrote more than a decade before New Mexico joined the American frontier, Presbyterian minister Lyman Beecher presented Catholic settlements as cause for alarm in the collection of sermons he published as *A Plea for the West*. Beecher was adamant that Protestant-guided education was the only solution for establishing American values in the nation's remote regions. "The thing required for the civil and religious prosperity of the West," he wrote, "is universal education."[38] He returned to this theme later in the tract:

> We must educate! We must educate! . . . If in our haste to be rich and mighty, we outrun our literary institutions, they will never overtake us; or only come up after the battle for liberty is fought and lost . . . as resources for inexorable despotism for the perpetuity of our bondage.[39]

For Beecher, Catholicism was the despotism that threatened to fill any educational vacuum left open as the United States expanded westward.

Although Beecher's plea was for Protestant missionaries to supervise education, by mid-century even missionaries were beginning to support publicly funded schools as the preferred medium for imparting the core tenets of Protestantism on children *and* for preserving the nation's exceptional character. For most Americans these objectives were one and the same. As Lamy began to build Catholic schools in New Mexico in the 1850s, his episcopal colleagues elsewhere in the country were preoccupied by common institutions that required all their students—Catholic ones included—to receive Christian instruction. The explicitly Protestant character of this instruction was reinforced through both curricula and devotional activities. American school children read from history textbooks that included biased discussions of the Inquisition and the Reformation, and geography textbooks that dismissed Catholic rituals as salves that did more to "to lull the conscience than to correct vice."[40] Many public schools required students to recite the Lord's Prayer in a Protestant style, and more of them mandated daily reading from the King James Version of the Bible. In 1839, the American Bible Society made sure of this when it undertook a campaign to introduce Christian scripture into every common classroom in the nation. It did so well aware that more students than ever before were Catholics. "The seeds of conflict," Ray Allen Billington remarked a century later in his study of American nativism, "were sown by this action."[41]

Catholics and Protestants came to blows over the character of public education in the 1840s. These conflicts were hottest on the Atlantic seaboard, where Catholics objected to the Protestant nature of common classrooms, and especially to rules requiring their students to read dutifully from the King James Bible.[42] The publicly funded schools in New York City had a longstanding rule to this effect. For years, New York's Common Council had funneled nearly all the educational money available in the city to a benevolent organization called the Public School Society for management. The Society was founded in 1805 to cater to children whose families were too poor to pay for private educations. In addition its Protestant membership pledged "to inculcate the sublime truths of religion and morality contained in the Holy Scriptures."[43] In keeping with its mission the Society implemented daily Bible reading, along with prayers and religious instruction, in all its classrooms.[44] In 1840 Bishop John Hughes (who would later become Archbishop of New York) protested the fact that Catholic children were being forced to read from the King James Bible and engage in the other religious activities within Society schools. Catholics who joined in the devotions of other faiths, he pointed out, were in grave violation of Church teaching. The bishop asked the council to rectify the situation by diverting educational funds directly to New York's Catholic schools. Worried that its members might refuse his request on the grounds that Catholic schools were sectarian, Hughes followed it up with a demand the council stop funding Society schools on the same sectarian grounds.

The Common Council denied both the bishop's petitions. A year later, when the situation for Catholic students in the city's schools had not improved, Hughes concluded that his only option left for fixing the system was to intervene politically. At a meeting at Carroll Hall in New York City in October 1841, the unyielding bishop proposed an independent ticket in an upcoming state election, and he rallied the city's Catholics to support a trio of handpicked write-in candidates. His hope was to unsettle Democratic politicians who relied—ungratefully, Hughes thought—upon the Catholic vote in New York. The bishop's ploy did nothing to ingratiate him to Protestant observers, who pointed to it as damning evidence that the Church would happily fiddle in affairs of the state. The political pressure it created, however, did have an effect. The following year the state legislature intervened to break the Society's monopoly on public education in New York City. It did so by divvying up control of the city's common schools among local districts. Many of those districts eventually agreed to ban the King James Bible from their classrooms.[45]

A similar dispute in Philadelphia took a darker turn three years later. Like the Public School Society, Philadelphia's school board mandated that students read from the King James Bible each day. The city's bishop, Francis Patrick Kenrick, appealed to the board, asking that Catholic students enrolled in the public schools be allowed to substitute the Church's own Duoay Bible during these sessions, or else be exempted from the Bible reading requirement altogether. He also requested that Catholic children be excused from reciting the Lord's Prayer.[46] The Philadelphia board consented to releasing Catholic students from both prayer and Bible reading, but it denied the introduction of the Duoay text, insisting that only Bibles "without note or comment" were acceptable within its system.[47] The board also agreed to penalize any schools that continued to require their Catholic students to read from the Bible. This apparent compromise between the city and the Church infuriated and inspired Philadelphia's nativist element. On the eve of the 1844 election season, the local branch of the Native American Party drummed up support for its candidates with rumors that Kenrick was plotting to ban the Bible from city schools entirely. Interreligious hostility in Philadelphia erupted in violence through the spring and summer months—Catholics opened fire upon nativists who paraded menacingly through their neighborhoods, and Protestant rioters fired cannons at churches and burned blocks of Catholic homes to the ground. By July the situation had become so bad that musket-carrying citizens groups, including the lawyers and clerks of the Philadelphia Bar Association, patrolled the streets at night to keep the peace.[48] "The city," one observer reported, "has worn in some measure the aspect of a military encampment."[49] When it was all over fourteen residents of Philadelphia, both Protestants and Catholics, had been killed in the violence and another fifty were wounded.[50]

Disputes over the Protestant character of public schooling lingered after the 1840s; they were ongoing as New Mexico explored the possibilities of its own public education system through the latter half of the nineteenth century. In 1852, the First Plenary Council of American bishops reminded Catholic parents of their duty to prevent children from reading Protestant translations of the Bible.[51] The next decade was peppered with episodes of students receiving corporal punishment for refusing to participate in Protestant prayer, even as some states had begun to grant Catholics exemptions from religious activities or—more rarely—to eliminate those activities from public classrooms altogether. Although not typical, a prominent example of the latter happened during the so-called Cincinnati Bible Wars of 1872. In Cincinnati a fight reminiscent of the conflicts in New York and Philadelphia resulted in the local school board resolving that "religious instruction and the reading of religious books, including the Holy Bible, are prohibited in the common schools."[52] Angry Protestants sued to restore the Bible and other devotional practices to the public system, but the state's high court rejected their claims. Though its decision rested on its finding that local officials should have authority over their school programs, the Ohio court also emphasized the importance of public spaces free from religious instruction. "Religion [lies] outside the true and legitimate province of government," it concluded:

> To teach the doctrines of infidelity, and thereby teach that Christianity is false, is one thing; and to give no instructions on the subject is quite another thing. The only fair and impartial method, where serious objection is made, is to let each sect give its own instructions, elsewhere than in the state schools.[53]

The Ohio court's 1872 decision made national headlines, but it was not widely imitated during the era. Although exemptions for Catholics from religion requirements became more common in public schools, prayer and Bible reading remained staples within American education for nearly another century.

Like their peers in New York and Philadelphia, most Protestants who arrived in New Mexico during the nineteenth century advocated for nonsectarian schools under the mandate of religious liberty. This upset Lamy like it had Hughes and Kenrick. When New York's Common Council denied Hughes' request for public funds in 1840, it argued that giving money to Catholic schools would violate a standard of church–state separation implicit in the state's constitution. "The purity of the Church and the safety of the State," a council committee wrote in response to Hughes' petition, "are more surely obtained, by a distinct and separate existence of the two, than by their union."[54] The same committee unhesitatingly defended the presence of the King James Bible in the Society's publicly funded schools. The distinction both it and the Philadelphia board drew between the Catholic Duoay Bible and the King James Version rested upon the latter's lack of "notes and commentary" (this despite the fact the King James edition included a preface and other distinguishing features).[55] This validation of "pure" Christian scripture over and against a Church-annotated equivalent is indicative of how most American Protestants, including those in New Mexico, understood religion's place within public education during the period—what traditions were compatible with religious liberty and what traditions were not. As Philip Hamburger explains the distinction, "Protestants tended to assume that, whereas Catholics acted as part of a church, Protestants acted in diverse sects as individuals."[56] The latter applied to prayer as well as to Bible reading; Protestant educators welcomed both in public schools and celebrated their capacity to guide students within their own free and individualized relationships with God and nation. Castigating Catholicism made it all the easier for Protestants to imagine these traditions as normative within a nonsectarian system—as benign, almost invisible alternatives to the Catholic Church's egregious texts and practices. In this way, disputes with the Church made the distinction between coercive Catholic and free Protestant religiosity true and self-evident for American school officials at midcentury.[57]

As Hispano New Mexicans would find out, Anglo-American conceptions of religious liberty were also closely tied to their concerns about assimilation and their faith in public education as the medium for that process. In New York officials recognized the generic Protestantism enforced by the Public School Society as the equivalent to language or civics lessons when it came to training immigrants how to behave as patriotic citizens. In New Mexico many Protestants held similar convictions about the curricula necessary to Americanize the territory's native-born population. In both locations, Catholic influence was troubling not only because it was sectarian in nature but also, and more alarmingly, because it came from a sovereign state. The Church appeared to demand—and elicit—political loyalties that contradicted those required by the United States government. From the perspective of nineteenth-century Americans, to be Catholic was something different from being strictly Irish or Mexican, but it was still to be foreign. To insist on nonsectarianism was to protect schools from influences that were at best alien and at worst traitorous. The hesitancy of the New York council to divert funds to Catholic schools in 1840 was also hesitancy to bolster a powerful bishop—a "vigorous, stormy individual, powerful in leadership and indefatigable in contest"—who seemed bent upon keeping the city's Irish segregated under his tight control.[58] Despite Lamy's own efforts to civilize the residents of New Mexico, public education advocates in the territory shared similar concerns about the political scope of the bishop's influence, and they worried about the ability of schools there to Americanize students should the Catholic Church in New Mexico retain access to public funds.

Meanwhile, Catholic leaders across the United States responded bitterly to officials who couched public schooling in the language of religious liberty. Bishop Hughes questioned how such language could be used to defend a *de facto* establishment of Protestantism, or what he referred to as "the justly obnoxious union of Church and State."[59] His complaint—along with the New York prelate's efforts to eliminate funding for the School Society should it keep the King James Bible in its classrooms—would seem to suggest that nineteenth-century Catholics advocated for a stricter model of religious freedom than their Protestant counterparts. The support of most Catholic leaders for religious freedom, however, was strategic at best. While a few Catholics of the era were inclined to defend religious liberty in principle, the bishop in New York appreciated it only insofar as it allowed students to avoid corruptive Protestant influence. As one scholar looking back on the episode put it, Hughes' bid to remove funding for Protestant practices from the city's schools was a "calculated risk"—the bishop had no desire to eliminate prayer and Bible reading *per se* from the common education system.[60] Even as he protested its mandatory Bible reading, Hughes also accused the Society's schools of being secular and atheistic because of their *lack* of sectarianism.[61] His position was not unusual for a Catholic prelate. At the end of the day, Catholics and Protestants in the nineteenth-century

United States had a lot in common when it came to the character of publicly funded education—nearly everyone wanted their schools to include resources for instructing children in their own faith traditions while excluding activities that could disrupt that religious formation.

Even though Protestants arrived in New Mexico with clear ideas about what schooling there should look like, formalizing public education in the territory was a long and uneven process. Between 1850 and 1891, New Mexico's government failed at multiple attempts to inaugurate a system of tax-supported schools.[62] Despite legislative proposals submitted for referendum vote as early as 1856, and even a board of education that convened briefly in 1863, a tenable tax-based system of public schooling became reality only in 1891. Many of its details remained inchoate well into the twentieth century. This delay was the result of a complicated set of factors, but religious and ethnic interests each figured prominently among them.[63] Early on, the Archdiocese of Santa Fe participated in public education in New Mexico. As time passed, however, Protestant educators and government officials in the territory agitated for nonsectarian schools that would emulate public institutions elsewhere in the country. As they did so the archdiocese became an outspoken critic of the nascent public system and began promoting its own schools as alternatives to it. At the same time, many residents of New Mexico harbored objections over Anglo-centric bias in the long succession of schooling initiatives. Distinct but overlapping considerations converged as New Mexico's clerical leadership and its Hispano people responded through the late nineteenth century to the schooling models imported by Anglo Protestants. Their two perspectives—the ambivalence of the archdiocese toward the territory's emerging public system, and the differently derived ambivalence of native residents toward that same system—coincided closely. Despite their history of disagreement, Church leaders and Spanish-speaking inhabitants found themselves expressing similar concerns about their territory's education prospects. By the twentieth century their shared unease would become an opportunity for cooperation.

Early interactions between the Catholic Church and the territorial government fluctuated when it came to education. Anglo-Protestant apprehension about Catholic influence motivated official scrutiny of the Church's role in schooling as soon as New Mexico became part of the United States. Members of the first territorial legislature expressed this concern, and the first draft of a territorial constitution in 1850 instructed that, in any education system established, no preference be given to "any religious society, [or] mode of worship."[64] Rather than clarifying future schooling arrangements, however, this failed piece of legislation was the start of decades of ambiguity. Within a few short years the Church was co-directing the territory's educational agenda. When New Mexico's first board of education convened in 1863, Bishop Lamy himself was included *ex officio* among its members. Soon

afterward schools taught by Catholic religious began to receive public funding—
some of the very first made available for education in the territory. The height of
reciprocity between Church personnel and territorial officials happened during the
1870s. In 1867 six members of the Society of Jesus traveled to Santa Fe from Naples,
Italy. The Jesuits opened a seminary, a boys' college, and several schools for younger
students after they arrived.[65] When the first tax-raised education funds became
available in the territory in 1872, the congregation's local superior, Father Donato
Gasparri, acted quickly to secure a portion of the money for Jesuit projects.[66] By the
mid-1870s, the Jesuits had become principal figures in New Mexican public education. They distributed a Spanish-language weekly with a teaching focus, and their
printing press, *Imprenta del Rio Grande*, supplied textbooks to many of the territory's tax-supported schools.[67] In 1878, Gasparri approached the territorial legislature
in hopes of formalizing his order's position in the region. Despite objections from
New Mexico's Anglo governor as well as criticism from its Protestant press, the legislature obliged the superior when it passed the so-called "Jesuit Act"—a piece of
legislation that legally incorporated the Society of Jesus as an educational institution within New Mexico.[68]

The first bids at tax-funded education in New Mexico in the 1870s resulted in the
appropriation of public money and the expansion of educational projects by Catholic communities like the Jesuits. Their activities in turn provoked angry opposition
within the territorial legislature. Between 1872 and 1889 lawmakers made a series
of attempts to codify the territory's *ad hoc* educational infrastructure. Each of these
proposals relied on the familiarly Protestant objection to sectarianism in a bid to
eliminate Catholic influence from publicly funded classrooms. A proposed constitution for New Mexico in 1872 instructed that no public funds should go to any
schools "controlled by any church of sectarian denomination whatever." Another in
1889 called for a school system "under the absolute control of the state, and free
from sectarian or church control." A proposed bill in 1875–76 attempted to exclude
religion from public education in terms that bothered even some Protestants by
requiring that schools "shall not be under the influence of any creed, religious society, or denomination whatever; that neither the Bible nor any sectarian book shall
be used in the public schools." The 1875 bill failed within the legislature itself, while
the two constitutional proposals were later defeated in referendum votes.[69] Despite
their failures, the persistence of measures like these through the later decades of the
nineteenth century—along with the strong nonsectarian language they proffered—
was evidence of mounting hostility between public education advocates and the
Archdiocese of Santa Fe.

The push for nonsectarian schools was also bound up with the quest for statehood. Statehood was a pressing issue for many Anglos living in New Mexico, and
by the last quarter of the century everyone understood that the territory's prospects for joining the Union depended upon the condition of its educational system. Above all, statehood would require schools free from Catholic influence.

Politicians in Washington had balked at the region's Spanish-speaking and Native American populations when New Mexico became a territory, and as the century wore on those officials voiced skepticism about the ability of its native-born inhabitants to meet the standards of civility and independence necessary for full membership in the Union.[70] With the exception of schooling for Native Americans, the federal government declined direct responsibility for education in its territories, but its representatives nonetheless promoted proper schools as instrumental for the Americanization of the people living there. Nowhere was this truer than in New Mexico. Like Lyman Beecher and the New York Common Council earlier in the century, Washington knew what types of schools would be effective at Americanization work and what types would not. By 1876 federal officials had concluded Catholicism was an unacceptable presence in the classrooms of any territory with aspirations of statehood. That year Congress passed a law requiring each new state admitted to the Union to include in its own constitution something the U.S. Constitution did not—a provision restricting educational funds to nonsectarian schools.[71] In New Mexico that provision served to strengthen the bond between two causes that many of the territory's Protestants already held dear.

Among the Protestants who spoke out in favor of nonsectarian public education during this period were individuals who had arrived in the region to found religious schools. The home missions movement of the Presbyterian Church in the U.S.A. sent its first representatives to northern New Mexico around 1870, and by the 1890s they were operating approximately twenty-five schools in the territory.[72] Like Bishop Lamy and the early Catholic religious in the region, these mainly female missionaries made educating native-born residents the centerpiece of their ministerial efforts. Unlike their Catholic counterparts, however, they brought with them a working appreciation of American common schooling, and an unshakable confidence in the compatibility between their own vision of Christian education and the "moral and political culture based on Anglo-American Protestantism" public schools instilled in their students.[73] Presbyterian missionaries denounced Catholic schools as a direct threat to the common Anglo-Protestant values both public and mission education provided. The denominational schools these women opened in New Mexico were a response to this threat. The concern among the missionaries was not only that the territory lacked Protestant schools, but that settlers had failed to provide adequate alternatives—either public *or* Protestant—to the antiquated and spiritually flawed Catholic system.[74] When state-sponsored schooling finally did gain a foothold in New Mexico, the focus of these home missions began to shift. The Presbyterian emphasis on private education gave way before the emerging public system as missionaries "hesitated to interfere or in any way impede its development."[75] Following the same principles that guided their earlier work, those residents became among the strongest advocates for keeping Catholicism safely out of the system taking shape.

As educational initiatives in late-nineteenth-century New Mexico targeted the Catholic Church, the Archdiocese of Santa Fe struggled to clarify its own position vis-à-vis the territory's growing number of public schools. A now-elderly Archbishop Lamy had defined his career by constructing a parochial system in New Mexico, and although he never prevented teaching orders from collecting public money for their work, he was wary of attempts to formalize public education in the territory.[76] Earlier in his career he had offered measured support for a public system, provided it allowed Catholic participation. As the archbishop aged, however, he recognized that efforts to build that system in New Mexico had become bound inextricably with the Protestant vision of nonsectarian schooling that predominated in the nation. This recognition compelled Lamy to state his opposition to public schooling in the strongest language of his career. In an 1884 pastoral letter he lamented the toll public education was taking on his beloved parochial schools. "After all this effort," he wrote, "it [causes] an intense pain to see that the result is not proportionate to our expectations; but the educational institutions existing among us are not appreciated and patronized as they can and should be." The bishop continued with a stern warning for parents who had abandoned parochial schools to send their children to the burgeoning public system:

> We who are obliged to watch over the education of the youth would find ourselves obliged to refuse the participation of the Sacraments to all those who, being able to education [sic] their children Christianly would prefer atheist or impious schools to those of their own religion.[77]

Like Bishop Hughes in New York, Lamy didn't object to public funds going toward parochial schools. He opposed a schooling model that excised Catholic influence and defied the objectives of Catholic education. That model was common throughout the United States and it was gaining supporters in New Mexico. In threatening to deny the sacraments to parents who capitulated to "impious schools," Lamy went beyond the Church's official stance at the time. Soon after penning the pastoral, and just before he resigned due to illness in 1885, the archbishop attended the Third Plenary Council in Baltimore.[78] There he was signatory to a joint decree from the American bishops on the topic of his schooling concerns. In words that echoed Lamy's instructions to his archdiocese the year before, the decree directed that all American Catholic parents were required to send their children to parochial schools "unless at home or in other Catholic schools they provide sufficiently and fully for their Christian education."[79] The bishops' joint statement remained nonspecific about the consequences for parents who disobeyed, however, and it left the decision to deny them sacraments to individual prelates like Lamy.

The Church in New Mexico remained uneasy about the character of public education after Lamy resigned. In 1889 the new archbishop, J. B. Salpointe, published an open letter in the territorial press. Responding to the legislature's most recent

attempt at a constitution, Salpointe voiced concerns that echoed those of his pred-
ecessor. The archbishop excoriated proponents of nonsectarian education as wolves
in sheep's clothing, calling their proposals "either sectarian, nonreligious, godless, or
agnostic." He demanded the proposed constitution's schooling clauses leave room
for a parent to educate his [*sic*] children "according to the dictate of his conscience."[80]
Even these remarks softened his full feelings about the latest campaign. Two months
earlier, an anonymously penned circular marked "Confidential" went out to Catholics across the territory. The pamphlet struck a provocative tone; it warned of "ene-
mies of our religion" who threatened to infiltrate the upcoming constitutional
proceedings. Those men, it predicted, would "so form the organic law as to force you
to deny your children all kinds of education excepting that of the world."[81] A rumor
attributed the circular to the archdiocese. Despite his last-bid efforts to influence
the character of this schooling proposal, however, when it came to the existence of
an independent system of schools the archbishop seemed resigned to the inevitable.
Salpointe knew a public system was all but a done deal in New Mexico by 1889.
Although the constitution he worried over failed that year in yet another referendum vote, the territorial legislature *did* pass a bill that finally created a public school
system in New Mexico two years later.[82]

The Archdiocese of Santa Fe's reluctance when it came to the territory's developing
public system was matched through the nineteenth and early twentieth century by
uneasiness on the part of many Hispano New Mexicans over the same system. At
times the position of the Church and the region's residents seemed to be one and
the same. In referendum votes, Hispano residents consistently rejected constitutions with education proposals that contained references to nonsectarianism. The
archdiocese appealed publicly to the territory's population to side with it on schooling debates; in the 1870s the Jesuit Gasparri tried to formalize this alliance when he
proposed an ethnically defined political party in New Mexico that would unite
Spanish-speaking residents against the educational initiatives of Anglo politicians.[83]
Despite the Church's overtures, however, New Mexico's Hispano people had their
own interests when it came to contests over education. For one thing, the territory's
native-born leadership included public schooling advocates among its ranks as early
as the mid-nineteenth century.[84] The majority of Hispano residents *did* resist public
education as it grew in the territory and later the state, but they did so for a variety
of reasons. As much as the archdiocese might have liked to presume otherwise, religion was not the population's only—or even its deciding—motivation.

Well into the twentieth century Anglos and Hispanos in New Mexico lived in
separate if overlapping worlds. If by the numbers the two groups were becoming
more balanced than ever before, they continued to make their homes in different
locations, speak different languages, and adhere to independent ethnic identities.[85]
While Americans who had relocated to New Mexico, especially since the 1880s,
tended to settle either on ranching land in the southeastern part of the state or in

urban centers, most of the state's Hispano population continued to inhabit traditional land grants in the state's northern counties, especially in the Rio Grande Basin and its surrounding elevations. Despite the arrival of a scattering of Anglos, the Basin remained a different place than the rest of New Mexico. Living in villages set apart on mountains and in hollows, the majority of its residents spoke only Spanish. As a testament to the region's cultural isolation, as late as 1935 accents varied between villages only a few miles distant from one another and expressions obsolete elsewhere in the Spanish-speaking world remained in usage.[86] The linguistic divide that separated Hispano and Anglo New Mexicans was compounded by their religious differences. While most of the state's Anglos were Protestant, nearly all its Hispano residents remained Catholic through the 1930s. In 1936 four out of five churchgoers in New Mexico still attended a Catholic church.[87] The most distinguishing feature of these Hispano villages through the early twentieth century, however, was their poverty. The four counties that made up the heart of the Rio Grande region were also the poorest counties in all of New Mexico in 1930.[88]

Religious loyalty coexisted with a host of concerns that informed Hispano residents' reactions to the education initiatives presented to them through the late nineteenth and early twentieth century. For Hispanos, the nonsectarianism asserted in many of those initiatives was not assayable in isolation; the religion issue was only one strand in the tangled web of expectations that was revealing itself as the American public school. The hesitancy of territory residents to embrace the schooling models imported by Anglo advocates was born from their Catholic faith, but it was born also from the reluctance of impoverished rural counties to pay new taxes, from concerns over state-instituted language requirements and enforced Americanization curricula, and from the lack of "community memory" when it came to publicly funded structures of education. As Lynn Marie Getz explains,

> Anglos brought with them ideas about how schools had been built, organized, and financed in older states. Hispanos had no such models and had to experiment with new methods of taxation, school administration, and curriculum suited to their own interests.[89]

Hispano people in New Mexico did not object to education as such. It was because they had a vested interest in education that they struggled with imported schooling models and tried to adapt them in ways "that made sense within the established patterns of their lives."[90]

New Mexico had a public school system in place in 1891, but it took another two decades for that system to standardize. During that time educational reformers continued to clarify the character and purpose of its schools. Like their predecessors over the latter half of the nineteenth century, these Anglo reformers had strong, loosely Protestant ideas about the place of religion within public classrooms.

More pressingly for most residents, they had equally strong ideas about the place of native culture in those classrooms. Some of these ideas were distinct to New Mexico, but most of them were borrowed from dominant American models of education. Theories about teaching children that were popular in places like St. Louis and Chicago translated into criteria for the New Mexican system. The civilizing impulses of early Anglo travelers to the region were supplanted by Americanization techniques—perfected by regional and national educators, scientifically justified, and applied meticulously to decisions about infrastructure, curriculum, and personnel.[91] The goal of transforming native behaviors through schooling remained. The Catholic priest and theologian Virgilio Elizondo, who grew up in a Mexican barrio in neighboring Texas a few decades later, remembered a similar Americanizing character in his public school system:

> The only institution in the area that was clearly Anglo-Saxon-Protestant-U.S.A. was the public school. . . . The school grounds were like a little island of the U.S.A. within Mexico. There the kids were forbidden to speak Spanish and even punished for doing so. While at home we heard about the Alamo traitors, at school they were presented as the Alamo heroes.[92]

As the proportion of Spanish-speaking people in New Mexico continued to decrease around the turn of the century, educational reformers in the territory conflated those people with new arrivals to the United States. Their classrooms became "incubators of republicanism"—replications of public institutions designed to cater to immigrants elsewhere in the nation during the Progressive Era.[93] The alienation many Hispanos felt toward the territory's public system arose because it was designed to treat them as just that—as aliens in need of Americanization. Because it was funded by tax money, the system Americanized them at their own expense.

More children were going to school in New Mexico at the turn of the century than ever before. While the 1870 census recorded only five public schools in the entire territory, by 1910 nearly two thirds of children in the soon-to-be state attended school.[94] Many of these students were Hispano. Within a generation Hispano students would grow up to be teachers themselves, and native-born educators would begin advocating to ensure that local concerns about curriculum and school funding policies reached state politicians. With a few exceptions, however, the early public system in New Mexico was neither representative nor reaffirming of the linguistic and cultural lives of the population who still claimed a majority in the territory. Instead, various theories about educating children prevalent in the United States during the era competed for an upper hand in that system. Some of these ideas were progressive in nature while others were more conservative strategies of Americanization.[95] The progressive impulse was manifested in New Mexico near the turn of the century in calls to professionalize teachers, modernize school buildings, standardize textbooks, and improve student hygiene. Meanwhile, Americanization advocates agitated for an English-only language requirement and for curricula that emphasized American history and civics. In practice, New Mexican educators and administrators often subscribed to both progressive and Americanizing impulses, and made them indistinguishable from one another in their work.

Both impulses shaped the new public system. In 1905, a nationalistically minded territorial legislature required the American flag to be flown outside of New Mexico's public schools on days of national significance—days that included the anniversaries of Civil War battles and the birthdays of Anglo-American notables like Louisa May Alcott and Eli Whitney. Anniversaries marking the native, Spanish, or Mexican histories and cultures of New Mexico's people were missing from the list.[96] Two years later the territory adopted another policy mandating the use of uniform English-language textbooks in its schools.[97] The legislature's concerted effort to transmit American culture and values through its new educational system was interspersed with more progressive policies as well, designed to cater to the distinctive needs and abilities of New Mexico's residents. Though well intentioned, these policies often reinforced an Anglo bias and were capable of alienating the population from its schooling as much as their more conservative counterparts. Hispano students, for example, were steered by progressive educators away from traditional academic subjects and into programs with special emphases on vocational training or, after the turn of the century, Spanish colonial arts like weaving and woodcarving—skills in which many reformers assumed the native population to have innate talent.[98]

The schooling policies that developed in New Mexico after 1891 represented national standards for the education of children applied to the special circumstances of the territory's native-born population. Those policies were reinforced when New Mexico became a state in 1912. New Mexico's new constitution included education clauses that singled out interactions between the region's school system, its Hispano residents, and its Catholic Church. The constitution echoed the U.S. Senate in its Congressional Enabling Act for New Mexico, and stipulated that the new state's schools "shall be open to all the children of the State and free from sectarian control, and [that] said schools shall always be conducted in English."[99] This clause clarified New Mexico's school system in opposition to both Catholic education and Spanish-language education. It echoed prevailing national concerns about the need to Americanize New Mexican people, and evinced the close supervision of the federal government in the delineation of an educational model for its newest state. It also reflected the nonsectarian language Protestant education advocates had been pushing for the last half-century. The constitution's overall posture toward both Hispano and Catholic interests, however, was more complicated. Other education clauses offered measured support for Hispano and Catholic participation in the state's schools by stipulating that "no religious test shall ever be required as a condition of admission into the public schools . . . either as a teacher or student," and that "children of Spanish descent . . . shall never be classed in separate schools, and shall forever enjoy perfect equality with other children in all public schools."[100] If the emphases (and ambivalence) of the 1912 constitution were any indication, Catholic religion and Hispano ethnicity were the two towering challenges facing the new state and its school system.

The Archdiocese of Santa Fe was in no rush to cooperate with New Mexico's public system at the turn of the century. Despite Salpointe's concerns to the contrary, Catholic communities had managed to retain access to tax funds after the territory's 1891 education law, and Catholic women religious still taught publicly in four communities when New Mexico became a state. By 1912, however, these examples of public–parochial cooperation were exceptions to the rule. The Church was conspicuously absent from the boom of public school construction and enrollment that occurred in New Mexico after 1900.[101] Instead the archdiocese chose to focus on its separate parochial system within the territory. While public school enrollment in New Mexico continued to grow—nearly doubling in the first decade of the twentieth century alone—Catholic schools lost enrollment to the public system between 1901 and 1905.[102] At statehood the archdiocese was operating only a modest twenty to twenty-five schools. In all, the Church was responsible for less than three thousand out of the approximately 50,000 students now attending school in New Mexico.[103]

In the two decades following statehood, however, the archdiocese's stake in public schools would change again dramatically. Between 1913 and 1935, at least eight communities of women religious arrived in New Mexico and began work in public classrooms. By the 1940s the number of Catholic religious communities teaching publicly in New Mexico had grown to thirteen.[104] Their arrival inaugurated a new era of public–parochial cooperation in the region, characterized by local projects in the style of Peter Küppers' school in Chaperito, but successful on a scale that would have been impossible during the territorial period. Through its participation in these projects the Catholic Church both found its place in the state system and revived its educational mission in New Mexico. Over a thirty-year period the Archdiocese of Santa Fe nearly quadrupled the number of students it was educating. Two out of every five of these children attended schools taught by Catholic sisters and supported with public funds.[105]

From a legal vantage point, the arrival of so many sisters after 1912 is oddly timed. New Mexico's constitution included language designed to exclude Catholicism from the state's schools. Historically the archdiocese had responded to nonsectarian education proposals by redoubling its efforts to steer Catholic children into a separate parochial system. This time, however, the educational reforms that came along with statehood created opportunities for cooperation between local residents, religious communities, and ultimately the archdiocese. By 1912, both New Mexico's Catholic leadership and its Hispano population had clear records of discontent when it came to schooling policy in their region. Although Church officials and Spanish-speaking residents had their differences when it came to what education should look like, the two groups shared wariness about the public system now

in place. Members of both groups also recognized, however, that pursuing their
interests within the state ultimately meant adapting to the realities of its structure. It
was serendipitous that the system had a structure in the decades after statehood that
allowed communities to engage it in their own ways. Even as the state's constitution,
and education statutes that followed it, sought to standardize the character of public
schooling in New Mexico, that character preserved a place for local decisions when
it came to things like facilities and teachers. Residents and clergy soon discovered
that even this limited autonomy was enough to give them collective control over the
day-to-day functions of the schools. Collaboration between them began in the
state's poorest communities. Just as a need for money had inspired Küppers' work in
Chaperito, the lack of educational resources in and around the Rio Grande Basin
motivated its residents to introduce sisters as public teachers there.

   Although the education clauses of New Mexico's constitution applied to Anglo
and Hispano parts of the state alike, the details of management and funding for the
new system that emerged after statehood reinforced old demographic divisions and
created an educational landscape that varied dramatically by location. Until at least
1940, two traits dominated the logistical side of New Mexican education: discrepan-
cies in the system's funding distribution formula that favored urban school districts
over rural ones, and the authority delegated to rural school officials for making decisions about buildings and personnel.[106] Taken together these traits encouraged
administrators in rural Hispano communities to experiment with schooling arrangements that conformed loosely (if at all) to state laws. The New Mexican legislature
officially distinguished between municipal and rural school districts in 1915, and in
doing so it inaugurated an era of educational policy that dictated, both directly and
indirectly, different treatment of the two.[107] Funding formulas during the period put
rural schools at a disadvantage. Rural districts were restricted by law to receive public
funds for shorter teaching terms than their municipal counterparts. State law also
dictated that teachers in rural districts receive lower maximum salaries, and that rural
classes enroll as many as fifty students before dividing.[108] These laws aggravated the
already difficult circumstances of most of New Mexico's rural communities. In 1916,
one of the state's top administrators took an exploratory trip across New Mexico and
reported that he found conditions in most of its rural schools "deplorable."[109]

   Laws stipulating where school money came from were especially paralyzing to
northern New Mexico's villages. Until the 1930s funding for rural schools was
derived almost entirely from county property taxes. This formula created a severe
disparity in educational resources between counties with urban centers and large
private landholders, and those with sparse populations, poor inhabitants, and large
swaths of land under federal ownership or trust.[110] To make matters worse, the limited tax revenue available to rural districts was distributed at the discretion of state
commissioners rather than on the basis of enrollment or other measures of need.[111]
Not surprisingly, the state's funding formula had an especially damaging effect on
the Hispano people, who resided disproportionately in rural counties. In all of the

Rio Grande Basin and its surrounding mountains there were only three municipal (or non-rural) districts in 1930.[112] Even after reforms to New Mexico's funding formula during the 1930s made statewide revenue the dominant source for educational funds, the Basin's public schools remained underfunded. During state board of education meetings during those years, accusations flew about the board manipulating its new distribution system in ways that continued to favor counties to the south.[113]

Through all of this, locally elected officials in northern New Mexico faced difficult decisions about how to spend the meager money available for their schools. The same educational code that deprived institutions of funding granted their administrators unusual authority over their management. Despite the state's control of purse strings, and the broad guidelines for the public system laid out in its constitution, the nuts and bolts of running a school remained a local responsibility into the 1940s. After 1915, the state board mainly wielded influence in two areas—it set the standards for teacher certification and it approved school curricula, including textbooks.[114] County and district officials held the power to build, purchase, or lease appropriate buildings for their schools and to make all hiring decisions, provided they limited their selections to teachers who were certified and spoke English.[115] Remembering the relationship of state and local educators during this period, one former state superintendent of public instruction recalled,

> There was really no state interest in local school affairs except where strong leadership demanded to be heard. The system had a distinct similarity to the feudal arrangement, where a few powerful barons challenged the state's authority, while others were entirely ignored.[116]

Officials in the rural districts of the Basin between 1912 and the late 1930s were those barons who were being ignored.[117] In northern New Mexico administrators and school boards neglected by the state government worked unnoticed along the margins of its educational system. Using the powers delegated to them, they developed schools that were both economically expedient and in sync with the desires of their constituency. A persuasive combination of factors—including local religious loyalties, the preexistence of a parochial infrastructure, and the prospect of teachers available at inordinately low salaries—prompted many of them to offer jobs to Catholic sisters. Their decisions to do so were welcomed and aided by the archdiocese, which recognized that these opportunities for public–parochial collaboration were a lifeline for the state's otherwise struggling Catholic school system.

Most sisters who taught publicly during the first half of the twentieth century were concentrated in New Mexico's impoverished rural counties.[118] For more than three decades, public schools taught by Catholic women religious were the solution to the educational challenges that plagued their mainly Hispano school districts. Wherever these schools opened they occupied a sort of bureaucratic no man's land—a space in between state laws and local practices, where the predominantly

Anglo-Protestant educational vision embodied by New Mexico's public system had given way to the web of concerns shared by its residents. The success of sisters' schools during this period was ensured by the Catholic officials and Spanish-speaking residents who worked together locating the religious to staff them and providing the material and financial resources they needed to function. A Hispano–Catholic alliance existed in early-twentieth-century New Mexico when it came to ideas about public schooling. That alliance, however, was neither perfect nor foreordained. Over the decades New Mexico's Spanish-speaking residents and its Church administration had acted on different and sometimes downright oppositional interests when it came to educating children. Those interests converged gradually over the course of the late nineteenth and early twentieth century, in the face of the tacitly Protestant and assertively Anglo educational models that became inspirations for New Mexico's public school system.

2

"We Live in a Valley Cut Off from the Outside World"

Local Observations on Sisters and the Separation of Church and State

Sister-taught public schools were always collaborations between residents, administrators, parish priests, archdiocesan officials, and the religious congregations invited to teach. In some places the schools began when administrators asked women already teaching parochially to make the transition to public work. In the city of Bernalillo, the Sisters of Loretto had taught in a parochial capacity since 1875. Their schools became public in 1891 at the request of New Mexico's first superintendent of public instruction.[1] When a change like this happened, the Archdiocese of Santa Fe leased buildings it originally intended for parochial use—often with Catholic names and often sharing property with a local church, convent, or rectory—to the local school board for a nominal fee. In other communities sister-taught public schools came about differently. Sometimes new districting laws required public education in villages that had none. Clergy, residents, or county officials would seek out a religious congregation willing to send its members to help. The local priest might oversee construction of a new school building as Peter Küppers had in Chaperito. On occasion parents themselves took initiative in these situations, petitioning the local board to hire sisters and to pay them from its budget. It was this sort of petition that prompted the most successful experiment in sister-directed schooling in New Mexico. Members of a Dominican community from Grand Rapids, Michigan, came to the state in 1925 to teach parochially, but a year later they agreed to accept public funds to work in the mountain village of Peñasco. By 1948 the Grand Rapids Dominicans had become the most represented religious community in New Mexico's schools.

The Dominicans came to the state as part of Peter Küppers' second effort to secure Catholic-led education for New Mexican children. By 1920 his school in Chaperito had closed and Küppers' relationship with some members of his parish had soured as a result of the failed experiment.[2] Aiming to give the energetic young priest a fresh start, Santa Fe's archbishop transferred Küppers to a new parish called Peñasco-Dixon in the heart of the Upper Rio Grande Basin. Küppers objected to the move at first. Although he faced problems in Chaperito, the thought of saying goodbye to his parishioners saddened him. In addition, the little he knew about his home to be was not enticing. He later wrote of Peñasco, "I only heard about it as a place where people had no spiritual foundation, and where annually people [got] secretly shot and killed."[3] Despite his misgivings, within a few short weeks the priest was living in Peñasco and presiding over a sprawling parish that encompassed thirteen missions. The setting for these missions was both beautiful and unnerving. Some of them were nestled in the narrow protected land along the Rio Grande while others—like Peñasco itself—were much higher, extending east into the elevations of the Sangre de Cristo Mountains. The steep unpaved roads that connected the parish's villages with one another helped create a feeling of isolation between places only a few miles distant. The trip from Santa Fe up to Peñasco was only thirty-five miles as the crow flies, but it could take five hours in 1920.[4]

The villages of Dixon and Peñasco were the dual hubs of Küppers' new parish. Each community was distinguishable by its post office, but in everyday life both comprised clusters of several small villages that functioned together as economic and social units. People in the communities were poor even by Basin standards. Exacerbated by overgrazing and water shortages characteristic of an overpopulated landscape, this poverty became most awful during the Depression years, when seventy percent of the region's residents fell dependent on federal relief.[5] Perched on the banks of the Rio Pueblo in Taos County, Peñasco was at the center of a group of villages that filled high wooded land in and near the Picuris Pueblo land grant and the Carson National Forest. These villages had names like Llano, Chamisal, and El Valle. The three thousand people who lived in and around Peñasco survived on high-altitude subsistence farming and selling railroad ties cut from the nearby forest.[6] More so than their counterparts in the valley, these residents had long cold winters to reckon with, and so the houses in Peñasco were small and thick-walled adobes with few windows and doors.[7]

Dixon was in Rio Arriba County, seventeen miles west of Peñasco and nearly a mile lower in elevation. Dixon had the name of its first postmaster, but in practice it was all but indistinguishable from the older adjacent village of Embudo. Embudo sat just where the Embudo River funneled into the Rio Grande, and Dixon itself was a mile and a half upriver. Land in the village was subdivided into subsistence farms that were irrigated through *acequias* hand-dug from the river and tightly controlled by local ditch bosses.[8] Most of Dixon's meager income came from men who worked in a nearby mine or—like men all over the Basin—who traveled several months of the year to labor as farm hands, sheep-herders, or railroad workers in states to the north. In the years Küppers ran its parish, Dixon had a reputation as the region's problem community. With only a half-dozen struggling stores and one automobile for every fifteen people, opportunities for both commerce and employment in the village were limited.[9] In the 1930s the local mine closed, itinerant jobs disappeared, and a three-year drought ravaged the local ecosystem. During that time most of Dixon's twelve hundred residents joined their neighbors up the mountain in relying on federal relief. Others went outside the law looking for ways to make ends meet. The bootleggers, marijuana dealers, and general rowdiness that cropped up in Dixon during the Depression years prompted one observer from the Works Progress Administration to describe "a general moral laxness which is unusual in the Spanish-American villages."[10]

In addition to its reputedly loose morals, Dixon was also known around the Basin—paradoxically—for its religious enthusiasm. The village had several churches and they competed hotly with one another to win over its more freewheeling residents. Küppers learned about this religious factionalism when he arrived in Dixon, and it gave his duties there a satisfying sense of urgency. The most remarkable thing about religious life in Dixon was that half of its people were Protestants. While the rest of the Basin was uniformly Catholic, Presbyterian missionaries had arrived in the village in the late nineteenth century as part of the outreach movement sponsored by their Board of Home Missions. By the twentieth century the fruits of their efforts were everywhere. In addition to maintaining a thriving church, in 1909 a group of missionary women founded a Presbyterian day school in Embudo. Seven years later they opened the Brooklyn College Hospital nearby. The Embudo hospital was a modest project; for most of the 1920s it functioned without a doctor, depending instead on the skills of mission nurses and local midwives. Despite its humble facilities, however, the establishment put Dixon-Embudo on the map by providing medical services to Catholic as well as Protestant residents throughout the Basin. By the time Küppers arrived in Dixon, the clinic had earned the nickname "baby catcher hospital" for the number of children its staff delivered.[11]

The village's Presbyterians were joined by other groups, including Seventh-Day Adventists, Mormons, Pentecostals, and United Brethren, so that by the 1930s a variety of small churches dotted the valley.[12] A Catholic sister who taught in Dixon during those years recalled catching glimpses of river baptisms in the Rio Grande and hearing stories about a local "Alluluia" chapel that was "equipped with a high steel rod along which the Holy Spirit was supposed to descend upon the faithful singing and rolling on the floor."[13] In this environment, Küppers realized that the greatest responsibility that came with his new job was to protect his parish's children from the enticement of Protestant sects. To do this work he knew he needed a school. Public and Catholic education were both largely absent from the Peñasco-Dixon missions when the priest arrived. Peñasco had no school at all in 1921, and the situation in Dixon was little better. Parents looking for an alternative to the Presbyterian institution in Embudo were obliged to send their children out of town at their own expense. Those children in the parish who did manage to attend school usually did not continue past the eighth grade. The rare student who went on to high school was likely to end up at a Presbyterian or Catholic boarding school in either Santa Fe or Albuquerque—not a single public high school existed in all of Rio Arriba County until 1917.[14]

Within two years Küppers had managed to create Dixon's first Catholic school. He collected money for the project wherever he could find it, even tapping into his personal funds. He cultivated the acquaintance of a Catholic ladies' group in Columbus, Ohio. Through a barrage of what he coolly described as "tear-jerking form letters" Küppers convinced the women of his worthy cause.[15] The priest soon found his most important supporters within his own parish. Rio Arriba County was a traditional stronghold of the *penitente* brotherhood. Although society membership was on the decline across northern New Mexico in the twentieth century, Dixon's unusual religious fervor extended to that corner of Catholic devotional culture as well. The independent Embudo *morada* was thriving when Küppers arrived there, and in Dixon the *penitentes* continued to enjoy an increasing membership through the 1930s.[16] The ever-practical Küppers understood the brotherhood's local influence, and even though archbishops since Lamy had officially denounced the *penitentes*, he wasted no time ingratiating himself with its members. In time, the priest would become one of the *penitentes'* most vocal advocates within the Catholic Church, saying annual masses on their behalf and writing sympathetic accounts of their activities for several publications. Even the archbishop himself acknowledged Küppers' intimacy with the estranged Catholic community when he asked him to write a book on the subject.[17] Dixon's *penitentes* gave the priest their support in return. The brotherhood's endorsement helped Peter Küppers not only build his school, but also make a name for himself politically and popularly in the region.

When it opened, St. Joseph's parochial school was housed in Dixon's old Catholic church.[18] As his next order of business Küppers began looking for sisters willing to staff the school. His initial solicitations to motherhouses across the country met little enthusiasm; the congregations he corresponded with had members who were already in high demand as teachers, and they could anticipate the financial burden that work in a poor and remote parish like Dixon-Peñasco would entail.[19] Then, on a 1925 visit to the University of Notre Dame, Küppers stumbled on a promising lead. Just a short trip north from South Bend, Grand Rapids, Michigan, was home to a Dominican community with a strong commitment to teaching. The prioress general there lately had been considering foreign missions work for her sisters, and Küppers guessed the community might be persuaded to come to the American Southwest instead.[20] Mother Benedicta O'Rourke received Küppers graciously when he visited the Dominicans' Marywood motherhouse in Grand Rapids, but she remained carefully noncommittal as the priest laid his case before her. The prioress was reluctant to commit her sisters to work in Dixon until she had the opportunity to travel to New Mexico and assess the situation for herself. Having put off a decision, however, Mother Benedicta wasted no further time. She traveled to Küppers' parish that April, and what she saw persuaded her to accede to the priest's request. Aside from a mission in dire need of teachers, the superior wrote her sisters that New Mexico offered a unique opportunity, "chiefly for the benefit of our delicate sisters who cannot stand this northern climate."[21] Upon returning to Grand Rapids Mother Benedicta selected four sisters from a group of volunteers. In July 1925, after a "formal missioning ceremony, with ringing of the tower bell and [an] 'honor guard' of sisters from the chapel to the property entrance," Sisters Amata Baader, Theodosia Foster, Mechtilde Cordes, and Ernesta Hogan departed Marywood by train for Santa Fe.[22]

The Dominicans' duties at St. Joseph's School began that autumn. The school experienced unexpectedly large enrollment during the sisters' first year on the job—one hundred twenty-five students, in grades one through nine—and it only continued to grow.[23] Catholic families from across the parish, frustrated by the lack of non-Protestant schools in their vicinity, began bringing their children to Dixon for instruction by the sisters. When road conditions made travel challenging, some families arranged for their children to live with friends or relatives in town. A few actually relocated to be closer to the new Catholic institution.[24] Although thrilled with their school's popularity, the four Dominicans were soon struggling with classrooms filled beyond capacity. They were undoubtedly relieved the following year when Küppers asked their superior to send additional members of the congregation to New Mexico. Mother Benedicta again obliged to the priest's request. Never one to rest on his laurels, Küppers contemplated the arrival of a second batch of sisters from Michigan as the opportunity for growth. He hardly waited for the women involved to consent to the relocation before proudly announcing his plan to open a second Dominican-taught school in his parish, up the mountain from Dixon in Peñasco.

The Peñasco school, when it opened in 1926, was as a public enterprise. A group of residents from that village had petitioned the Taos County School Board, asking it to fund the new school and to hire the Dominicans to teach in it.[25] Although Küppers certainly had his hand in making this request, the popular support for it was substantial. Many families in the heavily Catholic village were opposed to Protestants educating their children, and several parents were already sending their sons and daughters the seventeen miles to be taught by the Dominicans at St. Joseph's.[26] The school board assented to a school in Peñasco with one caveat—while it agreed to pay the sisters' salaries from its tax-funded operating budget, housing and equipping the school would remain the village's responsibility.[27] This time Küppers appealed to the archdiocese for help. Santa Fe's archbishop, Albert Daeger, agreed to provide building funds, and soon thereafter members of the community began work on a four-room schoolhouse. As promised, four Dominicans—Sister Theodosia Foster, along with Sisters Seraphine Wendling, Sienna Wendling, and Lorraine Gibson—arrived in Peñasco.[28] That autumn they began to teach, first in an abandoned schoolhouse that had been hastily repaired and, once it was completed, in the new building. St. Anthony's school—owned by the archdiocese but maintained and staffed with public funds—opened with Küppers as its director and the

Dominicans presiding over grades one through ten.[29] The sisters taught eight months of the year. For seven of those months, or the academic year required of rural districts by law, they received their $70-per-month salaries directly from the county. For the one additional month they were supported by parish funds.[30]

At its opening St. Anthony's School had just ninety-three pupils, but within a year that number had more than doubled to two hundred fifteen.[31] Two years later it became an accredited two-year high school, and in 1930 it received a full four-year accreditation from the state. With this achievement St. Anthony's became the first public high school in all of southern Taos County.[32] The archdiocese rewarded this milestone—and acknowledged the school's ever-increasing enrollment—by constructing a second building to house its higher grades.[33] The prominent stature of Peñasco's two educational institutions within northern New Mexico was affirmed beyond question in 1933. That year Peñasco successfully severed ties with the Taos County school system and became an independent educational district—a remarkable move for a village of its size during that era.[34] Amid all these exciting developments, however, some things remained unchanged in the Dixon-Peñasco parish. No one batted an eyelid when Peter Küppers himself stepped in to act as the first superintendent of the Peñasco Independent Schools.

After a decade spent working in Peñasco's public schools, one Dominican sister recalled the reception she and her companions received from *Peñasceros* upon their arrival in the mountain village years earlier:

> The same eagerness which had characterized parents in New York and Michigan when first "the white Sisters" arrived in their midst was manifest in New Mexico.... Here were starry-eyed children eager for what the Sisters were eminently qualified to give—opportunity to acquire knowledge.[35]

Despite its nostalgic tone, the sister's impression of the local reaction to religious like her was generally accurate. The Grand Rapids Dominicans, along with the dozen or so other communities of Catholic sisters who taught publicly in New Mexico in the decades before the *Zellers* suit, enjoyed strong support in the villages where they worked. The ambivalence Hispano Catholic residents harbored toward the rules and regulations of the still-new public system combined with religious loyalties and more worldly interests to create a vision of education in which the prospect of sisters doubling as public educators was unproblematic. The vast majority of residents in the Rio Grande Basin recognized potential in sisters' classrooms; they understood them to be places where their children would receive both the lessons in faith and morals necessary for a solid Catholic upbringing, as well as instruction in academic, vocational, and social skills that would bring them success in the world.

To say that residents approved of sisters in their schools, however, only scratches the surface of the relationship between New Mexicans and the women who taught them in the 1930s and 1940s. Just as an uneasy disposition toward public education in New Mexico predisposed residents of its rural northern counties to invite women religious into their classrooms in the first place, the dynamics of those classrooms could also produce uneasy feelings. Catholic religious were especially challenging figures for young people. In crowded quarters, Anglo sisters and Hispano children spent long hours together, five days a week, several months of the year, cultivating relationships that continued to shape both parties long after the school days ended. Six decades later, lifelong residents of Peñasco and Dixon still enjoy memories of the sisters who taught in their schools. To hear these men and women describe them, sisters shared a near-superhuman ability to inspire respect in their charges. Today that respect dominates the stories they tell. "You had to respect them, that was for sure," one Dixon resident affirmed of the sisters who taught him.[36] The respect that colors former students' memories of attending school with the sisters is a complicated sentiment. Children in New Mexico—like children everywhere— formed their respectful attitudes over time, as a response both to deeply seated pre-conceptions, and to hundreds of interactions with their teachers inside and outside of the classroom. While many of these episodes were pleasurable experiences, others in the short term produced feelings of confusion, fear, or shame. Students genuinely respected their teachers in Dixon and Peñasco, but to learn respect for someone was not always to enjoy their company. Interacting across differences in age, language, culture, and class, students and sisters built relationships out of conflicting emotions. Local children eventually came to recognize the full range of these emotions as evidence of their respect. That respect, in turn, became a key ingredient in the local population's support for sisters, and in its dismissal of the claims made against them during the 1940s by the *Zellers* lawsuit.

If the enthusiastic reception sisters received in New Mexico occluded the interior experiences of their classrooms, that enthusiasm also overwhelmed—at least for a time—the voices of a minority who were dissatisfied with the cooperative arrangements that characterized education in the northern part of the state. This minority comprised residents loyal to different Protestant faiths, and in most villages of the Rio Grande Basin it was small enough during the 1930s and 1940s to go almost unnoticed. In communities that were nearly entirely Catholic, the rare Protestant parent concerned about his or her son or daughter attending school with the sisters was likely to avoid confrontation with the status quo. When they had the financial means to do so, these Protestant families sometimes chose to send their children to denominational boarding schools downstate, much like Catholic parents were forced to in the days before sisters taught in their communities. Occasionally they had access to Protestant day schools—usually Presbyterian—in closer proximity that their children might attend. More often, however, these parents would send their children to the sisters for instruction and hope for the best. Faced with a Catholic school board and surrounded by Catholic neighbors on all sides, most Protestant parents assumed they had little choice in the matter. Some of these families came to value and even to defend the sisters' work. Those who did not kept their dissatisfaction to themselves.[37]

In Dixon things turned out differently. There Catholic sisters' eventual entry into the public schools was met with furious objections by parents. Dixon's Protestant community included energetic and articulate individuals who, though they lacked a hard and fast knowledge of constitutional law, were convinced that the tutelage of their children by Catholic sisters was wrong. Over time they came to suspect it was illegal as well. Spurred on by the anger of a young mother named Lydia Zellers, Anglo and Hispano Protestants in Dixon joined together to discuss what they found so disturbing about the presence of Catholic sisters in their schools. As they did so they clarified their own shared understanding of what the relationship of Catholicism to public education in their state should be. The vision of church–state relations that Dixon's Protestants developed as they reacted to the sisters in their schools in the 1940s was inherited in part from ideas imported by their religious forebears—the Anglo-Protestant educational reformers and missionaries who arrived in the region in the nineteenth century. But their valuation of church–state separation, as it appeared in response to the crisis of sisters teaching in their community, was also distinctly New Mexican. It was as particular in its own way as the disregard for separation and support for teaching sisters shared by their Catholic counterparts in the Basin. In time, the local value that they placed upon separation would motivate a group of Dixon's Protestants to action, and their actions would transform the shape of education in New Mexico.

Peter Küppers' tenure as superintendent of the Peñasco schools didn't last long. After Küppers resigned the post—it remains a mystery whether his poor health, conflicts with the archdiocese, or some combination of factors led to his departure—he was succeeded by a Dominican. Sister Maura McDonald arrived in Peñasco from Michigan in 1937, and the forty-year-old sister quickly demonstrated herself capable of filling the priest's administrative shoes. Born in West Virginia to hard-working Scottish immigrants, McDonald had followed her mother's advice as a young woman and delayed her decision to join the religious life until the relatively old age of twenty-five. The extra years of pre-vocational experience had given her a perspective unusual for a Catholic sister at the time. In her secular life, McDonald had been employed in both a factory and a freight office, traveled extensively, and even turned into an accomplished bowler. Upon entering the Order of Preachers, Sister Maura's thirst for new experiences didn't diminish but instead translated into a drive to continue her education. After acquiring her teaching certification—a standard accomplishment for sisters in her community—Sister Maura spent several summers enrolled in graduate courses at the University of Notre Dame, the University of Chicago, and Catholic University. She eventually completed her master's degree in school administration at the University of New Mexico in Albuquerque, where her thesis on the Dominican community's approach to teaching in the state received high marks.[38] Sister Maura had a sturdy build, a strong constitution, and a demeanor that was both sensible and beguiling. She presided as superintendent in Peñasco for the next twelve years.

Figure 2.1 Sister Maura McDonald, OP. Courtesy of the Dominican Sisters, Grand Rapids, Michigan.

With McDonald at their helm, Peñasco's schools emerged as models for the success of sister-directed education in the state. During the 1940s as many as three hundred seventy children were enrolled in school at Peñasco at any given time.[39] With only about seven hundred fifty residents living in the village itself, these enrollment numbers spoke to the reputation of Peñasco's schools in outlying mountain communities, and to the efforts of families in those more remote locations to send their children to the sisters for an education.[40] With primitive roads and winter snowfalls that could make walking impossible, parents went to great lengths to deliver their children to school. As one woman who grew up outside Peñasco in the village of Rio Lucio remembered:

> My dad had made a sled and he had horses. . . . he would take us on the sled all the way to the road. It was fun! The Rio Pueblo was frozen and we had to cross it. . . . Sometimes when we walked—when for some reason he couldn't take us—our feet were frozen it was so cold! We always had wood stoves and heaters. My mom would open the oven and make us take our shoes off and stick them in there to get warm.[41]

Sister Maura and the other Dominicans working in Peñasco made tremendous efforts to keep pace with their expanding student body. As time passed, they improved the infrastructure of both the elementary and high schools, so that by the 1940s the Peñasco campus boasted two domestic science workrooms and a new outbuilding erected by the high school's woodworking class. Most importantly the academic standards kept by both schools remained a point of pride. Peñasco High School, which had matriculated its first students in 1931, was producing successful alumni in a number of professional fields. Some Peñasco graduates had joined the armed forces, while others had gone on to pursue college degrees, and work as nurses and teachers. Much to the sisters' delight, a few students had also begun to study for religious vocations.[42]

As their reputation grew, Grand Rapids Dominicans were invited to staff public schools in other villages across the Basin. In the years after the community began working in Peñasco, additional sisters arrived from Michigan to open schools in Santa Cruz, the pueblo of San Juan, and Ranchos de Taos.[43] Before long thirty sisters from Grand Rapids were employed as teachers by the state; together these women oversaw the education of more than 1,600 students spread among five different public schools.[44] State officials in New Mexico celebrated the sisters' presence—they recognized the Dominicans' arrival as an injection of much-needed professionalism into their young system. Many of the women religious they employed had received both college degrees and formal training as teachers, educational achievements that surpassed those of most lay teachers in the region during the period. As early as 1931, the Peñasco Dominicans participated in their first state teachers' convention. During the proceedings, administrators appealed to the women to stage a demonstration of their methods for the benefit of teachers already at work in the state.[45] As word of their talents continued to spread with time, the sisters obliged a growing number of invitations to present at local, state, and national gatherings. By the end of the decade their schools in Ranchos de Taos and San Juan, along with Peñasco, each enjoyed the designation of a "key school"—an institution selected by state administrators to serve as a model for others in the public system.[46] In 1940 George Sanchez, native New Mexican and the foremost Hispano educator in the early-twentieth-century United States, distinguished the schools of Peñasco within his otherwise dire report of education in Taos County. Sanchez concluded their result was "important economies . . . to the taxpayers and, in general, a better education for the children."[47]

In spite of their success across northern New Mexico, the Grand Rapids Dominicans' time in their first New Mexican community proved short-lived. Again Peter Küppers catalyzed their movement. Although he was no longer superintendent in Peñasco, the priest continued to make educational decisions down the mountain in Dixon. By spring of 1941 his meddling influence in the school there had aggravated its religious enough that they wrote Santa Fe's newest archbishop, Rudolph Gerkin, a letter, informing him they would depart Dixon at the close of that year.[48]

The Dominicans' abrupt exit from St. Joseph's Catholic School after sixteen years of service left the archbishop in a difficult situation. Faced with the prospect of closing Dixon's hard-won school for want of teachers, he found himself scrambling to locate another religious order who might take the Dominicans' place. Quickly he wrote a personal letter to Mother Afra, the superior of the Third Order of St. Francis stationed in Amarillo, Texas. The archbishop had decided to reach out to Mother Afra because he was familiar with her sisters; Gerkin had worked with the Franciscan community years earlier while he served as the first bishop of Amarillo. Now he confided to its superior about the trouble Dixon was in, and laid out the stakes of the decision before her. "There is no place in the whole Diocese where it is so important we have sisters as at Dixon," he wrote, "because of the danger to the remaining Catholics from Protestant sects working."[49] The archbishop's message to Mother Afra sounded dire, but it was not exaggerated. In recent years Protestant groups around Dixon had laid new claim to education in the village. In addition to the community's successful Presbyterian school, a Seventh-Day Adventist institution had begun to compete for children in the area, and the United Brethrens had opened still another school nearby.[50] Without a Catholic school to compete in this heterodox environment, Gerkin knew Dixon's children would be more vulnerable than ever to the Protestant elements that had already succeeded in converting nearly half of the village's population.

Mother Afra promptly agreed to the archbishop's request. Her congregation already had a group of sisters living in the village of Aragon in the western part of the state, and sending an additional group into New Mexico was well within its means.[51] Over the next several months eight sisters, including Mother Afra herself, traveled to Dixon to work. The Franciscans who began to teach in St. Joseph's School in 1941 were an unusual addition to Catholic education in the Basin, and a sharp contrast to the Dominicans who were already familiar figures moving across its rocky landscape. The Franciscan Sisters of Mary Immaculate had gotten their start in Switzerland in the nineteenth century, but had relocated in the 1890s to Colombia, South America. They had settled in the United States even more recently, in the early 1930s, when their community accepted an offer by then-Bishop Gerkin to teach and train postulants in Amarillo.[52] The Franciscans who came to Dixon were a motley group, comprising both German and Spanish-speaking women—Swiss and *Tejano* novices who had joined the group during its time in Texas, as well as a handful of women from a Mexican religious order who had petitioned to join the community years earlier.[53] Whereas most of the Grand Rapids Dominicans came from hardy Midwestern stock, the Franciscan sisters had an air about them that was difficult to place; their English was accented and they brought with them a strange catalog of European rituals and songs.[54] For locals, even their appearance was a startling change—the Franciscan costume was constructed from somber brown wool, which gave them a simple appearance in contrast to the Dominicans' snow-white habit. Some residents also noticed that the group beginning work in Dixon seemed young and inexperienced relative to their predecessors. The oldest of the teaching sisters was in her early twenties; and although the women who took over St. Joseph's upper classes all had college degrees, the congregation soon began to send elementary teachers fresh from high school as it struggled to keep pace with the institution's rising enrollment.

Even with these differences, Dixon's Catholic residents received the Franciscans with the same enthusiasm they had shown the Dominican sisters in earlier years. In Dixon and across New Mexico, support for Catholic sisters' schools remained strong through the 1940s. In 1947—just a year before the *Zellers* case began—a graduate student at the University of New Mexico traveled to villages across the state with public schools taught by religious, and he interviewed residents to discover their attitudes toward the institutions. "Because of the widespread practice in New Mexico of offering public education by religious teachers," Frederick Bacon surmised, "a study should be of particular interest to the state."[55] During his research Bacon visited twenty-two of twenty-seven New Mexican communities with religious-taught schools, and he talked with some five hundred residents. Although the researcher could confidently identify only three hundred of his respondents as Catholics, the group he sampled expressed overwhelming approval of teaching sisters. When Bacon asked residents their general opinion of religious as public-school teachers, twenty percent of his interviewees expressed great enthusiasm, while another seventy percent maintained that religious were better than the "general run" of teachers available for their schools. Only one percent of respondents, Bacon reported, had criticism to offer.[56] In addition, four out of five residents who the student spoke with favored sisters' continued employment in their public classrooms. Among those expressing their support on this issue, the most common justification offered was straightforward: "Religious make better teachers."[57]

As litigation loomed in the 1940s, this widespread approval of sisters prompted one skeptical Baptist minister to speculate that the "Spanish Catholic laity" of New Mexico were little more than "dupes of an unfeeling Catholic system."[58] He was correct to notice that Catholicism acted as a powerful force in the lives of Basin residents as the mid-century mark approached, and that it shaped their ideas about education. For children especially, Catholic ideas and traditions provided an interpretive framework for all types of daily experiences. For a young Catholic person growing up in Dixon or Peñasco, even the passage of time was marked by a fixed cycle of religious observances, as reliably as it was by the agricultural cycles—the changing water levels in the *acequias* or the staggered plantings and harvestings— that denoted the annual rhythms of rural New Mexican life. Every Catholic child looked forward his or her favorite celebration, whether it was the reenactment of *los pastores* in the town square at Christmastime or the *fiesta* of a beloved saint. "There was St. John, *San Juan*," one resident of Rio Lucio remembered:

> We had a ditch just a few feet from the house. . . . And [when] it was . . .
> St. John's Day—*el dia de San Juan*—everybody went to . . . play in the

water because it was St. John's Day. The other day I remember was St. James. *Dia de Santiago*. On that day the boys would . . . saddle and ride their horses. . . . And then the next day is St. Anne's. And that was the girls' day. On the girls' day the girls would ride the horses.[59]

Important events, from births and marriages to illnesses and deaths, were answered with Catholic rituals both in the church and inside people's homes. Parents in Peñasco and Dixon brought their sons and daughters to Mass without fail, even when it meant (as it often did) walking several miles in bitterly cold temperatures. When Catholic women religious arrived to teach in the local schools, these residents accepted them as part of the already thick religious fabric of their lives. Children especially recognized the habit-clad figures as walking embodiments of the Catholic Church and its teachings. Just as the Church's celebrations and sacraments provided a foundation for experience most young people seldom questioned, so the Church's religious found their way easily into children's notions of community.

Even so, young people's reactions to the religious living and working among them went well beyond expressions of pious loyalty. Today those who attended school with sisters in Peñasco and Dixon describe their former teachers with real affection. Now in their seventies and eighties, most remember their relationships with these women as driven by an abiding sense of respect. Students "respected them very much," one Embudo resident remembered of the women religious who taught him in Dixon during the 1940s; "respect was a very big thing."[60] "I think everybody was very respectful at that time," surmised a resident of Dixon.[61] In these memories the respect students held is tied closely to the personal characters—to the talents and dispositions—of sisters themselves. While their authority as Church

Figure 2.2 Sisters with a class of fourth-grade students. Blanco, New Mexico, 1942.

representatives was important to building respect, it was not as important—if one takes students at their word—as the ability sisters demonstrated as teachers. As Bacon's survey also suggests, the quality of sisters' instruction elevated them in the eyes of locals, and perhaps young people most of all. "The sisters were very, very good teachers," Alfredo Gomez of Dixon remembered.[62] "My mother used to say [they were] the best thing that could have ever happened to this parish," his friend from Embudo added. "Because they were educated and they always tried to teach what they knew."[63] "Most of them had their degrees hanging on the wall," another former student emphasized.[64] When comparing them with lay teachers who staffed other public schools in the area, former students point to a marked difference in the quality of sisters' instruction. "The nuns always made sure you did your homework. . . . But in public school you were mostly on your own," Abelardo Jaramillo explained.[65] Edna Garcia, who attended school in Peñasco, agreed: "The level of education was lower in the public school."[66]

The traits that made sisters "good teachers," and built respect for them within the community, did not always result in pleasant experiences for the children who were their immediate beneficiaries. Many memories former students cherish recall episodes that were emotionally or physically painful for their younger selves. Both the Dominicans in Peñasco and the Franciscans in Dixon were formidable disciplinarians. In the Dixon elementary school, punishments for misbehavior included the ubiquitous ruler slap to the back of the hand ("not flat—sideways," one former student insisted) and requiring students to kneel at the front of the classroom. "I thought it was forever, but [it was] maybe five minutes," Edna Garcia recalled. Other students remembered the boredom of writing phrases like "I must not chew gum in school" repeatedly on the blackboard.[67] At the high school in Peñasco, sisters opted to separate difficult students from the general population by placing them in an optimistically named "opportunity room," where the women might keep close watch over those "who were the big troublemakers, the ones who didn't want to work, who were lazy."[68] For the more occasional mischief maker, a stern lecture and the threat of parent contact usually sufficed. Lucille Leyba, who attended school in Peñasco, reflected on sisters' use of discipline during her otherwise positive account of schooling with the Dominicans. "The times when it [was] negative it's because I did something that wasn't right," she concluded.[69] "They were a little strict," Abelardo Jaramillo agreed of the sisters in Dixon, "but that always helps when you're growing up—keeps you in line, keeps you straight."[70]

Sisters' disciplinary techniques are remembered approvingly by former students like Leyba and Jaramillo—now parents, grandparents, and great-grandparents themselves—as the tools of sound character formation. As children, however, the discipline that cultivated respect in an individual also produced feelings of anger and especially of fear. Sisters sometimes lost their tempers facing disobedient students. Francisco Romero recalled one episode involving an older student at the Dixon elementary school:

There was a guy in the eighth grade that got into a fight with one of our nuns here. He started yelling all kinds of language at her in Spanish and she ran after him! She went after him, but didn't catch him. And she turned red, and started coming in. And she said "Forgive me" when she came in. "I shouldn't have done that; but I did it."[71]

While a few sisters earned reputations for being hot-tempered or mean, former students recall the dispositions of others as softened by the capacity for gentleness or mercy. Lucille Leyba vividly recounted a time she faced disciplinary action from her teacher, also named Lucille, at Peñasco High School:

We went up to Tres Ritos where an old cabin was. . . . One of the girls had cigarettes and encouraged us to take a puff. . . . Somebody must have seen us and told [Sister Lucille]; when we cleared the trees and came back down into the open area she was standing there waiting for us. She went like this [slaps her thigh] and my knees went like butter. . . . She said "I know you were smoking. . . . Each one of you *must* bring your parents on Monday. And if you don't bring your parents don't even come back." I prayed all that weekend. I prayed and prayed that my parents would not find out. . . . On Monday morning I came to school and the first thing she did was call me to the office and she asked, "Where are your parents? I told you not to come unless you brought them." I cried and I knelt and I pleaded for forgiveness and I promised that I would never do it again. . . . And she heard me. She said, "Okay, I'm not going to tell them. . . . But don't do it again. Don't get in trouble again."[72]

The ability to scare wayward students into obedience without directly punishing them was a skill the Dominicans perfected. Of all the women religious working in the Peñasco school system, Maura McDonald is remembered most of all for her savvy exercise of discipline. "She was mean," remembered Anna Cordova with a laugh. "Now I think back, and I'd say she was not mean but she was strict."[73] "She was firm and serious," Leyba explained. "All you had to do was look at her, and you knew she meant business. . . . We were afraid of her because that look was enough to scare us."[74] Students' interactions with Sister Maura and their other teachers were punctuated by fear—sometimes even downright dread—of punishment for misbehavior. But those same relationships were also often marked by the reassuring sense their teachers were intelligent, reasonable, and on their side. This lively mixture of emotions that children felt around sisters formed the aura of respect now remembered approvingly by their adult selves.

The respect students felt toward their teachers also bore a complicated relationship to the cultural and linguistic differences that punctuated their interactions with the mainly Anglo and English-speaking sisters. Nearly all students who attended school in both Dixon and Peñasco spoke Spanish as their first language, and most only began to learn English once they joined the sisters in their classrooms. Alfredo Gomez recalled of Dixon in the 1940s that "at the time there were very, very few Anglos here.... There may have been two or three families only. Other than that it was all Spanish-speaking."[75] Margaret Atencio had a similar memory of the student body in Peñasco: "The only Anglos we had were the kids of the forest ranger," she recalled.[76] While the women who taught in both communities spoke what one student remembered as "real good English," most had little or no command of the Spanish language—a deficit that made communication with their youngest pupils difficult.[77] Abelardo Jaramillo, recalling his early years with the sisters, likened their frustrated efforts at conversation to an altogether different experience he had later in life while serving in the military. "I was in Korea for fifteen months and they had . . . Koreans serving in what they called the ROC army," he recalled. "They would start speaking Korean, and we would just . . ." Jaramillo laughed. "It was about the same way here with the nuns. We'd be speaking in Spanish when we were playing outside, yelling; and they would just look at us."[78]

Children facing the task of learning English often struggled with their teachers' expectations for them. A Dominican volunteered the story of a boy in the first or second grade at Peñasco who, when admonished by his teacher to speak in English, could offer only a perplexed query in return: "Do we have to laugh in English too?" he asked.[79] Because children began to study the language when they were five or six years old, most former students have trouble remembering the process in detail. Of those who do recall it, some acknowledge the difficulty it involved, while others give it a positive spin.[80] "They were very good at teaching English classes," Delia Garcia of Rio Lucio remembered about the Dominicans. "It was for our own good."[81] Lucille Leyba agreed wholeheartedly with her friend, although she also recognized some students felt otherwise:

> I've heard a few people who resent that we were punished for speaking Spanish in the classroom or on school grounds.... Some kids were punished by having to write on the board a hundred times "I must not speak Spanish in school." But I never saw it . . . as a real punishment. Because I understood, especially as I got older, that it was the only way that we were going . . . to get out of here and face the world.[82]

Even students who grew up to respect sisters' intentions, as so many of them did, had episodes as children that left them feeling ashamed or questioning their self-worth. Along with the English language, children in Dixon and Peñasco received instruction from their teachers about hygiene, clothing, and food. Abelardo Jaramillo remembered one awkward situation that arose when his mother ordered his older brother a pair of shirts from a catalog. "One was supposed to be brown, and one grey," he recollected. "And they sent the same color for both. So one of the nuns got after my brother and said, 'Don't you ever change your shirt?!'"[83] Leyba herself recalled being embarrassed about the lunch her mother packed for her each day:

> It was funny because all of us were . . . Spanish families, [so] all of us ate tortilla at home. Our mothers all made tortilla. So if we went to school and we took a lunch . . . our mothers didn't make bread. For some reason, tortilla was something to be ashamed of. If we took a sandwich with tortilla, then we'd take our little bag and go and eat our sandwich and hide. . . . We didn't want anybody to see us eat tortilla, even though everybody else had [it].

For Leyba the shame she felt as a girl sat uneasily with her memory of teachers whose expectations were nothing but admirable. "I don't think it had anything to do with the sisters," she continued. "I don't know where we got it. . . . I can't figure it out."[84]

The pressure sisters placed upon their pupils to speak English at a young age, and to dress, eat, and generally act more American as they grew up, inspired complicated responses in the children they taught. It produced feelings of confusion, anger, resentment, and shame, even as it also contributed to the abiding respect many of them had for their teachers. Despite the history of antagonism between Anglos and Hispanos over the shape of New Mexican education, a significant number of Spanish-speaking residents in the Basin in the 1940s recognized the adoption of the English language and Anglo customs as the surest way to economic and social success in a changing state. For their children, sisters' Anglo qualities became an outright source of admiration, a lifestyle model that might even lead students to disparage pieces of their own culture. As one former student put it, "we were very proud to have Anglos. My dad especially loved them. He said they tried harder to have what they had. They did everything. They weren't lazy."[85] Respect granted to sisters' Anglo-ness, however, was less common in Dixon and Peñasco than the respect sisters received *in spite* of their background. For every former student who reflects upon the teachers' Anglo qualities, others minimize sisters' ethnic differences in their memories. Most students remember their teachers as insiders—full-fledged members of the local community. "I think they were part of the community," Delia Garcia emphasized. "They were welcome."[86]

For some students, Catholic women religious even transcended the Anglo–Hispano binaries that typified much of public life in New Mexico. Despite the fact that sisters spoke and taught English, some students—then and now—stopped short of labeling them Anglos. Ethnic categories mattered in northern New Mexico in the 1940s, but they could also be tenuous with boundaries that were difficult for a young child to discern. In this environment, sisters' Catholic faith—and in particular the religious vows that were intended to separate them from the secular world—granted them a fluid identity in students' eyes. One Dominican sister volunteered an anecdote about the seventh graders she taught during the 1940s. "They said something about the gringos," Sister Carmella Conway remembered, "and I said, 'Well I'm a gringo.'" But her students disagreed:

> "Oh no! You're not a gringo!" [they said]. And I said, "Well I am too! I'm white." "But you're not a gringo." So in their minds, gringo stood for more than just being white.[87]

Students' own memories corroborate this sense that, for many children, their teachers' religious identity changed or even erased their ethnic character—in spite of the Anglo-American culture they taught. For some students, the names sisters took when they entered the religious life sounded culturally familiar. A Dixon resident who remembered the Franciscan Sisters Gilberta and Seferina as his favorite teachers in elementary school gave their names an easy Spanish pronunciation.[88] For others it was sisters' lack of surnames that freed them from ethnic certainty. A Peñasco woman recalled her teachers' ethnic backgrounds as always being a mystery. "I never knew," Margaret Atencio insisted. "We always wanted to know their last names and they wouldn't tell us. Later on I learned all of their names, but at the time we didn't know."[89] These memories suggest that the same markers intended by the Church to separate women religious from the non-Catholic world also loosened their ties to ethnic categories.

For children the most obvious symbol of a sister's religious vows was not her adopted name but her adopted clothing. The head-to-toe garb Catholic women religious of all orders wore in the 1930s and 1940s provided the first, and most lasting, impression that young students had of their teachers. Whether it was the Dominicans' white habit or the brown one of the Franciscan order, sisters' costumes played an important role in inspiring respect and all of its attending emotions among their charges. They wore "beautiful habits" that were "always spotless," Delia Garcia remembered admiringly.[90] "Habits have a lot to do with respect," Atencio surmised.[91] The habit was material evidence of all of the religious piety and authority students from strongly Catholic families of the Basin were raised to both admire and fear. Like religious names, habits also concealed distinctly Anglo traits sisters may otherwise have exhibited—a particular styles of dress, for example, or a shock of blond hair. Although sisters' faces were easily distinguishable from one another ("some of the nuns were [even] pretty!" Jaramillo remembered), from a distance or from the back the women appeared to local children as undifferentiated figures—ethereally removed from the trappings of ethnicity and even of gender.[92]

The habit's ability to conceal a sister's features helped cultivate respect among her students in another way as well. Most of the women religious teaching in New Mexico in the 1930s and 1940s were young, only a few months or years out of their novitiate. Many of them were in their early twenties and some may have been younger than that. For sisters overseeing high school grades, the age difference between teachers and students was often negligible. This was especially true in and around the Basin, where a migratory population—made up especially of men who spent months traveling north for work each year—meant that students' progress through school could be slow. In some villages it was common for young men in their late teens and early twenties to be enrolled in the upper grades. One Dominican remembered a telling exchange she had as a young sister with a male student who asked her age. "I'd always say, 'I'm past twenty-one,'" she recalled. "And one boy said one day, 'Well, that's good, because I'm twenty-one.'"[93] In situations like this, sisters' costumes distinguished them from their students and, by modestly covering their bodies and acting as silent reminders of their vows, deterred unwelcome attention from their male pupils. "Most of the time they looked old, but they were young," Alfredo Gomez remembered of the sisters in Dixon.[94] Anna Cordova shared a similar memory of the Peñasco Dominicans: "They didn't look too young because they're covered," she recalled.[95] Because they concealed themselves beneath their habits, sisters in their twenties were able to cultivate a respect among their students usually reserved for women twice their age.

Many adults who live in Dixon and Peñasco today—like their parents decades earlier—praise the sisters who taught them at school. When asked why sisters belonged in their public institutions in the 1940s, the answers they give aren't derived from interpretations of the law but rather from the respect these women inspired among the people who knew them. The respect local residents felt for their teachers, however, grew out of day-to-day interactions that were sometimes unpleasant and hardly ever straightforward. For a few families, the sisters' presence in local classrooms was outright troublesome. Even in the Basin's most far-flung villages residents were never of one mind, and in the absence of effective laws ensuring nonsectarianism, the popular Catholic sensibility expressed through local hiring decisions could seem aggressively imposed. Despite finding strong support for sisters, Bacon's 1947 survey acknowledged that the impulse to mix public and parochial education in New Mexico was *not* universal. Even in districts that enjoyed the practical benefits of sisters teaching, a full twenty percent of residents were reluctant to support the women in their schools. Of these residents, Bacon explained, just over half were ambiguously "non-committal" on the matter, while the remainder communicated their opposition to the public employment of religious. Bacon further separated the residents opposed to Catholic religious in their schools into three groups—those whose opposition was purely "political," those who admitted they were opposed to all things Catholic (Bacon labeled this stance as "bigotry"), and those whose reasons for opposing religious teachers were "sincere and conscientious." This last group of "conscientious" critics made up approximately five percent of all the residents Bacon surveyed.[96]

Bacon noted in his study that Catholics themselves were sometimes critical of sisters teaching. The vast majority of opponents to sister-taught public schools in New Mexico, however, were non-Catholic residents.[97] In villages throughout the

Basin and its surrounding mountains, the Catholic population shared classroom space with members of minority groups—with Protestants of both Hispano and Anglo descent, and more rarely with residents of no religious affiliation at all. To students who belonged to these groups, and more clearly to their parents, the women religious teaching in their local schools often represented a coercive and even sinister overture by the Catholic Church, rather than an educational opportunity achieved through on-the-ground compromise. Nowhere were the concerns of non-Catholic families expressed more clearly than in the village of Dixon, where Protestants made up a critical mass in the 1940s. Because these competing ideas about the value of sister-directed schooling coexisted in New Mexican communities, the best and the worst consequences of sister-taught schools—their greatest successes and their most serious failures—might play out down the road from one another, even in the same district. This explains what happened in Dixon, when Catholic support for the Franciscan teachers was matched by an earnest and effective opposition.

The Franciscans' arrival in the Rio Grande Basin wouldn't have created controversy had Dixon's schooling situation remained otherwise unchanged. St. Joseph's School was a privately funded enterprise in 1941, and non-Catholics in the village had no grounds for complaining about who ran it. But Peter Küppers had big plans for the Franciscans and their new school. Though Mother Afra was happy to bring her sisters to Dixon as a favor the archbishop, Küppers' difficult reputation had preceded him among her community. Concern about the priest prompted Archbishop Gerkin to write the superior again shortly after the congregation arrived in the village. Küppers "will be an entirely changed man," Gerkin tried to reassure her, "and there will be no difficulty in cooperating" with him.[98] Despite the archbishop's optimism, the priest continued to take an interest in St. Joseph's School. Although now retired from pastoral duties, in failing health, and working exclusively from his secluded orchards in Embudo, Küppers retained his ties in local politics. He declared it high time that Dixon's school receive the sort of public support its successful counterparts in Peñasco enjoyed. Even before Mother Afra was able to settle into her new living quarters, Küppers confronted the superior with his plan. St. Joseph's School would become a public institution, the priest advised her, and he would personally see to it that her sisters received salaries from the state, as well as the necessary accreditation for teaching in the public system. That November the priest met privately with what one observer would later denounce as the "weak and politically minded" Rio Arriba County school board. Soon after, St. Joseph's become Dixon's newest public school.[99]

The combined enrollment of Dixon's school, which included both primary and secondary grades, was approximately two hundred students during the 1942–43 academic year.[100] Teaching responsibilities were shared among a changing cast of Franciscan sisters and a few lay teachers. Grumbling could be heard from the village's Protestant community from the moment the Franciscans began to receive public money for their work, and its decibel increased yearly. Protestant residents were deeply disappointed by St. Joseph's tax-supported status, but a subsequent decision by the county board to consolidate several pre-existing public schools in the wake of its opening left them especially livid. By this time the Dixon area already had a central public school, built the previous decade with funding and labor from the Works Progress Administration. Located in the middle of the village, this WPA school functioned in tandem with several older one- and two-room schoolhouses that served children in the outlying settlements. After St. Joseph's School opened its doors to the entire community in 1941, the county board declared the WPA school redundant and it closed. Before long the board closed the little schoolhouses in places like Rinconada and Embudo as well, and students from these more remote locations began to travel into Dixon by bus for their classes. To the fury of local Protestants, by 1945 every student who attended public school in the greater Dixon area was enrolled with the Franciscans at St. Joseph's.[101]

The school board's decision to turn St. Joseph's into the only public school in the municipality had consequences that immediately distinguished the Dixon situation from that of neighboring Peñasco. While nearly every student enrolled in Peñasco's public schools was Catholic, the new student body at St. Joseph's included dozens of Protestant children. Presbyterian youngsters dominated this non-Catholic population. Siblings Lorraine and Donald Johnson, who began to attend St. Joseph's from their home two miles down the road from Dixon in the mid-1940s, were joined by Bertha Arellano, Teresita Alire, Clara Gonzalez, and other young members of their Embudo Mission Church. Children from other Protestant denominations enrolled in the formerly Catholic school as well. Even a minister like Leopoldo Martínez, who presided over the Apostolic Church of Jesus in Dixon, soon realized he had no choice but to send his four sons to the sisters for tutelage.[102] Many Protestant children whose families could afford to pay a tuition eventually transferred away from St. Joseph's, either to the nearby Embudo Mission School or to the McCurdy Mission School twenty-five miles away in Santa Cruz. The rest of the area's Protestant students remained at the public school under the Franciscans' care.

Dixon's school consolidation was especially painful for one local woman. Lydia Cordova Zellers was the mother of two school-aged boys, and until the consolidation she taught classes at the Rinconada schoolhouse. Zellers also happened to be deeply religious; her father Eliseo Cordova had spent his adult life as a Presbyterian minister in the region, and Lydia shared her father's strong commitment to their church. Born in northern New Mexico around 1877, the elder Cordova had converted from Catholicism to Presbyterianism along with several family members near the turn of the century. Zellers later remembered her paternal grandmother as the "worst Catholic I ever saw."[103] One of six children born to Eliseo and his wife Florida, Lydia grew up watching her father minister across the northern part of their new state, from Raton to Las Vegas. When she was old enough, she left home to attend the prominent Presbyterian Alison James School in Albuquerque, and eventually she traveled to North Dakota for college. Lydia met her future husband George Zellers after she finished her schooling, and the young couple moved back to New Mexico to start a family in 1934. They opted to make their home in Dixon, where Lydia's father was pastor at the nearby mission church. With her college degree Lydia had no trouble finding work as a teacher in the outlying villages. George—or "Doc" as he was known to his friends—opened a general store along Dixon's main road.[104]

George and Lydia Zellers sent their two boys to the Embudo Mission School rather than risk an education at the hands of the Franciscans. Even so, Lydia was hurt by the closure of her Rinconada classroom, and the idea of Catholic women religious teaching her former students made her angry.[105] Never one to back away from a problem, she began to imagine solutions—What would it take to provide her children with a public education away from the sisters' influence? Was it possible for an unhappy parent like herself to dismantle what Küppers and the board had built together? Zellers found a sympathetic audience for these questions among her Protestant neighbors. With Dixon's population split so closely between Catholics and Protestants in the 1940s, religious affiliation said a great deal more about a person than where he or she attended church on Sunday mornings. In a village where—with the exception of Lydia's husband and a handful of others—everyone was Hispano, religion played a role in determining everything from who a person's friends were to how she or he thought the community should be run. "Religious differences mattered more than ethnic differences," one Catholic resident of Dixon remembered. "My

Figure 2.3 George and Lydia Zellers in their general store. Dixon, New Mexico. Courtesy of Kathy T. Zellers.

dad used to say . . . somebody from the outside came in and started changing people, until [by the 1940s] we had two different groups"[106]

Relations between Dixon's religious communities fell short of outright hostility through most of the decade. The medical staff at the Presbyterian hospital safely delivered Catholic and Protestant babies alike, and neighbors did business together and helped each other out when times were tough. But limited social activity between Catholics and Protestants remained the rule of thumb. "Mostly we kept to ourselves, the Catholics and the Protestants," Abelardo Jaramillo remembered.[107] Parents discouraged their sons and daughters from pursuing both friendships and romance across religious lines.[108] Children (being children) sometimes defied their parents' instructions, but they were also good at recreating the antagonism of the older generation. Edna Garcia, a Catholic who grew up in Dixon, recalled these childhood rivalries:

> It's funny because my aunt . . . was Presbyterian. I used to go eat with her at noon, and I'd tell her that those children from [the Presbyterian] school . . . were the most horrible children in the whole wide world. . . . They'd say that our knees are peeled, because the nuns keep us kneeling and praying all the time. And we'd tell them that they sing to the devil! Because they kept on singing all the time. And . . . she'd tell me, "Don't ever say that, *mi hijita*, my child. Because you're calling them worse things than what they call you." "Well, they better stop calling us that!," [I'd reply]. Peeled knees. *Rodillas peladas.*[109]

Extending from church pews to school yards to kitchen tables, religion in Dixon had the ability to make or break social relations.

A person's religion also shaped his or her ideas about education. Just as most Catholic residents favored the Franciscans' school, many of the village's Protestants shared Lydia Zellers' objections to it.[110] By autumn of 1945 a loose group had resolved to act on those feelings, and they began to meet regularly to discuss bringing education free from Catholic influence back to Dixon. The group comprised prominent residents from various denominations. Its distinctly Protestant character was a sharp contrast not only to the Catholic sisters it opposed, but also to the Catholic-majority school board in the county, and the Catholic-majority municipal governments that prevailed throughout the Basin. The residents who rallied around Zellers' cause also came from different backgrounds; although most Protestants in Dixon by the 1940s were Spanish-speaking, the free school campaign drew Anglos and Hispanos in equal numbers. Dixon's small Anglo population had at its core a group of aging home missionaries, who had arrived in the Basin near the turn of the century to open the community's Presbyterian school and hospital. These included two sisters who worked at the hospital still. Sarah Bowen was an intelligent and dynamic woman in her fifties and was well loved by the community as its only physician. Her older sister Olive worked as the hospital's receptionist. Both women were close friends of the Zellers family.[111] The Bowen sisters were joined in their support for Zellers by more recent transplants to the Dixon area. Most prominent among these was the New York-born Arthur Montgomery. In the 1940s Montgomery was a mineral dealer and the operator of the Harding pegmatite mine, located just up the valley from Dixon. The Harding mine was one of the area's few sources of employment; Montgomery hired men from the village to chisel away at rock containing minerals like lithium and beryllium, which he sold to national defense programs.[112] The protesting group was also strengthened by the presence of J. Paul Stevens, who was a Presbyterian minister. Although he lived twenty-five miles to the north in Taos, Stevens kept abreast of the village's plight.

The Spanish-speaking Protestants, including Zellers herself, who made up the remainder of Dixon's complaining party were the first- and second-generation beneficiaries of missionary efforts. Although statewide the overall number of native-born Protestants was still small in the 1940s, Hispano converts had begun to unsettle Anglo-Protestantism's dominance in the region. As Susan Yohn explains it, when students trained in Presbyterian mission schools themselves became teachers and ministers in the twentieth century, they "reminded supporters of mission work that [native] cultural traditions . . . would persist even though people changed their religious affiliation."[113] The same applied, albeit on a smaller scale, to other denominations as well. This growing population of Hispano Protestants wielded disproportionate influence in Dixon, and its members quickly became the most vocal critics of its sister-taught school. Their objections disrupted the loose Hispano–Catholic alliance that over the decades had made sister-led education in the region successful; here were residents speaking Spanish while also arguing *against* the Catholic presence in their schools.

In addition to Zellers, her association of concerned citizens included several of Dixon's leading Hispano Protestants, including Amadeo Lucero, who was one of the few nonreligious teachers still employed at St. Joseph's, and Leopoldo Martínez of the local Apostolic Church. Lydia soon found her closest collaborator in another minister. In 1947 Porfiero Romero became the newest pastor of the Dixon-Embudo Presbyterian Church. Like Zellers, Romero was a native New Mexican with plenty of Catholics in his own family. He had been born in Taos, where his father served as president of the local *morada*. Although both his parents had been strong Catholics when Romero was a boy, his father eventually suffered a bitter excommunication from the Church.[114] Porfiero converted to Presbyterianism in the wake of this scandal, as a young man while boarding at the Presbyterian Menaul School in Albuquerque. After finishing high school at age twenty-three and completing a degree at the University of New Mexico two years later, Romero relocated to Chicago to attend seminary. He spent time in Indiana ministering to Mexican immigrants but eventually returned to his home state and settled in Rio Arriba County. He was pastor in Dixon for the next thirteen years.[115]

All the residents who met with Zellers to discuss the situation at St. Joseph's School shared anguish over the presence of women religious in its classrooms. Their complaints dwelt on the quality of the education children were getting from the Franciscans, and most of all on the Catholic dimension to that education. Individuals who described the problems they saw laid out a consistent set of grievances. The Franciscans in Dixon were untrained as teachers, they asserted, and unable to speak English competently. They failed to adequately prepare, challenge, and motivate their students. In addition, Zellers and her supporters listed examples of non-Catholic children being inappropriately pressured by the sisters—to participate in religious practices like prayer or confession, or to study religious lessons through Catholic texts and comics they made available in their classrooms. Ten-year-old Donald Johnson's mother reported that soon after her son began attending St. Joseph's he was told to attend confession and threatened with punishment if he did not. Leopoldo Martínez became worried after his son Leo came home from school one spring day with something black smeared across his forehead, "something like soot." The pastor's other children informed him that Leo had been in church with their teachers when he approached the altar to receive the ashes.[116] Instances when non-Catholic children were *not* included in the sectarian activities ongoing at St. Joseph's were just as troubling. The group pointed to ways in which those children were unfairly punished or excluded—like when students arriving to school early on buses were forced to wait around outside, while Catholic children were admitted indoors to attend catechism instruction in the sisters' classrooms.

As Dixon's Protestants began airing their grievances publicly they looked for ways to explain the anger they felt. Many denied any personal rancor, suggesting instead their objections were a matter of principle, born out of respect for the law and above all for the separation of church and state.[117] At the same time, their sense of this separation was itself part and parcel to a collective religious memory. Although no one within the group had legal training, deep-seated ideas about the purpose of state-sponsored education, the importance of religious freedom to that education, and the necessity of excluding Catholicism to preserve that freedom had existed within the Basin's Protestant community since the nineteenth century. Those ideas had origins in the popular American conceptions of public schooling that arrived in New Mexico during its territorial days, and they had been promoted with particular zeal in the Basin by the missionaries who worked in its Spanish-speaking villages. If the belief in public education's uplifting potential, and the corresponding feeling that Catholicism hindered the important moral work that went on within public schools, was a thoroughly American idea imported to northern New Mexico with the home missions, however, by the 1940s Lydia Zellers, Porfiero Romero, and other Dixon residents had inherited it and made it their own. The value that members of the group ascribed to church–state separation when they explained their objections to St. Joseph's School had a familiarly Protestant ring, but it was also a different vision of education than the one promoted by their missionary predecessors.

Among Dixon's Spanish-speaking Protestants, church–state separation had its own accent derived from the circumstances of life in northern New Mexico. Like the opposing attitudes toward separation that led most of their neighbors to support sister-taught schools, Dixon residents' assertions about the importance of Catholic-free schools were also inseparable from dominating concerns about poverty and other challenges distinct to the native-born population. As Zellers and her associates began to formally present their case for sister-free schooling to interested parties in the mid-1940s, they addressed these concerns using language that was a nod to the Hispano identity many (though not all) of them shared:

> Most of us are Spanish-Americans, and we live in a little valley cut off from the outside world. We are tillers of the soil; most of us are poor and ignorant of much that is new. But we do know that our school system is inadequate and narrow. We wish our children to have a chance at a more progressive education than we had, so that when they go out into the world they can hold up their heads, put themselves on equality [sic] with any other American citizen and not feel as if from an alien race because of difference in language, custom and enlightenment.[118]

Tapping into Anglo-American preconceptions of Hispano people, the Dixon group also cultivated a guileless quality in statements like this one that was intended to highlight the self-evident character of the separation it supported. In describing themselves, Zellers and her partners embellished a bit—the "we" behind their statement were teachers, ministers, and similar professionals, neither "tillers of the soil" (most of them) nor "poor and ignorant of much that is new." Yet details like these were central to their collective vision of church–state separation as they developed it through the 1940s. From early in its existence, the group opposed to the Franciscans' school realized that its Spanish-American members were well positioned to offer a unique vision of church–state separation—one that could appeal both to Anglo audiences and to other native-born residents of northern New Mexico.

When Zellers and her associates began to ask their neighbors in Dixon for help removing the Franciscans from public employment, they made their appeals along ethnic rather than religious lines. Religious loyalties, after all, sat uncomfortably close to the heart of the school controversy. When they spoke publicly, they spoke first and foremost as natives of northern New Mexico. People like Zellers, Romero, and Martínez could claim an intimate knowledge of the challenges their neighbors faced. Here were residents who had also grown up in the poverty of the Basin, who also spoke Spanish, and who also felt the negative effects of being cast as "an alien race because of difference in language, custom and enlightenment." Their religious orientation, however, made them see solutions to these problems differently. As Protestants, they integrated their local perspective with a profound faith in the state's educational system they inherited from the missionary generation. While their Catholic counterparts remained skeptical of the public system's structure, Dixon's Protestants turned their own skepticism toward the "inadequate and narrow" way their local school was being run—in violation of a public education model they believed had potential to uplift even the state's most destitute residents. As it developed its case against sister-taught education through the late 1940s, the Dixon group continued to stress the special role unbiased public schooling could play in the development of Hispano people, a population whom church–state collusion kept living in the past. By offering a local argument for why the Catholic Church should be kept away from public education, Dixon's Protestant residents joined their interests to those of their neighbors. In their pleas for separation they offered a compelling alternative to the Hispano–Catholic alliance that made St. Joseph's and other northern New Mexican schools possible.[119]

Lydia Zellers and her neighbors began their work to bring back free education soon after St. Joseph's became Dixon's only surviving public school in 1945. Their earliest efforts were dedicated to fundraising. The group was optimistic it could raise enough money to build a new public school building in the village—one free from the influence of Küppers and the Franciscans. That autumn, Zellers collaborated with Amadeo Lucero and Arthur Montgomery to write and distribute a Spanish-language circular entitled *Nuestra Nueva Escuela*. The circular had something for everyone in Dixon; it included community news and gossip, event listings, and bits of humor. It also included a list of prominent donors to the new school, and a solicitation for funds from readers. An editorial on the front page explained the importance of a new public school for the community:

> Everything in this world is changing. Nations have changed governments, leaders and borders. And so in Dixon we cannot follow in the same footprints as in years past . . . It seems incredible that our people in Dixon continue to live like they have lived in the past. The time has arrived when we should make a change. Let's break out of the shell that holds us in. We are going, as one, to build a school that expands our knowledge, and enables us, in some way at least, to keep pace with our quickly changing era.[120]

The article admonished Dixon's residents to act on behalf of their children's future by contributing money for the new building. In addition to their published appeals, Zellers and her group raised funds over the next several months by holding rummage sales and by sponsoring dances and movie screenings in the village.

The school campaign was a success; within two years the newly created Dixon Consolidated School Fund held nearly $12,000 in it. The group's members pointed proudly to the generosity their impoverished village demonstrated during the campaign; they celebrated it as evidence of "a little Spanish community coming awake, throwing off the chains of backwardness and narrow outlook, and asserting for the first time progressive ideas and ideals."[121] With the needed funds for a new school in place, Arthur Montgomery donated a two-acre plot of flat, cleared land for a building site, and construction of a spacious five-room schoolhouse was finished in the summer of 1947.[122] Zellers and her colleagues had already located several qualified teachers willing to work in the new building, and with this last hurdle cleared Dixon's new—and sister-free—institution stood ready to open its doors to the community that fall. Midway through the summer, however, Lydia Zellers' eagerness for the start of the new school year was shattered by a devastating piece of news. The Rio Arriba County school board had met to approve Dixon's new public school and—moving with uncharacteristic speed—it had already extended contracts to a group of women to teach in it. To Zellers' absolute dismay, every last one of those contracts had gone to a Franciscan. Despite her group's best efforts to free the village's public education from Catholic influence, the same community of Catholic sisters who already taught at St. Joseph's would now be responsible for Dixon's newest school as well.

3

A Space in Between Walls

Inside the Sister-Taught Public Classrooms of New Mexico

Carrizozo was a railroad town on the desert flats of Lincoln County, two hundred miles to the south of Dixon. Like Dixon, the community boasted two public elementary schools in the late 1940s. One of those schools was staffed by lay teachers while the other was run by the Sisters of St. Casimir, a group of Catholic women religious who had arrived in Carrizozo by way of Chicago a few years earlier.[1] St. Rita's School was housed in a low L-shaped building with a steep tin roof; the doors of its four classrooms opened out onto a dirt schoolyard with basketball hoops and a merry-go-round.[2] St. Rita's enrolled about one hundred twenty students in 1948, but because many of the children came from migrant families, enrollment figures fluctuated with the seasons.[3] It was common knowledge among Carrizozo's residents that St. Rita's was actually part public school, part parochial school—two of its classrooms received money from the government for their operations, while the sisters ran the other two as private Catholic enterprises. This arrangement had been status quo in Carrizozo for fifteen years; parents appreciated St. Rita's public classrooms as a convenient alternative to the town's other wholly public school, which sat across the railroad tracks on what some locals referred to as the "good side of town."[4]

An unfamiliar car arrived in Carrizozo on a September morning in 1948, and it drove straight up St. Rita's dusty driveway. At nine o'clock sharp two men and a woman stepped into the schoolyard, where they were greeted by the town's superintendent of schools. L. Z. Manire reluctantly escorted the group across the lot and over to the main building where classes were in session, and they walked down the row of doors until they paused in front of the seventh and eighth graders' room. The seventh and eighth grades at St. Rita's were taught by the school's principal, Sister Theodurette. Sister Theodurette's classroom was the largest space in the school, and Lydia Zellers and her companions had reliable information that St. Rita's entire student body—public as well as parochial children—gathered inside it for convocations throughout the year.[5] Convinced the classroom was being used as a public space, the visitors insisted upon seeing what sorts of things it contained. The group

77

ignored Sister Theodurette's objections and stepped through the low doorway into the building. As the trio looked around the classroom, one of them pulled out a camera and photographed the things they saw.

The photographs taken that day at St. Rita's eventually became the property of New Mexico's courts—a total of ten of them, handed over as evidence during the *Zellers* trial. Although grainy and blurred, the preserved images reveal classroom interiors the likes of which most American public school children would never have seen. Sister Theodurette's room is shown, crowded with people, objects, and decorations. Three rows of children sit at wooden desks—some smile unabashedly for the camera while others seem startled by the visitors' arrival. Carrizozo's parish priest, wearing a cassock that falls just short of his work boots, stands protectively beside the students. Father Vito DeBaca is visibly upset by the visitors' presence; he's staring into the camera with a cold glare and his arms folded defiantly. A cast iron stove fills the back of the classroom and posters and student artwork cover its walls. Some of the children's drawings depict the desert landscape dotted with cacti and others depict Catholic figures, including several portraits in crayon of a veiled Madonna with dark hair and eyes. A picture of Our Lady of Faith hangs on one wall, and a statue of Our Lady of Grace sits on top of a shelf in the room's corner, carefully arranged beside an American flag. The Madonna's arms are outstretched, and her gaze falls on a mounted globe of the world.[6]

Few sisters who taught publicly in New Mexico displayed religious objects as prominently as Sister Theodurette did. Zellers and her partners made the long drive from Dixon down to St. Rita's because they had heard that its rooms held an extraordinary number of Catholic sights. The types of images they photographed in Carrizozo, however—a statue of the Madonna here, an open catechism there—were hardly anomalies among the schools eventually named in the *Zellers* lawsuit. The Franciscans teaching in Dixon, the Dominicans in Peñasco, and all of the one

Figure 3.1 Statue of the Virgin Mary, St. Rita's School, Carrizozo, New Mexico, 1948. Photograph taken by the Dixon Free Schools Committee. Courtesy of Special Collections Research Center, Morris Library, Southern Illinois University Carbondale.

hundred thirty-one sisters eventually implicated in the litigation presided over classrooms that confronted students with an eclectic and sometimes precarious mixture of sights and sounds. The extemporaneous quality of sisters' classrooms indicated the variety of both their influences and their intentions. Participating in a society crowded with competing languages and cultures, the classrooms maintained traces of their students' backgrounds even as they asserted the Anglo bias of both teachers and school officials. When Anglo sisters and Hispano students met one another in these classrooms, however, they interacted in spaces that were already composites, unstable and charged. At its core each sister's classroom was an ongoing exchange between Catholic and civil ideas, techniques, and materials. This pedagogical encounter produced the bizarre mixture of sights and activities in Carrizozo, Dixon, and many of New Mexico's other public schools.

Sisters in New Mexico taught across educational models that touted encompassing strategies for children's formation, and that competed with one another in the early- to mid-twentieth-century United States. They received instructions about teaching techniques and visual aids from their different superiors in the Catholic Church as well as from the state government. They felt obligation toward all sides. Squeezed between two formidable institutions, one civil and one religious, and intended as mouthpieces for each of their respective ideas about educating children, these women worked in uncharted, interstitial, and highly contested territory. They went about their business with few historical precedents and they had no instructions waiting for them—no blueprints for what a public–parochial classroom was supposed to look like. Relying upon the tools made available by their congregations, the archdiocese, and the state, sisters worked as *bricoleurs*, assembling their classrooms piecemeal through endless decisions that tackled the mundane details of scheduling, lesson plans, and instructional material.[7] Considered together these decisions amounted to something unexpected—fortuitous to some, troubling to others, but unequivocally new. Sisters' classrooms stood as strange, hybrid creatures on the American educational landscape, Catholic and public at the same time.

While these classrooms thrived in New Mexican communities through the first decades of the twentieth century, supported by the Spanish-speaking and Catholic people who benefited from them, by the mid-1940s their existence had come under scrutiny. The objections of Protestant residents in Dixon threatened to breathe new life into older New Mexican efforts to excise the Church from public schools. As midcentury approached, an increasing number of New Mexico's citizens shared the assumption of Lydia Zellers and her neighbors that an educational system with two distinct and separate spheres—public and parochial—was both right and lawful. From this perspective, the Catholic Church and its sisters appeared to demonstrate a disregard for, or at least an insufficient appreciation of, the separation that others in the state and nation valued. This supposition was correct in part. New Mexico's sisters certainly did *not* share the viewpoint, posited so emphatically by Zellers' group, that publicly funded schools must be free from discernibly Catholic influences.

Those sisters did, however, inhabit their own complicated position in mid-century discourse about church–state separation. In fact, the Catholic sisters who oversaw public–parochial education felt pressure to separate acutely. Each day their classrooms occupied a tense space kept open only by the discordance between multiple impulses bent on keeping the religious and the civil in mutual isolation. Each of these impulses originated on a different side of the educational fault line along which they taught, and each strained in a different direction. In public schools, sisters regularly faced civil expectations to keep Catholic religion out of their classrooms. In a more immediate way, they also grappled with their Church's expectations that women religious, and to a lesser extent their students, live in pious separation from the secular world. While this early- to mid-century Catholic construction of separation did not require disengagement of the Church from the state *per se*, it did insist upon the danger of non-Catholic institutions, and it inspired policies that in practice required sisters to avoid many iterations of the civil sphere. For sisters heading into the mission field to teach, the lifestyle their religious vows demanded left them with a strong and embodied sense of separation's importance. For those hired on as public teachers, the pressure those vows exerted was both challenged and compounded by the additional, civil obligations toward separation they learned about as they worked. Schools taught by women religious in New Mexico did not suffer from lack of a separation ethic. Rather, they were marked by differently configured principles of separation that coexisted in a precarious balance in their hallways.

Luckily the women who worked in this environment had resources available to help them teach. The early- to mid-century world of American Catholic education was itself a varied place, home to multiple pedagogical models offered to and expected of sisters. These models sometimes disagreed with one another. Ongoing pressure to preserve sisters and their charges from the secular world was qualified during the era by a countervailing movement among some Catholic educators toward greater engagement with public models of schooling. Sisters in New Mexico took advantage of the teaching materials produced as part of this integrative trend, even as they continued the struggle to find their way at the limits to integration imposed by both their Church and the state. It was along those limits, and in the absence of protocols, that sisters' teaching demonstrated its ingenuity. By the end of the 1940s American courts would come abuzz with descriptions of a "wall of separation" between church and state. Catholic sisters employed in public schools were already teaching in a narrow space between two such walls—one state-imposed and the other imposed by their religion. Choices they made when they taught respected the weight of each these, even as they also sometimes defied—either advertently or inadvertently—the dominion of both state-derived and Church-derived ideals of separation.

Women religious who taught in New Mexico during the 1930s and 1940s had no choice but to reckon with the public nature of their employment and how it related (or failed to relate) to their religious vocation. The difficulty they had making sense of this peculiar relationship became evident years later when some sisters faced instructions to discuss it at length. On a Tuesday morning during the *Zellers* trial, Sister Mary Oda of the Sisters of St. Francis of Perpetual Adoration found herself thinking about the relationship between public employment and Catholic vocation as she sat on the witness stand. Sister Mary's attorney wanted her to clarify one issue on cross-examination. "Do you get any instructions on how you shall teach your classes in the public school from any Superior?"

Sister Mary was ready for this sort of a question, and she hardly skipped a beat before answering. "None whatever," she replied, "we are supposed to comply with our authority there and that is the County Superintendent."

Satisfied with her response, the attorney continued his line of questioning. "Now, you . . . stated that these Sisters have been trained?"

"Yes," Sister Mary explained. "They are trained as teachers just as any other teacher. . . . Some of them go to the University and get the same training in many respects that other teachers do."

Here Sister Mary's attorney took her by surprise, as he pressed on. "But most of them attend the college other Sisters are attending [who] are teaching in strictly parochial schools?"

Sister Mary paused before responding; she could not deny that most sisters she knew in New Mexico had completed their educations at schools run by and for women religious, and designed to train them in the religious formation of students. She chose her words carefully as she proceeded. "There is no difference in . . .," she hesitated and then continued, "between . . . [the] teaching of parochial schools and public schools."[8]

The reactions of the courtroom to Sister Mary's testimony—of the judge, her attorney, and her fellow sisters in the audience—are unrecorded. But her assertion that public teaching and parochial teaching were identical professions would have certainly raised eyebrows. The idea that women religious could cross back and forth between Catholic and public spheres, while teaching or doing any other activity, was difficult for non-Catholics and Catholics alike to swallow. In the first half of the twentieth century, the design of parochial education was tied closely to the special vocation of sisters. The women who trained as novices in religious communities across the United States learned the rules they needed to live by as sisters, as well as the skills required to teach children, within a convent culture—one that both emphasized sisters' own separation from the secular world and promoted a Catholic educational model with distinctive qualities that set it apart from American public schools. For a sister coming of age in this culture, the injunction to remain apart from secular influences underscored every lesson she learned about both her personal and her professional deportment. It dictated the minutia of her activities and it defined her work as a Catholic teacher. A sense of pious separation became foundational to her new religious identity. The young women who ended up in New Mexico's schools were no exception.

The typical Catholic sister teaching in New Mexico in the 1930s and 1940s was in her twenties. Almost all of them had taken their vows somewhere other than New Mexico. Of the thirteen communities teaching in the state's schools in 1948, ten maintained motherhouses in the American Midwest—in Kentucky, Indiana, Wisconsin, Missouri, Illinois, Michigan, and Nebraska. Most of the women had entered their communities as teenagers, arriving either from nearby towns or from more remote locations where the orders had established schools. Like other American Catholics in the first decades of the twentieth century, they were the children and grandchildren of European immigrants. Sister John Evangelist, for example, grew up in a family of Hungarian immigrants on a cattle ranch in Saskatchewan, Canada. She made her decision to become a Dominican after attending a high school taught by the order's sisters, and moved to Grand Rapids, Michigan, for her novitiate. "My parents were satisfied that I was going to be a sister, but they didn't quite like the idea that I was going so far away and out of the country," she recalled.[9] Sister Carmella Conway, from rural central Michigan, learned about the Dominicans who lived nearby when she was even younger. "I wanted to be a sister, but [I was in] a public school," she remembered. "So I waited a year and a half and the pastor helped me to find a school where I could be a sister." She enrolled in the order's Grand Rapids academy with the intention of joining the religious life when she was just fourteen years old.[10]

When girls like Sister John Evangelist and Sister Carmella took their vows at the Dominicans' Marywood Academy and at other Midwestern motherhouses, they became part of an insular society. Aspirants entering the novitiate between 1917 and 1950 participated in elaborate rituals—from donning the habit to adopting a new name—designed to mark their passage away from the outside world.[11] The new lifestyle they embarked upon was internally coherent and intended by superiors to provide women with a totalistic alternative to the nonreligious incentives and obligations that ordered people's behavior elsewhere in society. The Vatican-issued 1917 Code of Canon Law was the instrument that made this vision reality.[12] For nearly four decades following the 1917 Code, women religious from every congregation in the United States lived with an unprecedented number of rules applied to both their collective governance and individual activities. The daily lives of professed women were reconfigured around obligatory patterns of devotion and penance, and precise instructions delineating whom and what they could interact with and under what circumstances. Although the Code did not require communities of active sisters to remain physically separate—or cloistered—from the world at all times, it characterized the public spaces outside of convent walls as dangerous territory, to be engaged by sisters under only the strictest circumstances. The 1917 Code included instructions specifying the length of time sisters might remain outside of their convents, the reasons for which they might venture out, and how they should present themselves physically during their excursions. It also prohibited, except in instances of necessity, sisters from stepping out alone.[13] These canons were supplemented during the following decades by additional rules, drawn up within individual congregations, that restricted sisters' access to objects like televisions, radios, and newspapers that brought the outside world in. Communities even monitored sisters' personal letters for content. Each of these rules was directed toward the same purpose. While the world outside convent walls was recognized by the Church as needing the ministry of women religious, it was also a place tainted by secular culture and—so both Vatican authorities and community superiors agreed—it carried the potential to disrupt the religiously determined order of sisters' lives. The Church's rules were there to protect the women from public spaces and their influences.

If the separatist vision the Catholic Church had for its religious was embodied in the 1917 Code, and in the hundreds of additional rules that made up the constitutions of religious communities, those rules were made binding by the vow of obedience every sister pledged. The Code paid special attention to sisters' vows. "Each and every religious superior as well as subjects must not only preserve the vows that they pronounced faithfully and completely," it instructed, "but also arrange their life according to the rules and constitutions of their own religious [institute] and strive for perfection in their state."[14] The Code also discussed in detail what a vow of obedience entailed. Community superiors had "right of dominion" over member sisters. Those superiors were in turn required, with occasional exceptions, to obey local diocesan authority. At the top of the chain of governance, all members of religious communities were ultimately subject to the directives of the Pope as their "supreme Superior."[15] For a sister the stakes in all of this were high. Striving for righteousness entailed keeping one's vow of obedience, and obedience meant maintaining the level of separation from the nonreligious world the rules of the Church and one's community required. The women teaching in New Mexico understood these stakes clearly; nearly all took their vows in communities structured to conform to the 1917 Code.

Teaching also acquired new meaning in the wake of the 1917 Code. Echoing the words of the Third Plenary Council of Baltimore more than thirty years earlier, the Code warned against Catholic children attending "non-Catholic, neutral, or mixed schools, namely, those that allow non-Catholics to attend."[16] This formal prohibition contributed to a rapid increase in parochial school construction in the United States in the years after the First World War, and a correspondingly high demand for sisters to staff those new schools. Enrollment in Catholic schools more than tripled between 1917 and 1957, and four out of every five teachers responsible for this sea of young people were Catholic religious.[17] While this surging demand prompted some congregations to send members into classrooms while they were young and inexperienced, as early as the 1890s Catholic school expansion had begun to exert pressure in the opposite direction as well, motivating religious communities to make sure their teaching sisters had adequate professional training. The "credit craze" that became a characteristic of teaching communities around the turn of the century continued through the 1920s and 1930s.[18] As parochial education became subject to state accreditation requirements, more and more sisters worked toward

either certifications or higher degrees in education.[19] Most sisters earned these credentials by completing summer and Saturday courses at Catholic women's colleges
or normal schools. In 1911, the Catholic Sisters College in Washington D.C. opened
as the first institution of higher education dedicated entirely to sisters. An affiliate of
the Catholic University of America, the Sisters College offered courses to women
wishing to pursue both undergraduate and graduate degrees.[20] A similar program
began in Dubuque, Iowa, four years later, and by 1918 a summer school designed
specifically for sisters had opened at the University of Notre Dame as well.[21]

Over the next two decades, dozens of congregations opened teacher training
schools for their members.[22] Most of the sisters who taught in New Mexico received
their education in part or in whole from these small sister-run colleges. The Sisters of
Loretto, who taught in public schools in Socorro, Mora, and Bernalillo in the 1940s,
attended their order's Normal Training School (later called the Loretto Junior
College), and the Sisters of Divine Providence, who taught in the town of Pecos,
studied at their congregation's Our Lady of the Lake College in San Antonio.[23] The
prioress general of the Grand Rapids Dominicans had herself attended the first session at the Sisters College in Washington, and she made "intensive advanced schooling for sisters" one of the first goals of her tenure at the Marywood motherhouse.[24]
Her congregation opened Sacred Heart College as its own teacher training institution in 1923.[25] Dominicans teaching across the Midwest returned from their posts to
take courses at the college during the summers. Although travel costs made it impossible for the sisters in New Mexico to return home this regularly, an extension of
Sacred Heart was opened in Peñasco by the end of the decade.[26] The Dominicans'
prioritization of education resulted in a particularly high level of degree-holding sisters in the Grand Rapids congregation. Between 1925 and 1935, fifty Dominicans
held bachelor's degrees and nine held master's degrees, while another two hundred
fifty-five held life certificates in teaching received from normal schools.[27]

As Catholic sisters poured more energy into professional education, some leaders in the Church worried that too much teacher training could interrupt the spiritual work that was the priority of a religious life.[28] This was especially a concern
when training took place outside of the Church. Catholic colleges for women, and
especially sisters' colleges, were founded by provincials who worried about the
deleterious effects of secular education upon their young charges. Most Catholic
institutions of higher education still prohibited the enrollment of women in the
early twentieth century, and before the emergence of these women's colleges, sisters
in search of higher education often found themselves with no choice but to attend
non-Catholic institutions. This was particularly true in a mission region like New
Mexico, where many sisters pursuing degrees enrolled in courses at Las Vegas
Normal College and the University of New Mexico.[29] On a national level, sisters
preparing to teach attended non-Catholic colleges and universities in surprising
numbers during these years. Non-Catholic higher education among women religious actually peaked in the otherwise conservative aftermath of the 1917 Code.

Between 1925 and 1930 over ten percent of all sisters enrolled in higher education in the United States studied at non-Catholic institutions.[30]

Superiors who had sisters enrolled in non-Catholic institutions worried about the threat that interactions with teachers and fellow students might pose to their religious commitments. They also worried about the consequences a secular training could have when it came to the shape of sisters' future teaching. As one provincial put it:

> In visiting the classes of various schools I can always spot the Sister trained in a state university. There is a secular atmosphere about the room that is hard to describe but is very evident. I feel a qualm of conscience whenever I encounter it—but what can we do in the face of requirements today?[31]

These provincials were not alone in their worries; concern about the infiltration of secular influences into the Catholic classroom was expressed at all levels of the ecclesiastical hierarchy in the decades after the 1917 Code. Statements from the Vatican and American bishops concurred that Catholic educators needed to avoid offering religious instruction alongside secular teaching models. Rather, the parochial school should defy secular models by offering children an integrated curriculum with religious truths transmitted through every discipline.[32] The proper training of sisters—a training itself untainted by the secularism, materialism, and atheism endemic in public institutions—was universally understood as key to this endeavor. Although their own superiors were unusually permissive when it came to study at non-Catholic institutions, the Grand Rapids Dominicans nevertheless felt firsthand the consequences of this way of thinking. During the 1930s, their bishop in Michigan stepped in and imposed heavy restrictions on the sisters' ability to attend state schools. When the community ceded to this pressure and attained accreditation for its own junior college, the prelate's demeanor toward the group softened considerably. Bishop Joseph Pinten bestowed lavish praise, and described the new college as an institution that would finally educate students—and sisters especially—"in accordance with Catholic principles."[33]

No matter where they attended school, sisters who arrived in New Mexico did so expecting to work as Catholic educators. They quickly found themselves engaging people and policies that challenged their expectations. The hiring of sisters within the public system occurred through different channels. Occasionally, a sister applied for her teaching position in standard fashion, submitting paperwork for review by a district or country board. Other times a sister already working in a community in a parochial capacity was approached by local officials, and accepted their offer to teach. Most often, a sister was assigned to public employment by a superior who had negotiated with officials on her behalf. In order to be hired, however, each woman had to meet a uniform set of requirements. She first needed to send evidence of her teaching credentials to the proper state and local authorities.[34] State policy required that, along with her teacher's certificate, a sister also submit an official educational transcript and a certificate attesting to her sound health.[35] After these documents were approved a sister was required to sign a contract with the local board. By signing this contract the sister affirmed she was legally qualified to teach in public schools and promised to "be prompt, thorough and conscientious, judicious in punishment and watchful of the morals of the pupils." She also promised to abide by the rules and regulations of New Mexico's state board of education.[36] Every woman religious who taught in a public classroom agreed to these terms in her contract.

By pledging to comply with state rules, sisters signed on to a long list of civil expectations for how they were to conduct their classrooms. These expectations extended not only to the contents of sisters' textbooks and lesson plans, but also to the types of objects and images their students could be surrounded by, and even to the appearance of the teacher herself.[37] Along with state policies like those requiring teachers to conduct their classes in English and to display the American flag, sisters in public elementary schools in the 1940s were subject to a 450-page curriculum guide published by the state board. Along with providing teachers with lesson plans in a dozen different academic subjects, the state's curriculum advised them on how to manage every facet of children's classroom experience. According to the volume's 1947 edition, the classroom's appearance

> must be attractive and possess an atmosphere of order, beauty and serenity. There should be . . . not only textbooks, reference books, and recreational materials, but also an aquarium, a terrarium, a shrine of beauty, maps, globes, bulletin boards, a reading table, play materials and supplies for construction.[38]

The curriculum included equally detailed instructions for the teacher's physical appearance and comportment:

> The teacher must maintain proper personal appearance, possess good physical health, mental stability, a sense of humor, fairness in all occasions, and a professional attitude toward her chosen profession . . . the teacher must have the opportunity to live a normal life, have fun, travel, read widely, enjoy hobbies, [and] contact adults in the immediate and extended community.[39]

From the state government's perspective, its teachers were responsible for more than just textbooks and lessons plans; it expected them to bring an appropriate lifestyle with them into the classroom to share with students.

When they agreed to public employment Catholic women religious signed on to New Mexico's vision for what their classrooms should look like, and how they themselves should act both inside and outside of their schools. Fortunately for sisters, the language of these state-issued instructions left ample room for individual interpretation of their details. Leaving less room for interpretation was the state's most recent statutory language regarding educational nonsectarianism, directed specifically at the public school teacher:

> No teacher shall use any sectarian or denominational books in the schools or teach sectarian doctrine in the schools, and any teacher violating the provisions of this section shall be immediately discharged, his certificate to teach school revoked, and be forever barred from . . . employment in the public schools in the state.[40]

The state's expectation here was absolutely clear. Like public classrooms elsewhere in the country, New Mexico's classrooms needed to remain nondenominational spaces—free from sectarian religious instruction in any form. It was the responsibility of teachers to keep them that way. As public teachers, the sisters formally agreed to abide by this rule along with all the others. The fact these same women remained bound by vows of obedience to their orders—and expected to impart a Catholic education in fulfillment of those vows—complicated that agreement considerably.

Sisters who signed public contracts in New Mexico in the 1930s and 1940s insisted they adhered faithfully to the state's rules.[41] The uncomfortable position their dual allegiances put them in, however, was lost on no one—not on the women themselves, and certainly not on the citizens who eventually challenged their employment. Again, this recognition was articulated later in the exchanges of the *Zellers* trial. During one such back and forth, an attorney approached public teacher and Lorettine Sister John Ellen, and he asked her whether she was subject to the orders of her Superior. "Only in matters which concern my religious life," the sister answered him smartly, "but in school matters I am subject to [Principal] Torres and [Superintendent] Bell [of the Socorro school district]."

"Your entire life is devoted to your religious life, isn't it?" The attorney now angled his questions toward what he suspected was an inevitable admission. "That includes all of your time—[don't] you have to devote the remainder of your life to that religious life that you referred to?"

"Yes sir. . . . Yes sir, I do," the sister reluctantly responded.

The attorney swooped in for a final blow: "And you are subject to the direction of the Superiors of your Order?"

"Yes sir," Sister John Ellen now conceded.[42]

This tense encounter did nothing to resolve whether women like Sister John Ellen were obedient first to their civil employers' or to their religious superiors' instructions about how to teach. Later in the exchange Sister John Ellen reiterated her ability to obey school officials, insisting that in all decisions related to educational employment her order "would accede to Mr. Bell, whatever his decision was."[43] With her unqualified statement Sister John Ellen struggled to hide a much more delicate situation. Sisters' deference to the authority of the state sat in the most tenuous balance with the expectations of religious communities and their standing commitments to obey those expectations.

Congregations of teaching sisters were designing their own courses and curricula during the 1920s, 1930s, and 1940s. These tools were intended for the edification of members, and they emphasized religion as an integral and integrated part of the classroom experience. Despite their comparatively high tolerance for both the secular training of sisters and the public schooling of students, the Grand Rapids Dominicans took a lead in theorizing such a holistic approach to Catholic education. In 1929, Macmillan and Company published the congregation's own curricular guide for sisters engaged in elementary school work. The curriculum's preface explained that the aims of Catholic teaching should arise from entirely different assumptions than their secular equivalents:

> A program of instruction worked out from the point of view of a thoroughly Catholic philosophy of education, based on the supernatural teachings of Christ and His Church, ought to yield a practice characteristically different from that suggested by the principle of education based on naturalism and materialistic philosophy.[44]

Like its counterpart in New Mexico, the Dominican curriculum offered its readers guidance on covering a full range of academic subjects, but it did so employing a distinctly Catholic perspective. While it included advice for teaching religious topics to students, most of its chapters instructed sisters on how to incorporate Catholic themes into nonreligious lessons, from science and literature to history and civics. The curriculum advised sisters, for example, to introduce Jesus and the saints to children as examples of literary protagonists, and to teach about historical figures who demonstrated "courage, endurance and religious fidelity" alongside the canon of national heroes, as a strategy for demonstrating "how eloquently the pages of true history proclaims the presence of God in His own world."[45]

This guide would have competed for desk space with New Mexico's curriculum in the classrooms of the two dozen Grand Rapids Dominicans who taught publicly in the 1940s, and possibly in those of other sisters as well. The differences between the two volumes, one religious and one civil, demonstrate the opposing currents of thought these women found themselves working between.[46] Amid its calls for a holistic Catholic education, however, the Dominican curriculum also carried echoes of another voice gaining ground in parochial educational circles—one that would prove more helpful to New Mexico's sisters. In the curriculum's preface, the distinguished Catholic educator George Johnson articulated his vision for Catholic education in America:

> Eternal truths must be emphasized differently according to temporal con-
> tingencies . . . the Catholic school must . . . take account of the changed
> condition of modern living and strive to interpret life for the children in
> terms of what is, and not of what has been.[47]

This call for engagement with the stuff of modern life was strengthened by a second quote from Johnson, which the Dominicans deemed appropriate for inclusion in the curriculum's opening pages:

> The aim of the Catholic elementary education is to provide the child with
> those experiences which are calculated to develop in him such knowledge,
> appreciations, and habits as will yield a character equal to the contingen-
> cies of fundamental Christian living in American democratic society.[48]

Johnson's commentary was representative of a recent current of thought among American Catholic educators. This line of thinking de-emphasized separation and the preservation of an independently Catholic educational model, choosing to focus instead on situational propriety. In practice, this sort of thinking translated to closer collaboration and greater conformity with American public schools.[49]

Catholic educators like George Johnson promoted compatibility between Catholic and public education models in the United States as both desirable and necessary. Only a few years before the publication of the Dominican curriculum, the capacity—and the right—of Catholic schools to train American students had withstood a challenge in the nation's highest court. Just as Americanizing impulses showed themselves within New Mexican public education in the 1910s and 1920s, the United State generally had experienced a surge in what John Highnam referred to as "100 percent Americanism." As Higham explained it, "100 per centers regarded the maintenance of the existing social pattern as dependent on the indi-vidual's sense of complete identification with the nation—a sense of identification so all-embracing as to permeate and stabilize the rest of . . . thinking and behav-ior."[50] On the extreme end of this movement, citizens groups argued that manda-tory public education offered the only adequate medium for training American citizens. Their argument challenged the right and ability of Catholic institutions—even private ones—to teach children in the United States. In Oregon, an informal coalition of these groups, among them the Scottish Rite Masons and the Ku Klux Klan, fought for a referendum on the state's Compulsory Education Act in 1922. The referendum approved an amendment to the Act that effectively required all children between eight and sixteen years old in the state to attend public schools.[51] It was only after a group of private school providers, including the Society of Sis-ters of the Holy Names of Jesus and Mary, challenged the Oregon statute that the U.S. Supreme Court found it unconstitutional in its decision in *Pierce v. Society of Sisters* in 1925.[52]

In the years after *Pierce*, Catholic educators found themselves continuing to defend the Americanizing capacity of their schools against assaults from both the political right and left. Allegations Catholic schools failed as American institutions, and even that they were socially and politically dangerous, were always exaggerated. They were given some credence, however, by the behavior of a few Catholic religious orders. In Chicago as late as the 1930s, for example, congregations of Italian sisters were collaborating with their nation's foreign ministry to design and distribute pro-Mussolini lessons and textbooks to Italian American students enrolled in their schools.[53] The desire to silence critics of this sort of activity, combined with practical concerns about the ability of Catholic students to thrive within American society as adults, drove George Johnson and other educators of the era to argue for a standardized Catholic curriculum. This curriculum, they argued, should continue to develop students' faith and morals, but it should meet its objectives in a way that also complemented the aims of American public education.

An important early figure in this Catholic pedagogical turn was a priest named Thomas Shields. Like Johnson, Shields was professor of education at Catholic University, and he had been the founding force behind Sisters College there. In 1917 he published a volume entitled *Philosophy of Education*, with the intention of articulating a model of Catholic schooling that openly engaged recent, progressive developments within American educational models. Shields distinguished between the "ultimate" and "secondary" aims of Catholic education, and stressed that after adopting the former, the parochial school teacher needed to dedicate her time and energy to cultivating the latter.[54] To this end, he strongly advocated for the professionalization of parochial school teachers, the standardization of textbooks, and the incorporation into the classroom of teaching methods that relied upon scientific understandings of human biological and psychological development.[55] Catholic pedagogy, he argued, should take into account not only the religious character of the school but its public character as well:

> In contrasting the Catholic school with the state school, it should not be forgotten that they are both public schools and they must both minister to the needs of the home, of the state, and of society in general. In addition to those services, the Catholic school must include among its aims the teaching of religion and the upbuilding and perpetuity of the Church. These added services, however, do not in any way derogate from the public character of our Catholic schools.[56]

Like other Catholic educators of his day, Shields defended the public service parochial schools offered the community. He argued for a Catholic pedagogical model that took this public responsibility seriously.

Shields' influence was felt widely among Catholic educators of the period. Aside from his work with Sisters College, he began to publish the *Catholic Education Review* in 1911 (Johnson would also serve as an editor at the *Review*) and edited his own series of textbooks designed to put his pedagogical innovations into practice.[57] With some reservation, the Church hierarchy also began to acknowledge that Catholic education would benefit from "centralization and standardization . . . along public school lines."[58] Development of a system that not only fulfilled state accreditation requirements, but looked and performed more like its public counterpart, was deemed necessary both to attract students who might otherwise be tempted to attend public schools, and to train those students to be contributing members of American society. Although Catholics continued to disagree about how much public school influence was desirable, Shields' sense that Catholic education should conform to the demands of the society around it was ultimately reinforced at the highest level. In 1938, the Vatican itself issued instructions for the creation of a Commission on American Citizenship at Catholic University. The initiative's purpose was to help teachers in Catholic schools integrate religious learning with the more "immediate aims" of the American classroom.[59] The Commission published a national curriculum entitled *Guiding Growth in Christian Social Living* in 1944. Co-authored by Dominican Sister Mary Nona McGreal, from the order's Sinsinawa, Wisconsin, community, the similarities between *Guiding Growth* and civil curricula like New Mexico's are striking—right down to the American flags that grace the title plates of each.[60]

Every opinion about American Catholic education expressed within the Church during the 1920s, 1930s, and 1940s—from that of religious superiors worried about secular influence, to that of integrationist-minded educators like Shields—was intended have an impact "on the ground," to shape the actions of the tens of thousands of sisters who taught daily in the nation's Catholic schools. The sisters in New Mexico heard these opinions filtered through the training courses they attended, the instructions they received from superiors, and the curricula and textbooks they taught from. They considered them alongside the state's guidelines whenever they faced a decision about the contents of their classrooms or the lessons they would teach in them. If the Catholic voices pressing for their separation from the world presented a special challenge to publicly employed sisters, Catholic voices advocating for collaboration between public and parochial education models were unusually helpful. Although most sisters in New Mexico would not have read Shields' treatise at length, every day they employed tools and techniques that reflected his pedagogy and grew out of integrationist currents within the early-twentieth-century Catholic educational world. Sisters in New Mexico thrived in the areas of overlap between public and parochial educational initiatives. From this common ground they discovered they could teach with particular confidence, in a manner that satisfied state authorities as well as their superiors in the Church.

The school day in Costilla, a village south of the Colorado border in Taos County, was ordinary among sister-taught public institutions in New Mexico. The Sisters of Mercy ran both the high school and the elementary school in Costilla. At 8:30 every morning bells at both schools rang, summoning teachers to their classrooms. Buses carrying children from the surrounding villages arrived at school soon thereafter, and Catholic youngsters (all save half-dozen of the schools' three hundred students) filed into classrooms for religion instruction until shortly before nine. Public school officially began in Costilla at nine o'clock in the morning, as all of the students recited the Pledge of Allegiance and answered to a roll call. For the next seven hours, the schools' schedules conformed to the standards of the county, and public and Catholic instruction became indistinguishable from each other. In Costilla High School, students' course load included algebra, sociology, chemistry, typing, athletics, and Spanish. The sisters who taught there tended to specialize in one or two subjects. Sister Pancratia Phillips, for example, was the high school's principal, and she also taught the school's American history and English courses. Throughout the day students circulated between classes, taking breaks to eat hot lunches. They read in the school's six-hundred-volume library, and headed outdoors for recess, where the sisters sometimes joined in for a game of baseball. Students who had ridden to school on horseback took advantage of this free time to race their mounts across the dust flat that was their schoolyard. The school day in Costilla ended at four o'clock in the afternoon. After dismissal many students would leave while others stayed on to participate in extracurricular activities. On any given afternoon, these activities might include choir practice, Boy Scouts, or the monthly game of bingo organized by the sisters to raise money for causes like infant paralysis or the Red Cross.[61]

Like other northern New Mexican villages, Costilla had a student body that spoke mainly Spanish. Sisters turned to the state's curricular guidelines as they developed strategies for teaching these students. Women religious across New Mexico garnered respect from their charges, but they also participated fully in the Americanizing agenda that was a sore spot between state officials and many Hispano residents. Their insistence that students speak only English in their classrooms was not only a practical necessity—since most of the women were unable to speak Spanish fluently—it also fulfilled state policy.[62] Although sisters occasionally used music or drama to make the translation of ideas easier for both teacher and students, they mainly taught English through the direct method—permitting no Spanish, either during class or recess time, and insisting students learn through a regimen of immersion, recitation, and rote memorization. Women religious gained high praise from both state officials and outside observers for their effectiveness in teaching children the English language. A 1946 article co-authored by faculty from the University of New Mexico and the University of Chicago singled out one sister-run school for praise. Its authors made special mention of the school's success Americanizing students, describing its atmosphere as "charged with the constant pressure to instill in the children a drive toward institutionalized symbols of approval."[63]

Teaching children to act "American" didn't stop with changing their language. Sisters executed state lesson plans in areas ranging from hygiene to vocational arts to land conservation. The "whole child" vision of public schooling in early-twentieth-century

New Mexico extended far beyond the "three Rs"; it called for instruction in the techniques of home building, cooking, sanitation, and dress needed to bring the population into line with American mores. It also highlighted the training in traditional arts
like weaving and woodworking that administrators imagined would help the population to realize its earning potential.[64] Women religious took seriously the different
teaching responsibilities this comprehensive vision entailed, and they enjoyed
unqualified support from their religious communities as they tried to meet its goals.
From the Catholic side, the *Guiding Growth* curriculum explained that the promotion
of American citizenship was a "sacred charge" and advised:

> Our physical health, our economic well-being, our social and civic rela-
> tions, our cultural development, all are bound up in the most intimate
> manner with our moral and spiritual progress. To educate a child, conse-
> quently, means to promote his growth in all these spheres.[65]

This holistic vision for educating Catholic children resonated in a special way with
the holistic training Hispano students in New Mexico seemed to specially require.

New Mexico's state curriculum indicated that home life was an essential—if not
the essential—area of knowledge in which Hispano children were deficient. In
response, the Dominicans teaching in Peñasco in the 1930s received their prioress
general's support to convert an old home near their school into a two-room "home-
making laboratory." The sisters required all high school girls to take three years of
classes in the domestic arts. To motivate them to apply their acquired skills to the
routines of daily life, sisters made class credits contingent on the students trying out
new techniques in their own homes. They also encouraged the girls to invite their
mothers to school to observe home arts demonstrations.[66] For younger children,
the Dominicans designed course units with similar emphases on the skills useful in
home life. Sister Josefita, who taught the third grade in Peñasco, received special
commendation from her superiors after she implemented an elaborate unit explor-
ing the themes of home building and occupation. As described in a community
publication, the unit's lessons included:

> incidental arithmetic . . . in counting adobes and in measuring for furniture.
> Techniques of coordination . . . by such activities as: mixing mud, laying
> adobe, plastering, painting, sewing, hammering nails, sawing, cutting,
> pasting, and serving tables. . . . Excursions were taken to a home under con-
> struction and to the mountains to select vigas for the roof of the house.
> After marking the trees the children composed a letter to the forest ranger
> asking permission to cut those trees. . . . When the furnishings were com-
> plete, home activities were dramatized. The children set the table, served,
> washed dishes, made a bed, cooked, washed and ironed doll clothes, swept
> and dusted, etc. The unit culminated in a birthday party. The children

brought the ingredients for ice cream. . . . Most of the children had never tasted ice cream and as a result this healthful food was introduced into their diet.[67]

The Dominicans in nearby Santa Cruz also designed educational units around domestic and vocational trades. First and second graders under the direction of Sister Sienna learned about textiles by transforming their classroom into a wool and yarn store. Role playing as artisans, merchants, and customers, the children practiced business transactions alongside the techniques of cloth production— from the nitty-gritty processes of washing and dying wool to the more refined skills of weaving. Like Sister Josefita's students, Sister Sienna's youngsters also acquired unexpected kinds of benefits along the way. There was "elementary science work" occasioned by experimenting with vegetable dyes, and lessons in narrative imparted as each child assembled his or her own "wool booklet telling the story of wool and illustrating it with pictures and drawings."[68] Other learning units designed by Dominican sisters touched upon different emphases in the state curriculum by teaching children about personal health and hygiene, or sewage disposal and water sanitation.[69] The natural world was one more theme important to both the public and parochial curricula, as demonstrated by the special attention teachers like Sister Josefita paid to nature—and in particular land stewardship and resource conservation—in their classrooms and on school trips.[70]

Sisters' ability to execute the state curriculum was commended by the administrators who watched them work. By the late 1930s, Dominicans in the state-designated "key schools" of Peñasco, Ranchos de Taos, and San Juan were obligingly

Figure 3.2 Dominican sisters in Peñasco, New Mexico, in the late 1940s. Courtesy of the Dominican Sisters, Grand Rapids, Michigan.

leading county-wide discussions about the implementation of state programs. After attending one of their discussion groups, the state's superintendent of public instruction was duly impressed and recommended Santa Cruz as a potential site for the training of all teachers in the northern half of the state.[71] Although this accolade eventually went to a different school, the second-grade classroom in Santa Cruz was soon thereafter used to illustrate in the state's own guidelines. One of the few photographs included in the New Mexico curriculum depicted a sister and her students crowded around a microphone, contributing to a local radio program dedicated to land study.[72] Peñasco, already the centerpiece of Dominican education in the region, received similarly enthusiastic affirmation from administrators. Its sisters were invited to demonstrate their teaching methods at county and state conferences, and their students' handiwork was collected for display at a National Education Association meeting in Los Angeles.[73]

In addition to reinforcing the state's curricular guidelines, the integrative currents in Catholic educational circles also provided sisters in New Mexico with tools for their classrooms. Sisters teaching in public schools in the 1940s had the benefit of new textbooks designed by Catholic educators with the intention of giving parochial students an experience comparable to that of their public counterparts. For sisters already teaching publicly, these textbooks made it possible to substitute Catholic alternatives for state-approved teaching materials—alternatives that corresponded closely in content to the official state textbook list. Sometimes this correspondence was close enough that the Catholic volumes made the approved list themselves. One Catholic textbook series to make the state's list was published by L. W. Singer and another by Scott, Foresman and Company—two presses responsible for many of New Mexico's other textbooks. These special "Cathedral edition" series consisted of numerous volumes, each one closely replicating a different state-approved reader.[74] According to the estimate of Paul Masters, New Mexico's textbook director in the late 1940s, Cathedral edition texts were eighty percent identical to their non-Cathedral counterparts.[75] They also, however, included occasional stories or lessons highlighting Catholic themes. In the Cathedral edition of the primary reader *Our New Friends*, for example, the ever-present Dick and Jane count a Catholic priest among their friends, and their domestic adventures include a trip to Mass and a search for a lost rosary.[76] This volume and dozens of other Cathedral edition texts were included on New Mexico's approved textbook list during the 1940s and distributed to sisters' classrooms directly by the state board of education.

Another textbook series used by sisters in New Mexico was the *Faith and Freedom* readers. Like the *Guiding Growth* curriculum, *Faith and Freedom* texts were products of the Commission on American Citizenship designed for both primary and secondary schools. These books were intended, in the words of one of their authors, "to bridge the gap which has existed for so long a time between the teaching of religious truths and their translation into life situations."[77] *Faith and Freedom* texts explored American civic themes from an identifiably Catholic perspective; volumes highlighted the contributions of Catholic figures in American history, and the compatibility of Catholic teaching with American political values. The volume entitled *These Are Our Freedoms*, for example, was designed for the seventh grade, and its focus was antebellum American history. An excerpt from the U.S. Constitution introduced each of its chapters, often sharing space with a prayer or Bible verse. The book's third chapter, "We Worship God," was prefaced by the religion clauses of the First Amendment, accompanied by a verse from the Book of Romans.[78] The chapter's titular theme was then elaborated upon in several phases—by a radio play highlighting the contributions of French priest Pierre Gibault to the United States' acquisition of the Northwest Territory, by a story about the first Catholic mission on the Ohio frontier, and by several shorter pieces including George Washington's proclamation upon the first Thanksgiving and Walt Whitman's inimitable "Pioneers! O Pioneers!" Although sisters in New Mexico taught from these *Faith and Freedom* readers for only two years, the patriotic textbooks were an especially popular choice for their classrooms during that time. Between 1944 and 1946 sisters requested more than twelve hundred volumes for use in their schools.[79]

Sisters built their professional reputations on the common ground they found between the teaching instructions of the Church and the teaching guidelines of the state. The familiar quality of new Catholic textbooks, and the permissive attitude of state officials toward including those texts in their curriculum, gave these women a set of tools with which to work. Yet sisters also ran regularly into limits imposed upon that ground from both sides. Even the most successful and savvy sister in New Mexico occasionally found herself in the awkward position of offering a lesson that defied the expectations of her superiors in either the Church or the state. The opposing separationist impulses embedded in these institutions persisted along the edges of sisters' work, and these women faced the biggest challenges of their careers when the things they taught threatened to undermine the values of either one institution or the other. Sisters who found themselves in this position demonstrated incredible creativity, but it was expressed reluctantly, with the realization they had little other choice. In moments like this a sister's teaching became a delicate dance bent upon the all-but-impossible task of preserving her school.

Despite the permissiveness of state administrators when it came to Catholic textbooks, expectations of nonsectarianism built into New Mexico's education laws presented a formidable challenge for Catholic women religious. Even Maura McDonald, arguably the sister in all of New Mexico most skilled at playing by the public system's rules, admitted to the strain this expectation created. "One reason why the Sisters hesitated to accept public schools in the beginning," she remembered of her own Dominican community, "was the enforced deviation from their role as religious educators."[80] From the Catholic side, things could seem equally unforgiving; the same Catholic teaching tools that helped sisters engage the public system also set firm terms for that engagement. The pages of *Guiding Growth*, for example, were tempered by admonishments that cooperation with the public sphere should never translate into leaving Catholic teachings about God and Church out of education.[81] With a stern directive to remain nonsectarian speaking from one side, and equally stern instructions to preserve God in their classrooms coming from the other, sisters disagreed among themselves about how to proceed. They differed over how much, and what kind, of religion to retain in their teaching, and on the ways to make sure sufficient religion was included. Every sister who worked in a public classroom, however, took part in a process McDonald summed up candidly as lesson "modification."[82] Sisters altered the form and content of their instruction, in ways that departed from both their Church and the state's expectations, in their bids to avoid censure.

For all sisters' efforts to follow state guidelines, the complaints of residents like Lydia Zellers about Catholic influence in their classrooms had merit. Reports from Dixon were bolstered by the photographs Zellers brought back with her from Carrizozo. And neither Dixon nor Carrizozo was an isolated incident. Before all was said and done, Zellers and her neighbors photographed sixteen different schools across the state staffed by sisters. Their photographs—a total of eighty-two distinct prints—captured hundreds of objects and images that defied the nonsectarian directives of New Mexico's education statutes and its constitution. A portrait of the archbishop hung in the principal's office in the junior high school in Las Vegas, and a reproduction of the Last Supper hung above a blackboard in the elementary school at Blanco. On another blackboard, again in Las Vegas, the word "Religion" was scrawled in chalk. Iron crosses sat atop school roofs in Cuba and Park View, and in Lumberton a large stone grotto replete with a statue of Our Lady of Lourdes dominated a field adjacent to the high school.[83] Zellers and her associates also saw religious texts in many sisters' classrooms; after its photographic expedition the group assembled a "partial list" of sixty-seven "religious indoctrinated" books, comics, magazines, and pamphlets it had found in the schools it visited.[84]

Often sisters and clergy included these Catholic objects around their schools assuming—and correctly so—that local officials would look the other way. Other times, sisters integrated Catholic sights and sounds into their classrooms with care, in ways that balanced respect for state regulations with a willingness to test their limits. Finding this balance involved both liberally interpreting the letter of the law and altering forms of Catholicism present in the classroom. Because there was no protocol for what the balance should look like, sisters worked independently to achieve it. They made decisions about the details of their classrooms individually or in small groups, with only occasional guidance from local clergy. This sort of decision making was especially apparent in the visual culture of sisters' classrooms. Faced with detailed civil guidelines for the spatial organization of their rooms—the state's curriculum even included diagrams specifying furniture arrangement—as well as opposing pressure from their Church to fill those rooms with Catholic images, women religious in New Mexico were deliberate when they decorated their schools. Some included religious images among their decorations, but placed those images in private areas of the school only semi-visible by children. The Ursuline sisters teaching in Waterflow, for example, kept a grotto on their school's front campus but allowed their public students to play only on the east and west portions of campus.[85] The Sisters of Loretto permitted their public students in Socorro to walk through private classrooms on their way in and out of the school building. They did not, however (so one sister testified), permit children to linger in those rooms, for fear they might reflect upon the Catholic paintings hanging on their walls or over-hear the prayers other students sometimes recited in them.[86]

Other women found ways to fill their own classrooms with religious pictures while still meeting the requirements of the state. These sisters exploited ambiguities in the state's curriculum, namely its failure to distinguish between prohibitively sectarian images and those images sanctioned for classroom use as examples of fine art. In its section on art appreciation, the state curriculum invoked lofty language to describe the importance of exposing New Mexico's children to objects of beauty:

> The major objective in art appreciation is to awaken the child to a feeling for the beauty in the things about him. Early in the development of man he learned that when objects about him were harmonious in form, color, and arrangement, they gave him much more pleasure than when they were dis-harmonious, and so it has been his constant effort to secure harmony and beauty in life for himself.[87]

The curriculum also included a list of paintings sufficiently "harmonious in form, color and arrangement" to be recommended for display in public classrooms. In keeping with the Anglo tilt of the state's educational agenda, the works of European masters made up the bulk of this list. The fact that many of these paintings depicted Catholic subjects was unproblematic—a matter of historical rather than religious significance—to the officials who approved their presence in the state's schools.

Sisters decorated the walls of their classrooms with reproductions of Catholic-themed European masterpieces.[88] Franciscan Sister Natalina Fleckenstein, who was principal of the elementary school in Peña Blanca, displayed several of these prints in her school's auditorium in the late 1940s. During the trial she had an opportunity to defend her choice of artwork. Sister Natalina's attorney asked her whether the religious images she displayed on her walls were included in the curriculum as suitable art for the public classroom. Did her images include, he suggested, the "Madonna of the Chair" by Raphael or the "Madonna of the Magnificat" by Botticelli? Although she was unable to recount all the titles of the pictures she had collected, Sister Natalina hardly missed a beat: "I know they are masterpieces, but I don't know just [from] when."[89] Similar confidence marked the words of Ursuline Sister Eugenia Scherm as she talked during the trial about the artwork hung throughout her school. "Well,

Figure 3.3 "Madonna of the Magnificat" by Sandro Botticelli.

there are some masterpieces," she admitted. "Now in one [classroom], I recall ... the `Angelus' ... `Christ at Twelve' [and] `Christ in the Temple,' and in the other [class-room], Plockhorst's `Guardian Angel' and `Christ Blessing the Children.'" "They are all on the approved list," she added adamantly, "every picture."[90]

Women religious used loopholes in state policy to their advantage as they tried to integrate Catholic materials into their teaching. At the same time, circumstances often demanded that the sisters modify their religious offerings to conform to state law. As a result the Catholic objects and activities in New Mexico's public schools were different from their parochial counterparts. Some women were more willing to make these modifications than others—evidence abounded of recalcitrant sisters leading children through the Our Father or Hail Mary between classes, or asking them to donate nickels and dimes to the foreign missions for the ransom of "pagan babies."[91] More often, however, New Mexico's sisters relocated their religious activities to the periphery of the public school day. By the mid-1940s, most sisters restricted catechism and other religion classes to periods either before or after regular school hours. The schools in Costilla were again typical in this way. Sisters taught catechism to Catholic students between eight thirty and nine o'clock on weekday mornings, immediately before regular classes began. School buses arrived in Costilla early enough to accommodate these Catholic students' schedules, and the few non-Catholics who arrived with them were either supervised on the playground or sent to a library or study hall.[92] Conscientious sisters prohibited non-Catholic students from attending their early morning religion classes or—if a student displayed unusually keen interest—required the written permission of a parent.[93] In most cases, sisters omitted grades for these classes from children's official report cards.[94]

By compartmentalizing religious instruction in this way, sisters complied with state law, and in particular with several resolutions passed in New Mexico during the 1940s stipulating that religion classes were permissible when held on school property outside of regular class hours.[95] In instances where the building itself was owned by either the religious community or the archdiocese, sisters further defended this arrangement by pointing to the terms of the building's lease—often

Figure 3.4 Students praying, St. Rita's School, Carrizozo, New Mexico, 1948. The caption included with original photograph places the prayer at "beginning of school day," but does not specify before or after the start of normal school hours. Photograph taken by the Dixon Free Schools Committee. Courtesy of Special Collections Research Center, Morris Library, Southern Illinois University Carbondale.

schools were only rented to the district or county for public use between the hours of nine and four.[96] In cases where school buildings were public property, cautious sisters moved children to nearby private buildings for their religion classes, and a few communities even made sure those classes were taught by sisters not bound by contract to the state.[97] Religious cooperated with local clergy to make similar arrangements for Catholic students attending Mass or confession. Although occasionally students were excused or dismissed early for these religious activities, by the late 1940s such rituals often took place in a nearby church, and happened either before or after regular school hours, or during students' lunch hour.[98]

The changes Catholic sisters made to conform to state expectations resulted in the idiosyncratic creature that was the hybrid, public–parochial classroom. These spaces remained recognizably (and controversially) Catholic around the edges, but they also provided an education to both Protestant and Catholic students that was recognizably similar to their public counterparts—and different in several significant ways from parochial schools of the period. In many of these schools, a civil curriculum took precedence, with religious elements either cautiously integrated or else segregated to extracurricular periods of the day. As public employees, sisters were charged with acting in the interest of the state, and as they made decisions about their teaching—especially through the late 1940s—they felt the pressure of state expectations to keep things of the Church separate from their classrooms. They acceded to this pressure where they could, and the modified shape of Catholicism in their classrooms was the evidence of their concessions.

Community superiors worried a great deal about the consequences of state-sponsored education. Even parochial teaching could force sisters into a balancing act between their professional and religious identities.[99] The modifications sisters made to teach publicly put them in a far more dangerous situation—they not only distracted the women from their spiritual pursuits, but they could also throw those pursuits into jeopardy by exposing sisters to secular educational models and encouraging them to interact with people motivated by non-Catholic interests. Although mothers general permitted their sisters to work in New Mexico, women who taught regularly felt their superiors' apprehensions pushing back against their state obligations, reminding them of their commitment to remain distant from nonreligious aspects of the world in which they taught. This religiously derived sense of separation took priority over its legal counterpart in the minds of most sisters, just as it did with their superiors—this would become clearest amid the heat of litigation when sisters were forced finally to choose between the two. Until 1948, however, women religious continued to walk a thin line here as well. Even as they respected the separating impulse embedded in their vocation, the public nature of their jobs required sisters to test their orders' imperatives to reclusion.

In 1951 Mary Nona McGreal, co-author of *Guiding Growth*, wrote a dissertation defending the importance of her community's interactions with the non-Catholic world. Teaching, she explained, was a "career within a vocation," and collaboration with people outside of the avowed community was not only acceptable but integral to its aims. These people included members of non-Catholic civic and religious organizations, as well as the family members of students:

> There is a seeming paradox in the fact that Sisters who profess to withdraw from secular affairs . . . should visit the families of their pupils. Actually, however, this practice is in accord with the whole program of a religious, which is one of self-denial for the sake of God and others. Visits to pupils' homes are not made for recreation. They are limited strictly to charitable and professional purposes, which frequently coincide.[100]

McGreal also defended sisters who engaged with public schools and their teachers in the interest of meeting common educational challenges. She pointed out instances when these challenges required sisters' collaboration with state and federal governments as well.[101] Here McGreal's words seem directed at skeptics among the Catholic leadership, individuals still worried that such forays might damage a sister's fragile character. With a spirited tone, McGreal argued that sisters were full, *adult* participants in American social life: "The sisters take up responsible roles in this common life, not only as adult members of the community but more especially as teachers of its future citizens," she wrote. "They enter into the give-and-take of community life, conscious that for a time this is the sphere providentially given them for Christian teaching and action."[102]

Although McGreal had her own Dominican congregation in mind when she wrote, she no doubt knew about the work of her counterparts in New Mexico.[103] In the interest of their educational mission, those sisters developed unusual relationships within the wider society in which they taught. These relationships went hand in hand with the responsibilities of public employment. Sisters in New Mexico communicated regularly with students' parents—Protestants as well as Catholics—and they paid visits to their homes. They participated in retreats with sisters from other teaching communities, and in professional functions with nonreligious teachers. Those sisters who served as school principals had the additional responsibility of giving orders to lay teachers of both sexes, including male physical education instructors and athletic coaches.[104] As public venues, their schools were multi-use spaces that often served as *de facto* community centers during out-of-class hours. Sisters' classrooms doubled as meeting spaces for Boy Scouts and 4-H clubs. They hosted local elections, meetings of land grants and irrigation committees, and even on occasion a public trial. In addition, sisters regularly staged tutorials and screened movies in their classrooms, for the edification of adults and children alike.[105] Although most of these activities took place on evenings and weekends, it was not unusual for a school's civic functions to blend with its educational function during school hours as well.

Sisters also used their talents to help adults living in their communities. One Dominican exercised her exceptional penmanship, serving as the official correspondent between Santa Cruz residents and the young men from their village deployed to war.[106] Maura McDonald had the most visible public presence of all New Mexico's sisters for good reason—she not only served as both a principal and superintendent in Peñasco, but was also a rationing officer and a liaison for the Red Cross. In addition, she had the responsibility of registering all young men in her region for the draft. Because of these and other duties, Sister Maura had the advantage—or perhaps the burden—of keeping one of the mountain village's two working telephones.[107] Sister Maura's shadow was particularly long in New Mexico, but her political responsibilities were not unique. At least one other sister acted in the capacity of public official during the 1940s: Sister Irma Mariana of the Sisters of Divine Providence was both clerk of the Pecos school board and the superintendent of Pecos schools.[108]

Although stories of Catholic sisters participating in—and occasionally leading—community life in northern New Mexico are plentiful, their participation in the public sphere was tempered at every turn by the rules of their communities, and the respect the women harbored for those rules. The same young women who were positioned to enter public life on a level unprecedented among religious of their time also experienced a strong separation from that life—a sensation they felt acutely because of their proximity. Mary Nona McGreal, in advocating for sisters' visibility, made a clear distinction between purposes that were "charitable and professional" and unstructured recreation.[109] The same line between work and play was drawn on the ground in New Mexico, where superiors discouraged sisters from pursuing any relationships unrelated to their work. A former student, who recalled her teachers in great detail, emphasized she and other children never interacted with them outside the school day. "Never, never, never!" she insisted, "Once school was out they went to the convent and I guess they stayed there or they went to the church to pray. But never [did we see them]. . . . Now I see nuns all over, but then? No."[110]

The prohibition against mingling recreationally made it difficult for women religious to get to know the adults they encountered during their professional duties. Even as sisters developed intimate relationships with children, their interactions with the adults they met at meetings or in church continued at a guarded distance. Friendships between sisters and their Hispano neighbors, already made difficult by linguistic and cultural differences, were practically non-existent. One sister's recollection of *penitentes* during Holy Week in Ranchos de Taos is telling, framed as it is by their absence from her world rather than their presence. "My bedroom . . . faced west," Sister Carmella Conway remembered,

> and I could hear them coming from the hills. I don't know where, but they must have gathered far away and went in procession. . . . You go over to

church for the Easter Vigil, and they're not there. And Easter morning [in church] there are even less of them.[111]

During school hours, women like Sister Carmella were at the center of public life in northern New Mexico. At the end of their day's duties, however, these women returned to the shelter of their priories. For all the forays into civic life presiding over a village school entailed, sisters who taught in New Mexico still recounted "being confined to the classroom" and to their convents—marching, as one sister recalled it, out to church and back home again.[112] Sisters' vocational responsibilities demanded they engage an unusually broad array of people and professions across New Mexican society, and the women happily nurtured these collaborative relationships when the occasion arose. The same vocation that led them into public work, however, also pulled them away from the informal life of the surrounding community. And so in obedience sisters watched that life from a place apart.

The resolve to separate oneself from the happenings of the nonreligious world was one of two principles of separation that played off each other every day in sisters' classrooms. Pressure from these dueling principles opened up an educational landscape that resembled both its public and its parochial counterparts, but that was different in important ways from each. Poised in between these principles, sisters' success in New Mexico turned upon a seemingly impossible task—to keep Catholicism appropriately compartmentalized in relation to their public commitments, even as they took care to keep themselves and their students apart from the perceived secularity of public life. The culture of many New Mexican classrooms in the 1930s and 1940s was assembled from sisters' innovative successes in this regard and also from their failures—those instances when they were unable to make their teaching satisfy either the state's requirements or their orders' instructions.

Through the 1940s, the American legal principle of church–state separation gained traction in New Mexico. Its expectations were matched by rigidity on the part of religious communities when it came to their own separating impulses. By the opening of the 1947 school year, public–parochial education in towns across New Mexico was holding on only tenuously as the status quo. In places like Carrizozo, Peñasco, and—most brazenly—Dixon, Catholic sisters continued to mix and match the lessons from their vocation with pieces of the state's curriculum. It frustrated Lydia Zellers and her neighbors to no end that their classrooms—while patently public—left room for Roman Catholicism to intrude. The most recent developments in Dixon only added insult to injury. The prospect of Franciscans introducing their teaching style into a second, doggedly fundraised and newly built public school threw that village's Protestants into an unqualified rage.

In early September 1947, just days before classes were scheduled to begin, Zellers and several other residents drove the seventy-five miles to Tierra Amarilla to protest the county board's decision to hire the Franciscans. The group arrived in the county seat in the late morning and the mood in the conference room was tense when the school board members returned from their lunch. Zellers stood to speak on behalf of Dixon's residents, and she addressed county superintendent Albert Amador directly. The people in Dixon were out of patience, she informed him, and simply would not tolerate a Franciscan as principal of their new school.[113] There was no room for compromises; the newly built school *needed* to be staffed by lay teachers and lay teachers alone. As she made her appeal before the board, Zellers' voice tightened with anger. "The Sisters are already laughing [behind] our backs, and they would keep on laughing, if we were to allow them in our school, because they have the backing of you people."[114]

Zellers' outburst exposed the collusion Dixon's school proponents saw themselves up against, as they wondered at their failure to open a sister-free institution in the village. As the meeting dragged on through the afternoon their resentment only grew—the delegation found it could do nothing to sway the heavily Catholic board. Still, Dixon's residents had no intention of leaving Tierra Amarilla defeated. Late in the afternoon Lydia spoke again and laid before the board an ultimatum she and her neighbors had quietly agreed upon before the meeting. Their group, she suggested, was ready to take legal action if the board failed to keep Catholic sisters away from the new school. On this point J. P. Craig, a successful farmer who had accompanied Lydia from Dixon, was quick to join his friend. If legal action was needed, he suggested, their group could get "thousands of workers" to document evidence against the sisters. As he continued, the elderly man's own tone became defiant. "What we are after is the very best education facilities unhampered by anything.... We do not want this to go any farther, but if the Sisters want to put us in court, we will go there. I myself need no one to pray for me!"[115]

The board's members listened to these warnings soberly, but they were unwillingly to agree to the group's demands. Their responses vacillated during the afternoon between firm and evasive. Their hands were tied, Amador insisted to the delegation. The board had hired the Franciscans the previous May to teach during the 1947–48 year, and those sisters were protected by the tenure law that guaranteed employment for every teacher who renewed a contract after three years in the state. "The Sisters can turn right around, if we are to put them out, and sue the County Board and collect their money for the whole year," Amador tried to explain.[116] Hoping to avoid a sticky situation, other board members speculated they were ill equipped to make any decision at all about Dixon's schools. One man, correctly surmising the delegation's anger did not reflect the feelings of the whole of Dixon, suggested the board could make no determination unless it heard from the entire community.[117] The consensus that emerged among its members, however, was that the county simply lacked jurisdiction in such a complicated matter. The meeting adjourned with no action taken, but Amador did promise the delegation he would immediately refer Dixon's problem to the state board of education. Furthermore, to Zellers' satisfaction, the board agreed to allow any child not wanting to attend the new public school to remain at home until after the state board met to resolve the issue.

4

Captured!

POAU and the National Campaign against Captive Schools

Two weeks after the county meeting, the Dixon delegation had its promised hearing before the state board in Santa Fe. News of the group's trouble in Tierra Amarilla had spread throughout the Embudo Valley, and nearly fifty people traveled to the state capitol for the proceedings. All of the new school's strongest supporters made the trip, including Lydia Zellers, Porfiero Romero, the Bowen sisters, and Paul Stevens from Taos. This time, to be on the safe side, they brought with them twenty witnesses to testify about the sectarian nature of the Franciscans' teaching, and a pile of affidavits to speak for others who were unable to appear in person.[1] As the delegation gathered in the bustling city to present its case, the idea of taking legal action against the county seemed more real than it had in quiet Tierra Amarilla.

Zellers and her neighbors marched up the steps of New Mexico's capitol building shortly after midday, but they were stopped in their tracks and asked to wait outside the closed doors of the board of education's offices. Joining the crowd as it tarried together expectantly was a local lawyer named Harry Bigbee. Bigbee was only in his early thirties, but his serious dark brows and a taste for good suits made him a picture of confidence and success. His credentials matched his image. Bigbee was a Texan by birth and had a law degree from Southern Methodist University in Dallas. In Santa Fe he was a rising star; he had already served as assistant attorney general and recently completed a year-long appointment as district judge there. His energy and intellect—he enjoyed what one colleague described as a "bear trap of a legal mind"—won the young attorney plenty of admirers in New Mexico. When Lydia Zellers retained Bigbee to help her group with its trouble in 1947, he was settling comfortably into private practice with an office located prominently on Santa Fe's central plaza.[2]

The appointed time for the hearing came and went without word as the delegation mingled in the hall. When the doors finally opened forty-five minutes later, only Zellers and Bigbee were permitted access to the board's suite. As the pair walked in, State Superintendent of Public Instruction Charles Rose was presiding over a meeting in mid-session. The state board's chairman, Raymond Huff, was sitting in attendance along with the other members of the board. Among those unfamiliar faces, there was one aging face near the head of the conference table that Zellers recognized immediately. The young woman reacted with alarm to see Dixon's most famous Catholic resident, the priest Peter Küppers, glancing back at her. Küppers had been talking privately with the board, and now he joined its members as they greeted Zellers and her attorney and listened to their grievances. Had the entire Dixon contingent been permitted access to the hearing, it would have transformed the dynamic of the room—and probably also made it uncomfortably crowded. As it was, Zellers and Bigbee felt outnumbered. The board members refused to review the affidavits the pair had brought with them.[3] Their hearing was brief and the board dismissed the pair with a message much like the one Zellers had heard from the county two weeks earlier—its members concluded *they* had no jurisdiction over Dixon's teachers. The board referred the residents' complaints back once more to Tierra Amarilla, with instructions that the county board evaluate them immediately. The Dixon delegation left Santa Fe disappointed.

Despite handing responsibility for Dixon's problem back to the county, the state board was interested in the outcome of the teacher question. Huff and Rose wrote jointly to Rio Arriba County officials the next day, and passed along a strong recommendation for how the matter of Dixon's two public schools should be settled.[4] The county board followed their advice to a tee. In a follow-up meeting with the Dixon delegation—now numbering nearly eighty individuals—the county finally agreed the village's newest public school would open that fall with a staff comprising exclusively lay teachers. But it asked the delegation for a concession in return—while this lay-staffed school would serve children through the sixth grade, St. Joseph's would continue to house Dixon's public high school, and the Franciscans would continue teaching its classes. With this compromise in place, Dixon's new public school opened its doors to students the very next day.

Meanwhile, word of the state hearing traveled quickly from the capitol complex to the archbishop's residence just a few blocks away. Concerned about the Dixon delegation's tenacity, Chairman Huff passed along a word of warning to Archbishop of Santa Fe Edwin Byrne after the meeting. The entire practice of employing Catholic religious in the state system might be compromised, he cautioned the prelate, unless those religious began to pay more attention to avoiding Catholic influence in their classrooms.[5] Byrne, a Philadelphia native who had come to the archdiocese four years earlier, wasted no time responding. With the help of his own education director, the archbishop drafted a letter to all the religious teaching in New Mexico's public schools. The letter was to the point; it instructed sisters and brothers that "no religious instruction be given in public school buildings by the teachers on school days."[6] It directed that catechism—if it was taught to students at all—should only be taught on Saturdays and Sundays. Byrne also sent a more pointed letter to Sister

Emma, the current superior of Dixon's Franciscan community. The archbishop directed Sister Emma to immediately remove all religious emblems from St. Joseph's School in Dixon, and to ensure her sisters refrain from prayer and religious instruction there. Punctuating the weight of these orders, the prelate directed Sister Emma to report any sisters who failed to comply to him directly.[7]

By late September there was optimism in the offices of both the state board and the archdiocese that crisis in Dixon had been narrowly averted. Although the county board's compromise fell short of giving Zellers' delegation the completely sister-free public education it wanted, its members *had* seen the opening of their hard-won school, and only lay teachers were employed in it. The delegation had been quiet since the county board's decision, and it seemed plausible Dixon's Protestants had turned their attention to other things. On the Catholic side, the response of the religious to the archbishop's recent directive about their teaching was by no means enthusiastic, but most seemed willing to comply with his instructions.[8] The steady stream of communication between the board and the archdiocese during the month of September took on a tone that was both conciliatory and relieved. Charles Rose sent Byrne a letter offering his personal thanks, and Huff expressed his appreciation for the archbishop, calling him both diplomatic and broadminded in the face of such a challenging situation.[9]

At the end of the month, however, those hoping Dixon's school troubles would disappear from the radar received a jarring surprise. However improbably, the little village had found its way into the national news. Tucked away near the back of a late September issue of *Time* magazine, like a second thought beside a large advertisement for the Santa Fe Railway, was a short article. The article began:

> Catholic priests and nuns have been teaching in New Mexico ever since the 19th Century days of jolly Father Martinez, who taught reading, writing and the catechism to New Mexican schoolchildren, until he was excommunicated for having too many children of his own. State law prohibits religious instruction in public schools, but the law has long been winked at. Last week, in the remote town of Dixon, N. Mex., the winking stopped.[10]

Clear across the country, New Mexico's schools had caught the eye and, as the playfully irreverent tone suggested, the fancy of an editor. The article went on to recount the controversy surrounding the new school in Dixon, the delegation's actions, and the school board and archdiocese's responses. While there was no mention of how Dixon came to this editor's attention, the account was informed by the delegation's perspective and seemed sympathetic to its cause. It also concluded with a nugget of privileged knowledge. "Dixon's Protestants said they would not be satisfied," it reported, "until there were no nuns in the public schools."[11]

Whether or not Dixon's residents contacted the editor at *Time* themselves, they were grateful for the publicity the article offered.[12] Through the autumn of 1947, even as archdiocesan and school officials held out hope the school troubles had subsided, a growing group of residents from Dixon and surrounding communities were laying the foundation for a prolonged fight. In the weeks after the state hearing the group formally named itself the Dixon Free Schools Committee. Lydia Zellers, Porfiero Romero, and Olive Bowen became the committee's acting secretaries. The Free Schools Committee's purpose was to raise awareness about the situation in Dixon—namely the fact sisters were still publicly employed, in what was now the village's only high school—with the goal of attracting enough support, and raising enough money, to take action against the county. As their first orders of business, the committee's members began to assemble informational material for distribution, and they set about compiling a list of parties they hoped would take interest in their cause.

Through Romero, Stevens, and Zellers herself, the committee already boasted a network of allies among Protestant clergy in New Mexico. To reach an even larger audience it turned to the Home Missions Board of the Presbyterian Church—a national organization to which Zellers and Bowen, like many New Mexican Presbyterians, already had connections. Experienced in building spiritual and financial bridges between missionaries in places like New Mexico and Presbyterian donors across the country, the Home Missions Board had an infrastructure capable of delivering Dixon's story to a national following.[13] The Dixon committee reached out to the board through Olive Bowen's sister Sarah. Sarah Bowen was a missions spokesperson for the Board, and she traveled the country regularly to report on behalf of her Embudo hospital. That autumn Bowen began speaking to her Presbyterian audiences about Dixon's plight, and she referred interested parties she met back to the committee. Bowen also wrote to her extensive national contacts. She sent them leaflets, and implored they help Dixon's residents find an advocacy organization to assist their cause.[14] Both the *Time* article and Bowen's efforts made the committee optimistic about locating national support. None of its members, however, could have predicted how much support Dixon and its schools were about to receive.

The Dixon Free Schools Committee timed its appeal for national assistance perfectly. The autumn of 1947 was a fortuitous moment to solicit support for any action, legal or otherwise, against the Catholic Church's influence in American education. Sarah Bowen penned her request for help on behalf of the committee in late October, just one week after a different, sixty-strong group of men and women came together in Chicago to draft a manifesto. This new group comprised mainly Protestant ministers, and its own reason for existing was "to give all possible aid to the citizens of any community or State who are seeking to protect their public schools from sectarian domination, or resisting any other assault upon the principle of separation of church and state."[15] The following month the group adopted the name Protestants and Other Americans United for Separation of Church and State (POAU). By the start of the new year it had offered its support to the Dixon Committee.

With the intervention of POAU, Dixon's reputation grew between 1947 and 1951 into something much bigger than Lydia Zellers, Archbishop Byrne, or any resident of New Mexico could have anticipated. Within months the controversy in Dixon did take the form of a lawsuit, and the suit grabbed the nation's attention. By 1948, stories that described New Mexico's schools as prisoners, entrapped beneath a clerical Roman shadow, were titillating the imaginations of audiences who read them in magazines like *The Christian Century, Christian Herald*, and the Presbyterian monthly *Social Progress*. Coverage of the controversy expertly blended legal issues at play with colorful and poignant, if archaic, presentations of New Mexico's Spanish-speaking communities—rendering the legal and affective dimensions of Dixon's troubles indistinguishable in readers' minds. POAU realized early on that the persuasive blend encapsulated in Dixon's dispute made the case a provocative symbol; by the mid-1950s the organization had made the little village the centerpiece of its national campaign to defend American public education.

The public positions sisters held in New Mexico were products of that region's distinctive history and cultural mix, but they weren't anomalies in the United States in 1950. For decades school boards across the country had been forming cooperative arrangements with parochial schools and the sisters who worked in them. These situations tended to have several things in common. The communities involved were usually rural and, with the exception of New Mexico, in the American Midwest. They were always heavily Catholic, with a Catholic majority among local officials. As happened in Dixon and other New Mexican districts, school boards in these places reached agreements with clergy to purchase, rent, or simply assume use of local parochial schools. The boards then funded those schools and the sisters teaching in them, and began to call them public. Sometimes preexisting schools were closed, and their children transferred to these new public–parochial schools. Sometimes, but not always, religious education was removed from the curriculum or restricted to hours outside the normal school day. Sometimes, but also not always, religious images were removed from classroom walls, although the school might remain on a piece of land shared with the local church or convent. These arrangements had a history in the United States stretching back to the nineteenth century, and they became more visible than ever in Dixon's aftermath.[16] A decade after the Dixon crisis, a POAU-sponsored survey identified public–parochial agreements in twenty-one states, employing over two thousand Catholic sisters as teachers.[17] Around 1950 POAU began to talk about these arrangements as a unique challenge to American public education. It called them "captive schools."

POAU developed the idea of captive schools based on its involvement in the *Zellers* case. New Mexico's schools served as prototypes as the organization expanded its use of the "captive" label to describe analogous episodes and to indicate a pattern of public–parochial cooperation across the United States during the 1950s. The conversion of Catholic schools into public institutions, and the varieties of church–state collaboration this sort of transformation entailed, were enough to raise red flags under both state constitutions and the First Amendment by the mid-century mark. POAU developed its reputation as a separation advocacy organization by challenging these episodes in court. Through its efforts, the group made captive school lawsuits a major part of church–state litigation during the 1950s, as familiar to the American public as released time and bus transportation cases. While these other types of litigation targeted specific educational policies, however, captive school suits were true to their name by challenging a loose, undifferentiated state of takeover or control.[18] Captive schools were litigated systematically, but the suits against them included different combinations of allegations. They might cite the teaching of catechism or the distribution of religious textbooks, the presence of religious images in the classroom, or the Church's ownership of school buildings. In addition they always included complaints about the employment of women who wore religious garb. The indeterminacy of captive schools as a legal issue gave POAU flexibility as it developed tactics for fighting sister-taught schools within state courts. At the same time, this indeterminacy kept captive schools safely off of the U.S. Supreme Court's docket. The volume of captive school litigation during the 1950s, counterpoised with its absence from federal church–state rulings of the era, prompted Frank Sorauf to describe captive schooling as the "major 'nonissue' in the constitutional law of church-state relations" at midcentury.[19]

By 1960 captive schools made up a recognizable pattern of church–state cooperation in the United States, supported by a corresponding body of litigation. The category did more than point to a set of controversial arrangements, however; it also spoke to the motivations that drove public interest in separation of church and state. In the aftermath of *Everson v. Board of Education*, American separation proponents disagreed with one another about the implications of the principle they were fighting for. At POAU, some leaders believed in a separation standard that excluded all religion from public institutions. Among the organization's base, a more traditional, pro-Protestant reading of the principle dominated. Captive schools were the glue that held these interests together during the organization's first decade. From the beginning, POAU cultivated a populism that distinguished its advocacy mission and shaped all its work. While its dedication to upholding the Constitution was unwavering, the group committed itself to litigation and to public outreach in equal parts. To meet its dual ends, POAU sought out situations that called for legal recourse and also had compelling details it could exploit to mobilize its national following. The captive school was a muddy legal issue, but it was tailor-made for the young group's purposes. It provoked opponents from different walks of life, who had different preconceptions about what separation actually entailed. It violated secularist sensibilities about the First Amendment, but for many of its Protestant critics it stirred up more intimate misgivings as well.

A long public preoccupation with Catholic capture gained new life in the mid-twentieth-century United States. Evidence of church–state cooperation amid a climate of geopolitical fear and unsettling demographic change helped to revive vintage images of Catholic deceit and malicious design. New cultural proximity between Protestants and Catholics in the decade after World War II built ecumenical spirit, but it also spurred competition, especially over shared educational responsibilities. Even as American Protestants welcomed their Catholic neighbors, some of them continued to wonder about their loyalty to an undemocratic institution and its authoritarian hierarchy. These Protestants turned to centuries-old rhetoric of Catholic captivity to help them plumb the shape of a Church that was now living in their midst and more difficult to distinguish every day. POAU highlighted the late vestiges of Catholic difference in its campaign against captive schools. When its leaders published accounts of Dixon and episodes in its wake, they recalled a tried-and-true list of dangers. Captive schools not only threatened church–state separation, they were also nests of foreign influence, brainwashing, and bodily danger planted in America's heartland. The organization publicized these situations to evidence Catholic disregard for the First Amendment, but it also used them to affirm to its Protestant membership what many already suspected—that beneath its American veneer Catholicism still had terrifying and fascinating potential.

POAU drew fire from its opponents and occasionally its allies for using anti-Catholic language as part of its public awareness campaigns. Some of its critics knowingly linked the group's slippage into anti-Catholicism with its efforts to maintain rapport with its broad audience. The general public's interest in church–state separation, these critics insisted, lay less in the preservation of a principle of governance and more in unexamined fears of Catholic duplicity and aggression.[20] Captive schools, from this perspective, earned their reputation not because of any unique challenge they posed the First Amendment, but because of the drama suggested by their name. This appraisal had merit, but it also overlooked the foundational relationship between emotive captivity language and Protestant imaginings of separation at a time when the principle's meaning was unclear. POAU was a Protestant organization, and although its members disagreed about the implications of separation, they relied upon religiously grounded tropes they had in common to unite them in their work. In a legal environment where secular expectations were gaining ground, POAU's organization along religious lines was a stubborn assertion of the special significance separation still had for American Protestants, no matter how those Protestants felt about the principle's implications. Anxiety over religious authority had always found its expression within Protestantism through popular narrative forms devoted to Catholic captivity. No matter what ideas were circulating about the limits (or lack thereof) of separation during the 1940s and 1950s, those forms remained reliably potent reminders across the Protestant spectrum of the urgency of the separation cause. POAU's leadership introduced captivity accounts into legal conversations in a bid to unite its members, and also to prove to itself and to the Protestant public that church–state separation was still personally and spiritually relevant. Captive schools were more than an organizational strategy to translate an abstract legal concept into popular terms. The threat of Catholic capture gave the separation principle a fixed and familiar shape for POAU's leaders and its membership. In doing so it provided an opportunity for everyone involved to recommit themselves to the First Amendment.

POAU was founded in 1947 in an atmosphere rife with concern about the Catholic Church and its consequences for the American classroom. Discussion of "Catholic power" dominated American liberal circles in the era during and immediately following World War II.[21] In the war's shadow, the battle line between authoritarianism on one side and democracy and freedom on the other was sharply drawn. The Church's absolutist structure, and its apparent sympathy for Franco and fascist politics in Europe, led many intellectuals to wonder with alarm about its loyalties in the conflict.[22] Some speculated that Catholicism's rigid, top-down governance system, and the emphasis on obedience in its teachings, inclined the Church to act in tandem not only with fascism but also with communism across the Atlantic, like the middle head of an authoritarian Cerberus. Achievements of Catholic voting blocs and political maneuvering by the Church in the United States heightened these fears considerably. Political concessions to Catholic interests at home, including Franklin D. Roosevelt's appointment of Myron C. Taylor as his personal ambassador to the Vatican in 1939, seemed to forebode a parallel clash on American soil between an ambitious Church and the nation's democratic institutions.

John Dewey was one of those who worried about a domestic contest between democracy and authoritarianism, and he spent time thinking about potential battlegrounds. In his estimation, democracy was no foreordained trait of the American people, but rather depended upon the cultural institutions that instilled it as a shared value among the nation's citizenry. Those institutions, he argued, were far from invincible. In his 1939 book *Freedom and Culture*, Dewey included public education among the institutions he regarded as particularly vulnerable to authoritarian influence:

> The problem of the common schools in a democracy has reached only its first stages when they are provided for everybody. Until what is taught and how it is taught is settled upon the basis of formation of the scientific attitude, the so-called educational work of schools, is a dangerously hit-or-miss affair as far as democracy is concerned.[23]

Dewey was not alone in identifying the classroom as a strategic location in the struggle between American democracy and authoritarian threats. In 1944 he joined Sidney Hook and other participants in the annual Conference on the Scientific Spirit and Democratic Faith in New York City. The wartime theme of the conference, "The Authoritarian Attempt to Capture Education," was deemed necessary "to combat a growing trend toward authoritarianism in the life of the mind."[24] The conference's conveners agreed that while scientific inquiry in education promoted democratic sensibilities, education dependent upon guidance from "supernatural"

beliefs paved the way for authoritarianism. As participants discussed the importance of scientific method and free inquiry to the development of a "democratic
faith," they were careful to speak in abstract language and not single out the Catholic
Church for criticism.[25] The gathering's final panel on the "Teaching of Dogmatic
Religion," however, left little doubt about the major institutional source of their
concern, at least in the context of education within the United States.[26]

Concern the Catholic Church might encroach on American democracy by way
of public education grew steadily through the 1940s. The idea that the Church was
an opponent of public schools was hardly unfounded. In 1929, Pius XI had issued
his encyclical *Divini Illius Magistri* ("On the Christian Education of Youth"). Recalling Church documents from the decrees of the Third Plenary Council to the 1917
Code, the encyclical reminded Catholics of their educational obligations:

> The frequenting of non-Catholic schools, whether neutral or mixed,
> those namely which are open to Catholics and non-Catholics alike, is
> forbidden for Catholic children, and can be at most tolerated, on the
> approval of the Ordinary alone, under determined circumstances of
> place and time, and with special precautions.[27]

For decades the American hierarchy had taken this parochial imperative to heart,
overseeing the construction of Catholic schools across the country. By the 1940s,
prominent members of the hierarchy had also begun to issue strong public statements in favor of state and federal funding for those schools.[28] In some predominantly Catholic areas, local and state officials were responding to these calls, and to
the increased enrollments of Catholic schools in their municipalities, by diverting
public funds, buildings, equipment, and personnel for parochial use. This increase
in cooperation between public officials and Catholic schools in the United States
paralleled the spread of authoritarian influences throughout European institutions,
aggravating the concerns expressed at the Democratic Faith conference and laying
the groundwork for a domestic crisis.

The episodes that would define that crisis took place in the U.S. Supreme Court
in the late 1940s, as a series of cases that redefined the scope of the First Amendment's Establishment Clause. Catholics were demanding government support in an
era when constitutional law governing church–state relationships still permitted
religious influence inside public classrooms. Although most states had laws that
prohibited sectarianism; mandatory prayer, Bible reading, and other forms of Christian influence were still permitted and widely incorporated into public schools.[29]
The language of a separation of church and state had been part of the American
vocabulary since the nation's founding, but it was tied securely to the Constitution
for the first time in 1947, when the Court introduced it as the logical and applicable
extension of the Establishment Clause in *Everson v. Board of Education*. The *Everson*
case was brought by a New Jersey resident frustrated at his school district's practice

of reimbursing parents for the costs of bus transportation for their children to and from Catholic school. In what became one of the most influential—if easily miscon-strued—judicial opinions of the twentieth century, Justice Hugo Black upheld the use of state money for the transportation of parochial students. In doing so, how-ever, he created far-reaching precedent for the separation cause. He did this in two ways. First, the justice recognized the relevance of the Fourteenth Amendment's Due Process Clause to a case like *Everson*. By invoking Due Process, Black deter-mined that the First Amendment's Establishment Clause *did* apply to state laws like those in New Jersey that governed education. Second, Black concluded that—although busing was permissible support geared at individual children rather than their schools—the Establishment Clause at its core was "intended to erect 'a wall of separation between Church and State.'"[30] The import of the Court's decision became evident the following year in *McCollum v. Board of Education*. In the *McCollum* deci-sion Black—again writing for the majority—recalled his wall of separation model. This time he used it to declare the practice of released time religious instruction within public schools unconstitutional.[31]

POAU held its inaugural meeting in Washington D.C. three months after the *Everson* decision came down. The long-term consequences of *Everson* were still hid-den from the group's founders, who viewed the decision to allow public funds for bus transportation as a dangerous accession to Catholic pressure.[32] Nevertheless, the attention the First Amendment was getting in *Everson's* wake mobilized the group, and its agenda echoed Black's language in its commitment to laying down a hard separationist line. The group's objectives included:

> To enlighten and mobilize public opinion in support of religious liberty as this monumental principle of democracy has been embodied and imple-mented in the Constitution by the separation of church and state, . . . [and] to resist every attempt by law or the administration of law further to widen the breach in the wall of separation of church and state.[33]

Like Dewey and his contemporaries, POAU recognized American democracy as vulnerable to corruption in an authoritarian age, and it settled upon the First Amendment—and the principle of separation therein—as the key to its preservation.

Unlike many in Dewey's circle, POAU's members touted a commitment to defending democracy that had explicitly religious origins. POAU was a Protestant organization. Although the group was adamant that its mission included neither reli-gious teaching nor propagandizing, its interest in church–state separation reflected the spiritual as much as the constitutional commitments of its unusually broad alli-ance of Protestant members.[34] POAU was "instigated and organized" by the Baptist Joint Committee on Public Affairs, a collaborative effort funded by all four U.S. Bap-tist conventions in the 1940s, and dedicated in true Baptist tradition to intervening on behalf of its membership in political and legal matters related to religious liberty.

The Joint Committee lent the fledgling organization its office space and its executive director, Joseph Dawson, to guide it through its first year.[35] POAU's first round of meetings—at the National Baptist and Calvary Baptist churches in Washington, and later the Methodist Temple in Chicago—were attended by interested parties from across the Protestant denominational spectrum. Keeping company with the Baptists and Methodists at these early gatherings were Presbyterians, Christian Scientists, Lutherans, Congregationalists, Unitarians, and Friends. The president and secretary of the National Association of Evangelicals each attended, as did representatives from the religious liberty department of the Seventh-Day Adventists. These religious attendees dominated the proceedings, though they were joined in lesser numbers by various allies in the separation cause, including representatives of educational bodies, Masonic orders, and humanistic organizations.[36]

The Protestant character of POAU was made clear both by the denominations that spearheaded its formation and provided the bulk of its members, and by the conspicuous absence of non-Protestants from its leadership. Though the organization set out to develop "as broad a base of patriotic and public interest as possible," Catholics were missing from those early meetings, and Jews with an interest in separation mainly eschewed POAU for either the American Jewish Congress (AJC) or the avowedly secular American Civil Liberties Union (ACLU).[37] Even a representative from the ecumenically minded Federal Council of Churches declined involvement on behalf of his organization, citing a diversity of opinion at the Council.[38] POAU's Protestant membership was also disproportionately white. Although black Baptist groups lent measured support to the Joint Committee, African American Protestantism was not represented within POAU. Segregated schooling, coupled with the Catholic Church's relatively small ministry to African American communities during the mid-twentieth century, meant that black children did not attend the schools identified by POAU as in danger of Catholic takeover. Although many in POAU's leadership were early and strong supporters of desegregation and the Civil Rights movement, the organization made few efforts to recruit members from African American churches.[39]

POAU's leaders issued a manifesto to the national press in January 1948. Charles Clayton Morrison, a former editor of the journal The Christian Century, drafted the statement and added his signature. Joining him were John Mackay, the president of Princeton Theological Seminary, and Louis Newton, the president of the Southern Baptist Convention. Bishop G. Bromley Oxnam of the Methodist Church rounded out the group. As former president of the Federal Council of Churches and current president of the World Council of Churches, the "paladin of liberal Protestantism" seemed a natural choice to become POAU's first president as well.[40] Like its parent organization, POAU supported church–state separation because both its leadership and its membership believed in the principle as Christians. Its four leaders agreed that preserving public spaces outside the control of an ecclesiastical body made the individualized exercise of Christian faith possible. They took seriously the Protestant imperative that such freely cultivated faith was a necessary component of salvation. As they built the organization's public image, POAU's leaders spoke easily about God in their own lives, and they expressed support for the "public recognition of God, our dependence on His bounty, [and] our duty to follow his will."[41] True to its Protestant mission, the organization directed its early litigation efforts at eliminating government support for a church it contended suppressed personal faith. During its first two decades, POAU pursued Catholic violations of separation almost exclusively. Not only did the group decline to challenge parallel episodes involving Protestant educational influence; on occasion its litigators publicly defended Christian devotional practices within American public schools as consistent with the separation principle.[42]

Despite this Protestant public image, POAU's members disagreed privately with one another about what church–state separation demanded of public education. Just as its membership represented nearly the entire gamut of American Protestantism at mid-century, these disagreements reflected the different ideas that had come to characterize that spectrum. Most Protestants in the United States who thought about such matters continued to assert a loosely Protestant vision of church–state separation—one that trained its focus on Catholic sectarianism, while allowing for the "soft Christian" influences that had historically marked American public classrooms. Over the first half of the twentieth century, however, many liberal Protestants had adopted a more secular standard of separation. By the 1940s, this latter group was arguing that the First Amendment required the complete exclusion of religion, Christianity included, from state-supported education.[43] Bromley Oxnam was one Protestant leader who asserted a liberal view of church and state. "Personally," the bishop wrote during this period, "I do not want public money to be used to support Communist schools, Fascist schools, Roman Catholic schools or Protestant schools."[44] Oxnam's biographer described the church–state views of POAU's first president as coming "perilously close" to "absolutizing democracy [and] granting to the secular state an almost autonomous status."[45]

The differences between conservative and liberal interpretations of separation had already created tension within denominations like the Southern Baptists.[46] The pan-Protestant POAU was no exception. Its base worried about Catholicism, but they also worried about an American education system that had grown more secular over the course of the twentieth century.[47] Although *Everson's* implications were unclear immediately following the decision, by the time the Court decided *McCollum* in 1948, conservative Protestants were on the defensive. While the *Everson* lawsuit only challenged Catholic practices, the complaint in *McCollum* was brought by an atheist, and it targeted released time religious instruction by Jews and Protestants as well as Catholics. As Philip Hamburger puts it,

> The McCollum case made clear, as the Everson case had not, that the justices would go far beyond the Protestant version of separation. . . . Many relatively traditional Protestants felt stunned. . . . They had sought

their familiar Protestant separation and now suddenly found themselves confronted with a secular version.[48]

Twenty-one prominent Protestant ministers publicly questioned the Court's decision in *McCollum*, expressing collective concern that "whatever its intention may be, this hardening of the idea of 'separation' by the court will greatly accelerate the trend toward secularization in our culture."[49]

Protestants like these supported POAU's mission. By keeping the public spotlight on Catholicism, the organization was both curbing a dangerous social influence *and* delaying that secularization trend. While POAU's more liberal leadership continued to maintain that the requirements of separation extended beyond Catholicism, the Church dominated their concerns as well. In addition, they recognized Catholic power as the challenge that united their otherwise diverse membership. One early leader who understood Catholicism's importance to the group's Protestant coalition was Joseph Dawson. Dawson had agreed to split his time between POAU and his directorship at the Baptist Joint Committee. Although he joined POAU as its first secretary, within weeks he became its acting director. He served in the capacity until the fall of 1948, when his replacement could be found. Dawson was a Southern Baptist of the unapologetically liberal variety. The son of Texas cotton farmers, he was nearly seventy years old when he and his wife left their home state for Washington to fulfill his appointment to the Joint Committee.[50] Dawson spent most of his life in and around Waco. He studied for the ministry at Baylor University, and spent over three decades as pastor of the city's First Baptist Church. As a minister he was known for preaching racial tolerance and the social gospel, and he spoke in favor of Baptist colleges that employed Darwinist teachers. Like Oxnam, he also had a liberal understanding of his denomination's commitment to religious freedom and church–state separation.[51] It was under Dawson's leadership that POAU adopted the cause of the Dixon Free Schools Committee. Fortunately for Lydia Zellers and her neighbors, the acting director from Texas took an interest in their situation that was both personal and strategic.

Dawson had spent time on mission renewal work in New Mexico when he was a young man, and he had first-hand knowledge of the struggling Protestant missions in the northern part of the state. Even after his work there ended, Dawson remained a frequent visitor to New Mexico and a life-long admirer of the region's cultural mix.[52] It's likely that New Mexico's schools were brought to POAU's attention by Mackay or another Presbyterian member with ties to their denomination's missions network. Even so, their situation held special meaning for its director, who knew the rural communities between Santa Fe and Taos and who could sympathize with the challenges, spiritual as well as legal, the Free Schools Committee faced. When he learned about Dixon's trouble, Dawson didn't hesitate to act. Within a month of POAU's founding he traveled to New Mexico to assess the crisis there himself. He spent what he later remembered as "intense days"—meeting with members of the

Dixon Committee, traveling to communities with sister-taught schools, and conducting hearings to gather information from witnesses.[53]

Dawson shared the bulk of responsibility for New Mexico with two other members of his organization. Frank Mead became POAU's informal head of publicity on Dixon, while E. Hilton Jackson applied his legal knowledge to the situation. Mead was a Methodist minister and the recently retired editor-in-chief of the *Christian Herald*. He was also a prolific author; when he traveled to New Mexico to investigate reports of trouble there in late 1947, he was completing his latest work for publication—a missionary's guide to Hawaii, Puerto Rico, and the other U.S. territories.[54] The article he published recounting his trip to Dixon became the most famous or (depending on who one asked) infamous piece ever published on sister-taught schools. Mead was the sort of outspoken figure a young organization wanted on its side in 1948, and POAU soon asked him to serve as its executive secretary. Mead declined the offer, but stayed on the group's advisory council. He stepped into the role of reconnoiterer, "locating, describing and analyzing the various situations in America where it is charged that violations of church and state separation occur."[55]

The second man assisting Dawson in New Mexico was E. Hilton Jackson. Jackson was a Washington-based lawyer with expertise in constitutional law and a growing reputation built on the First Amendment. Dawson and Jackson knew each other well; their relationship stretched back to the Baptist Joint Committee, where Jackson served as chairman and did legal work on the committee's behalf. He had overseen the Joint Committee's brief for the Supreme Court in *Everson* and appeared before the Court during oral arguments in both *Everson* and *McCollum*.[56] When Dawson realized the potential for litigation in New Mexico, he assigned POAU's best legal mind to the job. Once the Free Schools Committee filed its lawsuit, POAU paid Jackson to oversee the litigation on its behalf. His role required traveling back and forth between Washington and Santa Fe to advise Harry Bigbee and to act as a consultant during the trial.

Dixon dominated POAU's first year of activity. Dawson realized the troubles faced by New Mexico's schools made a good debut project for his group because they gave credence to its unique mission. As its manifesto made clear, POAU had set out to defend the First Amendment by fighting Catholic power. Its two-pronged approach to that fight combined legal advocacy with awareness-raising campaigns. In the area of First Amendment advocacy, the organization shared a stage at mid-century with both the ACLU and the AJC. POAU collaborated with its counterparts to provide legal aid to groups like the Free Schools Committee interested in taking alleged violations of church–state separation to the courts. Together these three groups were the dominant litigating forces in the promotion of church–state separation during the twentieth century. POAU distinguished itself from the ACLU and the AJC, however, with the other half of its work. From its beginning, POAU emphasized building ties with local communities—primarily through the medium of hundreds of "scroll churches" that signed on to fund the group and distribute its message. By May 1948, more than six hundred churches and nine denominational magazines across the nation were actively supporting the organization's mission.[57] POAU worked closely with this network to implement a massive educational campaign focused on Catholic missteps. Through a steady barrage of traveling lecturers, pamphlets, and newsletters, the group informed the Protestant public about the importance of separation and the probable shape of Catholic attacks upon it. Its leaders hoped by doing this they could empower citizens to act on their own, to identify and correct threats in their communities.

This popularly oriented approach to defending separation drew the praise of some observers and the ire of others. It ultimately provoked charges of anti-Catholicism and prompted both the ACLU and the AJC to distance themselves from POAU.[58] The organization's leadership had this second strategy in mind when it began publicizing the details of New Mexico's education crisis. Dawson and other leaders wrote prolifically about the state's schools, and as they did so they described a scenario of capture and imprisonment. Their stories invoked rhetoric that was already familiar to generations of Protestants, and that reminded its audiences of the dangers inherent in Catholicism. This captivity language mobilized POAU's Protestant base. It trained the attention of its leaders and its ordinary supporters on a concern all of them shared, no matter what their ideas about the far-reaching consequences of the separation principle. The descriptive rhetoric POAU employed in the context of the Dixon situation in 1948 became the backbone of the organization's decade-long campaign against captive schools.

Captive school accounts struck a chord with Protestant audiences. The threat of Catholic captivity had a robust history in the United States, and youth and their schools had long been the targets of Romish design and Jesuitical conspiracy in this sensational corner of American Protestantism's imagination. The language of Catholic capture stretches back to the birth of Protestantism itself.[59] In the United States, it gained rhetorical momentum in the early nineteenth century. As Catholics began immigrating to the country in large numbers, an already flourishing genre of American captivity narratives shifted its lens from the American Indians colonists had wondered at, to the bishops, Jesuits, and mothers superior who were becoming a visible presence on American soil. The possibility of Catholic capture manifest itself culturally as both a dark fear and an enticing fantasy; by the 1830s the prospect had gripped large segments of American culture, simultaneously inspiring anti-Catholic riots and feeding a sensationalized publishing industry.[60]

The bestselling product of that industry was Maria Monk's 1836 *Awful Disclosures of the Hotel Dieu Nunnery*. A precursor to the dime novel, *Awful Disclosures* purported to recount the author's time at a nunnery run by the Religious Hospitallers of St. Joseph in Montreal. The voyeuristic account lingers with tantalizing detail upon the spaces, objects, and rituals of the religious life. Early on, Monk describes the veiling ceremony that joins her to the community:

I stood waiting in my large flowing dress for the appearance of the Bishop.... I then threw myself at his feet, and asked him to confer upon me the veil. He ... threw it over my head, saying, "Receive the veil, O thou spouse of Jesus Christ."[61]

Following the ceremony the young nun discovers she is a prisoner, entrapped physically and psychologically, and a victim to the perverse whims of her superior and the depraved sexuality of several priests. Though despairing, she is powerless to change her situation:

I could draw no other conclusion, but that I was required to act like the most abandoned of beings, and that all my future associates were habitually guilty of the most heinous and detestable crimes.... I would most gladly have escaped from the nunnery and never returned. But that was a thing not to be thought of; I was in their power, and this I deeply felt.[62]

The author of Monk's story intended for its audience to feel sympathy for its protagonist and anger at her institutional captors. *Awful Disclosures* also treated Protestant readers to the gothic thrills that came from following Monk into the nunnery's dark and forbidden spaces and discovering the unmentionable horrors they contained.

Catholic captivity in its fearful and fascinating forms was bound up through the nineteenth century with Protestant anxieties about Catholic difference. For Protestantism's American-ness, Catholicism seemed foreign; for Protestantism's individualism, Catholicism seemed communal; for Protestantism's domesticity, Catholicism seemed to promote alternatives to domestic family life. These underlying sources of Protestant worry translated into the vivid images—the dark confessionals, secret chambers, and leering priests—that thrilled and horrified. Such fantastical representations of Catholic difference reflected upon the Church's governing structure as well. Jenny Franchot identified the captivity genre in antebellum America as an early rhetorical challenge to democratic values: "The threat of captivity to Catholicism's dread interiors, to its alluring and perilous worldliness, gave shape and limit to American democracy; the menace also functioned ... subliminally, as a desirable alternative to the pressures disguised between the optimistic rhetoric of democracy."[63] If the Church's hierarchical face was an intriguing political alternative to some, public figures like Lyman Beecher and, later in the century, Josiah Strong and cartoonist Thomas Nast used tropes of Catholic invasion and captivity to incite democratic allegiance among their audiences.[64] In these later treatments, the convent prison often gave way to the endangered public school, while the predatory priests and bishops remained. The Catholic threat to American institutions seemed capable of proving itself anew with every generation.

The specter of Catholic capture revived once more in the 1940s and 1950s amid public fear of authoritarianism in all its forms. Captivity references during the era familiarly described women religious. Sisters were victims of "brain-washing and social pressure," wrote firebrand and POAU member Paul Blanshard in his 1949 bestseller *American Freedom and Catholic Power*, "In their personal and intellectual lives they are regimented almost as completely as convicts."[65] Sisters suffer a "social slavery," reformed theologian Loraine Boettner agreed in 1962. Boettner's dark description of sisters' enslavement bore more than passing resemblance to Monk's account of taking her vows more than a century earlier:

> Playing on [the] matrimonial instinct, the church deceives the nun with the fiction that she is the . . . "wife of Christ." . . . Furthermore, the priests have imposed on the nuns a medieval church garb consisting of a long, black dress, the very symbol of grief and death.[66]

Blanshard and Boettner were part of a generation of Americans who developed their critiques of Catholic power by drawing on a tried-and-true vocabulary of capture. At the same time, accounts like theirs struck a new tone as they contended with a Church that now seemed eerily familiar rather than dependably different. Anxiety over authoritarianism abroad was amplified by the collapsing concept of Catholic difference at home. The children, grandchildren, and great-grandchildren of Catholic immigrants were Americanizing; in many parts of the country they were becoming indistinguishable from Protestants in how they dressed and talked, and where they lived, worked, and played. As these men and women joined the cultural mainstream they brought their Catholicism with them. The religion that seemed more authoritarian than ever, more different than ever in its institutional structure, its governance, and its pedagogy, was also assimilating; its identifying markers were fading from the radar screen. Americans worried about Catholic capture in the mid-twentieth century had a transformed threat on their hands. The dangers of the Catholic Church in their era lay buried in the American appearance of so many of its projects and adherents.

In 1944, *The Christian Century* editor and future POAU member Harold Fey published the first article in a seven-part series with the heading "Can Catholicism Win America?" Although captive schools weren't yet in Fey's vocabulary, these articles explored acts of recent and ongoing Catholic encroachment into different sectors of U.S. politics and culture. Fey realized the Church he worried about no longer worked through ethnic enclaves and big-city political machines, and he chose to emphasize its strategies to win over a range of identifiably American populations, including rural communities, industrial laborers, and blacks. The standout article in his series was entitled "Catholicism Comes to Middletown." In it Fey returned to the site of the famous 1929 Robert S. and Helen Merrell Lynd case study of American culture, to find that Catholicizing elements had established themselves even in

that reputedly average Indiana community.[67] He traced the "progressive abandon-
ment of the 'inconspicuous course' which the Lynds saw Catholicism taking in Middletown, and the development of an aggressive and forthright strategy" by the local
Catholic hierarchy. He identified the "instruments of power" clergy had at their disposal, including hospitals and lay organizations, as well as parochial schools and the
nuns who taught in them.[68] The scenario Fey proffered was of complex institutional
machinery descending piecemeal upon the town, and of unwitting residents who
failed to notice the institution's architecture until it was ensconced in their community. The new Catholic invasion was dangerous because, with the exception of a few
revealing "tells," the enemy looked and acted just like anyone else.

Those "tells"—the traces of Catholic difference that still lingered at mid-century—
became valuable symbols for Fey, and everyone at POAU worried about Catholic
power, because they restored shape and character to a nearly hidden threat. The
Dixon story was full of such tells. With its severe landscape, home to a Spanish-speaking population on the margins of American culture, and to fully garbed sisters living
and working in public view, Dixon was no Middletown. POAU's leadership recognized the village's plight as a real-life story of Catholic invasion, one that could also
confirm to Protestants that the Church in their midst still had a strange and foreign
face. Even as Joseph Dawson and Hilton Jackson traveled to New Mexico to provide
on-the-ground support to the Free Schools Committee through 1948, others at
POAU used the organization's large network to tell Dixon's story. Over the course of
a few months, tens of thousands of Americans read and listened to these accounts of
the conflict in New Mexico, and committed those descriptions to their imaginations.

When POAU members wrote about Dixon, they slipped now and again into the
militant language that was familiar to them. Dawson himself described Dixon as
evidence of the Catholic Church "invading" public schools, and Clifford Earle of the
Presbyterian Board of Christian Education wrote about the "dissemination of Catholic teaching and propaganda" in New Mexican communities.[69] When Blanshard
introduced the New Mexico conflict in *American Freedom*, he wrote with alarm that
"the Catholic hierarchy has gone to extremes in capturing public schools."[70] The
piece that described the Catholic threat most vividly, however, was Frank Mead's
account of his visit to Dixon. "Shadows Over Our Schools" ran on page one of the
Christian Herald in February 1948. Over the article's title was a foreboding image—
a drawing of a public school beneath gathering clouds, overlaid by an outline reminiscent of the Vatican coat of arms, with a towering papal tiara and set of crossed
iron keys. Below the title was a photograph of a sister teaching in one of Dixon's
classrooms. The article began in the first person, as Mead described all he had seen
on his recent trip to New Mexico. "It seems," he wrote, "that the citizens of this town
woke up one dark grey morning to discover that their free public school had been
closed. Just like that!"[71] Mead went on to recount tribulations faced by the community—nuns unable to speak English; a public school left abandoned and crumbling
next to an untended *penitente* cemetery; Protestant children forced to stand in the

cold, walk into confessionals, and haul sand, water, and rocks at the end of the school day. His long list of concerns included the following anecdote, reminiscent of so many captivity tales:

> One Protestant youngster who refused to go to Confession was locked in a room after school and left there until 9 o'clock at night, when he jumped out through a window and went home.[72]

Mead described New Mexico's schools as places where glaring ineptitude was forced upon unwilling but malleable students. His account painted a landscape that would have felt remote and exotic to most Americans, but his suspicion—he confided to his reader—was that New Mexico was not an isolated incident. "You don't think it could happen in your town?" he wrote. "My friend, it already has begun to happen."[73]

Mead's juxtaposition of eye-catching details about life in Dixon with this universal caution—his bold insertion of Catholic difference back into the familiar—made an effective message. The *Herald* distributed his article to magazines nationwide for republication.[74] POAU handed out pamphlets based on Mead's work to members of Congress and sold reprints of the article through its newsletter for five cents a copy.[75] Back in New Mexico, Archbishop Byrne's office received inquiries from Catholics across

Figure 4.1 Front page of the *Christian Herald* magazine, February 1948. Courtesy of Princeton University Library.

the country who had read or heard about Mead's account and hoped the prelate would refute it. One especially anxious letter came from Bishop John Noll, who wrote from his editor's desk at the Catholic weekly *Our Sunday Visitor*.[76] Frank Mead's description of New Mexico and its people stirred up interest that went far beyond the scope of the state's legal conflict. "Shadows Over Our Schools" remained a conversation piece among some Americans years after the last sister had departed New Mexico's public schools.[77]

Looking back at the publicity surrounding Dixon in the late 1940s, Paul Blanshard remembered New Mexico as having the "most famous captive schools in America."[78] His memory was half-right. Although Mead and others sold Dixon's story using references to captivity in 1948, POAU only began to remember New Mexico's institutions as "captive schools" several years later. Dixon served as prototype for a captive schools crisis POAU first identified by name in the mid-1950s. This crisis took shape amid the wave of high-profile civil disputes, premised upon public–parochial arrangements and highlighting sisters as teachers, which followed in the New Mexico lawsuit's wake.[79] POAU's self-described captive schools crusade echoed the colorful language its members invoked during Dixon's troubles, even as its lawsuits became the medium for a new litigation strategy geared toward correcting violations of church–state separation within state courts.

A new executive director with a fresh organizational vision was responsible for POAU's captive schools agenda. His name was Glenn Archer. After a six-month search to secure a permanent director for the organization, its leadership settled on Archer's name in the spring of 1948. Archer was from Kansas and served as dean of the Washburn University Law School in Topeka. His past work on behalf of the National Education Association caught POAU's attention. Archer was initially reluctant about the prospect of moving east to take charge of a group and a cause he knew little about. His hesitancy dissolved, though, when one summer day he answered the telephone at home and heard the voice of Joseph Dawson:

> I just called to congratulate you for your acceptance of our position. You are to be our leader. The wife and I got the assurance of your coming at the family altar this morning, and I had to call you to tell you how happy we are that you will head this great cause.[80]

Archer was himself a devout Methodist, and he took the acting director's revelation to heart. He came to understand his future at POAU as the opportunity for God's work. He resigned his deanship two days after Dawson's phone call, and accepted the position of executive director immediately thereafter. One of Archer's first projects at POAU was to assist with the trial and appeal of the Dixon case. The new director had hardly unpacked his bags in Washington before he flew down to New Mexico to sit next to Harry Bigbee and Hilton Jackson in the courtroom.[81]

During his directorship, Archer built a legal strategy for POAU that took advantage of the organization's extensive local ties. He made it his priority to encourage community-based offshoots and affiliates of the national organization—groups like the Dixon Free Schools Committee. POAU reminded these groups that it was *their* responsibility to identify and initiate action against church–state violations in the places they lived. The national organization was happy to assist their efforts. C. Stanley Lowell, one-time associate director of POAU and Archer's biographer, defended the strategy:

> We have never gone into a community and created a controversy. The controversy was there first; then we were called in to help. This was the invariable procedure. We have never gone into a community unless we were invited in by responsible citizens. Having been thus duly invited, the organization would then dispatch a representative to make an investigation of fact.[82]

POAU stepped in with funding, personnel support, and legal assistance where it was requested. Because of its policy of supporting community-based initiatives, the organization sometimes found itself involved in messy local and state disputes that had little to no chance of creating useful judicial precedent. These were the sort of litigation other advocacy groups like the ACLU and the AJC were often reluctant to touch.[83] Disputes involving patterns of cooperation between public and parochial school systems were invariably some of the messiest church–state situations in the country. POAU's willingness to involve itself in these situations whenever satellite groups raised challenges allowed it to build a reputation on what it called captive school cases during the 1950s.[84]

Lydia Zellers and her colleagues put together a long list of allegations against New Mexico's schools. Along with nuns as salaried teachers, they mentioned catechism classes and benediction Masses, church-owned buildings, and Catholic textbooks, among other dubious practices. Most captive school challenges included similarly varied lists of allegations. Glenn Archer recognized that some Catholic activities were more legally dubious than others, and he knew litigation built upon a single issue—like Catholic sisters receiving public paychecks, for example, or the state leasing church property—could fail to sway a court. In contrast, POAU's working definition of captive schools, as institutions corrupted through a vague pattern of takeover, rather than through finite activities, encouraged litigation that pursued multiple allegations simultaneously.[85] Other advocacy groups of the era were more purity-minded—they sought out cases that could create precedent by prompting the courts to evaluate one controversial activity in isolation.[86] POAU saw no shame in lawsuits built from composite pictures. While a captive school suit might not raise one issue with the durability to stand up in court and be found unconstitutional, Archer knew the practical value in demonstrating a cumulative pattern of Catholic activity. As Lowell explained about captive schools,

If there were a single school practice that did not quite pass muster, the courts were reluctant to intervene. Considerable latitude in arrangement is given to local boards of education under our system. But if one could show a consistent pattern of sectarian encroachment and preemption of a school with any number of conspicuous sectarian practices going on, this was a different matter.[87]

POAU's strategy of targeting murky patterns of behavior, rather than single-issue violations of the Establishment Clause, is one reason the U.S. Supreme Court never agreed to hear a captive school case. The organization found Archer's strategy effective, however, when it came to what it considered to be its most important work—convincing individual state courts to correct public–parochial situations under their jurisdiction.

Archer kicked off his captive schools campaign around 1950. He began to travel the nation meeting Protestant citizens and listening to stories about the Catholic presence in their children's schools. A Missouri native by the name of John C. Mayne assisted him. As POAU's organization director, Mayne was responsible for maintaining the group's relationships with its local chapters.[88] His duties included keeping files on captive school situations across the country—in places like Indiana, Kentucky, Missouri, Michigan, Kansas, Minnesota, and Iowa.[89] Archer and Mayne also kept careful records on captive schooling episodes they could identify from the past. One notorious episode occurred the year before Dixon made headlines. North College Hill was a working-class suburb of Cincinnati with seventy-five hundred residents in 1947. Earlier in the decade, a school board split nearly evenly between Protestants and Catholics had approved the incorporation of the local Catholic school into North College Hill's system.[90] St. Margaret Mary School was leased by the Archbishop of Cincinnati to the school district for $3,500 annually, and it became Public School No. 3. The school was staffed by the Congregation of the Precious Blood, and its sisters received their $100-a-month salaries directly from the district. After a few years, an ongoing dispute between the city's board members and its Protestant superintendent of schools devolved into a public battle over the board's funding of School No. 3. At the time, critics like Harold Fey pointed to North College Hill as another example of Catholic "colonization," and described a community "savagely divided into two hostile camps . . . [with] lifelong neighbors refusing to speak to one another."[91] Students in three North College Hill schools went on a two-month strike to protest the board's activities, and many of them transferred to Protestant schools. The discontent in North College Hill culminated at a 1947 board meeting attended by more than a thousand of the city's residents. During the meeting, twenty-eight lay teachers read letters of resignation before the board. The atmosphere deteriorated as several residents stirred by their testimony rushed a gymnasium stage to attack the board members, and the members dove for cover beneath their tables. Five men were later arrested on charges including aggravated assault and attempted murder.[92]

North College Hill's crisis never turned into a lawsuit, but it did become part of POAU's cache of anecdotal evidence. The group's members recounted North College Hill's story alongside Dixon's as classic, cautionary evidence of captured schools. Situations that *did* end up in court—with Glenn Archer's help—multiplied over the next decade. After the *Zellers* lawsuit, two of the most publicized pieces of captive school litigation took place in Missouri in 1953 and Kentucky in 1955. *Berghorn v. Reorganized School District No. 8* began in the foothills of the Ozark Mountains. A group of parents there, acting on advice from POAU and a local affiliate, sued to end public–parochial cooperation in three schools. Two of the schools were run by communities of Catholic sisters—one by the Poor School Sisters of Notre Dame and the other by the Sisters of the Adoration of the Most Precious Blood of O'Fallon. Glenn Archer stepped in as the architect of the litigation. He employed his strategy of arguing a cumulative pattern of control, and the Missouri lawsuit met with success. In its decision, the Missouri Supreme Court endorsed Archer's big picture approach to sectarian influence. "We are not limited to a consideration of any particular fact separate and apart from all other facts and circumstances shown by the whole record," the court wrote. "We must consider the total effect of all of the facts and circumstances . . . in determining whether the schools in question are in fact free public schools."[93] Pointing to a pattern of Catholic influence determined largely by the sisters' presence, Missouri's court declared the contested schools in violation of its state constitution.[94] Archer and his colleagues at POAU were ecstatic over *Berghorn's* outcome. Stanley Lowell would later boast that the Missouri court's opinion probed "far more deeply into the church-state issue in schools" than either *Everson* or *McCollum*.[95]

The Kentucky lawsuit two years later departed from Archer's strategy, and from an organizational perspective it failed as a result. Like other captive school cases, *Rawlings v. Butler* was initiated by Protestant citizens who were angry over a local board's decision to close a struggling public school. The board in question diverted its funds to two sister-run schools instead. The Sisters of Loretto were teaching in both of the contested schools. Archer tried to intervene in *Rawlings* as he had in *Berghorn*; he hoped to build a case that replicated the "total effect" argument cited approvingly by the Missouri court. Local counsel in Kentucky, however, had other ideas. Disregarding Archer's recommendation, the plaintiff's attorneys chose to press their case in *Rawlings* around a single issue—the legality of the sisters' public employment.[96] The courts found their arguments on this issue unpersuasive. Lacking the cumulative evidence of Catholic control characteristic of other captive schooling litigation, the plaintiffs lost their case both in the lower court and before the Kentucky Supreme Court. It was only later—after a similar suit was brought in Kentucky on broader grounds—that the plaintiff's cause succeeded.[97]

The captive schools crusade culminated in 1959. That autumn POAU announced a surge of "grassroots" efforts to eliminate captive schools. Editors at the organizational newsletter *Church and State* praised the example of an "angry army of Protestant parents" who had recently descended upon Columbus, Ohio, to protest sister-taught public schools still functioning in their state. The editors' tone was triumphant. "Captive schools have continued for many years in certain places because Protestants lived in fear," they wrote. "Now fear's clammy hold is broken."[98] The editors' excitement over the swell in popular activism was mixed with pride in the role POAU played stirring it up. By the late 1950s, POAU had established itself as a leader in legal and educational advocacy in support of church–state separation. On the legal end the organization was energized by the addition of Blanshard as special counsel in 1956, and it boasted victories in dozens of court cases. The group's commitment to public outreach was even more impressive; by 1960 POAU claimed over 100,000 members. It planned to distribute eight million pieces of literature that year, or one for every seven households in the nation.[99] With this infrastructure in place, the group was ready for a final assault against captive education. In 1959, under Archer's direction, the organization began a media blitz to remind the American public about the lingering problem. It sponsored a nationwide survey, published a new body of literature on the topic, and produced and distributed a film it titled *Captured*.[100] After more than a decade investigating, mediating, and litigating disputes, POAU returned to its early experience in New Mexico to inspire the plot of its first film.

POAU advertised its 43-minute black-and-white production as a "semi-documentary based on actual legal files."[101] Following the captivity model developed by people like Frank Mead and Harold Fey, *Captured* engaged its audience by presenting a familiar picture of American life, punctuated by symbols of the Catholic threat hidden just beneath its surface. The film combined lurid details of Catholic coercion with a setting and a victim that spoke to the threat's ubiquitous quality. The audiences who flocked to view the movie expected to be taught a lesson in civics, but they expected to be entertained as well. *Captured* was advertised as an "exciting drama"; it won over its viewers with suspenseful encounters, a nightmarish dream sequence, and a renegade hero with an unquestionable moral compass.[102] Much of the film's dialogue would have sounded familiar to anyone in its audiences who had followed events in Dixon a decade before. The movie's screenplay was an at times verbatim rehashing of stories from New Mexico, translated into a more reliably "American" setting reminiscent of North College Hill.

The setting for *Captured* was the thinly veiled community of Pleasant Hill. The film's plot begins with the arrival of the town's newest residents. The Jacksons are a Protestant family; the film's narrator describes the father John Jackson admiringly as "an old-fashioned Protestant who thought a man's religion was his own private business."[103] As the family drives into town, the *mise-en-scéne* for the film unfolds. As described in the stage directions of the script:

It is like any other small town in America. . . . In the opening odyssey of this ride we see all the living elements of our life that we hold dear; the

Figure 4.2 John Jackson meets with Sister Corelli in the 1959 film *Captured*. Courtesy of Princeton University Library.

> Church, the Newspaper office, the Hospital, the statue dedicated to American soldiers, the School. We feel the music and the pictorial treatment, the enormous importance of these quiet, but symbolic things of the American way of life.[104]

The film's plot proceeds in a predictable fashion. Despite a few unheeded warning signs, Pleasant Hill seems like an idyllic place to the Jacksons, a place where their dreams are attainable. Their sense of well-being is shattered when the family's son, Richard, begins school and discovers that the local public institution is actually parochial. When a colleague of John's explains the situation to him at work the next day, his words echo the language Mead used to describe Dixon ten years earlier:

> One morning a blurry-eyed group of citizens in Pleasant Hill woke up to discover that their one and only free public school had a new core of teachers, eight Roman Catholic nuns. St. Joseph's parochial school had been closed as unsafe, and not one of us had shared in any vote to bring in the sisters.[105]

As the details of Pleasant Hill's crisis emerge over the next several minutes of film, they recall the more sensational allegations of Lydia Zellers and her neighbors. The school—also named St. Joseph's—is taught entirely by Catholic religious and the principal is a mother superior. Richard's own teacher is called Sister Corelli. When a committee of residents angry about the situation marches seventy miles to the offices of the state board of education, the state refers them back to the county for lack of jurisdiction in the matter. Meanwhile Protestant children at the school are required draw religious pictures, and to stand outside in the cold or wait in a basement during catechism classes. They are also pressured to attend confession and Mass.

Richard dismays his parents one evening by crossing himself at the dinner table. In a conversation with his confused son, John asks the boy to resist participating in the religious activities occurring at his school. The resulting strain on young boy's psyche is evident later that night as he begins to dream:

> The camera moves closer to him and appears to invade his preconscious thoughts or the dreams he is having. All the images and sounds are distorted, overlapped, superimposed etc. They include Richard's refusal to go to Mass. Suffering the jeers of the children, rejected by his friends, no longer on the ball team, sent to the coal bin, sitting out in the cold. He is ordered to cross himself, cross . . . and double cross.[106]

The scene builds quickly into a full-blown nightmare. Music reaches a crescendo as Richard cries out in his sleep, "I won't—I won't—I won't!" His father rushes into the room. "Don't worry," he assures the disoriented boy, "I'm not going to let you fight this all alone."[107]

John Jackson steels himself to take action. He's met by reluctance, however, from the few locals who might help him remove the sisters from their school. He soon realizes his family is on an unspoken blacklist, and a broken window at the home suggests his battle with the powers that be could easily take a darker turn. He persists in his cause anyway. "I just don't like being pushed around," Jackson exclaims. "I didn't like it in Normandy, or Casserine Pass or Anzio. Maybe if this were Madrid or South America somewhere I'd quit, but this is America!"[108] Once he recommits himself to the patriotic but seemingly impossible challenge of freeing Pleasant Hill's school from the Church's grasp, John's fortunes change. His colleague from work slips him a POAU pamphlet, and in the very next scene Glenn Archer himself (in a cameo appearance) answers Jackson's telephone call. Archer travels to Pleasant Hill and offers the Jackson family his organization's aid. As the film ends, the community's fears have abated. Jackson has not only received a promotion at his job; he is well on his way to winning back a free school for the residents of Pleasant Hill.[109]

Captured became POAU's best promotional tool. Copies of the film were distributed by the national organization and they circulated among regional branches and affiliated religious groups. The film played in civic centers, fraternal lodges, and churches, where in some cases it received official denominational endorsement. In the year following its release, *Captured* was shown over a thousand times to audiences

Figure 4.3 POAU's executive director Glenn Archer makes a cameo in the film *Captured*.
Courtesy of Princeton University Library.

averaging nearly one hundred fifty people. The largest of these events took place at
the Blue River Baptist Sunday School Association in Harrisonville, Missouri, where
a thousand locals turned out in one evening to watch the film.[110] The large groups
who gathered to view *Captured* made its screenings a good opportunity for POAU to
press its cause; the organization's representatives often stood on hand to answer questions, collect donations, and distribute literature. Audience members who left show-
ings of *Captured* did so with new or renewed concern about captive schools, as well
as armloads of material to use in studying the issue.[111]

   Captured brought the old discourse of Catholic captivity to a new generation of
Americans who crowded into churches and community centers out of patriotic duty,
but also for a thrill. Although the most sensational nineteenth-century tropes of kid-
napped nuns and priestly impropriety had faded by 1959, both the film and the
Dixon publicity it was based on drew upon a reserve of familiar images to tap into the
anxieties many American Protestants still had about the designs of the Church. By
the late 1950s, these Americans were used to seeing Catholics not only in their
schools and their neighborhoods, but also on their movie screens. The best-known
cinematic representations of Catholics from the era came from Hollywood, where
stars like Bing Crosby, Frank Sinatra, and Ingrid Bergman gave fans accessible and
endearing portrayals of Catholic clergy and women religious.[112] Amid this softening
of Catholicism's image within American media and culture, POAU stubbornly held

its ground. With *Captured*, its leaders redoubled their efforts to convince their fellow Protestants that—no matter how many heroic priests and nuns Hollywood produced—the Church was still undemocratic and capable of hurting the nation's schools.

Was POAU's captive school campaign anti-Catholic? Glenn Archer and others at POAU insisted it was not. The organization's liberal leadership took pains to defend their group against critics who inaccurately conflated them with the Ku Klux Klan or the American Protective Association, and to demonstrate they had no agenda against Catholic individuals. They stressed that Catholics were among their group's supporters, although they never mentioned those supporters by name. While the group's members had all sorts of private motivations for pursuing sister-taught public schools, its captive schools campaign was built upon a shared, and by all accounts deeply held, commitment to enforcing the First Amendment at a moment when the Catholic hierarchy wanted to limit the scope of its application. The campaign was designed to correct a recognizable and legally dubious pattern of cooperation between public and Catholic educators across the nation. It also held together a coalition of Protestants who differed about the implications of church–state separation during the 1940s and 1950s, but who all believed—most of them with great sincerity—that their common faith demanded separation advocacy.

It is also clear the charges of anti-Catholicism that plagued POAU through its first two decades were not unfounded. Although POAU officially shunned the label, some of its leaders and benefactors privately identified as anti-Catholic.[113] Furthermore, the group's populist vision often meant leaving behind the technical language of the amicus brief for a more familiar and imaginative tone, one capable of delivering a message to audiences with no training in constitutional law. As a consequence, literature and movies produced by POAU were sometimes appropriated by organizations with agendas less noble than the protection of the First Amendment. To defend POAU by distinguishing its interest in church–state separation from the colorful language it used to promote captive schools would be to simplify the character of its devotion to the law. While POAU's leaders read the First Amendment from different places, and came to different conclusions about the educational reforms it required, they all recognized among them a religiously informed commitment to its Establishment Clause. This commitment defined the mission of their organization and it permeated every aspect of their work, from their provocative captivity accounts to their most rigorous thinking on the scope and application of the clause. Whether or not the group was anti-Catholic, the vision of separation POAU defended was shaped by its members' common experience as Protestants, and that experience included, on some level, an inherited encounter with the Catholic Church. In this, it made no difference what its members believed the consequences, secular or otherwise, of the Establishment Clause to be. Establishment Clause battles of the mid-twentieth century were not reducible to anxiety about Catholicism. Legal perspectives of the period, however, *were* bound with how

Americans mapped a sense of right and wrong onto their worlds. Religious commitment and conflict did—as it still does—much of this mapping.

POAU's intervention in the Dixon case was foundational to its organizational
mission. In the late autumn of 1947, the group was still finding its footing in
Washington. In New Mexico, Lydia Zellers and the Dixon Free Schools Committee had dug their heels in for an uphill fight. They were uncertain still about many
things, including their ability to afford the type of legal action required to change
the status quo in New Mexico; the public's response to a lawsuit should they manage to bring it; and the willingness of the state's courts to entertain a challenge
against the Catholic Church. They were heartened to hear about POAU and its
interest in their cause, however, and as the new year arrived the committee was
happily surprised at the publicity pouring in from across the country. Frank
Mead's February article in the *Christian Herald* was an indicator of things to
come. By spring, sympathetic accounts of Dixon's situation were running in dozens of publications, from the *Herald* and *The Christian Century*, to the Masonic
New Age and the *Scottish Rite Bulletin*. Liberal journals like *The Humanist* and *Progressive World* were covering the developments in New Mexico, and so were magazines with more alarmist tones, including the Seventh-Day Adventist *Signs of the
Times* and *Converted Catholic Magazine*.[114] Many of these articles simply reiterated Mead's work, or reprinted verbatim statements the committee had sent its
supporters. Others claimed to uncover new details of New Mexico's troubled
classrooms. *New Age*, for example, published an affidavit from a student in Dixon:

> Because once I had been a Catholic, whenever there was confession, they
> were always begging me to go to confession. This happened during
> school hours. They used to tell me that I would go to hell when I died if I
> didn't confess. Once or twice the Sister tried to force me to go to religion
> and even pulled my hair. In the mornings, those of us who refused to go
> to religion had to stand outside in the cold because the bus brought eve-
> rybody very early so that they could go to religion. I will be seventeen
> years old in October and I am in the 10th grade (signed under seal).[115]

The editors concluded their article by appealing to their readers to donate money to
the Free Schools Committee.

Most journals that shared Dixon's story made similar requests, and soon contributions were pouring in from across the country. Some of these donations, like the
sum sent in an anonymous envelope and addressed to the "Dixon Fighters of Freedom," came from individuals.[116] Others came from the eclectic collection of organizations now monitoring the situation with interest. Groups who joined POAU
in making donations to the Dixon Free Schools legal fund included the American
Humanist Association, the National Liberal League, the Scottish Rite, the Knights

Templar, the Horace Mann League, the Jewish Congress of America, the Committee for the Defense of Democracy through Education (a subset of the National Education Association), the Unitarian Church, and the Evangelical United Brethren.[117] Lydia Zellers traveled to Seattle to speak before the annual meeting of the General Assembly of the Presbyterian Church, and soon the committee had secured funds from that body as well.[118]

In January 1948, the Dixon Committee made its intentions public for the first time. Although its formal membership remained modest—at just twenty-eight people—the group appeared confident. Attorney Harry Bigbee issued a statement on behalf of the committee to the New Mexican press. He was reluctant to disclose details, but Bigbee indicated its members had met in his Santa Fe offices and discussed plans to bring legal action against those responsible for the Catholic presence in New Mexico's schools. He also hinted at a new agenda that included more than removing the Franciscans from Dixon's high school. The Free Schools Committee's vision had "taken on state and national aspects," Bigbee suggested cryptically.[119] The scope of the committee's plans became clearer the following month, when a statewide council of churches convened to build support for its cause. Ministers from across New Mexico met at St. John's Episcopal Church in Santa Fe, and listened with rapt attention as Bigbee once more explained the troubles in Dixon's schools. Four Protestant children from the village accompanied him to the meeting, along with two carefully selected members of the press. When Bigbee had finished his presentation, a minister from Costilla stepped forward to describe similar problems with Catholicism in his community's schools. The mood throughout the gathering was calm and deliberate; the ministers who took turns speaking all agreed that Catholic influence in education was a statewide problem, and that it required a statewide solution. By the time the meeting adjourned, those in attendance had voted to support the Dixon Committee's efforts through their own specially convened Committee on Separation of Church and State.[120] The reporters Bigbee had invited to the proceedings brought this news of a statewide Protestant coalition back to their editors. A few days later, Bigbee contacted Lydia Zellers to let her know the right "psychological time" to press forward with a lawsuit had arrived.[121]

5

Habits on Defense

The NCWC and the Legal Debate over Sisters' Clothing

The Dixon Free Schools Committee was a growing headache for Archbishop Edwin Byrne of Santa Fe. The outward confidence the prelate displayed during the fall lingered long enough that one archdiocesan official maintained the "whole matter has been settled" in Dixon into 1948.[1] By February, however, this assured tone already sounded out of place. The archdiocese was scrambling to deal with the fallout from Frank Mead's article in the *Christian Herald* and the prospect of a lawsuit from the committee. Responsibility for managing the pending legal challenge, and its accompanying public relations disaster, fell to one of the archbishop's closest confidants, the Reverend William T. Bradley. Bradley was president of the Catholic Teachers College in Albuquerque and the director of parochial schools for the archdiocese. Soon the priest was working overtime, coordinating damage control on behalf of Byrne and the religious teaching in the state.

Bishop John Noll's January letter was the first of many addressed to Byrne requesting answers to Mead's allegations in "Shadows Over Our Schools." Some of these communications came from clergy worried by literature and rumors circulating among their parishioners, and others came from laity. One elderly Catholic in Santa Ana, California, wrote the archbishop for an explanation, complaining that Adventist acquaintances he knew had been "roasting Catholics" and showing him literature about Dixon.[2] A woman from New York wrote out of concern after a Presbyterian friend gave her a clipping about the situation.[3] While Bradley did his best to respond to these letters in turn, he also drafted a sixteen-point statement to answer the allegations. "The Truth about Sisters Teaching in the Public Schools of New Mexico" was the archdiocese's first attempt to systematically defend the Church's presence within the state's education system. The document included everything from clarification of the Dixon sisters' ethnicity ("The Sisters teaching . . . in Dixon are not German refugees. They were born in Switzerland and are American citizens," the statement confirmed) to assurances religion was not taught during school hours ("Neither is it given before or after school hours in the public school at Dixon," it

Figure 5.1 Archbishop Edwin Byrne of Santa Fe. Courtesy of the Palace of the Governors Photo Archives (NMHM/DCA), 65115.

added). The statement also asserted the archdiocese's right to collaborate with state officials. "If the Archbishop or his delegate cannot be requested personally by the State School Officials to lend the benefit of their advice on matters which affect the general welfare, then there must be an end to Freedom of Speech," the text exclaimed.[4]

William Bradley's effort was too little too late. The local press was already speculating excitedly about legal action, and it provided the Free Schools Committee with plenty of free publicity. Sensing its own vulnerability, in March the archdiocese retained the services of a Catholic advertising agent from Albuquerque. Robert Bissell's instructions were explicit—he was hired to study the goings on in the state's contested schools, and make any "facts" he discovered known to local press and radio.[5] Over the next few weeks Bissell traveled with a photographer to Dixon and several other communities, and in late April he submitted the first in a series of articles to the *Santa Fe Register*, the official newspaper of the archdiocese.[6] Like Bradley's memorandum, Bissell's article amounted to a point-by-point refutation of Mead's now-famous piece. "Too much is being written and not enough known about the question of Catholic religious teaching in New Mexico's public schools," Bissell cautioned readers. "This is often the case when stories about the Southwest are written from behind a desk in

New York City."[7] In the controversial sisters' defense, Bissell tried to explain the circumstances—"the hardships of a backward, primitive section"—that prompted them to come teach in the state. He also criticized Mead for inaccurate reporting and his refusal to acknowledge other viewpoints. He lamented the Protestant press's monopoly of the Dixon story, and like Bradley he warned of the threat to free speech that came with the censorship of Catholic voices.[8] Unfortunately, Bissell's own efforts to reclaim Dixon's story for the Church remained minimal—his investigation never went beyond a few articles in the pages of the *Register*. By summertime archdiocesan officials were expressing disappointment at his product and complaining about the hefty bill he sent them for his services.[9]

When he was not busy answering letters, Bradley worked frenetically with state officials to avoid litigation. In January, on the same day that Harry Bigbee announced the Dixon Committee's plans for a lawsuit, Bradley drove up to Dixon at the invitation of R. P. Sweeney. Sweeney was New Mexico's supervisor of secondary education, and he had agreed to make the trip on behalf of state superintendent Charles Rose. Sweeney had instructions to conduct an "immediate investigation" of Dixon's schools, and to report to Rose any evidence he found of religious instruction during school hours.[10] The fact that the superintendent suggested the priest as company for his delegate is evidence the state board and archdiocese held onto working ties even in the scrupulous climate of 1948. The two institutions that had been joined for decades by the cooperative arrangement of sister-taught schools now found themselves linked by the accusations leveled against them. After visiting Dixon's high school, Bradley and Sweeney submitted a joint statement to Rose asserting the school's classrooms appeared in compliance with the law. They also took affidavits from the district's bus drivers, attesting that students were dropped off on schedule and never required to stand outdoors in the cold, as Mead had alleged in his article.[11] Their findings were received with satisfaction at the highest levels of state government. A few weeks later, New Mexico's governor released his own statement on the Dixon situation. Governor Thomas Mabry, himself a Presbyterian, warned Catholics and Protestants to avoid "exaggerated stories" and disputes that may "stir up religious misunderstanding." He proposed that Dixon's controversy was being perpetrated by parties outside the state, and he expressed confidence in the ability of state officials to solve any problems that might exist:

> I am sure that the state superintendent of schools, an elected official and a thoroughly competent administrator (and a Protestant incidentally) and the members of the state board of education (also, predominantly Protestant) are unanimously opposed to instruction which introduces religious controversy of any sort and will strive to have corrected any isolated violations of the law in this respect.[12]

Beneath his conciliatory tone, Mabry was absolutely clear: he did not want the state's courts intervening to determine the shape of New Mexico's schools.

Despite public assurances to the contrary, by February it was clear to both arch-diocesan and state officials that a lawsuit was only a matter of time. With the recent gathering of the state council of churches, and with new sightings of people like Joseph Dawson and E. Hilton Jackson around Santa Fe, the suit's statewide scope was also becoming apparent. The situation took a serious turn in early March, when Byrne received a telegraph notifying him of the U.S. Supreme Court's decision in *McCollum v. Board of Education*. Like other bishops across the country, the Arch-bishop of Santa Fe had been following the *McCollum* proceedings closely. Now Hugo Black, writing for the majority, reintroduced his description of a wall of sepa-ration between church and state, and used *McCollum* as an opportunity to remind the Court and the public of the need to keep that wall "high and impregnable." The support the state gave to religious instruction through sanctioning released time arrangements, both by making its classrooms available for them and by ensuring through compulsory education laws that students would be present at them, consti-tuted a damaging breach of that wall.[13] Byrne and William Bradley joined Catholic leaders nationwide in expressing dismay when they learned about the Court's deci-sion. Both men recognized it had troubling implications for the similar sorts of peripheral religious activities that went on in New Mexico's schools.

Lydia Zellers and the Dixon Free Schools Committee recognized that *McCollum* was an opportunity to act. Two days after the decision, Bigbee filed the committee's complaint with the district court in Santa Fe. *Zellers v. Huff* was a class action lawsuit brought by each of the twenty-eight members of the Free Schools Committee. The suit listed two hundred thirty-five defendants—one hundred thirty-one sisters employed in publicly funded schools were included, along with thirteen brothers, two priests, members of sixteen local and county school boards, and all of the mem-bers of the state board of education. As head of the state board, Raymond Huff had the dubious privilege of being named first in the suit. The list of defendants went on to include Governor Mabry, Superintendent Rose, the state school budget auditor, and the state comptroller. It also mentioned Bradley, on the belief he "was delegated and exercises power" conferred by law for the exclusive use of state school officials.[14] The complaint was clear about the legal groundwork on which it stood. It wondered:

> whether or not a uniform system of free public schools sufficient for the education of, and open to all children of school age . . . has been estab-lished and maintained according to the provisions of Section 1 of Article XII of the Constitution of the State of New Mexico, and the Statutes of this state.

It wondered also whether there was separation of church and state in New Mexico as now required by the First and Fourteenth Amendments.[15] The complainants' contention, of course, was that separation did *not* exist, and over the next thirty-seven pages their document explained why. The religious it named as defendants had taken a vow of poverty, so that all of their salary "is received by them for the benefit of the religious orders." Under these conditions New Mexican residents, required by law to pay taxes to fund these salaries, were compelled to directly support religious congregations. The religious had also taken vows of obedience that demanded they devote their lives to the "advancement of a sectarian religious denomination."[16] State officials allowed them to engage in this sort of work, and the direct result—so the complainants argued—was pervasive sectarian religion in all twenty-seven schools cited in the suit.

The document meticulously itemized the materials and practices that made up this sectarianism. It cited teachers giving religious instruction "at a time when the children are at school" and requiring students to attend religious services during school hours or "immediately prior to or thereafter." It reported teachers distributing religious literature, placing "shrines and Holy pictures" in their classrooms, and opening their classes with prayers of a Catholic nature, "causing the children to kneel during the saying of said prayers and to make the sign of the Cross in the manner of the Roman Catholic faith."[17] The complaint also cited teachers wearing religious clothing, noting their clothing was "constantly reminding all students of the Catholic faith and vows of said teachers . . . thereby exerting a sectarian or denominational influence in the classrooms at all times." Finally, the complaint accused teachers of discriminating against and embarrassing non-Catholic children by singling them out and by withholding special favors or grades. This catalog of offenses did not indicate a cluster of isolated incidents, the complaint surmised, but rather spoke to a "general situation" existing across all sister-taught schools, and a pattern of cooperation between government officials and the Church.[18] Intervention by the court was the only remedy.

When Archbishop Byrne learned about the complaint he sent word to Bishops Sidney Metzger and Bernard Espelage of the neighboring dioceses of El Paso and Gallup. Both dioceses sat within the province of the Archdiocese of Santa Fe, and both contained schools named in the lawsuit. Metzger and Espelage traveled immediately to the capitol, where the three prelates met and drafted a statement. The statement, which the bishops released a day before the complaint's filing, defended the intentions of the Church in New Mexico:

> The authorities of the Church in New Mexico have in no manner whatsoever entertained the much haunted and often misunderstood idea of so called union of Church and state. It was only through a high sense of the duty of mission and to promote the welfare of human society that the Church permitted brothers and sisters to accept the office of teachers in public schools.[19]

The bishops assured the public they would see to it the religious involved in litigation "are neither misrepresented or abused." The statement concluded on a deferent

note as the prelates stressed they would "readily accept and concur" with any decision handed down by the courts.[20] While Byrne and the other bishops were hardly
resigned to a legal defeat so early on, their words carried a note of stoic resolve. By
March 1948, there was little either the archdiocese or the state could do to avoid
what everyone agreed was the most dreaded outcome of Dixon's crisis—the evalu-
ation of New Mexico's schools against the standard set by the Supreme Court. The
litigation ball had been set rolling, and the path ahead was ominous. Even as the
bishops' joint statement ran on the front page of the *Santa Fe Register*, county sher-
iffs across the state were already preparing to serve hard copies of the *Zellers*
complaint on defendants across New Mexico.[21]

As litigation began in New Mexico, the chatter of voices sounding off nationwide
over Dixon's schools became louder and angrier. Supporters of sister-led education lashed out at Frank Mead and its critics. The tenor of public sentiment was
measured in the April 1948 issue of the *Christian Herald*, which devoted its entire
letters-to-the-editor page to feedback from Mead's article. The printed letters
included several supporting Mead's provocative characterization of Dixon's sisters. Some of these were from citizens who reported finding similar patterns of
public–parochial collusion in their own towns. The collection highlighted a con-
gratulatory letter from Louie Newton, POAU member and president of the Southern Baptist Convention. Newton thanked the *Herald*'s editor for carrying Mead's
exposé and reminded his fellow readers that Americans "are asleep at the switch
as this shadow continues to spread over our land."[22] The *Herald*'s editor obligingly
printed several letters from readers sympathetic to the sisters as well. Their tone
ranged from indignant to furious. C. A. Minnaert of Iowa asked to discontinue
her *Herald* subscription because she discovered the magazine to be "very much
anti-Catholic." Others writers were less curt. A young Catholic woman who had
read Mead's article through a friend's subscription to the *Herald* described it as
"the most nauseated [*sic*] article I have ever had the unfortunate experience to
come into contact with." She challenged the editor to attend any Catholic school
in the country and "convince yourself that there is more civics taught in a Catholic
grammar or high school, than in a public school." Another reader from the Chicago suburbs was compelled to address his anger at Mead directly. "You are a
skunk when you say the nuns are not educated to teach," the man wrote. "They
have forgotten more than you will ever learn."[23]

These combative words came from men and women who felt personally insulted
by POAU's rhetoric. They captured the sentiments of thousands of Catholics who
spoke up objecting to the group's developing campaign against sister-taught schools.
Sometimes these angry voices were accompanied by physical protests: in New
Mexico, residents hurled rocks outside the district courthouse, and in Illinois and
Ohio hundreds of Catholic students walked out of their classrooms after their teachers' removal.[24] Catholics showed extraordinary loyalty on behalf of sister-taught

schools. These episodes entered the Catholic imagination just as they caught the fancy of the Protestants at POAU during the late 1940s and 1950s. The excitement that sister-taught institutions produced among both groups was due in part to the emotions Catholic women religious themselves evoked in people. Public–parochial classrooms often included lots of objects and activities that challenged church–state separation. The one thing they all shared, however, was a member of a Catholic religious order presiding as teacher. Usually that individual was a sister. In the middle of the twentieth century, the Catholic sister was a larger-than-life figure in the United States. While schoolchildren had feelings for their teachers built from daily interactions, most American adults considered these women from a distance. Informed by worries they had and rumors they'd heard, some adults continued to think of them as living subjects in a captivity drama—the simultaneous victims and conspirators of Catholic power. Other adults were driven by personal piety and nostalgia to revere them as living saints. Often, adult perceptions of American women religious were both less nuanced than those of children and more charged. Sisters provoked deeply rooted and largely unexamined reactions in Catholics and non-Catholics alike.[25]

For both groups, these responses were tied to the visual impression Catholic sisters made. With rare exception, in the 1940s and 1950s sisters wore a cloth habit that covered their bodies from head to toe. The habit was intentionally an overwhelming costume; it was the physical expression of a sister's separation from the non-religious world. It mediated her encounters with both children and adults, and shaped the perceptions of everyone who saw her. When sisters taught publicly their habits were contemplated not only by children, but also by the public who took an interest in their work. They also caught the attention of the American legal system. From a judicial perspective, sisters' garb presented problems and possibilities unlike other potential breaches of church–state separation. The same woolen tunic one judge might call unconstitutional, a wayward display of religious symbolism, another might permit or even protect as the free expression of a teacher's beliefs. The legality of sisters and their garb in public education was a recurrent, if open-ended, question in state courts through the first half of the twentieth century. By the late 1940s, American courts had reached a consensus—albeit a fragile one—that Catholic women religious could not be constitutionally prohibited from teaching in their habits. The New Mexico Supreme Court's decision in *Zellers* in 1951 turned that consensus on its head. *Zellers* and the captive school suits that followed it represented a new generation of litigation with outcomes that rested (if always in part) upon consideration of the habit's legality. Without clear precedent, justices hearing these cases wavered on the issue—the high court of Kentucky disagreed with the high court of Missouri, which disagreed again with the high court of New Mexico. Amid this confusion, POAU's own position on sisters bore straight as an arrow. In lawsuit after lawsuit the organization argued habits should be excluded from public schools. Whenever it could, POAU also encouraged the courts to take the sister issue a step beyond religious

garb—by pressing them to consider whether the very vows women took in the process of becoming sisters disqualified them from public teaching.

Despite the legal ambiguity of the habit question—and despite the angry Catholic response to public–parochial lawsuits—a well-developed defense of the habit
was missing from captive school litigation. Responsibility for articulating a Catholic
position on teaching sisters fell to a single organization. The National Catholic
Welfare Conference (NCWC) was the Catholic counterpart to POAU when it
came to mid-century church–state deliberation. It was the job of the NCWC's legal
department to aid American dioceses involved in lawsuits or otherwise targeted by
complaints of church–state collusion. Its team of Washington attorneys advised
prelates and women religious, and they worked closely with local counsel retained
to represent them. While the organization did speak on behalf of Catholic interests
in the era's Supreme Court litigation, the bulk of the NCWC's legal efforts during
the 1940s and 1950s went to helping religious personnel entangled in dozens of
lesser-known situations. The NCWC's aim was always the same—to preserve by all
reasonable measures Catholic educational interests. In New Mexico, members of
the NCWC's legal department arrived just a few days after the *Zellers* complaint was
filed. Its attorneys remained there on and off for the next three years.

From a twenty-first-century perspective, the NCWC's reluctance to defend the
right of sisters to wear religious garb in their classrooms suggests an oversight.
While other traits of the captive school—practices like reciting prayers and teaching catechism—are now prohibited by American courts, the place of religious
clothing within public institutions remains a live area of legal inquiry.[26] Facing an
issue cradled delicately between the First Amendment's Establishment and Free
Exercise Clauses, mid-century Catholics had an opportunity (it would seem) to
argue for a sister's right to wear religious clothing, and in doing so to test the limits
of the expanding separation principle. After all, even the courts themselves disagreed about whether the language of free exercise or disestablishment was more
relevant when it came to sisters' habits. For the attorneys who fought to save sisters'
employment, however, any chance of building a clothing defense was overwhelmed
by the Herculean challenges the advancing wall of separation brought with it. Legal
experts at the NCWC, like American Catholic intellectuals broadly, were in a dou-
ble bind at mid-century. First, the piecemeal efforts they did make to claim the First
Amendment placed them at a disadvantage. While Catholics were writing on the
religion clauses in unprecedented numbers during these years, most still had difficulty mastering this corner of American law. Unlike POAU's members, who
enjoyed the easy fit between their religious and their constitutional thinking, Catholics found that religious freedom and church–state separation were unwieldy—if
increasingly necessary—additions to their religiously governed intellectual endeavors. Second and more basically, the NCWC was thrown into a defensive posture by
the slew of lawsuits that followed in *Everson* and *McCollum*'s wakes, and this posture
had a troublingly reinforcing effect. Even if the NCWC *had* managed to put together

a compelling legal argument to support the habit, the defense work this barrage of litigation required made it impossible for the organization to adopt the concerted— and assertive—posture it needed to sell a new legal perspective. Captive school litigation had momentum, and it kept the NCWC's legal department on its heels through the 1950s.

The NCWC oversaw the legal defense of New Mexico's religious in 1948, but even as it did so it began rethinking its tactics for protecting sister-taught schools elsewhere in the country. It reoriented its focus, from crafting legal positions to the preemptive work of sheltering sisters from lawsuits and the logistical and psychological burdens they brought with them. In practical terms, this meant advising sisters to comply with a standard of separation strict enough to pass muster with POAU and other advocacy groups who might cause them trouble. Sometimes it meant asking the women to remove religious symbolism from their bodies while they taught. In many cases it meant encouraging bishops to remove their classrooms from the public system altogether. This strategy of compliance protected thousands of religious from the perils of litigation, and in doing that it met the NCWC's main objective. At the same time, it also had unintended consequences. Even as the American episcopacy condemned secularism—or what it described as the "exclusion of God from human thinking and living"—as the biggest threat to American education at mid-century, each woman religious who removed her habit or terminated her employment on the NCWC's advice helped to enact a *de facto* model of separation that *was* secular—more secular than most American courts demanded.[27]

The veiled face of Sister Corelli in *Captured* and the bumbling nuns of Frank Mead's article were two of the many portraits separation advocates offered of Catholic sisters.[28] These representations often included references to brainwashing, unhappy submission, and other reliable tropes of captivity. POAU had a special interest in using captivity language to describe sisters who worked as teachers because the group's most frequent complaint against captive schools—namely that the women teaching in them violated the Establishment Clause—rested upon its claim that sisters were bound by the Church in everything they did. Arguments to prohibit sisters from public classrooms turned upon the assertion they were, everywhere and at all times, walking advertisements for their religion. Sisters are molded by the Church inwardly as well as outwardly, Paul Blanshard explained to his readers in *American Freedom and Catholic Power* in 1949; they go through life like a "liquid, which has no shape of its own, but assumes the shape of the vessel in which it is put."[29] As a consequence, these women have lost all ability to use the "freedom of the unshackled, inquiring mind."[30] As evidence to support this assertion, Blanshard and other critics pointed to sisters' vows. Because sisters had promised to obey their superiors in all things, they were incapable of the autonomy needed to teach within a public system. Their obedience put them at odds with the American values that other public school teachers embodied. Their "medieval attitude of . . . feminine subordination," Blanshard suggested to his readers, "seems utterly alien to the typically robust and independent spirit of American womanhood."[31]

A sister's subordination to the Church was made material by her clothing. For captive school opponents the costume a sister wore while she taught was more dangerous even than her vows. The habit's message was clear, its presence in the classroom concrete, and its effect on students immediate.[32] Even when a sister instructed children in subjects having nothing to do with religion, these critics argued, her habit silently imparted its own lessons about the faith of the woman wearing it. Sisters' habits *were* unusual sights at mid-century. While female teachers around them donned the tidy, nipped-waist dresses that were the style of the day, women religious taught in shapeless tunics. A sister concealed her hands in folds that fell to the floor and children spent all year guessing at the color of the hair hidden beneath her veil. The habit's basic design had become standardized during the Middle Ages, and communities of women religious prided themselves on how little their outfit had changed during the intervening centuries. Items of clothing that had been familiar among thirteenth-century Italian noblewomen appeared alien in the United States in 1948. Critics condemned sisters' habits as "grotesque" and "unhygienic" costumes that were "awkward to wear and . . . totally unfit for either hot or cold weather."[33]

The habit was also universally recognizable; adults and children who saw it knew it was a manifestation of the Catholic identity of its wearer. That said, habits were complex and richly varied. In her historical treatment of the costume, Elizabeth Kuhns breaks down the components most sisters' clothing had in common. The habit refers to:

> the robelike tunic or dress that is the main garment worn over the body. The "veil" is the long cloth worn on the top of the head, extending down the back. Some veils are designed to be pulled forward over the face, and other veils are designed as thick linings to wear beneath heavier veils. The veil is usually attached to a cap underneath, or "coif," which is a close-fitting cloth headpiece that conforms to the shape of the skull. . . . A "wimple" or "guimpe" is the fabric piece that covers the neck and chest, and sometimes extends over the chin. A "bandeau" is the piece that stretches across the forehead, often attached at the ears behind the veil. A "scapular" is a long apron-like garment that is worn over the tunic. . . . A "cincture" is a belt worn around the waist of the tunic, and a "Rosary" is a string of prayer beads and other objects often attached to the cincture and worn at the side. A "cappa," cape, or mantle refers to a cloak worn over the tunic.[34]

While these esoteric elements made habits easy to identify, communities of women religious took pleasure in customizing the details of their design. In New Mexico, each of the orders boasted a costume with unique decorations, color, and silhouette, so that even sisters from communities who shared the traditional dress of black wool serge were distinguishable to a trained eye. The Sisters of Charity, for example, exchanged the common veil for a closely fitting black cap that tied at the neck, while the veil worn by the Sisters of Loretto was differentiated by a stiff white inner lining. The Sisters of Mercy all wore silver rings on their left hands, while the Sisters of St. Casimir wore gold ones. The Sisters of St. Casimir also adorned their habits with a blue cord that hung from the waist in honor of the Virgin.[35] The four congregations of Franciscans at work in the state's schools departed from the black habit altogether and instead wore a brown wool tunic that memorialized the poor raiment of their mendicant founder. Their habits were tied with a knotted rope cincture and accompanied by a seven-decade rosary of brown beads.[36]

The most distinctive costume in New Mexico belonged to the Order of Preachers. The Dominican habit was standardized in the thirteenth century. According to the order's own history, its design was suggested to St. Dominic by his disciple Reginald of Orléans, who had been shown a black-and-white dress by the Virgin in a vision.[37] True to its miraculous origin, the Dominican habit in 1948 consisted of a pure white tunic with a white scapular, a black leather belt, and a fifteen-decade rosary with black oval beads.[38] The Dominicans' black veils offered another striking contrast. The order's bright white habit came with both benefits and drawbacks in the mountains and deserts of New Mexico. While some Dominicans recalled the relief the reflective white cloth offered on hot summer days, others remembered the unforgiving way in which their clothing showed off the grime of rural living—the dust picked up from dirt roads, the grease of car wheels, and the oil that coated wooden schoolhouse floors.[39] "We'd scrub them," one sister recalled. "We'd roll them up and put soap at the bottom and just scrub them."[40] In villages where water was scarce and washing machines were unknown, the floor-length white garment of Blessed Reginald's vision seemed at those moments to be less-than-ideal professional attire. Whatever its practical merits, the Dominican habit did offer its wearer the benefit of unambiguous recognition. Even on those occasions when the tunic was covered by its requisite black *cappa*, the "white nuns" (as the Dominicans were called by people they met in New Mexico) could be picked out from a mile away—as different from the Catholic sisters in neighboring communities as day was from night.

While a habit's details were particular to the stories and values of the religious community who wore it, the discipline of wearing the habit was common to all mid-century Catholic women religious. In the nineteenth century, it was not unusual for American sisters to remove their habits when ordinary clothes better aided their travel or work.[41] The clarifications of Canon Law in 1917, however, emphasized the importance of sisters wearing their habits at all times. The Code left communities with explicit instructions:

> All religious must wear the habit of their religious [institute] both inside and outside of the house, unless grave cause excuses, [to be

assessed] in urgent necessity according to the judgment of a Superior, even a local one.[42]

A sister wearing ordinary, or secular, clothing in the first half of the twentieth century was a rare sight. Most women religious wore their habits agreeably and without question. For sisters, religious dress was a medium that allowed them to embody the religious life; the voluminous cloth of their habits was the natural, material extension of the commitment to worldly separation this life required. For their critics, however, habits transformed sisters from flesh-and-blood women into disembodied symbols of the Church. Habited sisters were reduced to "strange passing visions of flowing black," Blanshard wrote, "with maidenly white faces snugly bordered by white linen."[43] A costume with this sort of transformative potential, the critics reasoned, would necessarily provoke students to question its meaning.

The debate over whether sisters wearing religious clothing belonged in American classrooms began in the late nineteenth century, not long after the first women religious began to teach in publicly funded schools. The *Zellers* lawsuit was anticipated by a half-century of lesser-known contests over the habit. Courts that considered the issue during these years invoked state education laws prohibiting sectarianism, but each of them stopped short of making a definitive statement about the permissibility of Catholic garb. By the 1940s, the rough consensus among them was that habits were *not* unconstitutionally sectarian, but neither were sisters assured the right to wear them when they taught. The courts concluded state lawmakers could restrict the habit as part of their authority to regulate the uniforms of all state employees.[44] In 1894 the Supreme Court of Pennsylvania was the first high court in the nation to consider the garb question.[45] The case of *Hysong v. Gallitzin Borough School District* involved six Sisters of St. Joseph teaching in a publicly owned building in the mountainous center of the state. The eight-judge panel, with one judge dissenting, decided Pennsylvania's constitution allowed sisters to teach in their habits. The habit, the court concluded, did not amount to unusual sectarian influence. "The dress is but the announcement of fact that the wearer holds a particular religious belief," the court wrote, and "the religious belief of teachers . . . is generally well known to the neighborhood and to pupils, even if not made noticeable in the dress, for that belief is not a secret but is publicly professed." Furthermore, the court instructed, a Catholic sister should not be singled out from the variety of religious adherents who chose clothing in accordance with their beliefs:

> The religious belief of many teachers . . . is indicated by their apparel. Quakers or Friends, Ommish [sic], Dunkards and other sects, wear garments which at once disclose their membership in a religious sect. Ministers or preachers of many protestant [sic] denominations wear a distinctly clerical garb. No one has yet thought of excluding them as teachers from the schoolroom.[46]

The Pennsylvania court went a step beyond finding sisters' habits constitutionally acceptable; it instructed that disqualifying sisters from employment because of their beliefs would violate their right to worship in accordance with their consciences. "There can be, in a democracy," the court stressed, "no higher penalty imposed upon one holding to a particular religious belief, than perpetual exclusion from public station because of it."[47]

Despite its strong statement of support for sisters' beliefs, the court did leave opponents of the habit in Pennsylvania with one suggestion. The state legislature might enact a statute requiring all teachers to wear a particular style of dress, just "as we now see in the city police, railroad trainmen, and nurses of some of our large hospitals."[48] The next year Pennsylvania's legislature did just that; it passed a ban on public school teachers wearing any "dress, mark, emblem or insignia indicating . . . that such teacher is a member or adherent of any religious order, sect or denomination."[49] That the lawmakers intended to restrict the Catholic habit through the ban was obvious; the state's legislative branch had effectively accomplished what its judicial branch declined to do. When Pennsylvania's "garb statute" faced its own legal challenge several years later, the state's supreme court agreed it violated neither the state constitution nor the First nor Fourteenth Amendments. This time the court reasoned the law's dress requirements did not impede teachers' beliefs—only their actions while they fulfilled their professional duties.[50]

Between the second Pennsylvania decision in 1910 and the *Zellers* lawsuit in 1948, six other high courts heard cases involving allegations of religious garb in public classrooms.[51] In some of these, the habit issue was wrapped up with other alleged violations characteristic of public–parochial schools. As POAU discovered during its captive schools crusade later in the century, courts tended to base their rulings in cases like these upon the composite pictures that emerged of sisters' classrooms.[52] When the courts did evaluate the Catholic habit as an independent issue, they followed Pennsylvania's precedent, allowing that garbed sisters could teach under state and federal constitutions but also upholding state dress laws that effectively prohibited their habits.[53] By the mid-1940s, sisters' ability to teach in public schools while wearing habits varied by state. A 1946 survey conducted by the National Education Association found at least five states had laws on the books prohibiting habits in public classrooms. Sixteen states permitted the practice. In the middle were states in which the habit question had never been formally raised.[54]

One consequential judicial decision came from North Dakota in 1936. *Gerhardt v. Heid* started as a complaint brought by taxpayers against four Sisters of St. Benedict teaching in the western part of the state, along with several school officials. The lawsuit's list of allegations was similarly short. It made no claims about sectarian instruction; its only objective was to "restrain the teachers from wearing what is denominated 'a religious garb or dress.'"[55] The district court ruled in favor of the sisters in *Gerhardt* and the state's high court agreed. North Dakota had no garb statute, the supreme court reasoned, and its constitution ensured that "each person engaged in teaching in our public schools is . . . guaranteed the same religious liberty that applies to every other person."[56] Citing *Hysong*, the court concluded it had no business prohibiting sisters' habits. The *Gerhardt* decision inspired several legislative attempts to win a statute prohibiting religious dress for the state. These efforts failed, however, and the Benedictine sisters remained in their classrooms. Within a few years they had found additional company; by 1947 seventy-four Catholic women religious were teaching in twenty districts across North Dakota.[57]

In January 1948 a group of Lutheran ministers joined frustrated North Dakota residents to form a Committee for Separation of Church and State.[58] The committee intended to accomplish what the state's courts and lawmakers had not—the removal of Catholic habits from the public system. As one of its leaders remarked:

> The presence of nun's garb in the schoolroom predisposes the mind of the child toward the religion of the wearer. Nuns will never have children of their own. This deprivation leads them in many cases to lavish their affections on their pupils to a degree not matched by teachers with ordinary family ties.[59]

The North Dakota committee knew about the efforts of its counterpart in northern New Mexico.[60] Rather than continue to pursue legal action, however, the Committee for Separation hoped to accomplish North Dakota's ban on religious garb through a referendum vote. In just three months, the group collected more than ten thousand signatures backing the measure, and by late March it had successfully petitioned to have a ballot initiative on the garb question circulated that same summer.[61]

Bishop Vincent Ryan of Bismarck coordinated the sisters' defense. With help from Auxiliary Bishop Leo Dworschak of Fargo, Ryan started his own action committee.[62] Channeling the religious liberty arguments that already marked deliberations over teaching sisters in *Gerhardt* and elsewhere, the bishop named his group the Committee for the Defense of Civil Rights. In the months before the referendum, the bishop's committee answered the Committee for Separation with its own information campaign. It asked citizens to vote against the garb measure to preserve peace and ensure the state's children a quality education. It argued an anti-garb law would violate sisters' rights as citizens, and with them the intentions of the architects of the Constitution. "At the time the American Constitution was written," a committee booklet explained:

> there were sects in which all the members were known by their distinctive garb. There are sects that regard a certain garb as part of their religion. To disqualify them from any office because of their garb would be an infringement of religious freedom.[63]

While it's impossible to know how persuasive the bishop's message was, the results of the June referendum suggested that sympathy for the habit transcended religious loyalties in North Dakota. The anti-garb initiative passed, but it did so by surprisingly close margins. In a state in which four out of five residents were Protestant, nearly half of the voters had cast their ballots to keep sisters' clothing legal.[64]

With anti-garb law finally a reality in North Dakota, the Committee for Separation expected a quick end not only to religious clothing in classrooms, but to the public work of sisters themselves. It was all but unheard of for Catholic women religious to appear publicly sans habit in 1948, and garb statutes in other states had ended sisters' employment entirely. In North Dakota things would be different. Concerned about the referendum's outcome, Ryan had written in May to the Sacred Congregation of Religious in Rome with an unusual request. He asked that, in the event of a statute, sisters in his diocese be exempted from wearing their habits at work. The Vatican, in an even more unusual decision, agreed to let North Dakota's sisters don "modest lay garb, if necessity demands, while they are occupied in teaching in the public schools."[65] Negotiations between the bishop and motherhouses ensued, and by the end of the summer six communities, representing roughly sixty sisters affected by the new law, agreed to allow members to remove their habits. As a new year opened, sisters returned to twelve schools across the state dressed in ordinary clothes—outfits that, while modest, were in no way mistakable for uniforms.[66] On evenings and weekends they diligently changed back into their habits. This fragile solution held, ending the controversy one observer described as having split North Dakota "more deeply than had any issue done in years."[67]

Catholic leaders across the country monitored developments in North Dakota.[68] Few of them were as interested in the outcome of the state's garb initiative as Archbishop Byrne in Santa Fe. The creation of North Dakota's Committee for Separation closely paralleled the start of the Dixon Committee, and the similarities between the groups were hard to miss. Byrne and Bishop Ryan communicated regularly with one another about the problems in their dioceses.[69] While Ryan spent the spring of 1948 trying to shape public opinion in his state, the New Mexican archbishop turned to the different work of organizing a legal defense. For Byrne, organization itself was his biggest challenge. The two hundred thirty-five defendants of the *Zellers* complaint made up a group as large and diffuse as the suit's plaintiffs were self-selected and focused. The defense's chaotic quality became evident in the first days after the complaint, as clusters of defendants scrambled to secure legal representation, and the counsel they retained labored to communicate productively with one another. A dozen attorneys participated as *Zellers* made its way through the district court. State officials involved in the suit were represented by New Mexico's attorney general's office, in the person of a young district attorney named William Frederici. The sixteen county boards involved in the case retained a half-dozen of their own lawyers. The Catholic sisters and brothers who made up the bulk of the suit's defendants took steps to organize themselves, and they also received legal advice from multiple authorities.

Byrne summoned Brother Benildus of Mary to his chambers shortly after he realized the lawsuit was a sure thing. Brother Benildus was a Christian Brother and a native of Louisiana. He was also a giant of a man, weighing in at some three hundred pounds, and to those who didn't know the brother his portly frame and gentle drawl might have masked his great ambition and his energy. In the spring of 1948, Brother Benildus was busy as the new president of St. Michael's College in Santa Fe. Over the last year he had overseen the school's transition to a collegiate institution.[70] At Archbishop Byrne's request, Brother Benildus also agreed to act as spokesperson and legal attaché for the religious involved in *Zellers*. The archdiocese then hired William J. Barker, a prominent former judge from Santa Fe, to formally represent the religious.[71] Catholics within New Mexico's legal community had their own ideas about how to assist the sisters and brothers. An open letter from Byrne to Catholic attorneys in the state, inquiring about legal representation, received a flurry of energetic replies.[72] In late March, the state chapter of the Knights of Columbus assembled a committee of Catholic lawyers in Albuquerque to discuss strategy for the case.[73] An Albuquerque attorney named John Murphy, who also happened to be a prominent Knight, was selected by the group to work as co-counsel alongside the Protestant Barker.[74] Despite venerable reputations in New Mexico, neither Barker nor Murphy had experience with the legal issues surrounding church–state separation. The archdiocese made its hires with the understanding they would collaborate closely with the more experienced legal department of the NCWC.[75]

The NCWC was the first place any diocese facing legal trouble at mid-century would turn for support. It was the coordinating institution for American bishops and a mammoth clearinghouse for all things American and Catholic. Its ecclesiastic and lay members and employees shared responsibility for receiving, processing, and distributing a million bits of information as they managed the logistics of all imaginable encounters between the Catholic Church and its surrounding society. The organization began in 1919 as the National Catholic War Council, for the purpose of promoting "the spiritual and material welfare of the United States troops at home and abroad, and to study, coordinate, unify and put into operation all Catholic activities incidental to war."[76] By the time it became involved with *Zellers* in 1948, it had grown to represent American Catholic interests on many different fronts—everything from education and labor relations, to civil rights, missions, and international politics was fair game for the NCWC. It coordinated Catholic lay organizations like the National Conference of Catholic Women, and its busy media department issued press releases on behalf of American bishops covering social and political issues.[77] To support its work, the NCWC boasted a ten-story stone building prominently located on Massachusetts Avenue in the nation's capitol. It employed approximately two hundred fifty people distributed among its eight different departments.[78] In his widely read series on Catholic power in *The Christian Century*, Harold Fey described the NCWC's offices as "the real center of Catholic life" in the United States. He characterized its different agencies more ominously, as the tools with which each

American bishop "gears his diocese into the complex machinery of the Roman Catholic Church for the winning of America."[79]

While many of the NCWC's projects had no direct relevance to American politics, the organization wasn't shy about trying to influence the legislative or judicial process when it determined Catholic interests were at stake. During the organization's half-century of existence, most opportunities for this sort of political engagement stemmed from the government's stance on Catholic education. Two departments at the NCWC—the education department and the legal department—shared responsibilities in this area. The education department bore responsibility for the well-being of all the nation's Catholic schools, and its projects were proportionately broad. They included collaboration with the new Commission on American Citizenship, and oversight of the development of the *Guiding Growth* curriculum.[80] A great deal of the department's energy, however, was spent on matters of church and state. In the words of one historian of the NCWC, its staff:

> closely monitored and sought to influence state and federal education policy, served as a liaison between non-Catholic and governmental educational organizations and their representatives, and educated the American public, Catholic and non-Catholic, as to the nature and aims of Roman Catholic education.[81]

The education department was especially focused on funding sources, and securing whatever support it could for students who attended parochial schools. In the late 1940s, the department's assistant director, Father William McManus, divided his time between his own offices and Capitol Hill, where he testified before Congress that any federal funding proposals needed to include provisions for parochial students, to provide them with resources like buses and textbooks.[82]

The education department worked closely with the NCWC's legal department. In 1951 the legal department included a full-time staff of four attorneys and one registered lobbyist, as well as additional legal experts it retained in an advisory capacity.[83] Their responsibilities included assisting dioceses embroiled in litigation, analyzing all judicial decisions of interest to the Church, and articulating a coherent Catholic perspective on state and federal laws.[84] By the 1940s, education questions dominated the department's resources, and its attorneys had a joint résumé that included participation in several high-profile church–state cases. The NCWC had defended parochial schools before the U.S. Supreme Court as early as the 1925 in *Pierce v. Society of Sisters*. Thirty years later, a new generation of Catholic legal minds cut their teeth before the Court preparing the organization's amicus brief in *Everson*.[85] When the NCWC heard about the Archdiocese of Santa Fe's troubles in 1947, it offered Archbishop Byrne its assistance. The legal department sent its best attorneys to New Mexico. A young lawyer named George Reed, who was already well known at the NCWC for his expertise on educational issues, took the lead in the case. Assisting him were several lesser-known counsel and one attorney who was much better known. Charles Fahy was working as a legal advisor to the U.S. Department of State when he began consulting on the *Zellers* case. The elderly Catholic was well respected in Washington circles, having served as general counsel for the National Labor Relations Board, and more recently as U.S. Solicitor General.[86] The *Zellers* case was of personal interest to Fahy, like it was to Joseph Dawson at POAU. The former solicitor general had begun his career in New Mexico decades earlier, and once upon a time he and another young attorney named William Barker had shared a private practice in Santa Fe.[87]

Through the spring and summer of 1948 the NCWC legal team set its sights on New Mexico. Reed was especially committed to the case, traveling regularly between Washington and Santa Fe for conferences with local counsel and their religious clients, and to check in with Byrne and Brother Benildus.[88] Some NCWC attorneys doubted William Barker's ability to handle such important and complicated litigation on his own. Reed privately shared these doubts, and he saw his work in New Mexico as a careful balancing act—respecting the elderly attorney's authority as lead counsel, while encouraging him to follow the NCWC's recommendations at every step.[89] In the weeks before the *Zellers* trial, the team's other attorneys, Fahy included, began to join Reed on his trips to the Southwest. Back in Washington the group studied the plaintiffs' evidence against the teaching religious and wrote appraisals of the unfolding events. The NCWC's administrative department also monitored the litigation's progress and sent updates to interested bishops across the nation.[90]

The team's work on the Dixon case was part of a vigorous if uncoordinated Catholic response to the prevailing mid-century legal discourse about church–state separation. The *Zellers* lawsuit caught the NCWC's attention at a moment when Catholic intellectuals had been thrown off guard by both the Supreme Court's activity and POAU's formation, and were struggling to find their footing on the turf of church and state. George Reed and his team realized the unwanted publicity New Mexico's schools were receiving at the hands of POAU required a swift Catholic rebuttal. As the legal department bent to the task of crafting this response, however, it struggled with a scant rhetorical toolkit. In the late 1940s, American Catholic intellectuals at the NCWC and elsewhere were positing theories of church and state in noticeable numbers and piecing together interpretations of the First Amendment and Church teachings that emphasized compatibility between the two. Over the next decade and half a clear Catholic voice on these issues would emerge in the work of John Courtney Murray. The Jesuit priest's censure by Rome in 1954, however, meant that for the time being his church–state writings continued a precarious existence in the United States.[91] There was little to take their place. For the most part, Catholic thinking on church–state relations under the American Constitution was distinguished during the immediate post-*Everson* years by its tepidness and its unpracticed quality. Catholics displayed plenty of fire when they responded to POAU, but those responses inevitably failed to claim the First Amendment from separation advocates and to defend it on behalf of the Church and its teaching sisters.

Catholics who responded to POAU's separation campaign fell into two overlapping but distinguishable camps—those who reacted furiously to the group's provocateurs and their intentions and those who (on a more even keel) answered the substance of POAU's charges, and in doing so situated the Church within the separation debate. Articles published in and by the Catholic weekly *Our Sunday Visitor* were typical of the first camp. In 1951 Our Sunday Visitor Press published an undocumented exposé entitled *Who's Who in the POAU?* The book spared no opportunity to throw the titular organization and its leaders into disrepute—it compared POAU to both the Know Nothings of the nineteenth century and the Ku Klux Klan, and it supplied its audience with incriminating "biographies" of each of the group's prominent members.[92] The biographical sketch of founding member G. Bromley Oxnam, for example, framed the Methodist bishop's separation stance with references to his alleged Communist affiliations, and his promotion of artificial birth control during his time as president of the Planned Parenthood Federation.[93] "We wonder," the book's authors wrote, "whether Oxnam would heartily wish that his mother had used devices to prevent his birth."[94] To hammer its agenda home, the 160-page book concluded with a catalog of unscrupulous anti-Catholics who were unaffiliated with POAU but sufficiently titillating to be mentioned alongside the group—individuals like "Ethel, Sister Mary, alias Mrs. Helen Steep, Ex-nun, lecturer for the Klan."[95]

The NCWC also kept tabs on individuals who tried to curtail the Church's activities. The organization maintained an extensive file on Paul Blanshard, and it monitored public appearances by both Oxnam and Harold Fey. Its general strategy, however, was to fight POAU on the issues. Around the time POAU got its start, the NCWC established an internal Bureau of Information, both to debunk "anti-Catholic propaganda" and to educate the public about the Church's position on controversial points.[96] Members of the NCWC—and its legal department in particular—recognized that if Catholic leaders wanted to make any impact with the courts at mid-century, they needed to address the substance of charges being made against the Church. The Supreme Court had already decided in 1947 that a separating wall was the correct judicial model for interpreting the Establishment Clause; Catholics who remained interested in cooperative educational arrangements after *Everson* had more serious hurdles to face than the unsavory personalities at POAU.

Throughout the 1940s and 1950s, the NCWC never deviated from its claim that the First Amendment permitted—and even mandated—some level of government cooperation with religion in the educational arena. Its members joined prominent Catholic intellectuals in pointing out that while the Establishment Clause's design was to prevent the government from sponsoring one denomination to the exclusion of all others, the wall of separation promoted by POAU and affirmed by the Court in *Everson* threatened to erroneously prohibit religion itself—categorically and writ large—from American classrooms. In its defense of a religion-friendly interpretation of the Establishment Clause, the Conference struck a similar tone to the more conservative Protestants it was fighting against, who promoted the Court's wall in their campaign against the Church but who also worried about its restrictive capacity. Excluding all religion violated religious freedom and amounted to a different, more dangerous type of governmental establishment—an establishment of secularism. In the months after *Everson*, the NCWC issued a statement on secularism on behalf of American bishops.[97] Defining secularism as "the practical exclusion of God from human thinking and living," the bishops warned of its dire consequences for American education:

> In the rearing of children and the forming of youth, omission is as effective as positive statement. A philosophy of education which omits God, necessarily draws a plan of life in which God either has no place or is a strictly private concern of men.[98]

Godless education would invariably result in the amoralities of a godless citizenry. As it had for conservative Protestants, the trajectory of events after *Everson* intensified the bishops' concerns considerably. The Court's decision in *McCollum* had every appearance of enforcing of a godless standard upon American schools. In the months after *McCollum* the bishops aimed their words directly at the Supreme Court. They accused the Court of flirting with "the shibboleth of doctrinaire secularism" and distorting American history and law through its "novel interpretation" of the Establishment Clause.[99] In this climate, Catholic legal scholars began to echo the bishops' warnings. As one scholar writing in the Jesuit-affiliated *Marquette Law Review* in 1952 observed, "there is a secularist influence creeping into the law which is extending the interpretation of constitutional provisions far beyond their stated intent."[100]

John Courtney Murray developed by far the era's most sophisticated Catholic response to secular readings of the First Amendment. The Jesuit priest and theology professor at Woodstock College in Maryland wrote prolifically during the late 1940s and 1950s on the theological merits of American constitutional principles. Religious freedom—which for Murray ensured that men and women were free to conform to a higher law—was a key piece in his argument for the mutual sympathy between Catholic thought and the First Amendment. Church–state separation only affirms the spirit of the American Constitution, Murray argued, when it exists to serve the principle of religious freedom. The right to free exercise "is the more lofty provision, to which separation of church and state is instrumental," he wrote.[101] Separation that enforces secularism contradicts the "inner spirit" or *logos* that animates the Constitution—"the idea that the American is a free man under a limited government whose actions are themselves subject to a higher law which derives from the Eternal Reason of the Creator of all things."[102] Free exercise embodies that spirit. While certain moments in America's history have required a level of separation in order to nurture free exercise, in the long run religious freedom requires the government's unbiased and circumscribed support for public services that aid the religious lives of its citizens. "It has never been the tradition in America," Murray wrote, "for government . . . to regard the spiritual and religious needs of the people as being entirely outside the scope of its active concern."[103]

Murray's defense of the First Amendment rocked the Catholic world in the 1960s when the Second Vatican Council invited the priest to Rome to draft its own Declaration on Religious Freedom. In the decade before the Council, however, the priest's arguments on behalf of political freedoms stirred controversy within the Church, and the Holy Office of the Vatican censured Murray's writings on church–state relations in 1954.[104] Most Catholics who hoped to counter the secularist distortion they saw within First Amendment jurisprudence took on the less-ambitious (and nontheological) project of reconstructing the Constitution's "original intent."[105] The results of their efforts were mediocre at best. During the late 1940s and 1950s, scholar after scholar embarked upon historical analyses of the Bill of Rights and offered their findings to justify a religion-friendly contemporary reading of the Establishment Clause. The legal department of the NCWC spearheaded these efforts. In 1947 George Reed circulated a series of lengthy memos intended for attorneys at work on the *McCollum* case.[106] Reed's goal was to piece together a legislative history of the First Amendment, and each memo offered insights into the religion clauses based upon recovered evidence of the framers' intentions. Reed's research for the project was impressive; he included statements from the Constitutional Convention and the First Congress, and he also went deeper, digging in the national archives, delving into the papers of members of the First Congress, and corresponding with archivists in all thirteen original states. He perused newspapers from the late eighteenth century with the aim of learning "the reaction of the people who proposed the amendments" and the "combined attitude of all the states with reference to the relationship of church and state on a national level."[107]

The historical evidence, Reed thought, revealed an important theme—the language intended to preserve religious liberties in the First Amendment was "not designed to hobble religion."[108] Reed reasoned that the Court in *Everson* had erred by bending to secularist currents of the day and conflating the First Amendment with the Jeffersonian language of a wall of separation. The sources, he argued, "authoritatively demonstrate the proposition that the First Amendment, though influenced by, did not incorporate the whole concept of religious liberty as developed in [Thomas Jefferson's] Virginia."[109] The tenor of Reed's claim—that secularist trends in the courts were misinterpreting the pro-religious purposes of the Constitution's architects—was enshrined as the NCWC's formal position the following January, when its Bureau of Information responded to the publication of POAU's manifesto. "The First Amendment is being distorted today," the Bureau exclaimed, "especially by those who advocate secularism in education and in every department of our government. . . . Catholics join with all Americans in desiring to see the First Amendment preserved in its integrity."[110]

Kept busy by his responsibilities at the NCWC, Reed never published his research or distributed it widely. Over the next few years other Catholic scholars offered arguments for original intent that lacked Reed's scrupulous attention to historical detail. In 1949, a Catholic layman and Brooklyn College professor named James O'Neill received NCWC support to publish a lengthy critique of the Supreme Court's decision in *Everson*. In *Religion and Education Under the Constitution*, O'Neill echoed Reed's position that the Establishment Clause should be read narrowly and historically, and that this reading allowed the state to support religion in general, so long as it did not give official preference to one denominational form over another. "The complete and absolute separation of church and state," O'Neill wrote, "is an unreal political abstraction."[111] O'Neill coupled this by now familiar argument with a bolder claim. The Due Process clause of the Fourteenth Amendment, he argued, only ensured that citizens could not be deprived of "life, liberty, or property"—it did *not* offer an adequate basis for extending the federal Establishment Clause to govern the educational policies of the states.[112] In the *Everson* decision, O'Neill concluded, the Supreme Court had both incorrectly interpreted the Establishment Clause and incorrectly applied that interpretation to autonomous state governments.

Religion and Education received plenty of attention. Excerpts from the manuscript appeared alongside Reed's work in arguments for the defense in *McCollum*, and its prominence in Catholic circles prompted legal scholar Leo Pfeffer to call its thesis "the official position of the Catholic Church."[113] It also provoked scathing rebuttals from Pfeffer and his fellow separationists. Critics of O'Neill's book tore apart both the author's legal reasoning and his writing style. They dismissed O'Neill's reading of Due Process in particular as revisiting a question definitively settled by the Court, and as carrying completely untenable implications.[114] One critic scoffed that his argument advocated a "return to primeval chaos" and offered "a powerful and adroit presentation of a very vulnerable, already rejected thesis."[115] Even those who sympathized with O'Neill's basic position were hesitant to side with his arguments. One generally positive reviewer worried about his "extravagance of language" and his "inadequate appreciation of historic changes."[116] Another was less charitable: "The *Everson* case represents the Supreme Court as below average; the *McCollum* case represents it at its downright worst," Charles Lerche, Jr. conceded in a review in *The William and Mary Quarterly*:

> But [O'Neill's] reckless condemnation of the motives of all who oppose him has robbed the book of [its] potential value. The heat which discussions of this type engender will worsen an already bad situation.[117]

Amid all this negative press, even the NCWC received *Religion and Education* with reservations. When O'Neill proposed to write a second book as a direct response to Paul Blanshard, NCWC members worried privately to one another, although the organization once more lent its support.[118]

Other Catholic efforts at a historical defense of the First Amendment received similarly dismal receptions. In 1948 the NCWC sponsored the publication of a book entitled *The First Freedom* by Wilfred Parsons, a Jesuit priest and editor of the journal *America*.[119] Soon after the book's release, the organization's leadership admitted that Parson's work lacked intellectual heft. Bishop Howard Carroll, the NCWC's general secretary, could describe it only as a "popular treatise" that was half historical and half "polemic."[120] The book was also largely derivative; in its historical portion Parsons acknowledged a debt both to Reed and to an accomplished historian at Catholic University named Richard Purcell.[121] In its perennial search for a defensible treatment of church and state, the NCWC commissioned Purcell to complete his own study of the First Amendment the same year. Unfortunately, even Purcell's efforts had unsatisfactory results. When his completed manuscript, blandly entitled "Historical Research on Church and State," reached the desk of his Catholic University colleague John Tracy Ellis, Ellis recommended to the NCWC that it not even publish the work. Not only was Purcell's scholarship based almost entirely on secondary sources, the priest wrote in confidence, but its failure to extend its historical inquiry beyond the Revolutionary Era made it appear "unfinished."[122] Purcell's talents as a historian failed to translate to a project with the contemporary resonance the NCWC was desperately searching for. One can almost hear Ellis's disappointment in the manuscript reverberating in his 1955 essay "American Catholics and the Intellectual Life." The intellectual underachievement Ellis called out in his seminal essay was acute in the area of legal scholarship.[123] In the early 1950s, John Courtney Murray was on the verge of censure, and the studies of original intent Reed and others had proposed as part of a softer, pro-religious interpretation of the First Amendment were floundering—characterized by both non-Catholics and Catholics in the broader intellectual community as naive and insufficient for tackling the complexities of twentieth-century American society.

Early in its work in New Mexico, the NCWC's legal team hoped *Zellers* could act as a test case that resolved ambiguities left by the Supreme Court in *McCollum*.[124] Within a few months this optimism faded. As the team grew more familiar with the facts of the lawsuit, its members began to suspect *McCollum* was damning for the religious in New Mexico.[125] In private correspondence Reed speculated that sisters *were* sometimes violating the law, and in June General Secretary Carroll wrote to the American bishops to inform them of "certain practices" in New Mexico "which, technically speaking, violate the theory of separation of church and state as enunciated by the Supreme Court of the United States."[126]Although the team remained outwardly confident, privately the prospects of victory had dimmed enough by late spring that Reed wrote to Byrne, and suggested it might be best if the religious were to withdraw quietly from the state's public schools that summer.[127]

George Reed's suggestion was prompted by the damning evidence Lydia Zellers and her co-complainants were ready to offer against the teaching sisters. It also revealed a new mood at the NCWC—a pervading doubt that *any* of the dozens of sister-taught schooling situations POAU had begun to investigate would stand up in court. The challenge of producing a viable counter-argument to separationist readings of the First Amendment was becoming greater with each new judicial decision that favored a strict separation model. The *McCollum* opinion especially put Catholic–public arrangements across the country in jeopardy, and it compelled the NCWC to reroute its resources in anticipation of further litigation. The defensive posture the NCWC adopted after 1948, both inside and outside of the courts, made the already difficult work of promoting a coherent Catholic position on church–state relations all but impossible.

Reed laid out *McCollum*'s implications in a NCWC pamphlet intended for Catholic parents and published in the weeks after the decision.[128] The pamphlet's tone wavered between pedantic and provocative. The First Amendment, Reed explained, had been converted by the Court from a tool intended to preserve religion into a tool used to handicap it. "The religious atmosphere of the home," he wrote, "must now compete with the secularist atmosphere of the school."[129] The Court's opinion in *McCollum* was especially troubling because it suggested that released time instructors improperly relied upon compulsory education laws to draw students to their classes. Reed warned this reasoning held potentially dire consequences—compulsory education laws also governed children's attendance at religious schools; therefore the "judicial enshrinement of secularism" threatened the very existence of a parochial system in the United States.[130] Along with Reed's pamphlet the general secretary circulated a parallel letter to American bishops, warning them of potential implications of the decision in their dioceses. This letter's tone was less provocative and more practical. It made no mention of a parochial system at risk, but it did comment bluntly on the "wide opening" *McCollum* left and the probability of future lawsuits.[131] Over the coming months, the legal department identified two phenomena the *McCollum* decision rendered particularly vulnerable: surviving released time programs were one and sister-taught public schools were the other.

These communications were the work of an organization that understood the vulnerability of its clients. They also marked a shift in NCWC strategy, as the legal department reoriented itself to defend extant Catholic teaching practices from future lawsuits the Court's decision made probable. Assuming a thoroughly defensive posture brought with it new challenges to the department's work. As Frank Sorauf pointed out, groups responsible for counseling defendants in church–state litigation faced impediments to the already difficult project of building a case under the First Amendment.[132] Unlike POAU, which advocated primarily on behalf of plaintiffs through the 1950s, the defense-oriented NCWC was unable to choose either the situations that went to court or the issues a given lawsuit raised. In contrast to the shared objectives of POAU and its clients, the NCWC also had no choice but to contend with the often-conflicting interests of parties swept together unwillingly as defendants in the suits it responded to. Sorauf had these sorts of logistical challenges in mind when he wrote that the U.S. Catholic Conference (the NCWC's mid-1960s successor) "moves through these [church–state] cases as a somewhat shadowy presence, it is less by choice than by the logic of adversary litigation on church–state relations."[133]

This "logic of adversary litigation" was dishearteningly evident in 1948, as George Reed and his colleagues waded through the chaotic *Zellers* defense. While New Mexico's situation raised important questions about the ability of women religious to teach in public, the dozens of other allegations bundled together in the complaint compromised the sisters' position and diminished the chances any court would consider their presence in the classroom as its own issue. The suit's motley crew of defendants, and their only slightly less motley local counsel, made it difficult for the NCWC team to build a well-organized case on behalf of all the parties involved. Unlike the citizens who filed the complaint, each group of defendants was interested in furthering a different set of interests, and those interests were all more mundane than the clarification of a legal principle. Raymond Huff and members of the state board, for example, had agreed to sisters' employment because it saved the state money. Their local counsel would have little motive to join arguments on the sisters' behalf, should those arguments prove politically unpopular or otherwise jeopardize their clients' appointments. The circumstances of the *Zellers* defense were messy, but they were not unique; most other public–parochial litigation the NCWC's legal department intervened in was complicated by similar webs of factors. With *McCollum*'s precedent casting its shadow, and wary of the challenges these legal defenses entailed, the NCWC changed its tune. Even as Reed and his fellow attorneys concentrated on building a defense for the religious in New Mexico, elsewhere their department's focus shifted away from developing well-reasoned arguments for the courtroom, and settled on avoiding litigation at all costs.

After *McCollum*, the NCWC adopted an early intervention policy designed to diffuse incendiary situations within American dioceses before they reached court. This applied both to remaining episodes of released time, as well as to the more open-ended issue of sisters teaching publicly in their habits. The organization's approach was straightforward; it identified dioceses with potentially controversial schooling arrangements and it advised local religious leaders on how to modify the arrangements to remove them as litigation targets. The legal department followed this protocol whether or not it knew a diocese to be under investigation by POAU. These efforts to bring schools into compliance with opponents' expectations prevented lawsuits in dozens of communities through the 1950s. They also resulted in a *de facto* deference on the Church's part to the practical weight, if not the moral authority, of a strong—even a secular—standard of church–state separation. Nowhere was this give-and-take clearer than in the NCWC's position on publicly teaching sisters. The legal department began to recommend that women religious in garb leave their classrooms soon after *McCollum*. The voluntary withdrawals that followed happened even as courts themselves continued their back-and-forth about the legality of those sisters' employment.[134]

The captive school lawsuits of the 1950s put women religious at the center of public conversations about Catholicism and the state, but they did nothing to settle the debate over their ability to teach in religious clothing. The consensus that state courts had come to over the previous decades—that sisters in habits were constitutionally permitted to teach, but that legislatures could pass laws restricting their dress—dissolved with *Zellers* and the cluster of cases that followed it. The New Mexico Supreme Court's decision presented a new legal position on the Catholic sisters' habit. By the time the *Zellers* lawsuit found its way to the high court—three long years after the complaint was filed—New Mexico's own board of education had conceded to an anti-garb statute similar to those in North Dakota and other states. The court declared this statute insufficient. School board personnel might change, it reasoned; statutes might be repealed and the practice of garbed nuns teaching might resume in the future. "We feel compelled," the court concluded:

> to announce our decision that the wearing of religious garb and religious insignia must be henceforth barred, during the time the Religious are on duty as public school teachers. . . . Not only does the wearing of religious garb and insignia have a propagandizing effect for the church, but by its very nature it introduced sectarian religion into the school.[135]

The New Mexico Supreme Court's 1951 decision that the habit was *constitutionally* prohibited in public schools was a major victory for POAU, and it hastened the organization's efforts to bring captive school lawsuits in other states. For the first time, a high court had declared sisters' clothing vulnerable under the principle of separation.

Sisters' prospects took an even grimmer turn with the Missouri court's decision in *Berghorn v. Reorganized School District* two years later.[136] The *Berghorn* decision went a controversial step past its counterpart in New Mexico. Responding to the "total effect" of public–parochial cooperation within Missouri's schools, the court forbade sisters from public teaching in the state—regardless of their dress. Missouri's high court had laid legal groundwork for this bold banishment a decade earlier. In a 1942 decision, also regarding sisters, the court cited a state law that prohibited payment of public funds to ministers or other teachers of religion. Its justices concluded that Catholic sisters lived lives "dedicated to the training of children both in religion and education," and so fell within the parameters of this prohibition.[137] In *Berghorn*, the Missouri court recalled its earlier reasoning that disqualified sisters from teaching, and this time suggested it applied directly to the provisions of the state's constitution. It agreed with a lower court's determination that "because of the character of their obligations [the nuns in question] are disqualified from teaching in any public school in the State of Missouri."[138] Although the *Berghorn* lawsuit only involved sisters from two religious orders, the court intimated its decision's relevance for women religious generally when it cited Canon Law on the obedient character of all sisters.[139] Using language reminiscent of Blanshard, the trial court had posited that sisters act as "instruments and agents of their religious orders" and are categorically incapable of providing education free from the influence of their Church.[140] The high court agreed. It made no difference what clothing sisters wore, and it made no difference whether the state legislature had a relevant statute on the books. The Missouri court shared POAU's contention that a sister's profession put her unavoidably in violation of church–state separation.

By the mid-1950s the question of sisters in public schools was more unsettled than ever in the United States. Sisters' constitutional status was so tenuous that a group like the American Civil Liberties Union—which supported the right of women religious to teach publicly, though only in secular dress—found its stance on nuns squeezed awkwardly between two alternatives, both of which remained viable. While the ACLU's amicus briefs sat at odds with judicial precedent allowing sisters to teach in their habits in the absence of anti-garb laws, the group also disagreed with the categorical ban on sisters that POAU and other citizens' groups were pressing for.[141] Finally in 1956 another captive school case brought judicial thinking on the sister question back, however tentatively, to its pre-*Zellers* status. Like many other states, Kentucky still had no statute on its books regulating sisters' dress. In its decision in *Rawlings v. Butler*, the Supreme Court of Kentucky harkened back to the *Hysong* decision a half-century earlier:

> While the dress and emblems worn by . . . Sisters proclaim them to be members of certain organizations of the Roman Catholic Church and that they have taken certain religious vows, these facts do not deprive them of their right to teach in public schools. . . . The garb does not teach. It is the woman within who teaches. . . . The religious views of these sisters and their mode of dress are entirely personal to them.[142]

Disagreeing with its counterparts in New Mexico and Missouri, Kentucky's high court concluded there was no constitutional basis for removing sisters' habits.

George Reed's team worked alongside the defense counsel in both *Berghorn* and *Rawlings*, but church–state litigation was no longer the order of things at the NCWC.[143] In 1948, the conference's legal department, its education department, and its administrative board began putting together a comprehensive plan for dealing with sister-taught public schools. The controversies in New Mexico and North Dakota were front-page news when the board chose "Catholic public

schools" as the topic for its regular meeting. At its request, the education department distributed a questionnaire to diocesan superintendents across the country
in an effort to determine the extent and circumstances of these controversial
arrangements.[144] The results gave the organization a sobering picture of what it
was working with: the eighty-three dioceses that responded to the survey reported
over three hundred public–parochial schools. These schools employed some
twelve hundred teaching religious, and they were responsible for the education of
thirty-four thousand children.[145]

Secretary Carroll next asked the legal department to execute a study of the constitutional issues involved in sisters teaching.[146] The education department had circulated some cursory remarks on the matter earlier in the year, before the *McCollum*
decision. While it stressed that Catholic–public schools *must* obey the same laws
that apply to all public schools, the education department had concluded sisters
might continue to teach successfully since their habits were constitutionally permissible.[147] The legal department's read of the situation in August was different. In a
confidential memorandum distributed to all American bishops, the department
reviewed the case history on religious garb. Its analysis spoke from the perspective
of a post-*McCollum* era in which "practices which but a few year ago would not have
been considered objectionable will be given considerable weight." Turning to the
recent compromise that had allowed sisters to continue teaching in North Dakota,
the memo struck a cautionary tone:

> The stratagem of adopting a secular garb in the face of attack may serve
> to unduly prolong the "Catholic-public" school arrangement which
> admittedly is not an ideal system of caring for the religious education of
> Catholic children, and particularly since the McCollum decision.[148]

Rather than fight for the status quo like Archbishop Byrne in New Mexico, or
petition for the removal of sisters' garb like Bishop Ryan in North Dakota, the
department recommended bishops move toward eliminating Catholic–public
arrangements in their dioceses altogether. This could mean directing sisters to
withdraw from public classrooms in order to begin work in private ones, or it
could mean converting schools leased by the Church for public use back into
parochial institutions. The bishops should continue supporting sisters' public
employment only in extraordinary situations, the memo instructed, and in those
situations they should make every effort to eliminate their habits. "Resort by
religious to a secular dress in order to continue teaching in a public school
should only be made," it explained, "when the local conditions are [such] that
the religious education of a substantial number of Catholic children would be
jeopardized but for such action."[149]

The legal department relied on its guidelines as it intervened in public–parochial
episodes over the next decade. Between 1948 and 1954 the department's attorneys

advised diocesan officials in at least twenty different states.[150] In places like New Mexico and Missouri, where lawsuits had already been filed against a diocese or its schools, Reed and his colleagues helped the defense.[151] In many more situations, the team convinced dioceses to convert questionable public schools to private use before any legal action could begin. At the legal department's recommendation, public schools in Odanah and Lima, Wisconsin, and Lake Linden, Michigan, reopened as parochial.[152] In places like St. Donatus, Iowa, the transition took a bit longer, but even the Archdiocese of Dubuque eventually acceded to the NCWC's pressure.[153] In 1952 the education department circulated a memo reiterating the legal department's position on sister-taught public schools. Despite the NCWC's success in many dioceses, it reported two hundred twenty-five of these institutions still in operation around the country. POAU remained in hot pursuit, with fifty-two different cases pending either under investigation or formal litigation. The NCWC's recommendation remained the same: "Whenever practicable, Catholic public schools should be converted into Catholic parochial schools."[154]

Two years later—possibly in response to dioceses that still refused to comply with its recommendations—the NCWC softened its tone. It still refused to endorse sisters who taught in their habits. In a 1954 memorandum titled "Employment of Nuns as Public School Teachers," the legal department exchanged its advice on parochial transition for a set of practical recommendations aimed at sisters who wanted to remain in public schools. Sisters might continue to teach, the memo explained, so long as they meticulously erased all outward signs of religion from their work. The NCWC urged sisters to adhere closely to public school protocol:

> Nuns in arranging employment in public schools should follow standard public school procedure. . . . Nuns in public schools never should give religious instruction during school hours on public school premises; it is preferable that the Sisters give this instruction OFF public school premises at times when they have no duties whatsoever in their capacity as public school teachers.[155]

Although it made no direct mention of the habit, the NCWC did instruct sisters to carefully monitor what they wore. Nuns should refrain from wearing "what the courts have called 'distinctive religious symbols of a sectarian character,'" the document urged, "i.e. rosaries, crucifixes, medallions, etc."[156] The NCWC had sisters' interests at heart when it made these recommendations; its legal team knew any evidence of religion—habits included—carried the risk of litigation that could empty coffers and damage reputations. As it urged women religious to remove "distinctive religious symbols" from their bodies, however, the NCWC also worked against its own church–state vision. The organization that poured so much effort into developing pro-religion interpretations of the First Amendment during the

Everson era now found itself promoting schooling scenarios secular enough even for an organization like the ACLU.

The NCWC was constrained both by the logistics of adversarial litigation and by the theological-intellectual tools available to it when it intervened in sister-taught public schools. Working amid these restrictions, the organization's legal team had no choice but to forego a concerted defense of sisters teaching in their habits for a more tactical approach that involved working with religious communities and dioceses to preempt litigation. Catholics recognized their limited ability to steer the church–state conversation after *McCollum*, and so the NCWC's approach to sister-taught schools was as *ad hoc* as POAU's was deliberate. In its efforts to keep women religious away from lawsuits, the NCWC found itself endorsing schooling arrangements that conformed to its opponents' claims about the unconstitutional influences of those sisters and their clothing. In New Mexico, however, George Reed, Charles Fahy, and the rest of the NCWC's legal team had arrived on the scene too late to deter litigation. The *Zellers* lawsuit was the first sister-taught schooling episode the NCWC participated in post-*McCollum*, and as its attorneys began their work in Santa Fe in the spring of 1948 they still had no inkling of the twists and turns American law relating to sisters' habits would take over the next decade. What they did realize, almost immediately upon arrival, was that the one hundred thirty-one Catholic sisters employed by the state had slim chances of winning this particular dispute. Amid mounting evidence the women had filled their classrooms not only with clothing but also with objects and activities that appeared problematic in a post-*McCollum* light, the NCWC attorneys spent the spring and summer struggling to imagine a viable case for the defense.

6

Sisters and the Trials of Separation

During the summer of 1948 a small statue called the Pilgrim Virgin traveled from parish to parish across the Archdiocese of Santa Fe. The statue was a replica of the more famous image enshrined at Fátima in Portugal, at a spot where thirty-one years earlier the Virgin had appeared to a trio of shepherd children with dark warnings of war and the other punishments that awaited a sinful world.[1] The message of Fátima resonated with New Mexican parishioners who thronged to view the little statue every week and recite "Rosaries for the Russians" in its presence. The shadow of faraway conflicts had settled over their own state in recent years—it was insinuated in the bustle of secretive activity on a mesa just northwest of Santa Fe, at Los Alamos, and at an elusive testing site to the south near the city of Almagordo. Its dark weight felt heaviest in the absence of men who had left home to fight—New Mexico's young Hispanos and Native Americans had enlisted in disproportionate numbers during World War II, and their return home was slow and difficult.[2] The general restlessness of those years had finally spiraled to extraterrestrial proportions with reports of flying disks outside of Roswell the previous summer.

Hispano Catholics in New Mexico were witnessing upheaval in their religious lives as well. Some of it was for the better. Within the last year, Archbishop Edwin Byrne had surprised many of the state's Catholic residents by inviting the *penitente* brotherhood to become a sanctioned body within the Catholic Church. A majority of New Mexico's *moradas* accepted the prelate's gesture, and the result was unprecedented accord between lay and clerical Catholics in the state's northern villages.[3] By 1948, the minds of many in those villages were also trained on darker prospects. As Catholic residents learned about the *Zellers* lawsuit many of them recognized it as a direct threat to their children's schools. Throughout the spring and summer months the Catholic *Santa Fe Register* published updates on the litigation. It ran stories about communities rallying to support their sisters, like the members of one parish who "spontaneously" gathered and in two short hours collected $1,000 for the sisters' defense.[4] In March, the *Register*'s editors obliged the "many people [who] would like to know the names of those who are pressing the case" by publishing the full name of each of the suit's twenty-eight plaintiffs.[5] Publicity like this was incendiary—it identified targets for the deep hostilities the lawsuit inspired. In its weekly "Mr. Citizen" column, the *Santa Fe New Mexican* printed impassioned arguments from both sides. One reader who was sympathetic to the sisters sanctimoniously invoked the trial and execution of Jesus himself and warned of a "small scale version of that Supreme Tragedy" playing out right in New Mexico. Another reader, identifying himself only as "Mr. X" from Española, shot back by pointing out the "rotten things that are going on in a state where we are supposed to have freedom of religion and a complete separation of church and state."[6]

Back in Dixon, members of the Free Schools Committee were contending with a wall of Catholic fury. The little store owned by Doc and Lydia Zellers was a staple of the local economy, but the couple was forced to temporarily close it after its Catholic patrons abruptly stopped visiting. "I remember that there was a lot of fighting . . . and we were not allowed to go to the Zellers store," one Catholic resident remembered of her childhood in Dixon.[7] Another suggested the Zellers store boycott lasted longer than 1948. "Some of them never went back," Francisco Romero remembered.

> [The Zellers] had one of the better [stores] around here, because they carried just about everything and if they didn't carry it, they could get it for you. . . . But after this happened, my parents were some of the ones who said, "That's it." They didn't go, and I didn't go. There were just a couple of times I went to the store, even when I grew up. There were a few other small stores around here, and when my oldest daughters started working up at Los Alamos . . . they'd stop at the store [there] and bring whatever we needed for the week.[8]

Many Protestants and Catholics in town stopped talking to each other altogether. As ill will increased through the summer, Lydia Zellers even began to fear for her life. "They're going to hang you for this," her husband worried aloud to her one day. His concern was corroborated by an alarming conversation Zellers found herself in with a merchant she knew from Peñasco. "We're never going to be good friends again," Zellers later reported the man telling her, "and not only that, [but] you'd better not be on the highway at night because I'm going to have you killed. . . . I'll do anything for my church."[9]

Amid this bluster the litigation moved forward. In May, the judge originally assigned to the case was disqualified at the plaintiffs' request and a new judge named in his place.[10] In the interest of impartiality, the state's high court appointed a magistrate from outside Santa Fe's own judicial district to preside over the affair. The Honorable E. T. Hensley hailed from Roosevelt County near the Texas border—a part of New Mexico with a large Anglo-Protestant population and no sister-taught public schools.[11] By mid-June the defense had shot back with a motion to dismiss the suit, claiming a statutory remedy to the complaint already existed.[12] Ten different attorneys attended arguments on the motion, and the courtroom "was about three-quarters filled with an audience who listened raptly and silently to the dry legal discourses."[13] The motion failed, but Judge Hensley used the opportunity to strike nineteen paragraphs from the plaintiffs' complaint as "redundant, repetitious and evidentiary," and in doing so he cut the lengthy document in half.[14] The judge also settled on a starting date for the trial. Two attorneys for the defense had asked him to delay it until after October, noting they were running for office and that the proceedings might interfere with their candidacies.[15] Hensley opted instead to move the trial forward, and it was rescheduled to begin on September 27.

The Catholic sisters involved in the suit monitored this legal wrangling warily. The *Zellers* complaint was the culmination of a series of troubling developments they had witnessed over the 1947–48 school year. Since Archbishop Byrne's letter of caution the previous September, the women had labored under the archdiocese's expectation that they comply with strict requirements of church–state separation. By instructing sisters to refrain from religious instruction in public-use buildings on school days, the archbishop's letter had insinuated that recent developments within the American judicial system—and not religious motivation—should guide sisters' conduct in their classrooms at all times. The complaint asserted the need for a legal standard of separation more strongly, and it posited sisters' teaching against that standard in adversarial terms. According to the *Zellers* suit, it was impossible for religious in New Mexico to comply with Byrne's instructions because they were, by virtue of their oaths and clothing, themselves violations of the law. The lawsuit proposed a separation standard with fatal consequences for the public–parochial schools religious had built, and the more likely a plaintiffs' victory seemed in 1948, the more sisters found their backs against the wall. With their classrooms under scrutiny, the teaching opportunities sisters had relied on between state curricular requirements and the demands of their Church began to disappear. Many of these women continued to follow state policies when they could, but their priority became finding ways to defend the Catholic practices they would not or could not eliminate. By the spring of 1948, a number of religious had abandoned efforts to comply with the state's expectations altogether, choosing instead to develop justifications for noncompliant activities, or to cover them up through secrecy or evasion. When the *Zellers* trial began in September, most of the sisters who testified were aware their classrooms failed the standards of the legal system moving around them. Attorneys from both sides asked these women to explain their work anyway. They did so, but as they floundered for responses that conformed to the legal discourse of church and state, they balked, rationalized, and told half-truths. It was a discouraging experience, both for the sisters and for Judge Hensley as he sat on the bench listening to them.

Litigation was also difficult for the congregations who supported women religious. During the 1947–48 school year, the archdiocese and the state board seemed on the verge of erasing all identifiably Catholic elements from sisters' educational routines. Superiors in many communities worried that the loss of Catholic objects, prayers, and even clothing from their sisters' schools would cast those women irreversibly into the secular world, and force them to act in ways contrary to their religious lives. As the legal principle of church–state separation expanded and found enforcement through *Zellers* and suits like it, congregations of women religious responded by hardening their own, parallel commitment to church–state separation—by positing separate spheres, and by conflating, more thoroughly than ever before, the arena of the "state" with the prohibitively secular. The women's communities who arrived in New Mexico in the early twentieth century had not hesitated to enter public education. They treated it as a neutral space, ripe with possibilities for religious work at the peripheries of the Catholic world. By the time *Zellers* received a decision in district court, the leaders of those same congregations were rethinking public work as dangerous and damaging stuff. At their superiors' instructions, sisters in New Mexico began to withdraw from public employment two years before the state mandated it. Litigation left parties on both sides of the *Zellers* suit convinced that church and state were domains best kept separate from one another. For sisters, their commitment to remain apart from the world assumed a clearer form in the aftermath of *Zellers*; it was a mirror image of the new requirements of New Mexican law.

In his September 1947 letter to the state's religious, Archbishop Byrne had been specific that "no religious instruction be given in public school buildings by teachers on school days." Even catechism classes before or after regular school hours were no longer acceptable, Byrne explained; the religious should give catechism instruction on Saturdays and Sundays only.[16] Responses to the archbishop's directives varied widely. Some sisters quietly accepted his orders, and a few supported them with enthusiasm. The Grand Rapids Dominicans had the largest presence of any community in the state's schools, and they seemed happiest about the archbishop's instructions. On the same day Byrne's letter went out, a Dominican teaching in Santa Cruz wrote to the archbishop to recommend he warn sisters about including religion in their teaching. "We have to be very careful not to demonstrate our religion in public," Sister Claire Marie cautioned the prelate. She worried about two Dominican schools that still had crucifixes hanging on their walls: "I feel like a thing will happen in this state if some of the Sisters are not warned. I know, as in the above case, that the Sisters themselves are much to blame."[17] In the wake of the archbishop's communication, other Dominicans immediately began to restrict religious lessons and remove religious images from their walls. In Peñasco, Sister John Evangelist had just begun to outfit her room for All Saints Day when Sister Maura rushed in and ordered her to take the decorations down. "There were things you had to get used to teaching in public school," Sister John Evangelist conceded of the incident.[18] The same winter, Dominican

Sister Carmella Conway, who taught seventh grade in Ranchos de Taos, found herself changing the Christmas decorations on her blackboard three different times. Her principal acquiesced to the board only after Sister Carmella removed a nativity scene and replaced it with a picture of Santa Claus coming down a chimney.[19]

Not all Catholic religious in New Mexico were as ready as the Dominicans to obey the new restrictions. Many reacted to Byrne's instructions with surprise and dismay, and compliance over the school year was uneven. Some sisters contended that removing religion completely from their schools would anger residents in the villages where they taught. Others cited the unhappiness of children themselves. Sister Protasia Hofstetter, a Franciscan who taught the sixth through eighth grades in Aragon, recounted her students' reactions when in the spring of 1948 she relented and removed religious emblems from her classroom's walls:

> When the students arrived that morning...they missed the little crucifix on the wall and questioned its absence. With a choking voice I explained to them we were ordered to take it down.... Another surprise awaited us the next morning. One of the older boys in charge of sweeping the class-rooms after school had access to the key. Upon our arrival in the morning, we found no American flag nor the plaque with the Pledge of Allegiance on the wall. Instead, the walls of the classroom were literally plastered with religious pictures, large and small.... I actually had to beg them to take them down in order to avoid difficulties if someone were to come and check whether we had obeyed orders.[20]

Hofstetter celebrated her students for disobeying a directive neither she nor the children understood. Both sisters and brothers who taught publicly sent the archbishop letters objecting to the prospect of not offering religious instruction. A Christian Brother teaching in Las Vegas informed Byrne he still taught a class on "Manners and Morals"—outside of school hours but on school days. Brother B. Lewis insisted the people of Las Vegas wanted such instruction, and he boldly suggested the class complied with the spirit of the archbishop's instructions, if not the letter.[21] When William Bradley replied to Lewis on the archbishop's behalf, he reiterated the importance of removing religion from the schools. "State law must be followed strictly in this regard," he cautioned; "otherwise the positions of Religious who are teaching in all public schools of the State might be endangered."[22] On one point, Byrne's office capitulated to the protesting religious. If a school received unanimous written permission from the local board, Bradley offered, its teachers would be allowed to give religious instruction on school days, outside of regular school hours.[23] No sooner had Byrne conceded this point than his office received several letters indicating school boards around the archdiocese that gave their consent.[24] This compromise also seemed to satisfy Brother Lewis, who wrote the archbishop a week later to report his teachers had already stripped religious objects from their school's walls. "We will secularize everything except our religious garb and our hearts," he grandly assured the prelate.[25]

Whether or not they agreed with Archbishop Byrne, Catholic sisters understood the changes he expected of them, and the high stakes wrapped up in their ability to comply. Any woman who remained optimistic her classroom *could* meet the Dixon Free Schools Committee's expectations was sorely disappointed in March. Recipients of the *Zellers* complaint felt dread at the sight of their religious names attached to a legal document that was unmistakably accusatory but difficult in parts to understand. The tension that settled over Dixon and other villages during the spring and summer was magnified in convents, where religious struggled to make sense of their place in the lawsuit. One sister described feeling fearful about the legal proceedings and wondering how she could be punished for teaching in the way she was trained to teach.[26] Another wrestled with strong feelings of suspicion. "It was like living in a communist country," she recalled, "because you just didn't trust. The people you thought you could trust were betraying you, and it was so unjust; the whole thing. . . . It was like evil was triumphing."[27] Her sense of injustice was echoed by a sister from Pecos, who felt compelled to write a defense of sisters' schools, and who sent the piece to Bradley hoping to secure its publication.[28] Another woman felt something like betrayal when she privately blamed the "stupid Franciscans" in Dixon for compromising the work of her own community.[29] While sisters' reactions to news of the lawsuit varied, the formal response from their congregations was nearly unanimous. At the archbishop's request, superiors from motherhouses across the country began sending money for their members' legal defense—$150 for each sister named in the complaint.[30]

When they became defendants, the religious faced a new set of challenges. While the archdiocese and state officials had encouraged vigilance in their classrooms, litigation now turned an unforgiving spotlight upon everything sisters were doing—or had done—in those classrooms, and it demanded explanations. In April defense attorney William Barker sent each of the religious involved in the dispute a typed list of questions. In an effort to avoid a lengthy depositions process, attorneys on both sides of the suit had agreed that each of the religious would complete a uniform written interrogatory. Their responses would be admissible as evidence by both sides in the case.[31] In reality, however, the interrogatory was mainly Harry Bigbee's creation, and it included ninety-four questions designed to press the religious on every detail of their work with potential to bolster the plaintiffs' cause. Many of the questions probed either the content of the teacher's lessons, or the actions, objects, or textbooks that filled her classroom:

21. Do you now, or have you ever, conducted classes in religion or involving religious principles . . . during the period that you have been employed in tax supported schools in New Mexico?

70. Have you at any time during the current school year posted or seen a list of altar boys on the bulletin board or any blackboard in your school?

91. Do the children in your class kneel in a group at any time?[32]

A second class of questions focused on the teacher's religious allegiance, pressing her on the obligatory practices that accompanied membership in a religious order:

8. State the vows and obligations you took upon becoming a member or associated with such Order.

10. What proportion or percent of your time do your vows and obligations to your Order and Church require that you devote to your Order and its objectives?

12. Does your entire salary go to your Order?[33]

Among this series of more personal questions, one was especially important to plaintiffs' counsel—so much so that the attorneys submitted sisters' answers to it together, as a separate piece of evidence during trial. Question twenty-four pressed the religious to describe the sort of garb they wore and to further "explain the significance of the garb, what it denotes, and its purpose."[34]

The sisters were stumped by the interrogatory's questions. Whenever they could, they gave the answers they knew to be correct—that they did not pray with students, or that they did not distribute religious literature at school. Ultimately, though, no public–parochial classroom could match the standard of separation plaintiffs' attorneys were looking for, and no sister could answer the interrogatory in a way that was both truthful and satisfactory. Even the most disciplined Dominicans were still wearing their habits, living by their vows, and—truth be told—holding onto the stray catechism or Catholic comic. In a bind, the religious looked to the advice of counsel. The NCWC's legal team quickly drafted and supplied sisters with a list of sample answers, intended to help the women complete the interrogatory in a "non-embarrassing" way.[35] Despite Hensley's instructions that all forms be answered in full, the NCWC advised the religious to bypass many questions by simply writing "Refuse to answer, immaterial," or "Do not know."[36] For the most part sisters relied on these cookie-cutter replies, although occasionally the stress—or tedium—of writing answer after answer provoked them to supplement restrained non-responses with more colorful variety. Their spontaneous answers could be disarmingly frank one moment and devastatingly smug the next. Sister Claire Marie returned a set of responses that vacillated between the verbatim advice of counsel and her own irritated voice. "Give the names of all songs . . . that have been sung by the children in your class," the interrogatory instructed. "Life is too short," Sister Claire Marie quipped back. "Why did you resume teaching religion in violation of the Archbishop's instructions?" the document pressed her. "How could I resume if I never began?" was her retort.[37]

When it came to questions about their clothing, sisters had instructions from the NCWC to state only that it was the "distinctive dress of my choice."[38] Nearly every woman who submitted an interrogatory followed this prompt, but many took it upon themselves to add an extra sentence or two by way of explanation. Some sisters did this to justify their costumes' antiquated appearance, which they rightly suspected was a sore spot with the habit's critics. Franciscan Sister Mary Norbeta, for example, explained her outfit was fashioned "in the distinctive style of the gentlewomen at the time the Order was founded."[39] Other women included a visual description of their clothing. Another Franciscan, Sister Mary Elaine Binter, described her habit as a "brown woolen dress with a white headdress and black veil," and Lorretine Sister Ellen Mary explained her dress "consists of a simple black serge dress, and a black veil, lined with white, worn on the head." She too was adamant that "its only significance is that it is worn by all members of the Order."[40] A few of the women also thought it wise—or at least clever—to emphasize their garb's most basic use, like Franciscan Sister Noretta Otero, who wryly remarked her habit "has the same purpose as clothing worn by all civilized persons in temperate climate."[41]

The Free Schools Committee's legal team had high hopes for what the interrogatories might reveal, and they were disappointed by the evasiveness of their responses. The first questionnaires filtered back into counsels' hands during the second week of June, and throughout the summer Harry Bigbee levied complaint after complaint with the court about the defendants' failure to adequately answer his questions. Bigbee pointed out the religious had neglected to respond to a full one third of the questions on the returned forms. Many of the answers they did include were unacceptably vague. Only twelve of the interrogatory's ninety-four questions, Bigbee objected, were consistently answered.[42] During a pre-trial hearing in late August, Bigbee protested again, and this time he drew the court's attention to one question in particular. The question asked religious to provide a list of "materials, periodicals or books . . . that relate to or discuss the Catholic faith . . . that are now, or have been during the current school year, in the school building where you teach."[43] Exasperation crept into Bigbee's voice as he appealed to the judge:

> Out of 145 people with the possible exception of one school—which I don't know whether [it] is an exception or not—there hasn't been one of them [to] come out and say there are no such books—and yet not one [has] given a partial list or attempted in any way whatsoever to give any information.[44]

He then favored Judge Hensley with a sample of the maddening answers he had received regarding the presence of religious books. "Whether there is or not I wouldn't definitely say, possibly there are none," one sister had written. "I do not know, but do not mean to infer there are any," was another's response. "While one or two [sisters] used one of those variations I know of no such list," replied a third.[45]

Hensley reviewed Bigbee's interrogatory, question by question, and concluded only fifty-four of its queries demanded responses from the religious.[46] Once again, the court ordered the defense attorneys to ensure their clients answer these questions promptly and in full. If they did not, Hensley warned, the religious would be subpoenaed and required to answer the questions the following month in open trial.[47] At first, it seemed Hensley's warning had its intended effect; by mid-September nearly all the interrogatories had been handed back to the religious so they could reconsider their responses. Their attorneys collected the documents again in short order, and returned them to the judge as he had instructed.[48] When the court and plaintiffs' counsel reviewed the revised products, however, their consensus was that little in them had changed. In the end, sisters' replies to the interrogatory were still miserably insufficient.

As their answers (or non-answers) to Bigbee's questions made clear, by the summer of 1948 most religious were more concerned with defending their professional livelihood than accurately representing their classrooms. Litigation brought other inconveniences with it as well, and the women were soon matching the vague statements Bigbee complained about with similarly evasive behavior. That spring, religious across New Mexico found themselves face to face with a small band of investigators who had begun showing up uninvited to their schools. In March and again the following September, Free Schools Committee members and their supporters crisscrossed the state, making good on a pledge to visit the institutions named in their lawsuit. The group was composed in varying combinations of the committee's three officers—Lydia Zellers, Olive Bowen, and Porfiero Romero—along with Bigbee, Paul Stevens, and, when he was in town, Frank Mead. In March the group visited schools in Costilla, Ranchos de Taos, Peñasco, and Parkview. Six months later, they returned to each of these and paid visits to a dozen others as well. Zellers and her colleagues meant to see for themselves how the sisters taught, and the little group's modus operandi was always the same. Members would arrive in town early and wait quietly outdoors until the beginning of the school day. Then, asserting their right to access public property, they would enter the sisters' building. As the visitors toured each school they took pictures of incriminating evidence they found. Porfiero Romero later explained the group's tactics:

> Whenever we saw a crucifix, . . . Mrs. Zellers and Miss Bowing [sic] [would] go ahead with the nuns and we [would] stay back and snap a picture. When court came . . . the sisters were very much surprised that we had a picture of their own rooms . . . with a crucifix.[49]

Although Romero remembered the women he encountered as behaving pleasantly, privately sisters responded to these intrusions with anger. On an early trip to the high school in Costilla, the group discovered Catholic periodicals on the library shelves.[50] After the plaintiffs carried some of this evidence away with them, the school's principal wrote bitterly to Bradley. "Another group swooped down upon us," Sister Pancratia seethed, "and without permission or authority searched through everything they could get their hands on."[51] The local priest contacted the district attorney's office to ask whether such a seizure of school property was legal. In reply he received only a counsel of patience and the suggestion that little could be done.[52]

During the whirlwind tour Zellers' group made in September—which included visits to seventeen communities in a span of five days—any patience its religious hosts mustered in the spring was wearing thin. In Ranchos de Taos, a spirited middle-aged priest named Paul Hatch had acquired a deep dislike for Paul Stevens, his neighbor and fellow man of the cloth in Taos. Hatch was "determined to take care of everything" when it came to the local school, one sister remembered. Upon learning that the committee, Stevens included, was planning a visit to Ranchos, the priest took to spending his mornings as sentry, pacing back and forth in front of the school building.[53] Hatch was, in Romero's recollection, "rabid" on the morning the visitors' car finally approached the school. He strode out to confront the group and hotly informed them they were trespassers until the building and its property became public. "He came out very belligerent," Romero remembered of Hatch:

> "Well, you want me to pose for a picture?," [he asked]. "Well," we said, "we already took one." We took a picture of him going into the church . . . [and] he was real mad. I thought he was going to hit Paul Stevens.[54]

Romero and his traveling companions conceded to the priest's demand they leave the property—but not before they caught the sound of the Our Father being recited in unison, behind the closed door of one of the school's classrooms.[55]

As news of the visitors spread among New Mexico's religious communities, sisters waited grimly for their turn under the microscope. Just as reports of children locked in classrooms and intimidated into attending Mass enraged the Free Schools Committee and its sympathizers, women religious contemplated different rumors— reports of slick cars cornering children on their way home from school, and bribing them with candy in exchange for the catechisms or comics they carried.[56] When the Zellers group arrived at a school, sisters who had failed to remove religion from their classrooms and their schedules, whether through defiance or neglect, scrambled to appease their guests. Often the investigators found religious materials stuck hastily into closets, removed to empty classrooms, or sectioned off with handwritten signs indicating "private." In San Fidel, the plaintiffs caught Sister Paulina, a member of the Poor Sisters of St. Francis of Perpetual Adoration, rushing to cover up a chart the second they walked into her classroom.[57]

Figure 6.1 Students with a copy of the Baltimore Catechism, St. Rita's School, Carrizozo, New Mexico, 1948. Photograph taken by the Dixon Free Schools Committee. Courtesy of Special Collections Research Center, Morris Library, Southern Illinois University Carbondale.

Even in Peñasco, where under Sister Maura's watchful eye the Dominicans had taken steps to comply with the archbishop's regulations, the investigators' arrival meant hasty preparation and cover-up. Sister Maura wrote her superior of a March visit:

> Last week their lawyers made a tour of our schools in company with some sly troublemakers. . . . We were quite concerned for the Thursday and First Friday always mean "extra-curricular" activities. We had to cut everything, as it was sure they would arrive here either of those days.[58]

By the time the plaintiffs' group revisited Peñasco six months later, McDonald and her sisters had grown more cautious. Even so, the seasoned principal still found reason to hold her breath and pray:

> I discovered Romero looking inside the stove in the study hall and the others standing guard. . . . Could they see the school? [the visitors asked].

Certainly[,] come with me was my sharp and short response. It did not take me long to get them through. . . . A big box of books had come from the library in Santa Fe, and they scrutinized them carefully. I calmly informed them that there probably would not be found so much as the name of God in the whole lot so they need not worry. . . . Only yesterday I discovered that right inside of an unlocked door on the stage was a whole snag of pamphlets, the Holy Bible and several others of like nature. Had they opened it, and be sure they would have had I not been there, we surely would have been sunk with the evidence. Could they see the Grade School? [they asked]. Surely, for I thought they would be safe enough there, for Sr. Lucille has been very careful. . . . I stayed in the chapel and prayed.[59]

For the most part, the Dominicans had done their job well. With the exception of two photographs depicting stray catechisms, the visits to Peñasco turned up little of use to the plaintiffs' case.

The September episode did provide one sister an opportunity to get the stress of scrutiny off her chest. As the investigators approached Peñasco's elementary school, its principle Sister Lucille noticed that one member of their group remained back in the car. When she inquired, she was told the man was the by now infamous attorney Harry Bigbee. Sister Maura recounted what happened next:

Sister said she would like to meet the man who put all those silly ques-tions in the interrogatory. [Bigbee] got out to ask her what she meant. She told him, too. Well, they stayed there for more than an hour arguing back and forth. . . . They finally went on their way when Bigbee told Sister that her very habit was an influence—good women, you know, and all that sort of thing.[60]

As he drove tiredly back to Santa Fe that evening, Harry Bigbee's overall impres-sion of the "good women" he had met—in writing and person, in Peñasco and all across the state—was stronger and more complicated than he had imagined it could be.

Down the mountain from Peñasco, the Franciscans in Dixon were feeling the heat of the lawsuit ferociously. Like their counterparts at other schools, Sisters Dor-othy, Emma, Gilberta, Seferina, and Wendelina—the five Franciscans from the village named in the complaint—faced interrogatories, visits, and the possibility of subpoenas. They also grappled daily with the anger of their town's Protestant residents, as well as more distant disdain, both from Americans who followed them in POAU-affiliated publications and from sisters in New Mexico who blamed them for the suit. The strain on the sisters was palpable at the close of the school year when their superior general wrote to them from Amarillo. The superior directed the sisters to quietly depart their teaching posts in Dixon. She issued similar instructions to her sisters working in village of Aragon. One woman remembered her community's departure from Aragon the same May:

> We left Aragon in the early dawn forever, without the opposition and arguments we had feared if the pastor had realized what was happening. The only persons ... that appeared on the scene were a boy and a girl who had graduated the day before. How they knew is still a puzzle. They begged the sisters not to leave—to come back. What else could the sisters do but respond with a final embrace and a grateful goodbye.[61]

The Franciscans' departure from Dixon was not so seamless. When Archbishop Byrne learned belatedly of the congregation's plan, he angrily forbade the sisters to leave.[62] After they refused to obey his order the archbishop took another approach, this time urging the sisters to remain in Dixon in a parochial capacity. The congregation replied to Byrne with a series of adamant communications: it had had enough. The superior general and her council were insistent the sisters would not remain in Dixon.[63] In July the archbishop finally relented to the superior's wishes. In his disappointment, he punished them in the only way he could; he informed the sisters the archdiocese would not purchase their school from them, and forced the congregation to take a financial loss as a result.[64] That summer the sisters who sparked the Dixon controversy left New Mexico—and the jurisdiction of the state courts. Some returned to Texas, while others took employment further west in California.[65] By August, Archbishop Byrne had mended their absence as best he could by persuading a group of Dominicans teaching in Abiquiu to accept employment in Dixon.[66]

In September 1948 a new school year opened and the sisters remaining in New Mexico resumed their teaching duties. The trial was scheduled to begin at the end of the month. As its start date day grew closer, the women who had returned their interrogatories prayed they would be spared further scrutiny. A week ahead of the proceedings, however, sisters began to receive subpoenas. Sixty years later, Sister Carmella Conway remembered the afternoon a local sheriff delivered one to her. It was Friday. The school day had ended, and the twenty-five-year-old woman had joined two of her fellow sisters for evening prayers in the small chapel attached to their convent. As Sister Carmella recalled it:

> The doorbell rang, so I went to answer it. We were praying the rosary. I don't think we'd gotten to the [Divine] Office yet.... So I get to the door and here stands the sheriff. He said, "Sister Carmella Conway?" And I said, "I'm she." And he said—he had this paper [and he said] "You are hereby subpoenaed to appear in the district court in Santa Fe on

Wednesday." . . . And then I went inside and went in the little chapel door and I stood in the back and I said "Oh my God!" That's what I said out loud—they were praying, but I said it. And they stopped, and they asked me what [happened], and I said, "I gotta go to Santa Fe, I gotta go."[67]

Thirty-eight women from ten congregations were directed to travel to Santa Fe over the following week to testify. The quality of the answers they had submitted with their interrogatories now seemed irrelevant; the sisters selected for subpoena represented a cross-section of the religious defendants in the case. At least one sister from each school cited in the complaint was summoned to speak in court. The only exceptions were the school in Tucumcari and—it came as no surprise—those in Aragon and Dixon. Without any religious to provide evidence in those jurisdictions, the case was quietly dropped.

The trial opened at ten o'clock on a Monday morning. Judge Hensley, who had made the long commute to Santa Fe from his home in Roosevelt County, presided over a crowded courtroom. The group gathering in the room exhibited uncertainty and agitation, and reports of residents throwing rocks outside in protest added to the tumult.[68] No one present knew how long the trial would last; some guessed it would be over within a week and others feared it could drag on for months.[69] To begin building the plaintiffs' case, Harry Bigbee had on hand twenty subpoenaed witnesses that opening day.[70] These witnesses included school officials, like Rex Bell, superintendent of the Socorro school district, and women religious from some of the more remote communities involved in the case—dusty places to the south like Carrizozo and Belen. The first sister scheduled to testify was Sister Theodurette. Like the judge, Sister Theodurette had traveled over two hundred miles to Santa Fe from her home in Carrizozo. Now she sat quietly and waited to be called to the witness stand.

Along with school officials and Catholic women religious, the room was filled by attorneys, journalists, and other interested onlookers. At the plaintiffs' table Bigbee worked largely alone during the trial—grilling witnesses, filing objections, and submitting evidence. On that morning, however, he was joined by Lydia Zellers and other members of the Free Schools Committee who had traveled down from Dixon for the hearings. Bigbee also had support from his Washington allies. E. Hilton Jackson was there on behalf of POAU, and his presence gave the proceedings an air of national import, at least for anyone who managed to recognize him for his recent work on the *McCollum* case. The other side of the courtroom was crowded by the large and complicated representation for the defense. William Barker was there to represent the religious, with assistance from the younger John Murphy. The pair was joined by the various counsel hired to represent the school officials named in the suit. Finally, the NCWC had flown in its own legal team in the persons of George Reed and Charles Fahy.

In the end the *Zellers* trial lasted only nine days. Hensley was eager to return home, and he put the proceedings on an accelerated timetable with regular admonishments to the attorneys to speed up their questioning. After the first week he added evening sessions to step up the pace further.[71] Seven of the trial's nine days belonged to the plaintiffs, as Harry Bigbee laid out the Free Schools Committee's evidence piece by piece, witness by witness. Bigbee was meticulous. By the time he rested his case, he had called ninety-five different witnesses to the stand—forty-six religious (the thirty-eight sisters plus three brothers and five priests) in addition to school administrators and board members from across New Mexico. Father Hatch received a subpoena up in Taos, and so did William Bradley. Bigbee also elicited testimony from members of the Free Schools Committee, from Protestant parents and teachers, and from nine children who had attended sister-taught schools. In addition to these witness accounts, the plaintiffs submitted nearly two hundred pieces of physical evidence, including photographs the committee had taken during its tours, and materials it had confiscated from sisters' classrooms.[72] The defense's case was spare in comparison. When their time finally came, attorneys for the defense put together a combined presentation that included testimony from only nineteen people. They made their case in just over a day. Closing arguments in the trial began after Barker abruptly announced he had run out of witnesses.[73]

Testifying before a judge is never an easy thing. For women religious, the prospect of sitting in a courtroom and disclosing information about themselves was horrific. Although the sisters had spent time in public as teachers, speaking in court took public visibility to an alarming level. The same women forbidden by their superiors to own cameras now saw their photographs circulated as legal evidence and published in newspapers during the trial. Women prohibited from interacting familiarly with lay adults found themselves in front of a sea of unfamiliar faces, both Protestant and Catholic. When they spoke, their words were transcribed by the court reporter and reprinted in the press.[74] The prioress general of the Grand Rapid Dominicans summed up the feelings of many religious when she described the whole experience as "torture," and wrote to her sisters in New Mexico, "My heart aches to think of you being dragged before the public eye in such a way."[75] In addition to troubling publicity, sisters on the witness stand were also forced to revisit the quandary that had dogged them over the last year—in the archbishop's letter, in the "silly" interrogatories, and in the visitors combing through their schools. Again they confronted expectations about their activities, derived from the assumption of a separation of church from state. Everyone around them, from Bigbee to Judge Hensley, and even their own attorneys, spoke as if that assumption carried the weight of law. Again the women were asked to reconcile the reality of their teaching with the expectations separation brought with it. As always, that reality resisted reconciliation. Because sisters felt their backs against the wall, they acted uncomfortably when they spoke in court. They moved between tactics of disclosure and noncompliance, explanation and evasion, as they tried to cast their work in an acceptable light. It was an impossible task even when they knew the stakes to be unmistakably high.

Every sister faced a similar pattern of interrogation. Sessions opened with a lengthy examination by Bigbee. His inquiries were followed by a shorter cross-examination, usually by Barker or Fahy, followed in turn by a brief re-direct and if necessary a re-cross. Direct examinations were made up of several often-returned-to lines of questioning. Bigbee always began by asking a sister to sum up her professional experience and her responsibilities as an educator. Having set the scene, he then settled into asking questions designed to prove the plaintiffs' allegations. Did the sister teach catechism, and where and at what time? Did the sister display religious imagery in her classroom or distribute Catholic literature during school hours? Did the sister excuse children to attend confession or lead them in Catholic prayers throughout the day? Did the sister wear her habit when she taught? Bigbee's questions highlighted those parts—and only those parts—of a sister's routine he expected the court would interpret as uniquely Catholic. The nonsectarian activities that religious included in their classrooms as part of the state curriculum were irrelevant to the plaintiffs' case. With their scripted quality, these direct examinations dictated sisters' responses before they spoke. Bigbee had no reason to sit back and allow witnesses to explain teaching in their own terms; his job was to steer the women to reflect only upon the most controversial activities their teaching involved.

Some sisters had an easier time on the stand than others. One relative success story came from Maura McDonald, who summarized her experience in a letter to her motherhouse in Michigan. Nine Dominicans from Grand Rapids were subpoenaed to testify during the *Zellers* trial, and it came as no surprise that Sister Maura—with her work as superintendent in Peñasco and her years of teaching in the state—was one of the women selected. Sister Maura received the news on a Monday, one week into the trial. Like other subpoenaed sisters, she prepared for her debut in court by attending a series of exhaustive prep sessions in Santa Fe, staged by Barker and the NCWC legal team. Sister Maura did not enjoy the sessions. "I had my conscience examined in fine shape if I ever did," she recalled sourly.[76] It seemed like everyone the sister met had a nugget of advice for her to take to court. Most worried the seasoned McDonald would appear *too* confident on the stand. Bradley cautioned her to act humbly as she responded to questions, while a fellow sister recommended she resist folding her arms for fear of appearing "too pugnacious." Her attorney's secretary even poked a bit of fun at Sister Maura's predicament, warning the strong-willed sister "not to let them get me mad."[77]

All of this chatter fed her jitters, and the sister spent a sleepless Sunday night and a Monday morning with butterflies fluttering madly in her stomach. She was finally called to the stand after mid-afternoon recess. As she left her seat in the gallery, Sister Maura felt her emotions change abruptly. Her self-assurance returned:

> As I walked up the length of the courtroom to the witness stand I felt a
> mighty urge [sic] of confidence. Never in my life have I felt so definitely
> and so consistently the effect of prayers. I was completely at ease. Remem-
> bering Sister E's advice, I fixed myself in the chair as comfortable as I
> could. . . . From then on the victory was mine. . . . [Bigbee] kept me there
> for thirty-five minutes, through which I smiled consistently. He was nice,
> too, and we got along well. The nuns said I looked as if I was really enjoy-
> ing myself. I was at certain points . . . Zellers and Bowen and two minis-
> ters kept whispering directions and passing papers to Bigbee telling him
> things he had evidently forgotten. Finally he just pushed them aside and
> paid no attention. I think he must have seen my smiles at their antics.[78]

While testifying, Sister Maura did have to make one admission about excusing
students for confession, but she prided herself for acting as though she thought
nothing of it. "In this way," she explained to her sisters, "they did not press us for
explanations that could have been worse than they were." "God was good to us,"
she surmised.[79] Sister Maura's steadiness in the face of questioning was not lost on
her audience. A sister who shared the courtroom with her that day still remembered her performance six decades later, recalling that even the "enemy" was "just
enthralled with her."[80]

Not all women religious shared the Dominican's confidence; the frayed nerves
Sister Maura put behind her were probably closer to the norm for most women
when they testified. Each sister arrived on the witness stand with well-rehearsed
answers to some questions but found herself ill prepared to tackle others thrown
her way. While Sister Maura had been able to fall back upon her experience and
poise, different religious responded to hostile questioning differently. When boxed
in by evidence they had taught Catholicism, some women admitted to it on the
stand, but then tried to re-contextualize the allegations against them. These sisters
offered the court justifications—all of them original and some of them sincere—for
acting in the ways they had.

Sister Seraphine, who taught in Santa Cruz, tried to justify her work in this
way. At trial Bigbee confronted the Dominican with evidence her students had
recited prayers of Grace and Thanksgiving over their lunch hour. Sister Seraphine
conceded the point, but argued that such devotions were not her doing. Children,
even Protestant ones, have a natural interest in religion, she insisted. They're
inclined to pray spontaneously, without a teacher's influence. This line of argument might have sounded dubious to listeners, but Sister Seraphine's conviction
was clear as she reached for anecdotal support. To her attorneys' dismay, the sister
volunteered stories about other pious children—the Protestant girl who had
asked her for a crucifix as a "souvenir," and a non-Catholic boy who crossed himself at lunch, but only after reassuring a worried sister that "well, I want to."[81] For
many in the courtroom, Sister Seraphine's testimony sounded like proof positive

of an invidious Catholic influence.[82] The Dominican, however, seemed oblivious to this damning interpretation of her stories. "I think [children] hunger for religion of some kind," she appealed to Bigbee, in an effort to make him understand.[83] Other women who testified at trial made similar attempts to justify religion among their students. Like Sister Seraphine's account, these explanations always rested upon highly particular logic. What seemed like common sense to Catholic sisters was often irrelevant in court and deviant to others following the case.

The religious often compensated for their confusion within the legal system— and their inability to provide the answers it demanded—by eschewing candid responses altogether. Even their non-answers, however, said things about their stake in the conflict. Sometimes women religious responded to hostile lines of inquiry with comebacks that were sarcastic or smug. Other times they displayed flourishes of wit. On the second day of trial, Franciscan Sister Mary Cyrill, a high school teacher with a career that spanned three decades in New Mexico, was losing patience with her interrogator. Tired of fending off Bigbee's questions about a gate located on her school's property, Sister Mary Cyrill finally retorted, "Well, . . . if you say it is locked, it is locked!"[84] One can only guess that the scriptural echo in her words was intentional—in the sister's mind, there would have been few occasions more suitable for recalling the exchange between an accusing Pontius Pilate and Christ decorous under pressure. And what episode from Christian scripture could better intimate the confusion of the *Zellers* courtroom—a confusion born of one party's failure to understand the categories privileged in the life of another?[85] While Sister Mary Cyrill's biblical allusion might have been lost on Bigbee, there were others present in the courtroom who appreciated it a great deal. Moments after the sister's comment, Hensley halted proceedings to brusquely admonish the audience: "There is no cause for merriment, there has been no cause for merriment, and if there is cause for merriment the person responsible will have to leave the room!"[86] His reprimand suggests there was at least one sister, and probably more than one, who appreciated Sister Mary Cyrill's comment so much that she sat laughing at it as she waited her own turn to testify. The sister returned to her quips later when Bigbee tried to extract information from her about the time school buses arrived to her village. "They usually arrive by 8:30?" Bigbee asked, attempting to establish a correlation between the bus schedule and the beginning of catechism at her school. "Not all of them," Sister Mary Cyrill answered. "Sometimes they come at 10:00, sometimes 10:15, sometimes 11:00. We have lovely roads up in our district." This time Bigbee managed to keep up with the sister's banter. "And sometimes they don't come at all?" he asked her. "Exactly," she responded.[87]

The next day, another woman responded to Bigbee's questioning with a subtle mixture of pedantry and sarcasm. Bigbee had asked Sister Carmelita Mattingly, an Ursuline from Blanco, to comment on a photograph he presented to her. The image depicted a Catholic Church viewed through what Bigbee suggested was a public classroom window. The attorney hoped he could persuade the sister to confirm the proximity between the church and the public building. Sister Carmelita looked at the photograph skeptically. "The distance [can be] judged better than the distance in the picture," she surmised,

> because of the position in which the picture is taken. Now, there is another way of getting a picture. I happen to have one at home. If you get in another position on [sic] the back, ... if you take [a picture] from the mesa, from the back ... your distance relationship will look different.[88]

Bigbee had no use for Sister Carmelita's lesson in perspective as he pressed her on the image, "But that gives an approximate relation, doesn't it?" The sister remained firm: "Judging from the picture that does not give me a true picture of the distance between the church and the school."[89] Sister Carmelita had made her point. While she was at it, she was happy to draw attention to the blunder of out-of-towners, who had burst in to take pictures of her school and its surroundings with only rudimentary knowledge of the local landscape.

A confrontation between Harry Bigbee and the next witness over photographs resulted in one of the trial's most dramatic exchanges. From the beginning of her testimony, Sister Genevieve of the Poor Sisters of St. Francis was an unaccommodating witness. After the sister had avoided answering several questions, the court suddenly realized she had not been properly sworn in. Sister Genevieve was sworn in mid-testimony, but she remained unresponsive. The final straw in her interrogation came when Bigbee asked the sister to identify objects in a series of photographs. In the first exhibit, he asked her to confirm the appearance of a cross above the entrance to her school. Her reply was to the negative: "I cannot, that is the support of the electric light."

"It wouldn't be your testimony that there is no cross, would it?" Bigbee asked Sister Genevieve incredulously. "I have not seen it," was her smug reply, "the picture doesn't show it is a cross."[90]

Refusing to be misled, Bigbee brought out a second photograph, which—he suggested to this witness—depicted a shrine in the school's front yard. "And this shows the approximate relation of those two objects, doesn't it?" he asked her.

"You say it does," answered Sister Genevieve, recalling her fellow Franciscan's quip from earlier in the trial.

"I asked you if it did." Bigbee could hardly contain his anger. Still Sister Genevieve refused to budge. "I do not understand what you mean by relation, approximate relation."[91] At this point Hensley interjected and made his own exasperation with the sister's replies evident: "This examination will go no further. The witness will be excused."[92] Hensley ended Wednesday's hearing without warning, when he dismissed Sister Genevieve in the middle of her examination.

Harry Bigbee called the last sister to the stand on Monday evening. He spent one additional day interrogating witnesses sympathetic to the plaintiffs' cause, and then rested his case on Wednesday morning, the eighth day of the trial. The defense exhausted its stock of witnesses soon afterward. On Thursday, Hensley listened to closing arguments from both sides. Instead of reserving his comments for a written decision, the judge took the opportunity while the facts were fresh to make some general remarks, both about how the litigation had proceeded and about how he planned to rule. The judge surprised some in his audience when he noted first he did *not* agree with the Free Schools Committee that the "wearing of cloth creates a sectarian influence." He did, however, express a strong inclination to side with the plaintiffs on most of the issues presented in the case:

> Here we have things in addition to sectarian dress. We have the teaching of catechism; the teaching of prayers particular to one sect; literature of one sect, works of art depicting the scenes found only in the stories of or legends, or illustrations, of one sect. . . . Buildings where playgrounds are dotted with statuary and grottos peculiar to one sect. . . . In the midst of these indoctrinating influences, to say that there is still a separation of church and state in our school, we must say that they are separated only by the sound of a bell, or a sign marked "private." To any reasonable person that would be a mirage.[93]

In a moment of candor, Hensley conceded to those present that he could not altogether escape "humanistic, realistic, or idealistic impulses" that might favor the maintenance of sister-taught schools in New Mexico. He stressed, however, that the court's standard needed to be legalistic. It was not his job to determine whether separation was a desirable or an efficient standard in the state, the judge explained. Higher courts had already made that decision, and so the situation would be "measured by the yardstick handed down by [the] United States Supreme Court no later than this last Spring."[94]

Hensley also had choice words for some present in the courtroom. He had reached his conclusions about the complaint, he lectured, in spite of the lamentable behavior exhibited by parties on both sides during trial. He complimented the attorneys for their work but pointed to a deep "prejudice" permeating the parties they represented, "particularly among those who have not really studied and thought of the situation" on either side.[95] The judge also singled out the difficult demeanor—he described it as a lack of frankness—displayed by testifying witnesses. Although he spared the sisters any direct mention, Hensley offered an example of courtroom behavior that was typical for the Catholic religious. The judge reminded the audience of an exchange between Harry Bigbee and a member of the Christian Brothers during the trial. When Bigbee had asked the man to explain a photograph depicting a star-shaped decoration on his school building, the brother's only response was to suggest, improbably, that the star on his New Mexican school might actually be the state symbol for Texas.[96]

In the absence of a written decision in *Zellers*, the Archdiocese of Santa Fe maintained an outwardly hopeful disposition through the winter. Church officials hailed comments by Hensley that suggested his verdict might only extend to select defendants proven indisputably to have violated the law.[97] Privately, however, William Bradley and the NCWC legal counsel were already considering what a broader judgment against the religious would mean for public–parochial schools in the state.[98] Any lingering hopes among the defense were extinguished in early March, when the court's written decision finally appeared. Hensley's twenty-seven-page opinion was a painful blow—not only did it hold against religious instruction in public schools in all its forms, but it permanently debarred one hundred thirty-seven religious found guilty of such instruction from employment by the state. This number included nearly all the religious still teaching publicly in the New Mexico; the only sisters excepted were three Dominicans in Abiqui.[99]

Hensley also took additional steps aimed at making public–parochial compromises untenable in the future. He enjoined the use of church-owned buildings for tax-supported education. And in a pair of statements that dealt a blow directly to the archdiocese, he prohibited both textbook distribution to parochial students and the transportation of those same students on public buses.[100] In the interest of not disrupting students' schedules too severely, the plaintiffs agreed to delay the declaratory judgment enacting the reforms until the end of the 1948–49 school year.[101] A delay of this sort seemed the only reasonable course of action, given the magnitude of the work ahead. One local journalist, who offered an early estimate of the decision's material costs, predicted that along with hiring new teachers, at least twenty public school buildings would require replacement. On the parochial side, some ten thousand children would be left without textbooks, and eight hundred students without bus transportation.[102] Everyone understood the message sent by the district court's decision—it was a resounding admonishment to both church and state leaders in New Mexico, and it demanded big changes. The news dismayed residents in affected communities. After the trial, all but "about six" of the people living in Chama signed a petition expressing satisfaction with sisters' work there.[103] In response to the decision, residents of Mora, Cuba, and Guadalupita submitted similar petitions, which they addressed directly to the judge. They pleaded with him to change his mind and allow the sisters to continue teaching.[104]

Even amid these public pleas, and the scramble to locate resources for the upcoming year, defense counsel did recognize a silver lining in Hensley's decision. While the judge barred religious already teaching in the state from future employment, he had declined to prohibit religious teachers as a class. Nor had he banned the clothing that was a nonnegotiable part of most sisters' religious commitments. Under the terms of Hensley's decision, new sisters unsullied by the lawsuit might—at least in theory—come to New Mexico to teach, so long as they adhered to all the court's requirements. Before long the archdiocese began to explore the possibilities the district court's decision preserved. During the second week in March, each motherhouse that had sisters involved in the lawsuit received a letter from Bradley informing its superior of the court's findings. This communication was followed in short order by another letter, signed by Archbishop Byrne himself. The archbishop asked each superior about her inclination toward future work in New Mexico. Would she consider sending new sisters to replace those women barred from the public schools? If she would not, would she at least allow the prohibited sisters to continue teaching in the state in a parochial capacity?[105]

Both the archbishop and the NCWC's legal team were cautiously optimistic about these scenarios. They supposed superiors would feel sympathy for both the church and state in New Mexico, and that they would agree to replace the barred sisters. Their optimism, however, was short lived. By late April Byrne had received replies from several superiors, all unwilling to send replacements for the public schools. The Franciscans from St. Louis flatly refused to send another group of women to New Mexico, while the Franciscans from Oldenburg, Indiana, responded that replacements were uncertain. The Sisters of Mercy, based in Bethesda, Maryland, were indisposed to sending sisters, so much so that Byrne wrote a personal letter to Archbishop Francis Keogh of Baltimore to ask for his help persuading them to return to work in Costilla.[106] The refusal of so many communities to remain in New Mexico's public schools troubled Byrne and his advisors deeply. Communicating privately with the prelate, George Reed predicted a dire future for the contested schools "if the Mother Generals [*sic*] persist in their attitude," and if currently teaching sisters were not reinstated through a successful appeal.[107] The archbishop agreed. Byrne kept up his efforts to persuade motherhouses through the summer months, but he fared little better in the negotiations. By August he was forced to report mainly "hurtful" results.[108]

Superiors knew their sisters were in demand as parochial teachers, in New Mexico and elsewhere, and they had little incentive to send their members back into the battlefield that was the state school system. Requirements they remove religion from their classrooms put a strain on the religious mission that sisters shared, and superiors already disposed to worrying about exposure to the secularized atmosphere of public education saw no reason to prolong the ordeal. Mother Mary Victor, the new prioress general of the Grand Rapids Dominicans, summed up this sentiment when she wrote her sisters after the trial: "Our presence in the schools of New Mexico or any other schools is for only one purpose," she counseled them, "to bring God into the lives of the children. If that purpose is thwarted in the public schools it will be accomplished in some other way."[109] Of all the congregations in New Mexico, the Grand Rapids Dominicans had dedicated the most—both in resources and in personnel—to the state's schools. Now its leadership was resolute the time had come to leave. Elected to her position as the case neared trial, Mother Victor had listened to the painful stories of sisters caught up in the litigation. When Sister Maura placed a long-distance call to the motherhouse in March with news of the court's decision, Mother Victor acted quickly to bring her religious home. "God's ways are not our ways," she wrote to the Dominicans in New Mexico in the days after the decision. "His field of labor is vast: He may have other work for us to do."[110]

There was little Byrne could do to change the prioress general's mind. She did, however, agree to travel to Santa Fe to discuss the matter with the archbishop. On Holy Saturday, accompanied by a fellow sister, Mother Victor met with the prelate in his offices and explained the congregation's position. Byrne later described the prioress as being "quite decisive in informing me that no replacements will be sent."[111] For her part, Mother Victor left the meeting worried about the effect her words had upon the weary prelate. "At one time we both thought he had tears in his eyes," she confided to another sister. "Just keep in praying that what we told him was not too offensive. I'm sure I would not want to be responsible for his death."[112] In an episode that only made sense within the maze-like logic of ecclesiastical governance, Archbishop Byrne—the same man who when he sanctioned the *penitentes* had demonstrated his authority over New Mexican Catholicism with easy magnanimity—now faced the elderly prioress from Michigan with tears of disappointment in his eyes. The archbishop's hands were tied, and Mother Victor and her sisters made the decision to walk away.

Mother Victor decided the services of the Dominicans working in New Mexico were needed elsewhere. She instructed sisters not to make improvements to their convents, nor to enter into any local arrangements that would require them to remain teaching in a parochial capacity.[113] Her decision was both financial and personal. In the past, the public salaries of sisters in New Mexico had supported lay teachers in the parochial schools of their home diocese. Without these salaries, sisters themselves were needed for this work.[114] The prioress also had every desire to save her sisters from the hostility they had encountered during litigation. Even in Catholic Peñasco, where residents desperate to keep the religious petitioned the prioress general directly, and ensured her the women would be well compensated as parochial teachers, Mother Victor was resolute her decision would stand.[115] Sisters might return in a year or two, she offered, "when the bitter feeling that exists in some quarters has subsided."[116] In the meantime the congregation would keep its property in the village, and send some Dominican-educated girls (not sisters) from Michigan, to apply for jobs in the public school.[117] The sisters' departure from Peñasco in August 1949 was by every available account a sad day. "When we left they cried," one sister remembered. "And we cried."[118] While a few congregations *had* capitulated to Byrne's request to send replacements, and sister-taught public schools would persist in a diminished capacity in New Mexico over the next year and a half, the Dominicans' exit marked the end of an era. As the white-robed sisters boarded trains returning north, they joined an exodus of women religious already underway across the state.

Epilogue

Even though most Catholic religious had departed New Mexico's schools by the autumn of 1949, the *Zellers* litigation continued. Supporters of the sisters had shown early signs of relief at the district court's decision. "We consider that the Catholics—not the Protestants—have won the so-called Dixon school case," Father Küppers boasted to a local newspaper.[1] At the NCWC offices in Washington, there was consensus that Judge Hensley's unwillingness to extend a blanket ban on sisters amounted to a partial victory. This satisfaction was tempered, however, by concern over the decision's implications for parochial textbooks and bus transportation, and even more so by fear the Church might lose additional ground if the decision were appealed by either side. George Reed and others in the legal department recognized the devastating potential if the *Zellers* suit made its way to a higher court. Writing to Archbishop Byrne after the decision, the NCWC's General Secretary Howard Carroll stated the Conference's apprehension in no uncertain terms. "There is great peril for all the dioceses of the country," he wrote, "if there is an appeal ultimately to the Supreme Court of the United States."[2]

Of the district court's findings, its decision to prohibit the state from issuing textbooks to parochial schools caused the most short-term trouble for the Archdiocese of Santa Fe. The financial burden on Catholic families stood to be immense. Archbishop Byrne worried in a letter to the NCWC that without state-supplied texts "hundreds of our children, now attending parochial schools, will leave them for public schools because their parents will be unable to pay for textbooks."[3] In response to his concerns the NCWC's legal team briefly considered appealing the court's decision on this issue, but everyone in Washington recognized the defense had more to lose on appeal than it had to gain.[4] Sisters who had moved to New Mexico since the time of the lawsuit were still allowed to teach publicly in the state, and both the NCWC and the archdiocese understood this privilege could be revoked, should the plaintiffs win an appeal in a higher court on the issue of sisters' garb.[5] With religious garb so fragile an issue in the American courts in 1949, the NCWC team also worried that a decision against the habit in New Mexico might tip judicial favor against sisters' clothing nationally. These reservations were compounded by logistical challenges. Illness had forced William Barker to retire from the case after the trial, and further litigation would require the defense to reorganize and retain new local representation.[6] With these risks and challenges in mind, the defense resigned itself to Judge Hensley's ruling.

Deliberations among the plaintiffs bore different results. Although the Dixon Free Schools Committee admitted Hensley's decision "on the surface appears like a complete victory," within a few months its concessions to Catholic interests appeared glaringly evident.[7] During the summer of 1949, New Mexico's attorney general effectively invalidated the court's ban on state-funded parochial textbooks. By determining the ban's language only enjoined Catholic schools from receiving public money directly, the attorney general deemed parochial students could continue to receive state books, so long as they were not sectarian in nature.[8] Lydia Zellers and the committee were even more distressed at the news that Catholic religious were arriving in New Mexico to replace their banned counterparts, and that some had begun to teach publicly.[9] In September the plaintiffs announced their intention to appeal the district court's ruling. Their reasoning, as Harry Bigbee explained, was that Hensley's decision was not "broad enough to effectuate the doctrine of separation of church and state" in New Mexico.[10] Their target remained Catholic sisters, and their goal was still to disqualify them from public teaching—not as individuals, but as a class. Religious should be barred "not for their religious alignment," the Free Schools Committee clarified to its supporters, "but because by virtue of their vows of obedience and poverty, they are not free agents."[11]

The appeals process stretched the dispute that began in Dixon an agonizing two more years. Before the state's judicial system resolved the *Zellers* case, even the few remaining sister-taught public schools in New Mexico bent beneath the arc of separation sentiment and closed their doors. In March 1951 the state board of education quietly passed a resolution similar to that in North Dakota and other states, stating that "members of any . . . sectarian religious group, wearing clothing of religious significance, should be removed from the public schools throughout the state as expeditiously as circumstances (of) each locality allow."[12] The same month, on the NCWC's advice, Archbishop Byrne wrote to the half-dozen religious communities still involved in the state's schools and asked them at last to remove their sisters.[13] At the prelate's instruction each motherhouse wrote to inform the state board of its intention to withdraw from the public system, and in mid-April the board answered by introducing a second resolution, thanking the religious and praising their past work in the state.[14] The parting was treated as mutual, and when classes dismissed for the summer the last of New Mexico's public school sisters departed her post. When the New Mexican Supreme Court brought the *Zellers* case to an end the following September, by declaring habits worn by women religious unconstitutional in the state's classrooms, it was both offering its judicial two cents to a national conversation and laying cautionary protocol for future generations of New Mexicans, but it was not affecting any behavior that survived on the ground. Sister-taught public schools were a thing of the past in New Mexico.[15]

During the *Zellers* litigation the Catholic *Santa Fe Register* published several political cartoons. One drawing carried the caption "Well, We Got the Nuns Out!" and depicted two thin men—"Separation Boys"—marching in self-satisfied tandem. Between them they carried a judicial gavel the size of a battering ram, and in their wake they left the pitiable, shattered remains of a public schoolhouse.[16] The reality of schooling in New Mexico after *Zellers* was less fantastic; the lawsuit transformed public education in the state but did not topple it. The disentanglement of the parochial and public systems included disruptive episodes to be sure—like in Mora, where an assailant set fire to a public school still being run by the Sisters of Loretto in 1949, or in Dixon, where new lay faculty were dogged by accusations of gross moral laxity.[17] Residents of one Rio Arriba town even filed a counter-suit, accusing Protestant public teachers of indiscretions that paralleled those of the Catholic religious—including inviting missionaries to their classrooms, holding commencement exercises at Baptist and Presbyterian churches, and making Presbyterian literature available to students.[18] Upon reviewing this second piece of litigation, the district and high courts in New Mexico agreed the offending Protestant teachers should also be barred from public employment.

Despite these growing pains, most communities made the transition to dual school systems without major incident. In some towns, public schools or classrooms were converted or reconverted into parochial spaces and sisters continued to teach in them. In other locations, sisters withdrew from the local public schools and moved into privately funded and newly built parochial buildings. Often sisters brought their students with them, causing public enrollment in certain villages to decline dramatically. Public schools that lost students consolidated and towns that lost their only public schools to the parochial system began sending their remaining students by bus to nearby (relatively speaking) consolidated schools. A growing network of paved roads in the state made the work of consolidation easier. The odd public student who remained in Parkview began to travel to school in Tierra Amarilla, while in Villanueva a school that had lost nearly its entire student body when its religious teachers left gained new life as a consolidated building.[19] After St. Joseph's School in Dixon closed, its students began attending public high school twenty miles downriver in Española.[20] Meanwhile Peñasco officials found lay teachers to replace the Dominicans in their schools, though they also held onto a lease agreement with the local parish against the court's orders. Their rented building became home to a consolidated public institution for the region.[21] The thinned-out public system in New Mexico would eventually recover its enrollment and, with the help of improved salaries and retirement benefits, attract a new generation of teachers. For many observers, however, the immediate success story in New Mexico seemed to be that of parochial education.[22] Parochial enrollment in the state boomed after 1948 as students followed their teachers out of the state system. Even without the benefit of public funds, twenty-six Catholic schools opened in the Archdiocese of Santa Fe in the five years after Hensley's decision—an increase that more than doubled the number in existence before the *Zellers* lawsuit began.[23]

Leaving public employment was a relief for many women religious. Most were happy to relinquish the responsibility of looking for compromises between their religious vocation and the laws of the state. Though she wrote a decade before the last sister departed New Mexico's classrooms, Bertrande Meyers predicted the alienating experience public education became for these women:

> A definite amount of control was asked in exchange for a definite amount of aid. Relegation of Religion to outside-of-school hours, elimination from the classroom of symbols of Religion save where a "Madonna" could claim exemption as a work of art, the use of non-Catholic textbooks, all would combine to deprive a Catholic school of that spirit of the supernatural . . . and place its teachers in a practically alien atmosphere.[24]

In her 1941 study *The Education of Sisters*, Meyers lamented the sacrifices women religious like those in New Mexico made as they struggled under secular educational models. Proximity to the public system, she argued, limited sisters' ability to work in their own style and in doing so develop a sophisticated and coherent Catholic pedagogy. It even made sisters incapable of appreciating the resources public education had to offer. "Too long we have either imitated secular teacher training and tried to make our theology of education merely an adjunct to it or underestimated the value of genuine finds of secular educators," the Daughter of Charity wrote. "Our need today is a great Catholic synthesis of teacher training which will bring into our work of education the fullness of our Catholic education ideal."[25]

Meyers' work, which also included a proposal for training novices before they entered the classroom to teach, became a catalyst in the lives of American women religious in the mid-1950s. The founding of the Sister Formation Conference (SFC) in 1952, a sister-directed initiative affiliated with the National Catholic Education Association, marked a new drive among congregations to increase opportunities for professional development available to novices and young sisters, and to improve both the intellectual and spiritual quality of those opportunities.[26] Through regular meetings and workshops, a published bulletin, and curriculum development, the Conference encouraged superiors across the country to grant sisters a period for study beyond the novitiate, and it advised congregations and Catholic women's colleges to broaden the scope of sisters' training to include subjects like sociology, political science, and current events.[27] The Conference's impact upon religious life in the United States extended beyond the educational sphere. In the words of historian Mary Schneider, the SFC "afforded the first opportunity for serious and extended cooperation among religious communities on both the regional and national level . . . [and] was the most influential factor in preparing for and initiating change within religious congregations in the 1950s and 1960s."[28] This forward thinking and pan-congregational effort coincided closely with the end of sisters' work as public educators nationwide during the mid-1950s. Without a doubt, Bertrande Meyers and her protégés at the SFC applauded the exodus of women religious from public schools, as a move that freed sisters from the onus of "imitating secular teaching" and allowed them to commit their intellectual energy to the internal housekeeping of the formation movement. At the same time, there is an irony to the timing of their departure amid the enthusiasm of sister formation. The congregational directives that *ended* women's formal engagement with the public sphere were part and parcel to the formation efforts that historians praise as foundational to the publicly engaged "new nuns" of the Vatican II era.

The religious formation project of the 1950s also paralleled the unremitting efforts of Catholic legal minds to compose a doctrinally coherent reading of American constitutional law, and in particular of the relationship between the church and the state. Each of these Catholic impulses—to religious formation and to constitutional theory—developed within an American Church unsettled by allegations of anti-intellectualism, and their agendas carried added urgency as a result. It would be several years before John Courtney Murray's theological interventions rescued a generation of floundering Catholic constitutional scholars. In a dramatic reversal of the priest's decade-long silencing on church–state topics, the Vatican Council invited Murray to Rome in 1963 to participate in its second session. During his visit Murray agreed to assist in drafting the Council's own Declaration on Religious Freedom, *Dignitatis Humanae*. The Vatican's 1965 Declaration found it "greatly in accord with truth and justice" that "constitutional limits should be set to the powers of government, in order that there may be no encroachment on the rightful freedom of the person." It is necessary for the preservation of both peace and human dignity, the Council concluded, "that religious freedom be everywhere provided with an effective constitutional guarantee."[29] This belated but resounding endorsement of Murray's scholarship on religious liberty gave American Catholics—for the first time—a doctrinally sound framework for claiming their collective rights under the First Amendment during the 1960s. Among its promising potential, the Declaration presented a new opportunity for Catholic legal advocates to build a religious freedom defense of the still-unsettled existence of sisters' habits in public classrooms.

By the time Catholics found their voice in American conversations about religious liberty, however, the national debate over sisters' clothing had ended. The flexibility the Church had shown when it permitted sisters to remove their garb to teach in North Dakota in 1948 turned out to be a portent of attitudes changing at the highest level. A series of Vatican communications, first from Pius XII in 1952 and later from the bishops' council, made it easier and more acceptable—even expected—for women religious to modify their traditional garb or replace it altogether.[30] In its Decree on the Adaptation and Renewal of Religious Life, *Perfectae*

Caritatis, published in the same year as its Declaration on Religious Freedom, the Vatican Council instructed:

> The religious habit ... should be simple and modest, poor and at the same time becoming. In addition it must ... be suited to the circumstances of time and place and to the needs of the ministry involved. The habits of both men and women religious which do not conform to these norms must be changed.[31]

A decade after sisters were banned from wearing religious garb in New Mexico, fewer and fewer women religious felt pressure to work in the habit at all. This changing fashion was a monumental shift in the lives of many American sisters; adopting ordinary clothing revolutionized how Catholics and non-Catholics thought about and interacted with them, and it altered how the women thought about themselves.[32] The outward transformation of sisters was of secondary importance, however, in the chain of events that made the habit's legal status obsolete. Habits or no habits, religious congregations had already pulled nearly all their members from public employment during the decade following the *Zellers* suit. Motivated by pressure from the NCWC, and by their own desire to protect sisters from situations that carried potential to corrupt their characters and their commitments, superiors across the country transferred their teaching members to cut-and-dried parochial work. The erasure of mandatory clothing among women religious was preempted by a simple fact—by the 1960s sisters were all but gone from American public schools.

The two decades after the *Zellers* lawsuit also brought big changes for the national advocacy groups involved in the litigation. By the end of the 1960s both the NCWC and POAU were nearly unrecognizable, and the stolid opposition that characterized their early relationship with one another was gone. The NCWC formally divided in 1967 into two different but related organizations—the National Conference of Catholic Bishops (NCCB) and the United States Catholic Conference (USCC).[33] The NCCB, which as its name suggests was composed wholly of American ecclesiastics, turned its attention to developing policy to guide the nation's hierarchy. The USCC provided the administrative muscle needed for that policy's implementation among Catholic laity, and continued to manage the American Church's general social engagement. George Reed remained of counsel for the USCC until at least 1980, but as the Church's relationship to American culture changed, so did the emphasis of his legal department. As time passed other areas of legislative and judicial activity—particularly those dealing with abortion rights and other "life issues"—redirected the department's attention from its intensive early focus on public money and the schools.[34]

By the late 1960s, POAU had endured a transformation more radical than its Catholic counterpart. That decade arrived with new tests for the First Amendment's

Establishment Clause. The captive school litigation that had energized POAU during the 1940s and 1950s was replaced by the next generation of lawsuits targeting prayer and Bible reading. When the U.S. Supreme Court took up these issues in *Engel v. Vitale* in 1962 and *Abington v. Schempp* in 1963, it invoked separation and found both activities unconstitutional in public classrooms. For many Americans, the Court's back-to-back decisions cast Protestant religiosity and First Amendment jurisprudence against one another in a definite way.[35] POAU supported the Court's position in both *Engel* and *Schempp* as consistent with its pledge to defend separation, and its decision to do so irreparably fractured the alliance of conservative and liberal Protestants that had characterized the organization's early Catholic crusades. By the mid-1960s, members of the conservative and evangelical churches that had formed POAU's popular base during the 1950s began to acknowledge they had more in common with Catholics in their anti-secularist interpretations of the First Amendment than with their former colleagues. Meanwhile the 1972 decision of POAU's liberal leadership to shorten the organization's name to Americans United for Separation of Church and State was symbolic—both of a conscious self-distancing from the group's Protestant roots, and of an intellectual reorientation away from its binary relationship with the Catholic Church.[36]

The rapid exit of Catholic sisters from American public education, and the overhaul of the advocacy organizations that called attention to their teaching, make it difficult to imagine the cultural visibility of these women just a few decades ago. The steep decline in congregational membership since the mid-1960s has meant that today sisters are out-of-the-ordinary figures in most American public spaces. Catholic habits are even rarer occurrences—in the twenty-first century one is hard pressed to find a habit in a parochial school, much less a public one. Despite the fact that women religious and their costumes have faded from prominence and controversy in the United States, the public debates they inspired still have cultural relevance—more so today, in fact, than at any time since the 1950s. Clothing remains one of the most recognizable and most contested markers of religious commitment within civil society. Contests over religious dress within public spaces have persisted since the decline of captive schools, and especially in Europe those fights are more acrimonious than ever. In the United States, laws written to prohibit sisters' habits more than a century ago apply to teachers wearing other types of clothing today.

In the past decade France has grabbed international headlines with laws that target the outfits of Muslim women. In a 2004 move aimed at restricting Islamic headscarves, the French legislature prohibited the wearing of "conspicuously religious symbols" by both teachers and students in public schools.[37] Recently the legislature approved a broader ban on full facial veils in public places, from government offices to hospitals to mass transportation.[38] This new law enjoys strong support among the French people; its advocates argue the enveloping *niqāb* worn by a small percentage of Muslim women poses a security threat by concealing the identity of its wearer.[39] These safety concerns are joined inextricably in supporters' arguments with loftier appeals to the values of French Republicanism. Islamic veils, their opponents assert, are at odds with the nation's responsibility to preserve public spaces where citizens can contribute fruitfully and freely to their society.[40] The veils defy this ideal by fostering communalism and denigrating women. French president Nicolas Sarkozy took a popular line in 2009 when he remarked that "the problem of the burqa [sic] . . . is a problem of liberty and the dignity of women. It is a sign of servitude and degradation."[41] André Gerin, a Communist Party member who was instrumental in the creation of the latest statute, adopted a more alarmist tone when he cautioned that "Islamism really threatens us. . . . It is time to take a stand on this issue that concerns thousands of citizens who are worried to see imprisoned, totally veiled women."[42] This coupling of values—national security with personal freedom and women's equality—has proven a compelling mix across the political spectrum and across Western Europe, with lawmakers in Belgium and elsewhere pushing for similar legislation in recent years.[43]

American secularism is not the *laïcité* of French Republicanism.[44] Regardless of opposition to Islamic garb in some quarters of society, the First Amendment's free exercise guarantee makes any equivalent to France's public clothing ban impossible in the United States. Because the Constitution's protections extend to public education, students across this country wear headscarves and other items of religious apparel in class with minimal controversy.[45] For American teachers the situation remains more complicated. As of 2011 forty-eight states permitted public teachers to wear religious clothing in their classrooms. Two states, Nebraska and Pennsylvania, maintain garb statutes originally designed to restrict Catholic sisters' dress when they taught.[46] Pennsylvania's law is the same one its legislature passed shortly after the *Hysong* decision in 1894. Despite the tenuous constitutional terrain these anti-garb statutes tread, the U.S. Supreme Court has (still) never commented on their legality. The only federal opinion on religious clothing in the United States came in 1984 in the case of Alima Delores Reardon, a devout Muslim who lost her job in Philadelphia after she refused to remove her *hijab* while teaching. Considering Reardon's case on appeal, the Third Circuit agreed with the precedent set by most, though not all, state courts that evaluated sisters' habits earlier in the century. It concluded that garb laws like Pennsylvania's *are* constitutional, citing they "advance a compelling interest in maintaining the appearance of religious neutrality in the public school classroom." State governments, the court determined, may restrict their employees' clothing—even when those regulations explicitly prohibit religious dress.[47]

The concerns that inspired Pennsylvania's statute, and those that fed the captive school litigation of the mid-twentieth century, are analogous in some ways to European protests of the Islamic veil today. It's important to be cautious here—after all, not only is French *laïcité* different from American church–state separation, but Islam is not Catholicism, and the fears of post-9/11 Europe are not those of a post-World War II United States. Still, the parallels that exist are meaningful. Groups looking to restrict clothing on both sides of the Atlantic have expressed concern about the expanding political influence of religious traditions that value non-transparency and radical submission. Both have questioned the ability of those religions' most loyal adherents to participate within civil society. Like their French counterparts, Paul Blanshard and other American critics of garb evoked specters of female imprisonment and servitude when they described their opponents. And like Sarkozy they cast themselves proudly as defenders of both national security and women's freedoms. In France and in the United States, arguments against the veil have shared a raw, sometimes even derisive, character that is indicative of the high stakes of the conflicts recognized by those involved.

In the United States, the Catholic habit was provocative not only because it was a religious influence, but because it disturbed a set of closely held sensibilities—and visual proclivities—among people who beheld it. By mid-century these proclivities were extensions of a civil imagination as much as they were a religious one. Like the French, Americans hold common if not universal assumptions about acceptable dress, about the proper appearance of figures who populate their public spaces. The importance of appearance to American identity was never more evident than during captive school litigation. Facing threats overseas, men and women were looking for tangible ways to feel a part of their nation's higher purpose at mid-century. In an era when the character of that purpose wavered uncertainly between older Protestant and new secular articulations, Americans with differing ideas or private ambivalences relied upon common symbols, and visual cues in particular, for grounding that otherwise unsettled civil identity. Nowhere were patriotic sights held in greater prestige—or understood as more powerful imaginative occasions—than in the nation's public schools. If a civil religion exists, then mid-century classrooms were the locations where American children were catechized visually into its mysteries.[48] For parents and lawmakers intent on guiding students toward lofty democratic principles, the minutiae of classroom interiors—from the flag in the corner, to the map on the wall, to the cut of the teacher's dress—mattered immensely. Catholic habits were arresting sights when they showed up in these public schools, and Protestant Americans in particular feared they would spark children's imaginations toward a troubling set of religious *and* civil possibilities. Like the Islamic veil in France today, the habit with its air of concealment and submission represented the limit (or at least one limit) of what many considered appropriate clothing for American democracy at mid-century.

Considered alongside Islamic veil controversies, disputes over the Catholic habit contribute to a cross-cultural commentary on the role of correctly appointed bodies within the construction and maintenance not only of religious identity, but also of national identity. Whether that national identity is oriented around the quasi-Protestant liberalism of the 1940s United States or twenty-first-century

French Republicanism, clothing controversies suggest its common markers are not only a set of abstract tenets, but also a field of images and other sensory phenomena that orient individuals as loyal parties to their American or Francophone worlds. Everyday objects can inspire reflection on a nation's higher purpose and they can also inspire visceral fear on that nation's behalf. As in conventional religions, the appearance and comportment of the human body especially, including the clothing that adorns it, acts in civil societies as an occasion for this sort of elevated contemplation as well as the deep disquiet that can result. As POAU's opposition to the Catholic habit made clear, clothing sometimes does its work in ways that also end up exposing the indeterminate boundaries between the civil and the conventionally religious for many citizens. The Dixon case spoke to the high civil stakes involved in bodily appearance, as they existed for the American public in 1948. Debates over the Islamic veil suggest similar stakes involved in bodily appearance in Western Europe today.

Memories of the Dixon litigation faded slowly in New Mexico. Even years later, after a new public school had opened in Peñasco and the Grand Rapids Dominicans had returned to teach in its parochial counterpart, locals still talked remorsefully about the sisters' departure from their high school.[49] In Dixon itself, the *Zellers* case remained a sore subject long after the lawsuit's main protagonists had gone. "It hurt a lot," former student Delia Garcia remembered.[50] Children forced to travel to other public schools in other towns after the Franciscans left resented the lifestyle change. "I thought it was very unfair as a child," Edna Garcia explained, "very unfair that we had to go to the public school."[51] Ten-year-old Francisco Romero was sent by his parents to stay with a cousin in Española during the week, so that he might attend classes there. "It was kind of hard," he recalled. "I remember I used to watch the traffic go by and I would cry."[52] Though still a child, Romero was aware of the animosity that lingered between religious groups in Dixon after the lawsuit ended. "It was a long period before we got back to where we were before all this started—and that was both sides," he remembered. Relations between Presbyterians and Catholics in the village became so strained there was talk of a schism or rift between the churches for decades after the decision.[53] Young people who had never known either Peter Küppers or the Franciscans held onto their parents' stories and to their parents' anger over the feud that had torn the community in two. Children growing up in Dixon in the 1950s, 1960s, and 1970s learned that religious allegiance came with complicated social codes and expectations in their village.

Dixon's troubles finally ended—symbolically at least—on a stormy May afternoon in 1999. On the Sunday of Pentecost, residents from the village gathered to heal old wounds. In what one observer declared a "historic reconciliation," several hundred Catholics and Protestants walked together between the Embudo Presbyterian Church and St. Anthony's Catholic parish, across the road from one another, and paused respectfully to listen to sermons inside of each.[54] Both the Archbishop of Santa Fe and the regional presbyter of the Presbyterian Church were in attendance, and the two men smiled broadly as they signed an agreement affirming their intent to work for the common good of all New Mexicans. Also sitting in attendance were several special guests—white-haired women who, as young sisters fifty years earlier, had run the classrooms that fomented so much division. It was a reflective event, but it was also a pleasant one. People commemorated the past and applauded how far the little town had come in the half-century since Judge Hensley's fateful decision. Some shed tears. "It's a big thing," one elderly Embudo resident mused of the reconciliation to a reporter on the scene. "I never thought it would happen."[55]

NOTES

Introduction

1. Transcript of Testimony, *Zellers v. Huff*, no. 5332, legal documents on microfilm, Clerk's Office of the Supreme Court of New Mexico, Santa Fe, New Mexico (cited hereafter as *Zellers* documents), 1557–58.
2. Transcript of Record ("Complaint"), *Zellers* documents, 1.
3. According to the National Catholic Welfare Conference, 1,218 sisters were teaching publicly in 1948. This figure is likely low, since dioceses were reluctant to report the extent of the practice and the number was taken from a survey to which less than three quarters of American dioceses responded. A decade later POAU estimated that over two thousand sisters were teaching publicly, and this was after ten years of litigation and threatened legal action had already forced hundreds if not thousands of sisters from public schools across the nation (Howard J. Carroll, "'Catholic-Public' School Arrangement," memorandum, National Catholic Welfare Conference/United States Catholic Conference Collection, American Catholic History Research Center and University Archives, Catholic University of America [cited hereafter as NCWC Collection]; "Protest at the Grass Roots," *Church and State* 12, no. 10 [1959]: 2).
4. Gordon, *The Spirit of the Law: Religious Voices and the Constitution in Modern America* (Cambridge, MA: Harvard University Press, 2010), 78.
5. Transcript of Testimony, 1827–28.
6. *Zellers v. Huff*. 55 N.M. 501 (1951).
7. Ibid.
8. Frank J. Sorauf, *The Wall of Separation: The Constitutional Politics of Church and State* (Princeton: Princeton University Press, 1976), 247.
9. Although the terms "nun" and "sister" are often conflated with one another, even in scholarly work, they reference different categories of Catholic women religious. While a *nun* is a member of a cloistered order, a *sister* is a member of an active order. Although the women who taught in New Mexico all came from active orders, they were referred to as sisters and nuns interchangeably by residents, by the courts, and even in Catholic journals like *America*.
10. See Clifford Geertz, "Local Knowledge: Fact and Law in Comparative Perspective," *Local Knowledge: Further Essays in Interpretive Anthropology* (New York: Basic Books, Inc., 1983); Robert Cover, "Nomos and Narrative," Foreword, *Harvard Law Review* 97, no. 4 (1983). I follow Geertz and Cover in two premises here: (1) that a legal principle like church–state separation, and its underlying normative assumption of a public–parochial distinction, have differently derived resonances in the varied cultures and religions that participate in America

legal system, and (2) that legal ideas are always in conversation with apparatuses of government but hardly ever coextensive with them. Geertz proposed the relativity of law working on a deep, epistemological level: "Law . . . is local knowledge; local not just to place, time, class, and variety of issue, but as to accent—vernacular characterizations of what happens connected to vernacular imaginings of what can" (Geertz, "Local Knowledge," 215). For Geertz a culture's legal knowledge is premised upon a shared sense of what is possible, and that sense of possibility is tied to a framework of what is right. This model of law, as an *a priori* yet culturally grounded set of sensibilities that give events meaning, was extended to American constitutional law by Cover. The foundational plane of possibility that Geertz called *the real*—"a deeply moralized, active, demanding real"—Cover defined as a *nomos* (Ibid. 188; Cover, "Nomos and Narrative"). Cover confined his model to religious communities; a nomos is assembled from the elemental narratives that bind people around a religion. The nomoi of American religious groups are responsible for their respective relationships to First Amendment principles. The correlation between communities' "vernacular" legal systems and the nomoi underlying them, and the codified American laws they share between them, is an idea I carry forward from Geertz and Cover.

11. My use of the terms "secular" and "secularism" throughout this book recalls the ways in which they were used during mid-century education debates. "Secular" was used by both its critics and its supporters to describe an educational model that excluded elements distinct to Christianity and other major religious traditions from state-funded classrooms. For critics especially, "secularism" further implied a closed ideological system, hostile to religion and competing against it for control of American education. Recent scholarship has demonstrated that secularism itself is a historically situated and culturally relevant category. One can argue with good reason that secular standards were enforced (if differently understood) in the United States before the mid-twentieth century. One can argue with equally good reason that after the 1960s—and even today—public classrooms remain anything but secular. Tracy Fessenden, for example, argues that Protestantism itself fostered the development of secularism during the nineteenth century as it began to fade into the woodwork as an "unmarked" if dominant influence within American public life (Tracy Fessenden, *Culture and Redemption: Religion, the Secular and American Literature* [Princeton: Princeton University Press, 2006], 6). On the internal dynamics of secularization, see also Christian Smith, ed., *The Secular Revolution: Power, Interests and Conflict in the Secularization of American Public Life* (Berkeley: University of California Press, 2003). On the global relationship of religion to secularism in the twentieth century, see Jose Casanova, *Public Religions in the Modern World* (Chicago: University of Chicago Press, 1994).

12. See James Davison Hunter, *Culture Wars: The Struggle to Define America* (New York: Basic Books, 1991).

13. The geographer Richard Nostrand famously referred to this region as the "Hispano homeland." Using nineteenth- and twentieth-century census records of surnames, racial designations, and parentage, Nostrand argued for the ethnic distinctiveness of northern New Mexico's Spanish-speaking residents. Scholars after Nostrand have made damaging criticisms of his characterization, pointing out the one-dimensionality of his method, his exclusion of Native Americans, and his assumption of Hispano as a naturalized rather than a cultivated identity (Richard Nostrand, *The Hispano Homeland* [Norman: University of Oklahoma Press, 1992]).

14. For a succinct explanation of the New Mexican land grant system, as well as the long history of litigation arising from it, see Robert J. Torrez, "New Mexico's Spanish and Mexican Land Grants," New Mexican Genealogical Society, http://www.nmgs.org/artlandgrnts.htm (accessed Sept. 27, 2007); "Land Grants," New Mexico Commission of Public Records State Records Center and Archives, http://www.nmcpr.state.nm.us/archives/land_grants.htm (accessed Sept. 27, 2007).

15. In addition, the Christian Brothers were responsible for public schools in the community of Las Vegas.

16. Frederick Mason Bacon, "Contributions of Catholic Religious Orders to Public Education in New Mexico Since the American Occupation" (M.A. thesis, University of New Mexico, 1947), 72, 77, 93.

17. Qtd. in Harold E. Fey, *With Sovereign Reverence: The First Twenty-Five Years of Americans United* (Rockville, MD: Roger Williams Press, 1974), 9.

18. Philip Hamburger, *Separation of Church and State* (Cambridge: Harvard University Press, 2002), 192.

19. *Engel v. Vitale*, 370 U.S. 421 (1962); *School District of Abington Township v. Schempp*, 374 U.S. 203 (1963). The Court assumes a "wall of separation" in the former, and in the latter grounds its reasoning in *Everson* and *McCollum* directly. Although the trajectory toward the removal of formal religious influence from public classrooms guides my story, the Court acknowledged that—particularly when it came to activity located outside the walls of public schools—its "wall of separation" had limits both before and after *Engel*. In its 1952 decision in *Zorach v. Clauson*, the Court determined students were able to leave public schools during class time for private, off-campus religious instruction (*Zorach v. Clauson*, 343 U.S. 306 (1952)). In its 1971 decision in *Lemon v. Kurtzman* the Court decided against a state law allowing public reimbursement for secular textbooks and salaries of teachers who taught secular subjects within parochial schools, but in doing so it acknowledged that "total separation is not possible in an absolute sense. . . . the line of separation, far from being a 'wall,' is a blurred, indistinct, and variable barrier depending on all the circumstances of a particular relationship" (*Lemon v. Kurtman*, 403 U.S. 602 (1971)).

20. Hamburger, *Separation of Church and State*, 391–478.

21. Patricia Byrne, "In the Parish But Not of It: Sisters," *Transforming Parish Ministry: The Changing Roles of Catholic Clergy, Laity, and Women Religious*, eds. Jay P. Dolan, R. Scott Appleby, Patricia Byrne, and Debra Campbell (New York: Crossroad, 1990), 133.

22. Gordon, *Spirit of the Law*, 84.

23. Hamburger, *Separation of Church and State*, 360.

24. The decision recognized the incorporation of the First Amendment into the Fourteenth Amendment's due process clause. *Everson v. Board of Education*, 330 U.S. 16 (1947), 16.

25. See my estimate of two thousand sisters teaching publicly at any given time in the United States (see Introduction, note 3). If each sister presided over a class of twenty students (a low estimate by post-World War II Catholic educational standards), then 40,000 students were attending public–parochial schools during any year in the late 1940s and 1950s. The actual total is likely higher. Adding parents to this number puts the estimate of lay Catholics directly invested in public–parochial education closer to 100,000.

26. During the nineteenth century the federal government distributed funding to religious communities, including Catholic religious, to run Indian schools, but this practice was discontinued at the turn of the century. In 1912 the U.S. Commissioner of Indian Affairs issued an independent order that any Catholic sisters still teaching in federally run Indian schools must remove their religious garb while teaching. Although a very few American Indian children did eventually attend New Mexico's sister-taught public schools, the large majority was enrolled in federal boarding or day schools during the first half of the twentieth century and therefore did not participate in the dispute over the character of the state system. On the history of American Indian education, in New Mexico and the United States broadly, see Margaret Szasz, *Education and the American Indian* (Albuquerque: University of New Mexico Press, 1974); Jon Reyhner and Jeannne Eder, *American Indian Education* (Norman: University of Oklahoma Press, 2004); Sally Hyer, *One House, One Voice, One Heart: Native American Education at the Santa Fe Indian School* (Santa Fe: Museum of New Mexico Press, 1990). On Catholic Indian schools, see Theresa McNeil, "Catholic Indian Schools of the Southwest Frontier: Curriculum and Management," *Southern California Quarterly* 72, no. 4 (1990): 321–28.

27. My use of the term "Hispano" in this book refers to the collective, self-consciously Spanish identity of many residents of nineteenth- and twentieth-century New Mexico. It is not synonymous with all Spanish-speaking New Mexicans, as some American Indians in the region have spoken Spanish for centuries. Nor is it synonymous with a broader category like "Latino." New Mexico's Hispanos have historically distinguished themselves from "Mexicans" living to the south as well as more recent "Mexican" immigrants to their region. For historical analyses of Hispano identity in New Mexico, see John Nieto-Phillips, *The Language of Blood* (Albuquerque: University of New Mexico Press, 2004); Charles Montgomery, *The Spanish Redemption* (Berkeley: University of California Press, 2002).

28. Byrne, "In the Parish," 135, 141.

29. This conservatism has prompted historians to dismiss the period between 1917 and the 1950s as a "virtual ice age" and a "process of fossilization" for Catholic women religious (Carol Coburn and Martha Smith, *Spirited Lives: How Nuns Shaped Catholic Culture and American Life, 1836–1920* [Chapel Hill: University of North Carolina Press, 1999], 225; Byrne, "In the Parish," 117). While I don't reject the characterization of the post-1917 years as conservative or even repressive, I believe it's important to question the assumptions that underlie the scholarly dismissal of sisters who lived during them. Feminist scholars looking for evidence of self-governance, subversion of gender norms, or other forms of empowerment; as well as scholars interested in social activism or ecumenism, are among those who skirt this era when considering women religious. For scholarship that focuses on sisters and public activism during earlier and later periods see Maureen Fitzgerald, *Habits of Compassion: Irish Catholics and the Origins of New York's Welfare System, 1830–1920* (Urbana, IL: University of Illinois Press, 2006); Amy Koehlinger, *The New Nuns: Racial Justice and Religious Reform in the 1960s* (Cambridge: Harvard University Press, 2007). See also Lora Ann Quinonez and Mary Daniel Turner, *The Transformation of American Catholic Sisters* (Philadelphia: Temple University Press, 1993). Kathleen Sprows Cummings also stays in the immediate pre-1917 period but highlights tension between Catholic and American notions of gender during this era, as well as less obvious locations of social power (Kathleen Sprows Cummings, *New Women of the Old Faith: Gender and American Catholicism in the Progressive Era* [Chapel Hill: University of North Carolina Press, 2009]). Scholarship on women in other (non-Catholic) conservative religious communities reveals the limitations of analytic models that take as normative categories like "empowerment" or "choice." These approaches privilege the non-feminist frameworks of value women often inhabit. They open up new possibilities for studying Catholic women religious during the post-1917 era and for thinking about the conservative elements of their religious practice, including their habits, their cloister, and their vows of obedience. See R. Marie Griffith, *God's Daughters* (Berkeley: University of California Press, 1997); Saba Mahmood, *Politics of Piety* (Princeton: Princeton University Press, 2005); Carolyn Rouse, *Engaged Surrender: African American Women and Islam* (Berkeley: University of California Press, 2004).

30. I see no inherent difference between lived and intellectual approaches to history; the "breach" described here appears in light of the divergent themes each tends to take as its own. For an example of a "lived" approach see Robert Orsi, *Between Heaven and Earth: The Religious Worlds People Make and the Scholars Who Study Them* (Princeton: Princeton University Press, 2005); for an "intellectual" approach see John McGreevy, *Catholicism and American Freedom* (New York: W. W. Norton & Co., 2003). Orsi and McGreevy's studies of pre-Vatican II American Catholicism capture different sets of voices (Orsi's the underrepresented voices of women, children, and cripples; McGreevy's the voices of Catholic intellectuals and activists, underrepresented albeit in a different context) as well as practices (private devotions or family dramas on one hand; public conflicts played out in the press or the courts on the other). When read against one another, Orsi's and McGreevy's historical subjects seem to inhabit different worlds. At its inception the lived religion model promised to collapse these

very sorts of high /low distinctions. On lived religion's commitment to studying laity without displacing institutional voices and influences see David Hall, "Introduction," *Lived Religion in America: Toward a History of Practice* (Princeton: Princeton University Press, 1997) from Pierre Bourdieu, *Outline of a Theory of Practice*, translated by Richard Nice (Cambridge: Cambridge University Press, 1977).

31. These activities are described by Pierre Bourdieu as the foundations of habitus. "The structures constitutive of a particular type of environment . . . produce habitus, systems of durable, transposable dispositions, structured structures predisposed to function as structuring structures, that is, as principles of the generation and structuring of practices" (Bourdieu, *Outline of a Theory*, 72).

32. On the liberal Protestant bias within the American academy see, for example, George Marsden, *The Soul of the American University* (New York: Oxford University Press, 1996); Robert A. Orsi, "Snakes Alive: Resituating the Moral in the Study of Religion," *In Face of the Facts: Moral Inquiry in American Scholarship*, eds. Richard Wightman Fox and Robert B. Westbrook (New York: Cambridge University Press, 1998). On post-Reformation bias toward interiority within academic constructions of religion, see especially Talal Asad, *Genealogies of Religion: Disciplines of Reason and Power in Christianity and Islam* (Baltimore: Johns Hopkins University Press, 1993). Scholarship on religious subjects participating in the legal system usually considers the First Amendment's Free Exercise Clause. Unlike Establishment Clause litigation, free exercise cases lend themselves to accounts that emphasize the beliefs of the religious/legal subject. Plaintiffs in free exercise cases often justify their claims with theological articulations of the value of religious freedom. See, for example, Shawn Francis Peters, *Judging Jehovah's Witnesses: Religious Persecution and the Dawn of the Rights Revolution* (Lawrence, Kans.: University Press of Kansas, 2000); Peters, *The Yoder Case: Religious Freedom, Education and Parental Rights* (Lawrence, Kans.: University Press of Kansas, 2003). For analysis of the First Amendment as a site for negotiation between minority religious groups and the dominant cultural order, see Eric Michael Mazur, *The Americanization of Religious Minorities* (Baltimore: Johns Hopkins University Press, 1999).

33. Lucille Leyba, personal interview, July 22, 2010, Rio Lucio, New Mexico.

34. Geertz, "Local Knowledge," 170.

Chapter 1

1. Peter Küppers, "The Pastor of New Mexico," trans. Tomas Jaehn (unpublished memoir, private collection), 40–41. The only historical treatment of Küppers to date is in the work of Tomas Jaehn. The biographical information in this chapter is taken both from Jaehn's published work on Küppers (Tomas Jaehn, "The Priest Who Made Schools Bloom in the Desert," *Seeds of Struggle/Harvest of Faith*, eds. Thomas J. Steele, SJ, Paul Rhetts, and Barbe Awalt [Albuquerque: LPD Press, 1998]) and from his unpublished translation of the priest's private memoirs, which were originally written in German.

2. Jaehn, "The Pastor," 40–41.

3. "Theory of Preservation," n.d., n.p. Robert Jones Papers, New Mexico State Records Center and Archives, Santa Fe, New Mexico (cited hereafter as Jones Papers).

4. Jaehn, "The Priest," 293.

5. Jaehn, "The Priest."

6. Küppers, "The Pastor," 74.

7. Ibid., 79–80.

8. Ibid., 81.

9. Ibid., 82.

10. Bacon, "Contributions of Religious Orders," 61, 72, 130, 133.

11. Ibid., 164.

12. For an example of scholarship that traces education in New Mexico back to the Anglo arrival, see Tom Wiley, *Public Education in New Mexico* (Albuquerque: Division of Government Research, University of New Mexico, 1965). For an example of scholarship that assumes a natural affinity between Hispanos and the Catholic leadership in New Mexico, see Diana Everett, "Nativism, Catholicism and Public Education in New Mexico, 1870–1889" (M.A. thesis, Eastern New Mexico University, 1973).

13. Education in New Mexico is as old as the succession of civilizations that have inhabited the region. Here I distinguish between older native modes of conveying knowledge across generations and formal European-style schooling, which arrived with the first Franciscan missionaries in 1598 and which was required in different forms by both the Spanish and Mexican governments. For education in New Spain, see David Weber, *The Spanish Frontier in North America* (New Haven: Yale University Press, 1992); Bernardo P. Gallegos, *Literacy, Education and Society in New Mexico, 1693–1821* (Albuquerque: University of New Mexico Press, 1992). For education under Mexican rule, see John B. Mondragón and Ernest S. Stapleton, *Public Education in New Mexico* (Albuquerque: University of New Mexico Press, 2005), 8–12; David Weber, *The Mexican Frontier, 1821–1846* (Albuquerque: University of New Mexico Press, 1982), 232–234.

14. Mondragón, *Public Education*, 10; Gallegos, *Literacy*, 32. The financing of public schools during the Mexican period was left to individual communities and often involved some combination of tithing, subscription, and appropriations. Only the largest communities in New Mexico had schools, including Santa Fe, Albuquerque, Taos, and Belen (Mondragón, *Public Education*, 9–10).

15. On Martínez the political figure see Juan Romero, "Begetting the Mexican American: Padre Martínez and the 1847 Rebellion," *Seeds of Struggle*.

16. Weber, *The Mexican Frontier*, 73.

17. Robert Arthur Moyers, "A History of Education in New Mexico" (Ph.D. dissertation, George Peabody College for Teachers, 1941), 151. By Lamy's own estimation there were 68,000 Catholics, two thousand "heretics," and thirty to forty thousand "infidels" upon his arrival, as well as eight or nine thousand Catholic Indians, and 30,000 non-Catholic Indians (Paul Horgan, *Lamy of Santa Fe* [Middletown, Conn.: Wesleyan University Press, 1975], 127).

18. Moyers, "A History of Education," 196. For accounts of New Mexican Catholicism during the Mexican period, see Robert E. Wright, OMI, "How Many Are 'A Few'?: Catholic Clergy in Central and Northern New Mexico, 1780–1851," and Jerome J. Martínez y Alire, JCL, "The Influence of the Roman Catholic Church in New Mexico under Mexican Administration, 1821–1848," *Seeds of Struggle*. According to Wright there were as many as nineteen clergy in the region in the years preceding Lamy's arrival.

19. On the priestly indiscretions Lamy encountered see Horgan, *Lamy*, 147–154, 169–172.

20. Marta Weigle, *Brothers of Light, Brothers of Blood: The Penitentes of the Southwest* (Santa Fe: Ancient City Press, 1976), 53–56. Rules issued by Lamy in 1857 included his admonishment that "the Penance must be done, as hidden as possible, without giving scandal, to the rest of the faithful according to the Spirit of the Church and without doing it with vain-glory" (qtd. in Ibid., 203). These regulations were the seeds of division between lay and clerical Catholic leadership in the region as the brotherhood disregarded Lamy's authority and, over the course of the nineteenth century, acted increasingly outside the purview of the diocese.

21. Jane C. Atkins, "Who Will Educate: The Schooling Question in Territorial New Mexico" (Ph.D. dissertation, University of New Mexico, 1982), 288; Horgan, *Lamy*, 169–181.

22. Horgan, *Lamy*, 230–236, 240–251.

23. Ibid., 177, 227; Atkins, "Who Will Educate," 288.

24. Qtd. in Moyers, "A History of Education," 204.

25. For a complete account of the educational endeavors of the Sisters of Loretto in New Mexico, see M. Rose Theresa Soran, OL, "Lorretine Educational History in New Mexico" (M.A. thesis, University of New Mexico, 1949); Patricia Jean Manion, *Beyond Adobe Walls* (Independence, Missouri: Two Trails Publishing Press, 2001).

26. Moyers, "A History of Education," 201–202; Soran, "Lorretine History," 34; Manion, *Beyond Adobe Walls*, 71.

27. Qtd. in Moyers, "A History of Education," 202–203.

28. Hal Russell, *Land of Enchantment: Memoirs of Marian Russell Along the Santa Fe Trail*, ed. Garnet M. Brayer (Evanston, Ill.: The Branding Iron Press, 1954), 43.

29. Soran, "Lorrentine History," 74.

30. Frederick Mason Bacon, "Contributions of Catholic Religious Orders," 34; Phyllis Burch Rapagnani, "A Tradition of Service: Roman Catholic Sisters in New Mexico" (M.A. thesis, University of New Mexico, 1988).

31. The Sisters of Loretto remained an educational presence in New Mexico well into the twentieth century. At the start of the *Zellers* case the community was celebrating the seventy-fifth anniversary of its public school in Mora and its sisters had expanded their public employment, teaching at schools in the communities of Bernalillo and Socorro as well.

32. On the arrival of Anglo Protestants in New Mexico, see Susan M. Yohn, *A Contest of Faiths* (Ithaca: Cornell University Press, 1995).

33. Nieto-Phillips, *The Language of Blood*, 116. Although many Anglos in New Mexico referred to the region's inhabitants as "Mexicans," immigration from Mexico remained low during this period, especially relative to migration from the United States after 1880. The immigration that did occur from Mexico was confined largely to the southern part of the territory, away from the traditional Hispano communities to the north (Ibid., 111–116).

34. Robert W. Larson, *New Mexico's Quest for Statehood* (Albuquerque: University of New Mexico Press, 1968), 70–71; Atkins, 11–12; Moyers, 152.

35. Qtd. in Atkins, "Who Will Educate," 12; Larson, *Quest*, 71.

36. Qtd. in Moyers, "A History of Education," 152.

37. On nineteenth-century American nativism see Ray Allen Billington, *The Protestant Crusade, 1800–1860: A Study of the Origins of American Nativism* (New York: MacMillan Company, 1938).

38. Lyman Beecher, *A Plea for the West* (New York: Leavitt, Lord and Company, 1835), 13.

39. Ibid., 21–22.

40. Billington, *Protestant Crusade*, 144–145; Qtd. in Joan DelFattore, *The Fourth R: Conflicts Over Religion in America's Public Schools* (New Haven: Yale University Press), 25.

41. Billington, *Protestant Crusade*, 143.

42. The following account of nineteenth-century conflicts over public education relies on existing historiography, including Billington, *Protestant Crusade*, 142–237; Hamburger, *Separation of Church and State*, 193–251; Fessenden, *Culture and Redemption*, 60–83; and DelFattore, *Fourth R*, 12–61. For a close study of the New York dispute, see Vincent P. Lannie, *Public Money and Parochial Education* (Cleveland: Case Western Reserve University Press, 1968); on the Philadelphia riots, see Michael Feldberg, *The Philadephia Riots of 1844: A Study of Ethnic Conflict* (Westport, Conn.: Greenwood Press, 1975).

43. Billington, *Protestant Crusade*, 143; Qtd. in Hamburger, *Separation of Church and State*, 220.

44. Billington, *Protestant Crusade*, 144.

45. DelFattore, *Fourth R*, 27–29; Hamburger, *Separation of Church and State*, 228; Billington, *Protestant Crusade*, 151–156. Billington points out that Hughes privately "detested" the idea of a separate Catholic political party and saw the creation of an independent ticket as a last resort (Ibid., 152).

46. DelFattore, *Fourth R*, 33.

47. Ibid., 35.

48. Ibid., 38.

49. Qtd. in Ibid., 41 (*Catholic Herald*, Aug. 1, 1844: 243).

50. James O'Toole, *The Faithful* (Cambridge: Harvard University Press, 2010), 92.

51. DelFattore, *Fourth R*, 43.

52. Qtd. in *Board of Education of the City of Cincinnati v. John D. Minor Et Al*, 23 Ohio St. 211 (1872). Unlike the earlier disputes in New York and Philadelphia, Archbishop John Purcell of Cincinnati was joined prominently in his push by Jews, Unitarians, Universalists, and Quakers. DelFattore, *Fourth R*, 56. For an overview of debates regarding the relationship of Catholicism to public education through the latter half of the nineteenth century, see also *Daniel F. Reilly, The School Controversy (1891–1893)* (Washington: The Catholic University of America Press, 1943), 1–38.

53. *Board of Education v. Minor.*

54. Qtd. in Hamburger, *Separation of Church and State*, 223. Although the committee only read the principle as implicit in the state's constitution, Hamburger cites this episode as the first in which the idea of separation of church and state attracted national attention in the United States (Ibid., 219).

55. DelFattore, *Fourth R*, 21, 24, 35.

56. Hamburger, *Separation of Church and State*, 228.

57. Tracy Fessenden argues that the singular focus on Catholicism in places like New York and Philadelphia allowed Protestantism to fade as an "unmarked category" into a proto-secular vision of American education. Displacing Catholic sectarianism allowed a Protestant consensus to cast itself as the preserver of both religious liberty and diversity. Her argument develops Hamburger's claim that Protestant ministers struggling to comply with new expectations regarding disestablishment (men like Lyman Beecher, one might argue) deflected criticism by turning their attention on Catholics (Fessenden, *Culture and Redemption*, 6, 60–83; Hamburger, *Separation of Church and State*, 201).

58. Billington, *Protestant Crusade*, 146; DelFattore, *Fourth R*, 18–19.

59. Hamburger, *Separation of Church and State*, 241.

60. DelFattore, *Fourth R*, 17.

61. Ibid. On Catholic reservations about liberal notions of freedom during this era (including religious freedom and the absence of religious influences from public schooling it entailed) see McGreevy, *Catholicism and American Freedom*, 19–42 (esp. 36–42). McGreevy places these reservations within the context of the ultramontane Catholic revival of the nineteenth century.

62. Often these efforts were in conjunction with constitutions proposed in an ongoing effort to win statehood status. For a discussion of these efforts see Wiley, *Public Education*, 23–35. For a thorough history of these efforts in the broader context of territorial politics and statehood efforts, see Larson, *Quest*.

63. New Mexico's school system was a late arrival even by western standards; tax-supported funding structures for education were in place in Texas and California by the time they became states in 1845 and 1850, respectively, and a public system was established in the Arizona territory in the 1870s. Along with ethnically and religiously aligned opposition, scholarly explanations of the delay include the lack of federal support for territorial education and the concentrated ownership of taxable property in the territory among large landholders, including the federal government and the railroads (see Mondragón and Stapleton, *Public Education*, 1–2; Wiley, *Public Education*, 25; Atkins, "Who Will Educate," iv–v).

64. Qtd. in Larson, *Quest*, 35.

65. Ibid., 213–215. For an extended discussion of Jesuit participation in New Mexican education, and its political repercussions, see Everett, "Nativism"; Atkins, "Who Will Educate," 337–374. See also Gerald McKevitt, *Brokers of Culture* (Stanford: Stanford University Press, 2007); M. Lilliana Owens, SL, *Jesuit Beginnings in New Mexico, 1867–1882* (El Paso: Revista Católica Press, 1950); Dianna Everett, "The Public School Debate in New Mexico, 1850–1891," *Journal of the Southwest*, 26.2 (Summer 1984): 107–134.

66. The first public school fund was successfully initiated in New Mexico in 1872; money was raised through a general property tax of one percent on all families with property over $500 (with only one quarter of that dedicated to educational purposes) as well as a poll

tax. In 1876, revenues collected from fining persons selling liquor to the underage, and persons violating Sunday observance laws, were added to the school fund. This fund, albeit limited, made possible the first significant wave of public school construction in the territory. It supported the Jesuits' projects and the first sister-taught public schools as well (Moyers, "A History of Education," 169–170, 176). By 1873, Jesuits were teaching in publicly funded schools in several communities in the territory, including Bernalillo, Albuquerque, Las Vegas, and Santa Fe (McKevitt, *Brokers of Culture*, 201); Atkins, "Who Will Educate," 338.

67. Owens, *Jesuit Beginnings*, 66; Moyers, "A History of Education," 364.

68. McKevitt, *Brokers of Culture*, 202. Other Catholic communities were similarly incorporated as educational organizations in the state without the same political backlash. See Moyers, "A History of Education," 218–219, 376; Mona Schwind, OP, *Period Pieces: An Account of the Grand Rapids Dominicans, 1853–1966* (Grand Rapids, Mich.: West Michigan Printing, 1991), 138.

69. Larson, *Quest*, 101, 159; Qtd. in Atkins, "Who Will Educate," 367; Everett, "Nativism," 57.

70. Larson, *Quest*, 123–123, 148–155.

71. Atkins, "Who Will Educate," 371.

72. Yohn, *A Contest of Faiths*, 11, 178.

73. Ibid., 76.

74. Ibid., 43, 44.

75. Ibid., 178.

76. His position sometimes put him at odds with the Jesuits in his archdiocese; although Lamy defended the Jesuits in the face of heated criticism of their work in the 1870s, members of the Society of Jesus in New Mexico acted largely independently of his jurisdiction and his relations with the order were sometimes strained (Everett, "Nativism," 77; Atkins, "Who Will Educate," 348, 393).

77. Qtd. in Atkins, "Who Will Educate," 386.

78. Ibid., 386–387.

79. Qtd. in Timothy Walch, *Parish School* (New York: Crossroad Publishing Company, 1996), 61.

80. Qtd. in Everett, "Public School Debate," 130; Larson, *Quest*, 159.

81. Qtd. in Larson, *Quest*, 159.

82. Atkins, "Who Will Educate," 397–403. Notably, the legislation that finally passed was missing any specific reference to nonsectarianism.

83. Everett, "Nativism," 67. There are also recorded reports in 1889 of clergy preaching sermons that advised people to vote against statehood and the constitution (Larson, *Quest*, 167).

84. The first state constitutional convention in 1850, which drafted the first (failed) provisions for public education in New Mexico, had many Hispano members, including at least one priest (Larson, *Quest*, 31–35). As late as 1889 the constitutional delegation still had thirty Hispano members that voted in favor of the document's educational provisions (Ibid., 167). For discussion of the relationship of New Mexico's political parties to the Hispano population through the late nineteenth century, see Ibid., 70–71, 167–168, etc.

85. The exact population of Hispanos in New Mexico is difficult to glean from census data from the period because while the census distinguished "Mexicans" (those born in Mexico, or the children thereof) it did not distinguish native New Mexicans of Hispano ethnicity (George Sanchez, "The Education of Bilinguals in a State School System [1934]," *Education and the Mexican American*, ed. Carlos E. Cortés [New York: Arno Press, 1974], 12). We do know that according to a 1931 school census of New Mexico fifty percent of all school children were Spanish-speaking (Sanchez, "Education of Bilinguals," 13).

86. Marta Weigle, ed., *Hispanic Villages of Northern New Mexico: A Reprint of the Volume II of the 1935 Tewa Basin Study* (Santa Fe: The Lightening Tree, 1975); Margaret Atencio, personal interview, July 19, 2010, Peñasco, New Mexico.

87. Randi Jones Walker, "Protestantism in Modern New Mexico," *Religion in Modern New Mexico*, eds. Ferenc Szasz and Richard Etulain (Albuquerque: University of New Mexico Press, 1997), 34–35. Walker's numbers are taken from U.S. Bureau of the Census, *Religious Bodies: 1936* (Washington D.C.: Government Printing Office).

88. Based on per capita assessed wealth. The only other county in the state with similar poverty levels was San Juan County, in the northwestern corner of the state. The population in San Juan was mainly Native American (Sanchez, "Education of Bilinguals," 43). Although approximately half of the state's population spoke English as its first language in 1930, over ninety percent of residents in these four counties—Mora, Rio Arriba, Sandoval, and Taos counties—continued to speak Spanish as their first language (Ibid.).

89. Lynne Marie Getz, *Schools of Their Own* (Albuquerque: University of New Mexico Press, 1997), 7.

90. Ibid., 8.

91. David M. Key, "Progressivism and Imperialism in the American Southwest, 1880–1912" (Ph.D. diss., University of New Mexico, 2005), 85–86, 90–93. See also Yohn, *A Contest of Faiths*; Getz, *Schools of Their Own*. For more on Progressive Era Americanization efforts through education see Frank Van Nyes, *Americanizing the West* (Lawrence, Kans.: University Press of Kansas, 2002).

92. Virgilio Elizondo, *Spiritual Writings* (Maryknoll, NY: Orbis Books, 2010), 42.

93. Nieto-Phillips, *Language of Blood*, 116; Key, "Progressivism," 68.

94. Moyers, "A History of Education," 164, 298; Getz, *Schools*, 7.

95. I take my distinction between progressive and nationalistic perspectives from John Higham, who discusses both in relation to how Americans engaged immigrants in the United States during the same period. See John Higham, *Strangers in the Land: Patterns of American Nativism, 1860–1925* (New York: Atheneum, 1981), 116–123, 234–263.

96. Key, "Progressivism," 139–140.

97. Getz, *Schools of Their Own*, 21.

98. Ibid., 23–24, 42–43, 108–109.

99. *New Mexico Historic Documents*, ed. Richard N. Ellis (Albuquerque: University of New Mexico Press, 1975), 76. The Constitution further stipulated that "the legislature shall provide for the training of teachers . . . so that they may become proficient in both the English and Spanish languages, to qualify them to teach Spanish-speaking pupils and students in the public schools and educational institutions of the state, and shall provide proper means and methods to facilitate the teaching of the English language." It also stated that "no student . . . shall ever be required to attend or participate in any religious service whatsoever" (Ibid., 127–128). See also Wiley, *Public Education*, 28: Larson, *Quest*, 266.

100. Ellis, *Historic Documents*, 127–128. The language prohibiting a religious test for teachers was likely included to protect Catholic teachers within the public schools (Getz, *Schools of Their Own*, 26–27; Rapagnani, "Tradition of Service," 70).

101. Moyers, "A History of Education," 341–344. In 1891 the Archdiocese oversaw fifteen schools, run by four orders of religious, with a total enrollment of approximately 2,100 students (Ibid., 223–224). While several of these schools received some public funding, they were a diminished presence in the expanding state system. In 1893, there were 519 public schools in the territory, with a total enrollment of more than 21,000 students. Catholic enrollment saw only modest gains through 1910, while public enrollment tripled during the same period (Ibid., 298, 303, 323, 336–337). In 1912 sisters were teaching in Mora, Bernalillo, Socorro, and Peña Blanca.

102. Enrollment in public schools in 1901 was 31,500. By 1911 this number had increased to 61,027. Catholic school enrollment was 2,207 in 1901. Enrollment decreased to 1,798 in 1905 (Ibid., 323, 336).

103. There is a slight discrepancy among sources. According to Moyers the archdiocese was responsible for twenty-one schools in the territory in 1911, with an enrollment of 2,510

(Ibid., 336–337). According to an entry from the 1911 edition of *The Catholic Encyclopedia*, the archdiocese was responsible for twenty-three schools, but with an enrollment of only 1,500 pupils, one year earlier (Aurelio Espinosa, "New Mexico," *The Catholic Encyclopedia* v. xi [New York: Robert Appleton Company, 1911], http://www.newadvent.org/cathen/11001a. htm [accessed April 13, 2008]). Part of this discrepancy may be the result of different criteria used to count schools as Catholic.

104. The Sisters of Loretto and the Sisters of Charity had both been teaching in publicly funded schools since the nineteenth century, and they were joined in 1904 by the Poor Sisters of St. Francis of Perpetual Adoration from Denver. These three orders were joined in their public work between 1913 and 1935 by the sisters Küppers invited to Chaperito, along with seven additional communities: Sisters of the Third Order of St. Francis from Oldenburg, Indiana; Sisters of the Sorrowful Mother from Milwaukee, Wisconsin; Sisters of Divine Providence from San Antonio, Texas; Ursuline Sisters from Louisville, Kentucky; Sisters of the Atonement (origin unknown); Dominican Sisters from Grand Rapids, Michigan; and Sisters of Mercy from Detroit, Michigan. By the time of the *Zellers* lawsuit all of the above orders remained in public schools with the exception of the Sisters of Charity, the Chaperito sisters and the Sisters of Atonement. As defendants they were also joined by more recent arrivals— members of the Third Order of St. Francis from Pasto, Columbia; Dominican sisters from Adrian, Michigan; Franciscan Sisters of Our Lady of Perpetual Help from St. Louis; and Sisters of St. Casimir from Chicago. They were joined as well by members of the Christian Brothers, who continued to teach in public schools in the state.

105. In 1940 Catholic religious orders were teaching in fifty-four schools, with 374 religious as teachers, enrolling nearly twelve thousand students. Twenty of those schools were public, employing 119 religious with an enrollment of 4,600 pupils (Moyers, "A History of Education," 585).

106. New Mexico's public education system was refined between 1912 and 1923. The system instituted in 1891 was detailed in the state's constitution in 1912, and again in a series of laws culminating in the state's first school code, passed by the legislature in 1923. Even after the passage of the school code, important details remained open for debate, including the system's funding formula. For an extended analysis of public education laws in New Mexico during this period, see Wiley, *Public Education*.

107. Ibid., 33.

108. Ibid., 38–39.

109. Ibid., 27.

110. Sanchez, "Education of Bilinguals," 83–84; Wiley, *Public Education*, 36–46.

111. The disjuncture between the needs of local districts and funds made available to them was effectively standardized in the 1923 school code, which stipulated that the funding for rural districts, though gleaned from county tax money, would be distributed at the discretion of budget commissioners working for a state auditor, rather than in conjunction with local school boards. In the words of Tom Wiley, former state superintendent of public instruction in New Mexico, this exercise of state control "effectively separated the control of educational finance and revenue from the board which had the responsibility for the educational program" (*Public Education*, 43).

112. Sanchez, "Education of Bilinguals," 71, 75.

113. See Wiley, *Public Education*, 46–67. Despite a majority of revenues coming from state sources by 1938–1939, the four counties of the Basin were still among the five counties in the state with the lowest amount of money budgeted for use per classroom (George Sanchez, *Forgotten People* [Albuquerque: Calvin Horn Publisher, 1967], 72).

114. Wiley, *Public Education*, 42–43.

115. Ibid., 32. During this period there was also a series of proposed resolutions requiring teachers, particularly teachers in rural schools, to receive training in Spanish as well. Such resolutions met with little enthusiasm from state education officials, and bilingual instruction, although used in some local districts, was not officially promoted (Getz, *Schools*, 31–32).

116. Wiley, *Public Education*, 51.
117. Rural school districts did find allies during the 1930s in federal New Deal programs, in particular the Works Progress Administration. Working in cooperation with state officials, and with building material supplied by local communities, the WPA provided labor for the construction of over three hundred new or remodeled school buildings during the decade (Getz, *Schools of Their Own*, 103–105).
118. Schools in twenty-seven communities were implicated in Zellers. Fourteen of these were in the four Basin counties mentioned earlier in the chapter, and several others were in communities closely adjacent to the region. Nearly all of the schools not located in the Basin served smaller Hispano populations concentrated in other parts of the state. For an extended analysis of economic relations between Hispanos and Anglos during the early twentieth century, with an added focus on gender, see Deutsch, *No Separate Refuge: Culture, Class and Gender on the Anglo-Hispanic Frontier, 1880–1940* (New York: Oxford University Press, 1987).

Chapter 2

1. Mary Clare McGee, SBS, "The Causes and Effects of the 'Dixon Case,'" (M.A. thesis, Catholic University of America, 1955), 50–51.
2. The priest lost a bid for a new school building and the sisters he had invited to Chaperito departed after the archbishop and certain residents complained they could not speak the English language (Jaehn, "The Priest," 297).
3. Küppers, "The Pastor," 93.
4. Schwind, *Period Pieces*, 117.
5. Weigle, *Hispanic Villages*, 36.
6. Ibid., 206, 209.
7. Ibid., 211.
8. Ibid.,189.
9. Ibid., 184, 192.
10. Ibid., 185, 193.
11. Virginia Voorhies to Friends, September 14, 1939, Menaul Historical Library of the Southwest, Menaul School, Albuquerque, New Mexico (cited hereafter as Menaul Library).
12. M. Protasia Hofstetter, FMI, *The History of the Franciscan Sisters of Mary Immaculate in the United States of America, 1932–1992* (Amarillo: Miller National Corporation, 1992), 118.
13. Ibid. The sister was referring to the"Allelujahs," a common name for New Mexico's Spanish-speaking Pentecostal churches, especially La Asamblea de Dios (Marta Weigle, *Brothers of Light*, 99–100).
14. Jaehn, "The Priest," 300; Sarah Deutsch, *No Separate Refuge*, 65.
15. Qtd. in Jaehn, "The Priest," 300. For the next decade the group reliably sent money to support Küppers' schools.
16. This increase was due to the formation of progressive branch in addition to members of the traditional "old guard." Weigle, *Hispanic Villages*, 185. On northern New Mexico's *penitentes* during this period see also Weigle, *Brothers of Light*.
17. Jaehn, "The Priest," 301, 310 (fn. 45, 46).
18. Bacon, "Contributions of Religious Orders," 98.
19. Maura McDonald, "Contributions of the Dominican Sisters of Grand Rapids, Michigan to Education in New Mexico" (M.A. thesis, University of New Mexico, 1942), 30, 31.
20. Schwind, *Period Pieces*, 115. On Mother Bendicta's governance and the activities of the Grand Rapids Dominicans during this era, see Ibid.
21. Qtd. in Ibid.
22. Ibid., 117.

23. Ibid. The school did not receive public money for its operation; support for the sisters' work came from their motherhouse and other Dominican convents back in Michigan, with the archdiocese turning over what funds it had available and local residents providing donations of firewood and other essentials (McDonald, "Contributions," 34–36).

24. Ibid., 37; Ann Perpetua Romero, OP, videotaped interview, n.d., Marywood Archives; Bacon, "Contributions of Religious Orders," 100.

25. McGee, "Causes and Effects," 66.

26. Jaehn, "The Priest," 301.

27. Ibid., 300; McDonald, "Contributions," 38.

28. Schwind, *Period Pieces*, 118.

29. McGee, "Causes and Effects," 66.

30. Ibid.; Schwind, *Period Pieces*, 142.

31. Schwind, *Period Pieces*, 118; McGee, "Causes and Effects," 67. With an enrollment of two hundred fifteen students, the average daily attendance at St. Anthony's was one hundred fifty-six—a rate the sisters considered a success given the fact many of the children were shepherds and at home only part of the year.

32. McDonald, "Contributions," 43.

33. Ibid., 40; Jaehn, "The Priest," 300.

34. Jaehn, "The Priest," 302; McDonald, "Contributions," 45–46; McGee, "Causes and Effects," 66.

35. McDonald, "Contributions," 34.

36. Francisco Romero, Personal interview, July 20, 2010, Dixon, New Mexico.

37. There were two instances in which sisters' public employment was challenged by tax-payers in New Mexico before *Zellers*. One occurred in Chama and the other Belen in 1939. In the first case, the complaint was taken before the State Department of Education, and in the second it was brought before the district court. In each case the issue was deemed not reviewable by the courts, and the petitioners' requests were denied. A challenge by a local school board itself, in Albuquerque in 1892, did lead to a resolution requiring sisters in that district to remove their garb while teaching. The mandate resulted in the *de facto* elimination of sisters from those schools (Bacon, "Contributions of Catholic Religious Orders" 11–12).

38. "Life of Sister Mary Maura McDonald of the Sacred Passion," biography, n.d., Marywood Archives.

39. McGee, "Causes and Effects," 66.

40. Bacon, "Contributions of Religious Orders," 101.

41. Edna Garcia, personal interview, July 21, 2010, Dixon, New Mexico.

42. Bacon, "Contributions of Religious Orders," 103.

43. Sisters reported that the superintendent of Santa Fe County schools influenced their em-ployment in Santa Cruz, while a local pastor requested them at San Juan (Schwind, *Period Pieces*, 138–139). In contrast to Peñasco, Santa Cruz is another example of community that had a preexisting public school, and buildings owned by the school district (McDonald, "Contributions," 48).

44. Transcript of Testimony, 1935, 1936, 1938, 1941; McGee, "Causes and Effects," 69. Student enrollment in these schools was likely even higher in the early 1940s. The two different branches of Dominicans teaching publicly in New Mexico (Grand Rapids and Adrian, Michigan-based) were together responsible for 2,813 pupils in 1941 (Moyers, "A History of Education," 583).

45. Bacon, "Contributions of Religious Orders," 103.

46. McDonald, "Contributions," 74.

47. Sanchez, *Forgotten People*, 76.

48. While it is uncertain what prompted the Dominican departure, there is ample evidence of a troubled history between Küppers and the Dominicans. In 1934 Küppers attempted to seize sisters' salaries and redirect them back into the schools rather than allow sisters to hand them

over to their community. The archbishop ultimately intervened, prohibiting Küppers from taking sisters' salaries without the approval of their superior (Schwind, *Period Pieces*, 142). See also Hofstetter, *Franciscan Sisters*, 117.

49. Qtd. in Ibid.

50. Ibid., 118.

51. The Franciscans had begun to teach in Aragon, in what would become the Diocese of Gallup, in 1938 (Ibid., 113–114).

52. Ibid., 4–14.

53. Ibid., 81, 118.

54. One sister remembered: "I still gasp at the boldness I had in asking the principal to have a band ready to accompany the First Communicants in procession from the school to the church. This was the way I was accustomed to seeing it in my childhood in Switzerland. During Mass, the older children did their best singing, 'Jesus, Jesus, Come to Me,' 'O Lord, I Am Not Worthy,' and 'Mother at Your Feet is Kneeling' as a recessional. Luckily liturgists had not as yet banned such hymns as sentimental" (Ibid., 34).

55. Bacon, "Contributions of Catholic Orders," 2. Bacon mentions his own experience teaching in New Mexico's public schools, including one or more communities that employed religious teachers (Ibid., 163). Although he presents his findings as the result of systematic and unbiased inquiry (and I find no reason to question their validity), it is worth noting that—based on his teaching experience and familiarity with the topic—Bacon himself may have been a member of a religious order, pursuing an advanced degree under his secular name.

56. Ibid., 164.

57. Ibid.

58. Lewis A. Myers, "Controlled Hierarchy Resents Enlightenment," *Baptist New Mexican* (June 17, 1948): 3.

59. Leyba interview. Resident Anna Cordova described the enactment of *los pastores* in Peñasco: "For Christmas we would have Mary and Joseph and the burro and all the people—the apostles and the kings and all that. We did what we had seen and knew had happened. It was like a drama" (Anna Cordova, personal interview, July 22, 2010, Dixon, New Mexico).

60. Alfredo Gomez, personal interview, July 19, 2010, Dixon, New Mexico.

61. Cordova interview. See also Edna Garcia interview; Margaret Atencio, personal interview, July 19, 2010, Peñasco, New Mexico.

62. Gomez interview.

63. Abelardo Jaramillo, personal interview, July 20, 2010, Dixon, New Mexico. Of nine former students I spoke with (eight Catholics and one Protestant; five of whom attended school in Dixon in the 1940s, four of whom attended school in Peñasco), every one remembered with approval the sisters' presence in their local school.

64. Francisco Romero interview; see also Gomez interview.

65. Jaramillo interview.

66. Edna Garcia interview.

67. Ben Valdez, personal interview, July 21, 2010, Dixon, New Mexico. See also Jaramillo interview; Gomez interview; Edna Garcia interview; Francisco Romero interview.

68. Leyba interview.

69. Ibid. "There was God in that building," Delia Garcia recalled of the Dominicans' high school in Peñasco, "there was love, and there was also discipline!" (Delia Garcia, personal interview, July 22, 2010, Rio Lucio, New Mexico).

70. Jaramillo interview.

71. Francisco Romero interview.

72. Leyba interview.

73. Cordova interview. See also Delia Garcia interview.

74. Leyba interview.

75. Gomez interview.
76. Atencio interview.
77. Valdez interview.
78. Jaramillo interview.
79. Elizabeth Barilla, OP (formerly Sister John Evangelist), personal interview, January 12, 2006, Marywood Motherhouse, Grand Rapids, Michigan.
80. "It was very difficult. Because it was the only time we spoke English. Most of the kids, our first language was Spanish and so at home it was Spanish. We used very little English" (Jaramillo interview).
81. Delia Garcia interview.
82. Leyba interview.
83. Jaramillo interview.
84. Leyba interview.
85. Cordova interview.
86. Delia Garcia interview. See also Jaramilo interview.
87. Carmella Conway, OP, personal interview, January 12, 2006, Marywood Motherhouse, Grand Rapids, Michigan.
88. Gomez interview.
89. Atencio interview.
90. Delia Garcia interview.
91. Atencio interview.
92. Jaramillo interview.
93. Barilla interview.
94. Gomez interview.
95. Cordova interview; see also Edna Garcia interview.
96. Bacon, "Contributions of Religious Orders," 164. The author does not disclose his criteria for determining these categories of opposition.
97. Ibid.
98. Hofstetter, *Franciscan Sisters*, 118.
99. Arthur Montgomery to the Editor of TIME, September 25, 1947, Jones Papers. The priest's early advocacy on behalf of the sisters gave way to a tempestuous relationship similar to his relationship with the Dominicans. Sisters remember Küppers as an increasingly unreliable ally through the 1940s. At times he assumed domineering ownership of the school's governance, while at other times he loudly renounced his involvement in school affairs, and shifted the blame for failed projects onto the sisters themselves (Hofstetter, *Franciscan Sisters*, 119–120).
100. Ibid., 118.
101. Ibid., 121; Lydia Zellers, transcribed interview, 1980, Lydia Zellers Information File, Menaul Library.
102. Transcript of Testimony, 1548–1549, 1556, 1558, 1561–1562, 1566–1567.
103. Zellers interview.
104. Ibid.
105. Ibid.
106. Francisco Romero interview.
107. Jaramillo interview.
108. Leyba interview.
109. Edna Garcia interview. A Protestant resident of Dixon had a more positive memory of interactions between the groups. "We did [hang out together]. . . . A lot of us were very close friends" (Valdez interview).
110. There were also Protestants in Dixon who accepted the sisters' presence in their school. As one Presbyterian student who attended school at St. Joseph's remembered, "My [parents] thought it was alright, because it would probably bring me up into a straight kind of life" (Valdez interview).

111. Cordova interview.
112. Rodney C. Ewing, "Memorial of Arthur Montgomery, 1909–1999," *American Mineralogist* 85 (2000): 1848–1850. Montgomery would go on to receive a doctorate from Harvard and join the geology faculty at Lafayette College in Pennsylvania
113. Yohn, *A Contest of Faiths*, 202. Yohn has described Hispano-Presbyterians and other Hispano-Protestants during this period as representing a "third culture" on New Mexico's still relatively bifurcated ethno-religious landscape (Ibid., 201).
114. In Porfiero's own memory his father's excommunication was solely the result of his decision to send his son to a Protestant school, although one wonders if his *penitente* activities also played some role. Porfiero Romero, transcribed interview, 1974, Menaul Library.
115. Porfiero Romero, transcribed interview, 1986, Menaul Library.
116. Transcript of Testimony (testimony of Leopoldo Martínez), 1557, 1562–1563.
117. See for example, "Appeal for Free Schools: The Dixon Case Continues," pamphlet, n.d., Jones Papers: 3.
118. "Free Schools," pamphlet, n.d., Jones Papers; see also "pamphlet #2," pamphlet, n.d., Jones Papers.
119. As the conflict progressed the group would reinforce its bid for ethnic solidarity by emphasizing the ethnic difference of Dixon's sisters. Reports written by Dixon's Protestants about the Franciscans highlight the sisters' foreignness. Although the sisters were Swiss and Latino, their literature described them as German refugees from the war, untrained as teachers and unable to speak either intelligible English *or* Spanish ("Basic Facts about the Dixon Case," manuscript, n.d., Jones Papers; Frank S. Mead, "Shadows Over Our Schools," *Christian Herald* 71, no. 2 [1948]). This foreignness eventually came to define the sisters in people's memories of the case. Even other Catholic sisters, from other orders involved in the case, remember the Dixon sisters as German refugees (Barilla interview; Conway interview). Porfiero Romero, remembering the case in 1986, removed them even further geographically and ethnically by recounting the nuns "were not teaching nuns; they were working nuns from an order from somewhere in the Middle East" (Porfiero Romero interview, 1986).
120. *Nuestra Nueva Escuela*, 1 no. 2 (October 1945), Menaul Library.
121. "A School for Dixon," pamphlet, n.d., Jones Papers.
122. Lydia Zellers to Raymond Huff, September 6, 1947, Menaul Library.

Chapter 3

1. McGee, "Causes and Effects," 79.
2. Transcript of Testimony, 1849, 1850 (plaintiffs' exhibits 4, 7).
3. Ibid.
4. Transcript of Testimony, 101 (testimony of L. Z. Manire). While most of Carrizozo's Hispanos and Catholics lived on the west side of the railroad tracks, in the vicinity of the sister-taught school, most of the town's Protestants and Anglos lived on the east side of those tracks (Ibid., 89–90, 98–99).
5. Ibid., 109 (testimony of Sr. Theodurette).
6. Ibid., 1584–85, 1850–53 (testimony of Paul Stevens, plaintiffs' exhibits 6, 9, 11, 12).
7. Sisters did *not* have unqualified agency in decisions about the structure of their classrooms. They received instructions from many parties, including local and state school officials, local clergy, religious, and lay school principals, and superiors within their congregations. Amid this volley of direction, however, each sister was ultimately responsible for the minutia that made up her own classroom and the daily proceedings therein.
8. Ibid., 305–306 (testimony of Sr. Mary Oda).
9. Barilla interview.
10. Conway interview.
11. Byrne, "In the Parish," 128–129.

12. The 1917 Code was a legal volume written for the instruction of Catholics around the world and was unprecedented in its thoroughness and attention to regulating the details of Catholic life. For American Catholics the Code punctuated the end of the United States' period as a relatively unorganized mission territory of the Church, and indicated the advent of a new era—one of strong government and closer oversight from Rome (*The 1917 or Pio-Benedictine Code of Canon Law*, in English translation, Curator Edward N. Peters [San Francisco: Ignatius Press, 2001]). Canons 487–672 apply specifically to men and women religious. The Code's restrictions built upon the 1900 papal bull *Conditae a Christo*, which elevated non-cloistered or "active" religious communities from their former status as Third Order laity, incorporating them strictly into the religious state of the Church for the first time (Elizabeth M. Cotter, *The General Chapter in a Religious Institute* [Bern, Switzerland: Peter Lang, 2008], 32).

13. *1917 Code*, 231–233 (Canons 600–607).

14. Ibid., 228 (Canon 593).

15. Ibid., 194–196 (Canons 499–501). The Grand Rapids Dominicans were one congregation that worked tirelessly (and eventually successfully) in the post-Code era to circumvent restrictive diocesan authority. On superiors' efforts to this end, see Schwind, *Period Pieces*.

16. *1917 Code*, 462 (Canon 1374).

17. Harold Buetow, *Of Singular Benefit* (New York: The Macmillan Company, 1970), 225, 249.

18. Ibid., 249. Historical characterizations of teaching sisters from this period tend to stress they were overworked and ill prepared. Kathleen Sprows Cummings offers a fuller picture of these sisters by documenting their interest in professionalization during the earlier 1890–1915 period (Cummings, *New Women*, 130–153). On the post-1917 years see Mary Oates, "The Professional Preparation of Parochial School Teachers, 1870–1940" (*Historical Journal of Massachusetts* 12, no. 1 (1984): 60–72). Scholarship that dismisses the era's sisters as ill prepared usually considers the years between 1917 and 1950 from the vantage point of the Sister Formation Movement of the 1950s. The "ill-preparation" claim relies on the work of that movement's early advocate, Sr. Bertrande Meyers (*The Education of Sisters* [New York: Sheed and Ward, 1941]). Meyers herself, however, was not concerned with sisters' lack of professional preparation so much as with the lack of spiritual nourishment the resulted from sisters' *emphasis* on professional training.

19. When New Mexico laid out educational requirements for teachers in its 1923 school code, it joined states across the country that were demanding teacher certification in order for schools, both parochial as well as public, to retain accreditation (Byrne, "In the Parish," 118–119). By the mid-1920s, the National Catholic Educational Association was also requiring that all parochial elementary school teachers take at least one normal school course after high school graduation, and that high school teachers graduate from a standard college (Buetow, *Of Singular Benefit*, 247). By 1927, two years of education beyond high school was typical among sisters teaching at the elementary-school level, and three quarters of sisters teaching in parochial high schools in the United States had four years of college training (Ibid., Byrne, "In the Parish," 120).

20. Catholic University finally allowed sisters to pursue graduate work there in 1929, and all courses were transferred from the Sisters College to Catholic University by 1951.

21. John F. Murphy, "Professional Preparation of Catholic Teachers in the Nineteen Hundreds," *Enlightening the Next Generation*, ed. F. Michael Perko (New York: Garland Publishing, Inc., 1988), 248; Schwind, *Period Pieces*, 130.

22. Buetow, *Of Singular Benefit*, 248.

23. Soran, "Lorretine History," 44–45; Roberto R. Treviño, "Facing Jim Crow: Catholic Sisters and the 'Mexican Problem' in Texas," *Western Historical Quarterly* 34, no. 2 (2003): 146–150.

24. Schwind, *Period Pieces*, 94, 96.

25. Ibid., 108. The college's opening was directly related to fact that Michigan began to require certification from all its teachers in 1921 (Ibid., 101). Before the opening of Sacred Heart College sisters had primarily attended Central and Western State Normal Schools to receive

teaching certificates, occasionally attending the Sisters College and the University of Notre Dame as well. Sacred Heart became Catholic Junior College in 1931, a two-year program accredited through the University of Michigan. By 1940, the school's name had changed to Aquinas College, and it had received state approval to offer four years of course work. The college was fully accredited as a four-year liberal arts institution in 1946 (Ibid., 102, 176, 233, 245).

26. Ibid., 139. Congregational policy stipulated that, under normal circumstances, sisters would not return to Michigan from New Mexico for six years (Ibid., 142).

27. These numbers were relative to approximately four hundred fifty professed sisters in the congregation in the late 1920s (Ibid., 102, 120–121).

28. Cummings, *New Women*, 136.

29. In 1930 the Grand Rapids Dominicans purchased a city block adjacent to the College of St. Joseph on the Rio Grande (later University of Albuquerque), run by the Franciscan Sisters, in order to provide a residence for sisters enrolled in courses there. In 1935 fourteen Dominican sisters were attending University of New Mexico while six attended Las Vegas Normal College (Ibid., 142).

30. Meyers, *Education of Sisters*, 43, 69. This number decreased to less than four percent by 1935–40 (Ibid., 43, 69, 76–77).

31. Qtd. in Ibid., 72.

32. Beutow, *Of Singular Benefit*, 232, 263.

33. Schwind, *Period Pieces*, 175, 191.

34. Transcript of Testimony, 749 (testimony of Sr. M. Claire). Certification requirements changed over time in New Mexico. In 1933 all sisters were required to either have a normal school degree, or have completed one year's experience teaching in the state, plus six semester hours of college work in the state (Schwind, *Period Pieces*, 140).

35. Transcript of Testimony, 1978 (defendants' exhibit 12).

36. Ibid.

37. David Morgan has written on the importance of the visual elements, and in particular patriotic sights like the American flag, to promoting "civil religion" within American public classrooms during the late nineteenth and early twentieth century. See David Morgan, *The Sacred Gaze: Religious Visual Culture in Theory and Practice* (Berkeley: University of California Press, 2005), 230–244.

38. *Curriculum Development in the Elementary Schools in New Mexico*, issued by State Superintendent Charles L. Rose (Santa Fe: Santa Fe Publishing Company, 1944), 1.

39. Ibid.

40. *New Mexico Statutes 1941 Annotated Official Edition*, excerpt (n.p.), Dixon papers, Collections of the Archdiocese of Santa Fe, Santa Fe, New Mexico (cited hereafter as Archdiocese Collections).

41. Barilla interview.

42. Transcript of Testimony, 159 (testimony of Sr. John Ellen).

43. Ibid., 169.

44. Dominican Sisters, *Curricular Studies: Practical Applications of the Principles of Catholic Education* (New York: Macmillan and Company, 1929), 2.

45. Ibid., 64–65, 208–209.

46. While the Dominican curriculum emphasized the inclusion of religion within every subject, explaining that "Religion should live in that part of a child where hobbies and interesting lessons live, where there are day-dreams of the sort that get worked out; where formation of character along practical lines is going on" (Ibid., 22), the civic curriculum was as adamant in its exclusion of obviously religious language. While the Dominican curriculum's reading units included vocabulary referring to church architecture and sentences on saying one's prayers, for example, the equivalent units in the state curriculum excluded Christian language almost entirely. Even an included unit on the Christmas season in the state curriculum pared down any Christian allusions, save spare vocabulary references to "church" and "star" (*Curriculum Development*, 40).

47. Qtd. in Dominican Sisters, *Curricular Studies*, vii. George Johnson was a professor of education at Catholic University of America and director of the Department of Education at the National Catholic Welfare Conference.

48. Qtd. in Ibid., 3.

49. This current of thought did have some nineteenth-century precedents, particularly in the ideas of Catholic Americanists like Archbishop John Ireland of St. Paul. It's also important to note that these two impulses—between Catholic educational distinctiveness and collaboration—were never mutually exclusive. Although their respective proponents often disagreed, advocates of collaboration still desired to preserve Catholic truths through the educational process, and advocates of Catholic distinctiveness were never proponents of absolute isolationism. See Mary Charles Bryce, OSB, "Four Decades of Roman Catholic Innovators," *Enlightening the Next Generation*.

50. Higham, *Strangers in the Land*, 205.

51. See Hamburger, *Separation of Church and State*, 408–415.

52. *Pierce v. Society of Sisters*, 268 U.S. 510 (1925).

53. Peter d'Agostino, *Rome in America: Transnational Catholic Ideology from the Risorgimento to Fascism* (Chapel Hill: The University of North Carolina Press, 2003), 254–256.

54. Thomas Shields, *Philosophy of Education* (Washington: Catholic Education Press, 1917), 180.

55. See Bryce, "Four Decades," 226–229; Murphy, "Professional Preparation," 245.

56. Shields, *Philosophy of Education*, 346. Shields offered an expansive definition of public education: "whatever is done by the state or in the state's interest, whether it is carried out by a governmental agency or not, is public" (Ibid., 346–347).

57. Bryce, "Four Decades," 228.

58. Marvin Lazerson, "Understanding American Catholic Educational History," *Enlightening the Next Generation*, 347, 349.

59. Buetow, *Of Singular Benefit*, 230–238.

60. Mary Joan Smith and Mary Nona McGreal, OP, *Guiding Growth in Christian Social Living: A Curriculum for the Elementary School* (Washington: Catholic University of America Press, 1944).

61. Transcript of Testimony, 1044–1089 (testimony of Sr. Mary Adelina Gallegos, Sr. M. Pancratia Phillips); McDonald, "Contributions," 79, 80; Barilla interview.

62. See Barilla interview; Conway interview; Sr. Donata Judis, OP, personal interview, January 12, 2006, Marywood Motherhouse, Grand Rapids, Michigan. Although most sisters would have been unable to conduct classes bilingually or in Spanish, some were unsatisfied with the English-only policy, and deviated from it. This may have particularly been the case for sisters who were raised with a first language that was not English. As an ethnically Hungarian sister remembered, "[The teachers would] always say 'Speak English! Speak English!' And I never said it 'cause I was used to a different pattern" (Barilla interview). Sisters also sometimes employed Spanish-language editions of textbooks, particularly catechisms.

63. Dorothy Senter and Florence Hawley, "The Grammar School as the Basic Acculturating Influence for Native New Mexicans," *Social Forces* 24, no. 4 (1946): 398–407.

64. On New Mexican educators who advocated for this sort of education as part of a progressive agenda, see Getz 78–86. See also the "Home Unit for First Grade" of New Mexico's state curriculum (*Curriculum Development*, 131–134).

65. Smith and McGreal, *Guiding Growth*, 4, 6.

66. McDonald, "Contributions," 78.

67. Ibid., 67–68. This particular project very closely reflected the state curriculum's "Home Unit for the First Grade," which also suggested making a trip to see a home under construction, building a playhouse, and making books about houses, families, furniture, etc. (*Curriculum Development*, 132–133).

68. McDonald, "Contributions," 68–69.

69. Ibid., 75. On hygiene emphasis in the Dominican's own curriculum, see Dominican Sisters, *Curricular Studies*, 462–465.

70. As Sr. Maura McDonald remarked, "the young people were seemingly unaware of the duties incumbent upon people living in a national forest" (McDonald, "Contributions," 73). See New Mexico's curriculum on irrigation, and closeness of children to nature (*Curriculum Development*, 185–186); see also section in the curriculum's revised edition on "conservation of wildlife" (*Curriculum Development in Elementary Schools in New Mexico*, second and revised edition, Issued by State Superintendent Charles L. Rose [Santa Fe: Santa Fe Publishing Company, 1947], 135–240). Also *Toward Better Teaching of Soil and Water Conservation*, University of New Mexico Publications in Education, no.1 (Albuquerque: University of New Mexico Press, 1947). See also Dominican sisters on collecting insects, conserving resources (Dominican Sisters, *Curricular Studies*, 103–106, 466–467). "The man who has been educated to understand the importance and the value of our natural resources; who has learned to like and appreciate nature; who sees in every living thing a message from his Creator, will take care that the natural source of wealth is not exploited through mere commercial greed or some similar motive" (Ibid., 466).

71. McDonald, "Contributions," 74.

72. *Curriculum Development*, second ed., 223.

73. McDonald, "Contributions," 43.

74. The publication of Cathedral edition readers began in 1931 (Buetow, *Of Singular Benefit*, 238).

75. Transcript of Testimony, 1396 (testimony of Paul Masters).

76. Rev. John A. O'Brien, *Our New Friends*, Cathedral Basic edition (a revision of William S. Gray and May Hill Arbuthnot, *Our New Friends*) (Chicago and New York City: Scott, Foresman and Co., 1942).

77. M. Marguierite, SND (Qtd. in Buetow, *Of Singular Benefit*, 238).

78. "'Who shall separate us from the love of Christ? . . . Neither death, nor life, nor angels, nor principalities, nor things present, nor things to come . . . will be able to separate us from the love of God, which is Christ Jesus Our Lord.' (Romans viii, 35–39)" (Qtd. in M. Charlotte, RSM, and Mary Synon, LLD, *These Our Are Freedoms*, Book Seven, Catholic University of America's *Faith and Freedom* Series [Washington, DC: Ginn and Co., 1944]), 115.

79. Transcript of Testimony, 1945–47 (plaintiffs' exhibit 155).

80. McDonald, "Contributions," 64–65.

81. Smith and McGreal, *Guiding Growth*, 4–6.

82. McDonald, "Contributions," 58.

83. Transcript of Testimony, 1873, 1887, 1890, 1891, 1892, 1905 (plaintiffs' exhibits 37, 70, 85, 87, 91, 117, 118).

84. Transcript of Record, 29–30 ("Plaintiffs' Complaint"), *Zellers* documents.

85. Transcript of Testimony, 561–564 (testimony of Sr. Eugenia Scherm).

86. Ibid., 163, 173 (testimony of Sr. John Ellen).

87. Transcript of Testimony, 472 (testimony of Sr. Natalina Fleckenstein).

88. On the use of Raphael's Madonna as picture study in art see *Curriculum Development*, 306. The list of artwork approved by the state for display in public classrooms also included "Holy Night" by Correggio, "Divine Shepherd" and "Virgin and Infant Jesus" by Murillo, "Christ Blessing Children" and "Guardian Angel" by Plockhorst, and "Star of Bethlehem" by Zotzka (Transcript of Testimony, 95 [testimony of L. Z. Manire]). For a complete list of approved images, including those with Christian and Catholic themes, see "Masterpieces Suggested for Study by Grades" (*Curriculum Development*, 294).

89. Ibid., 475.

90. Ibid., 571 (testimony of Sr. Eugenia Scherm).

91. Hofstetter, *Franciscan Sisters*, 116.

92. On catechism arrangements see Transcript of Testimony, 177–178, 180–182, 459–462, 656–657, 788, 1052–1053 (testimony of Sr. Natalina Fleckenstein, Sr. John Ellen, Sr. Rita Maria, Sr. M. Pancratia Phillips, Sr. Elizabeth Ann Ray). Occasionally, catechism was taught after the end of the school day instead (Ibid., 1201–1202 [testimony of Sr. M. Lucia]).

93. Ibid., 439–440, 656, 1225–1226 (testimony of Sister Ann Thomas, Sister Maura McDonald, Sister Elizabeth Ann Ray).

94. There were always exceptions. Plaintiffs submitted as evidence the report card of one young man in Taos County that included marks for catechism class (Ibid., 1893 [plaintiffs' exhibit 94]).

95. The Sandoval County, Pecos, Peñasco, and San Juan school boards all passed resolutions to this effect in October 1947 (Ibid., 445, 1074, 1212, 1958, 1982, 1983, 1993 [testimony of Sr. Ann Thomas, Sr. M. Pancratia Phillips, Sr. Maura McDonald; defendants' exhibits 2, 14, 15, 24]).

96. Ibid., 349 (testimony of Sr. Mary Cyrill).

97. Ibid., 107, 660, 821–823 (testimony of Sr. Theodurette, Sr. Elizabeth Ann Ray, Sr. Irma Walker).

98. Ibid., 434–435, 704–707, 1244 (testimony of Sr. Ann Thomas, Sr. Carmelita Mattingly, Sr. Maura McDonald). Sisters adopted a similar policy when it came to the use of some religious texts, particularly comic books and periodicals like the *Junior Catholic Messenger* and *Treasure Chest of Fun and Fact*. While some sisters insisted on stocking these materials in their classrooms, and others insisted they did not use them at all, a third group allowed children to subscribe individually, receive issues on their way out the classroom door, and read them on their own time (Transcript of Testimony, 327, 656, 791 [testimony of Sr. M. Gerardine, Sr. Elizabeth Ann Ray, Sr. Rita Marie]).

99. Kathleen Sprows Cummings explores the relationship between professional and religious identities, both in how parochial teachers were perceived by others and in how they perceived themselves. Canon law, she points out, was clear in distinguishing between the primary and secondary ends of religious vocation, and asserting the importance of personal sanctification over aiding in the sanctification of others. In practice, however, religious who taught saw the relationship between the two in complicated ways (*New Women*, 135–139).

100. Mary Nona McGreal, OP, "The Role of a Teaching Sisterhood in American Education" (Ph.D. diss., Catholic University of America, 1951), 19–20, 98.

101. Ibid., 112–113, 124.

102. Ibid., 102.

103. The Dominican congregations shared close ties through the early twentieth century. The Grand Rapids Dominicans actually adopted the Sinsinawa congregation's constitution for several years, using it until their own constitution was approved by Rome in 1941 (Schwind, *Period Pieces*, 213).

104. McDonald, "Contributions," 73, 81.

105. Transcript of Testimony, 326–327 (testimony of Sr. M. Gerardine); McDonald, "Contributions," 73.

106. Bob Bissell, "Teaching Nuns Answered State's Biggest Problems," *Santa Fe Register*, May 15, 1948: 4.

107. McDonald to Marywood Sisters, October 1948, Marywood Archives: 3; "Sister Maura Makes 50th Jubilee," *The New Day*, April 29, 1973, Marywood Archives. When the *Zellers* litigation began, McDonald also struck up a correspondence with attorneys in Washington and lent her academic work to assist with their legal preparations. NCWC attorney George Reed assured McDonald that her master's thesis on the Dominicans' experiences as public teachers would serve as an important resource for oral arguments before the New Mexico Supreme Court. See Reed to McDonald, July 22, 1949; Reed to McDonald, January 23, 1950; Reed to McDonald, February 7, 1951, Marywood Archives.

108. Transcript of Testimony, 1135, 1984 (testimony of Sr. Irma Mariana; defendants' exhibit 16).
109. McGreal, "The Role of a Teaching Sisterhood," 98.
110. Cordova interview.
111. Conway interview.
112. Judis interview; Conway interview.
113. "Minutes of the Meeting of the Rio Arriba County Board of Education," September 2, 1947, Archdiocese Collections: 1.
114. Ibid., 3.
115. Ibid., 3–4.
116. Ibid, 5.
117. Ibid.

Chapter 4

1. "Free Schools," manuscript, n.d., Jones Papers: 5.
2. Sally Eauclaire, "Vignette, Harry L. "Judge" Bigbee," *The Santa Fean Magazine* (December 1990): 38–40; "Basic Facts About Dixon, New Mexico," manuscript, n.d., Jones Papers: 2.
3. "Basic Facts About Dixon, New Mexico," 2.
4. Charles Rose and Raymond Huff to Rio Arriba County Board of Education, September 16, 1947, Archdiocese Collections.
5. William Bradley to Bernard Lewis, September 24, 1947, Archdiocese Collections.
6. Edwin Byrne to Religious, September 18, 1947, Archdiocese Collections.
7. Byrne to Sr. Emma, September 18, 1947, Archdiocese Collections.
8. Br. Bernard Lewis to Byrne, September 22, 1947; Sr. M. Cordia to Byrne, September 23, 1947; Sr. Claire Marie to Byrne, September 18, 1947, Archdiocese Collections.
9. Charles Rose to Byrne, September 25, 1947; Walter Washila to William Bradley, September 28, 1947, Archdiocese Collections.
10. "Compromise in Santa Fe," *Time*, September 29, 1947: 70.
11. Ibid.
12. Arthur Montgomery to Editor of *Time*, September 25, 1947, Jones Papers.
13. See Yohn, *A Contest of Faiths.*
14. Zellers interview; Sarah Bowen to unnamed recipients, October 21, 1947, Jones Papers.
15. Qtd. in Luke Eugene Ebersole, *Church Lobbying in the Nation's Capital* (New York: Macmillan Company, 1951), 72.
16. This history stretches back to Poughkeepsie, New York, where in 1873 a compromise allowed the local school board to rent out a parochial school for public education during school hours, allowing religious instruction to take place there at other times. In the Midwest Archbishop John Ireland of St. Paul drew attention for the similar compromises he orchestrated in the towns of Faribault and Stillwater, Minnesota, in 1891. Ireland's ambitious plan of public–parochial cooperation lasted only a couple of years before folding in the face of both Protestant opposition and skepticism from many of his peers in the American hierarchy. See Robert Cross, *The Emergence of Liberal Catholicism in America* (Cambridge: Harvard University Press, 1958), 139–141. For a full account of Ireland's school plan and the controversy surrounding it, see Reilly, *The School Controversy.* Although the religious involved in twentieth-century captive school cases did not identify with their nineteenth-century precedents, some separation advocates of the period did make this connection. See Leo Pfeffer, *Church, State and Freedom* (Boston: Beacon Press, 1953), 449–450; Paul Blanshard, *American Freedom and Catholic Power*, second ed. (Boston: Beacon Press, 1958), 125–126.
17. *Church and State* 12, no. 10 (1959): 2.

18. Definitions of the captive school were always vague, with the exception of the "take over" language they shared. One POAU member summarized it simply as "a public school that has been taken over by a sectarian group and operated for sectarian purposes" (C. Stanley Lowell, *Embattled Wall* [Washington DC: Americans United, 1966], 96). Other proffered definitions of captive schools included the "control of public schools by [a] religious group" (Sorauf, *Wall of Separation*, 246); and "situations in which Catholic nuns [have] taken over the public schools and were running them at public expense" (Fey, *Sovereign Reverence*, 7). These one-line explanations invariably reversed the usual sequence of events on the ground—as in New Mexico, the public school board was always the prime mover, acting to assume control (at least formally) of the parochial school.

19. Sorauf, *Wall of Separation*, 247. Despite its use by legal organizations, the captive school label was never incorporated into the language of the courts. The idea of captivity did influence judicial language, particularly in the legal doctrine of a "captive audience." References to the Catholic Church aside, during this period the U.S. Supreme Court acknowledged captivity as an effective category for describing people, particularly children, in locations that make them vulnerable to the dissemination of religion. The court's first use of captive audience language was in a 1951 case regarding street worship meetings (*Kunz v. People of the State of New York*, dissenting opinion, 340 U.S. 290 [1951]). Ten years later the Court used the same language to articulate the grounds on which official prayer in the public classroom constituted a violation of the Establishment Clause (*Engel v. Vitale*, concurring opinion).

20. Leo Pfeffer, one of the period's most respected legal voices on separation, spoke about POAU's audience choice, its message to that audience, and the consequences of that message. He explained the ability of his own group, the American Jewish Congress, to avoid the anti-Catholic image POAU fell victim to lay in its decision to appeal to "the elite—the opinion leaders and the decision-makers—rather than the masses." He joined other scholars in connecting POAU's use of "anti-Catholic" language with its need to appeal to a mass audience uninspired by the abstract principle of separation (Qtd. in Mary Beasley, "Pressure Group Persuasion: Protestants and Other Americans United for Separation of Church and State, 1947–1968," (Ph.D. diss., Purdue University, 1970), 191–194). See also Sorauf, *Wall of Separation*, 34; Ebersole, *Church Lobbying*, 178.

21. McGreevy, *Catholicism and American Freedom*, 166–188.

22. On the Church's arrangements with fascist regimes in Europe see Frank J. Coppa, *Controversial Concordats: The Vatican's Relations with Napoleon, Mussolini, and Hitler* (Washington: The Catholic University of America Press, 1999).

23. John Dewey, *Freedom and Culture* (New York: G. P. Putnam's Sons, 1939).

24. Sidney Hook, "Democracy and Education: Introduction," *The Authoritarian Attempt to Capture Education: Papers from the Second Conference on the Scientific Spirit and Democratic Faith* (New York: King's Crown Press, 1945), 11–12.

25. Ibid., 11.

26. Ibid.

27. Pius XI, "Divini Illius Magistri," *Online Papal Archive of the Vatican*, http://www.vatican.va/ holy_father/pius_xi/encyclicals/documents/hf_p-xi_enc_31121929_divini-illius-magistri_en.html (accessed July 6, 2006).

28. McGreevy, *Catholicism and American Freedom*, 183.

29. Before 1962 religious observances were required by law in twelve states and forbidden in only nine. Other states left the decision to local districts. Before 1962, seventy seven percent of public schools in the American South provided students the opportunity to read or hear passages from the Christian Bible. See DelFattore, *The Fourth R*, 53; E. Katz, "Patterns of Compliance with the Schempp Decision," *Journal of Public Law* 14 (1966): 405.

30. *Everson v. Board of Education*.

31. *McCollum v. Board of Education*, 333 U.S. 203 (1948). The ambiguity of this language became evident soon after *McCollum*; in 1952 the Court denied an Establishment Clause claim that

questioned the constitutionality of released time programs occurring off school grounds (*Zorach v. Clauson*). This decision, however, didn't negate the broad impact of *Everson* and *McCollum* when it came to enforcing a new legal standard of separation on things happenings *inside* publicly funded classrooms.

32. *Church and State* 1, no. 1 (1948): 1; Joseph Dawson, *Separate Church and State Now* (New York: Richard R. Smith, 1948), 53. Black reportedly did have a private conversation with founding member Joseph Dawson in which he endeavored to alleviate the latter's worries about *Everson* by emphasizing the decision did not favor religion in any broad capacity (Hamburger, *Separation of Church and State*, 469).

33. Ebersole, *Church Lobbying*, 72.

34. POAU made the point against religious propagandizing in its manifesto (Joseph Dawson, *A Thousand Months to Remember* [Waco: Baylor University Press, 1964], 199).

35. Ebersole, *Church Lobbying*, 67 (from interview with Joseph Dawson). The committee is now called the Baptist Joint Committee on Religious Liberty. Initiated by the Baptist conventions' joint signing of a pronouncement on religious liberty in 1941, the Joint Committee was dedicated to upholding what organizers believed was a common and fundamental Baptist commitment to protecting religion from governmental persecution both in the United States and abroad. The same year the pronouncement was signed, Rev. Rufus Weaver, the founding force behind the committee, organized a Baptist-sponsored conference on church and state. The conference was attended by several future POAU members, and it saw the appointment of a commission dedicated to keeping alive public interest in church–state separation. Although this commission was interrupted by war, upon Weaver's death and Dawson's nomination to the Joint Committee it was reborn under different leadership as POAU. Its motivations and much of its core membership remained the same. Interestingly Hugo Black was a Baptist and had been an original member, albeit briefly, of the Southern Baptist committee that was a progenitor of the Baptist Joint Committee (Hamburger, *Separation of Church and State*, 388). For a detailed history of Baptist Joint Committee, see C. C. Goen, "Baptists and Church-State Issues in the Twentieth Century," *American Baptist Quarterly* 6, no. 4 (1987): 226–253.

36. Nonreligious organizations represented included the American Ethical Union, the American Humanist Association, the National Education Association, and the National Parent Teacher Association. Rounding out the group was Elmer Rogers, of the Supreme Council 33rd-Degree of the Southern Jurisdiction of the Scottish Rite Masons (Ebersole, *Church Lobbying*, 68–70; anonymous to John Pitzer, November 28, 1947, Americans United for Separation of Church and State Records, Public Policy Papers, Department of Rare Books and Special Collections, Princeton University Library [cited hereafter as AU Records]). The interest of the Scottish Rite Masons became particularly significant for the group; while Rogers joined the group's executive committee, John H. Cowles, the Sovereign Grand Commander of the Council, demonstrated his commitment to POAU's mission by becoming its founding benefactor, donating $38,000 in start-up funds on behalf of his Order (anonymous to Grand Commander Cowles, January 6, 1948; minutes (POAU executive committee meeting), February 12, 1948, AU Records).

37. Edwin McNeal Poteat, qtd. in Robert Moats Miller, *Bishop G. Bromley Oxnam: Paladin of Liberal Protestantism* (Abington Press, 1990), 406. The organization did include some Jewish members on its national advisory board (Ibid.).

38. Ebersol, *Church Lobbying*, 69.

39. In North College Hill, Ohio, for example, teachers in the community's African American school did not take sides in a dispute involving religious teachers at one of the area's other public schools (Pfeffer, *Church, State*, 453–454). On Catholic ministry, and lack thereof, to African Americans in the mid-twentieth century, see John McGreevy, *Parish Boundaries: the Catholic Encounter with Race in the Twentieth-Century Urban North* (Chicago: University of Chicago Press, 1996).

40. Miller, *Bishop G. Bromley Oxnam*; Edwin Gaustad and Leigh Schmidt, *The Religious History of America: The Heart of the American Story from the Colonial Times to Today*, revised ed. (New York: Harper One, 2004), 340.

41. POAU publicly went to further pains to distinguish separation from secularization. The group's secretary defended separation as "insurance of religious liberty and goodwill among the sects.... It produces a keen sense of obligation to strengthen ... the high moral and spiritual values now being taught under the democratic process of the public school" (*Church and State* 1, no. 2 [1948]).

42. Of the thirty cases POAU formally participated in between 1951 and 1971, only two did not involve the Catholic Church. This reflects a more targeted approach to separation than that of either of its counterparts, the ACLU (with less than half its cases during that period involving the Church) and the AJC (with roughly two thirds of its cases involving the Church) (Sorauf, *Wall of Separation*, 61 [Table 4–1]). In one notable case, a local POAU-supported attorney actually cited in his complaint the failure of Catholic sisters teaching in a public school to read daily chapters from the Bible (Sorauf, *Wall of Separation*, 35).

43. Hamburger, *Separation of Church and State*, 372, 361.

44. Miller, *Bishop G. Bromley Oxnam*, 431.

45. Ibid., 399.

46. Hamburger, *Separation of Church and State*, 375–386.

47. Ibid., 384.

48. Ibid., 476–477.

49. Miller, *Bishop G. Bromley Oxnam*, 431.

50. Dawson, *A Thousand Months*, 1–6.

51. Hamburger, *Separation of Church and State*, 387.

52. Dawson, *A Thousand Months*, 146–148.

53. Dawson, *Separate Church and State*, 44.

54. Frank S. Mead, *On Our Own Doorstep* (New York: Friendship Press, 1948).

55. Joseph Dawson to Edwin Poteat, March 23, 1948, AU Records; *Church and State* 1, no. 1 (1948): 1.

56. Hamburger, *Separation of Church and State*, 464.

57. *Church and State* 1, no. 1 (1948): 2. By the mid-1960s there were over a thousand churches across the country that donated funds annually to POAU and distributed *Church and State*, the organization's newsletter, to their members (Lowell, *Embattled Wall*, 142).

58. Sorauf, *Wall of Separation*, 81.

59. Martin Luther himself wrote of a church that "has been taken prisoner" by Rome ("The Pagan Servitude of the Church," *Martin Luther: Selections from His Writings*, ed. John Dillenberger [Garden City, NY: Anchor Books, 1961], 284); Jenny Franchot, *Roads to Rome: The Antebellum Encounter with Catholicism* (Berkeley: University of California Press, 1994), 88.

60. In well-known examples, the climate of fear and anger that fostered the burning of the Ursuline Convent in Charlestown, Massachusetts, in 1834 also manifest itself as intrigue, turning the horrific and sensational account of convent captivity written by self-proclaimed Ursuline escapee Rebecca Reed (1835) into a best-seller. For a thorough discussion of nineteenth-century Protestantism's obsession with captivity, see Ibid., 87–196. See also Barbara Welter, "From Maria Monk to Paul Blanshard: A Century of Protestant Anti-Catholicism" *Uncivil Religion: Interreligious Hostility in America* (eds. Robert Bellah and Frederick Greenspahn) (New York: Crossroad Publishing, 1987), 47.

61. *Awful Disclosures by Maria Monk of the Hotel Dieu Nunnery of Montreal* (New York: Francis F. Ripley, 1836), 44–45.

62. Ibid., 48, 50.

63. Franchot, *Roads to Rome*, 108.

64. See Beecher, *A Plea for the West*; Josiah Strong, *Our Country*, ed. Jurgen Herbst (Cambridge: Harvard University Press, 1963); Thomas Nast, *Miss Columbia's Public School* (New York: Francis B. Felt & Co., 1871).

65. Blanshard, *American Freedom*, 89.

66. Loraine Boettner, *Roman Catholicism* (Philadelphia: The Presbyterian and Reformed Publishing Company, 1962), 6. In the Supreme Court's 1971 decision *Lemon v. Kurtzman*, Justice William Douglas cited Boettner's remarks on education, from the same book, in his concurring opinion—"The whole education of the child is filled with propaganda.... [They] are regimented, and are told what to wear, what to do, and what to think." *Lemon v. Kurtzman*, concurring opinion, 403 U.S. 602 (1971); McGreevey, *Catholicism and American Freedom*, 264. On mid-century captivity language used in describing women religious, see also Helen Conroy, *Forgotten Women (In Convents)* (Agora Publishing Company, NY, 2nd ed., 1946); Emmitt McGloughlin, *American Culture and Catholic Schools* (New York: L. Stuart Press, 1960), 196.

67. Robert Lynd and Helen Merrell Lynd, *Middletown: A Study in Modern American Culture* (San Diego: Harcourt, Brace and Company, 1959).

68. Harold Fey, "Catholicism Comes to Middletown," *The Christian Century* 61, no. 49 (1944): 1410.

69. Clifford Earle, "Dixon, N.M.—Testing Ground for Democracy," *Social Progress* (December 1949): 1–5; Joseph Dawson, "Public Schools, Catholic Model," *The Christian Century* (June 1948): 627–629.

70. Paul Blanshard, *American Freedom and Catholic Power*, first edition (Boston: Beacon Press, 1949), 98.

71. Mead, "Shadows Over Our Schools," *Christian Herald* 71, no. 2 (February 1948): 1.

72. Ibid., 2.

73. Ibid., 4.

74. Carroll M. Wright (public relations, *Christian Herald*) to Editors, n.d., Archdiocese Collections.

75. *Church and State* 1, no. 1 (1948): 4; Archbishops John T. McNicholas and Howard Carroll to U.S. Bishops, June 30, 1948, NCWC Collections.

76. William Bradley to Bishop John Noll (in response to Noll's inquiry), January 16, 1948, Archdiocese Collections.

77. POAU continued to draw upon Mead's article intermittently. Independent of POAU, the article was still being circulated as an alarmist tract in 1958, intended to dissuade California residents from voting for the Catholic candidate for governor. See Frank Mead, "Shadows Over Our Schools," pamphlet (Los Angeles, CA: Heritage Manor, 1958).

78. Paul Blanshard, *Religion and the Schools: The Great Controversy* (Boston: Beacon Press, 1963), 164.

79. By 1955 POAU's new executive director was using "captive school" as a descriptive category in speeches (see, for example, "Church Unit Scans Religious Freedom," *Christian Science Monitor*, October 15, 1955: 15). The evolution of the term is also traceable through a comparison of successive editions of Blanshard's *American Freedom and Catholic Power*. While Blanshard does not use the term in the original 1949 edition, he does include the term in his second, revised edition in 1958 (Blanshard, *American Freedom*, second ed., 126).

80. Qtd. in Lowell, *Embattled Wall*, 32–33.

81. Ibid., 99.

82. Ibid., 95–96.

83. Sourauf, *Wall of Separation*, 95.

84. Lowell, *Embattled Wall*, 96.

85. See Lowell, *Embattled Wall*, 96; Fey, *Sovereign Reverence*, 7.

86. For an explanation of the differing goals of the AJC and the ACLU in this regard, see Sorauf, *Wall of Separation*, 96.

87. Lowell, *Embattled Wall*, 106.

88. Ibid., 142.
89. Folders on violations by state, n.d., AU Records.
90. Harold Fey, "Preview of a Divided America," *The Christian Century* (May 28, 1947): 682–684; Pfeffer, *Church, State*, 450.
91. Fey, "Preview," 682.
92. The disastrous condition of North College Hill's schools improved only after the National Education Association effectively blacklisted the entire district. At the recommendation of its Commission for the Defense of Democracy through Education, the NEA declared the city an unprofessional place for teachers to work, and it urged teachers to refuse employment there. As a result of this crippling move, the local school board resigned. A probate judge assumed responsibility for the situation; he cancelled the city's contract for Public School No. 3 and scheduled board elections. Soon after, a safely Protestant majority was elected onto the board. The superintendent, William Cook, went on to become an active member in POAU. Sources used to assemble this account of North College Hill include Fey, "Preview"; Pfeffer, *Church, State*; "Parochial Schools Made Issue at NEA," *New York Times*, July 11, 1947.
93. *Berghorn v. Reorganized School District No. 8*, 364 Mo. 121 (1953), 46.
94. The court only considered issues under the scope of the state constitution because the school district failed to cite the federal provisions in question in the appellate brief.
95. Lowell, *Embattled Wall*, 104. Other sources used to assemble this account of Franklin County include Joint Appendix ("Agreed Statement of Facts"), *Berghorn v. Reorganized School District No. 8*.
96. *Rawlings v. Butler*, 290 S.W.2d 801 (1956).
97. Lowell, *Embattled Wall*, 107–108; *Wooley v. Spalding*, 293 S.W.2d 563 (1956).
98. *Church and State* (November 1959).
99. "Lit Distribution," memorandum, n.d.; Glenn Archer to Board of Trustees, August 21, 1959, AU Records.
100. See "Captured," promotional flyer, n.d., AU Records; C. Stanley Lowell, "Captive Schools: An American Tragedy," pamphlet (Washington, D.C.: Protestants and Other Americans United, 1959); "Bradfordsville—Ten Years Later," pamphlet (Washington, D.C.: Protestants and Other Americans United, 1959).
101. "Captured," promotional flier.
102. *Church and State* (February 1959): 5.
103. *Captured*, DVD, private collection (Washington: Protestants and Other Americans United for Separation of Church and State, 1959).
104. "Captured on Pleasant Hill," film script, AU Records: 1.
105. *Captured*.
106. "Captured on Pleasant Hill," 16.
107. *Captured*.
108. "Captured on Pleasant Hill," 22.
109. *Captured*.
110. John C. Mayne to Paul Duling, April 13, 1960, AU Records.
111. The literature distributed at screenings of *Captured* included over 250,000 publicity flyers and 70,000 pamphlets about captive schools ("Film Department Report for Year Ending August 21, 1960," memorandum, n.d., AU Records). Employees working on behalf of the Nixon campaign in 1960 even contemplated using *Captured* to rally Protestant support for their candidate. The campaign worked closely with POAU, and *Captured*'s screenings regularly shared venues and personnel with meetings convened to question Kennedy's electability as a Catholic (Shawn Casey, *The Making of a Catholic* President [New York: Oxford University Press, 2009], 107).
112. On representations of Catholicism in Hollywood during this era, see Anthony Burke Smith, "America's Favorite Priest," *Catholics in the Movies*, ed. Colleen McDannell (New York: Oxford University Press, 2007). On the representations of Catholic sisters in Hollywood, see

Rebecca Sullivan, *Visual Habits: Nuns, Feminism, and American Postwar Popular Culture* (Toronto: University of Toronto Press, 2005).

113. Although the organization officially went to great efforts to avoid the anti-Catholic title, some of its members were privately more receptive to the label. The group's founding ben-efactor, for example, wrote to Dawson about his personal anti-Catholicism, confessing "it is very difficult for me to keep from showing it more than I do" (John H. Cowles to Joseph Dawson, September 16, 1948, AU Records). Paul Blanshard reflected on his relationship with the term in his autobiography. Although he distanced himself from the label, he also remembered it with pride, writing that those who called him anti-Catholic did so with "appropriate fury" (Paul Blanshard, *Personal and Controversial* [Boston: Beacon Press, 1973], 216).

114. See, for example, "Serious School Problem," *New Age* (December 1947); "New Mexico Public Schools Disgraceful Mess," *New Age* (March 1948); Edwin H. Wilson, "The Sectarian Battlefront," *The Humanist* (Spring 1948): 179–180; Edwin H. Wilson, "The Sectarian Bat-tlefront," *The Humanist* (Summer 1949): 100; "Two Valiant Women," *Progressive World* (April 1949): 83; "Victory Is Complete in New Mexico School Case," *The Converted Catholic Magazine* (May 1949): 130; Frank Mead, "Shadows Over Our Schools," reprint, *Signs of the Times* 75, no. 14. The founding editor of *Converted Catholic Magazine* was a former priest turned evangelical Christian. Other publications offering sympathetic coverage of the com-mittee included *The Nation*, the free thought-oriented journal *Truth Seeker*, the Presbyterian *General Assembly Daily News* and *Presbyterian Life*, the *Christian Beacon*, the *Christian Science Monitor*, *Liberty*, *The Churchman*, and *The Baptist New Mexican*.

115. "New Mexico Public Schools Disgraceful Mess." *New Age* was the official journal of the Supreme Council 33rd-Degree Scottish Rite Freemasons.

116. Porfiero Romero interview, 1986.

117. "Free Schools," manuscript, n.d., Jones Papers. The list also included various groups of Bap-tists, Lutherans, and Methodists.

118. Zellers interview.

119. "Dixon Group Ponders Action Over School," n.p. (January 1948), Jones Papers.

120. Anonymous to William Bradley, February 19, 1948, Archdiocese Collections; "Move to Ban Catholic Instructors in NM Public Schools Begins Soon," *Albuquerque Tribune*, February 19, 1948.

121. Dixon Free Schools Committee to Supporters, February 27, 1948, Jones Papers.

Chapter 5

1. Bradly to Bishop John Noll, January 16, 1948, Archdiocese Collections.

2. Anonymous to Byrne, n.d., Archdiocese Collections.

3. Bradley to Bernadine Keefe, May 15, 1948, Archdiocese Collections. See also Auxiliary Bishop Leo Dworschak of Fargo to Bradley, April 12, 1948; Bradley to Steve K. Vaught, April 8, 1948, Archdiocese Collections.

4. "The Truth About Sisters Teaching in the Public Schools of New Mexico," memorandum, n.d., Archdiocese Collections.

5. Byrne to Robert Bissell, March 31, 1948, Archdiocese Collections.

6. Press release, n.d., Archdiocese Collections; Robert Bissell, "Dixon School Case Distorted By 'Christian Herald' Article," *Santa Fe Register*, April 23, 1948: 1.

7. Ibid.

8. Bissell, "Teaching Nuns Answered State's Biggest Problems," *Santa Fe Register*, May 14, 1948. See also Bissell, "Confusion Still Rampant on Religious Schools," *Santa Fe Register*, May 28, 1948.

9. Bissell to Rev. C. C. Shepner, 8 July 1948; Archdiocese to Bissell, 9 July 1948, Archdiocese Collections.

10. "Official Probes Fuss in Dixon Area," n.p., n.d., Jones Papers.

11. R. P. Sweeney and William Bradley to Charles Rose, January 20, 1948, Archdiocese Collections.

12. "Religious Rows Hurt All in State—Mabry," *Santa Fe New Mexican*, March 5, 1948. See also "Governor Replies to Minister: 'State Makes No Distinction As to Religion of Teachers,'" *Santa Fe Register*, February 20, 1948; "Taos Pastor Questions Mabry in Dixon Stand," *Santa Fe New Mexican*, March 4, 1948.

13. *McCollum v. Board of Education*, 212.

14. Transcript of Record, 5 ("Complaint").

15. Ibid., 14, 18.

16. Ibid., 13.

17. Ibid., 27–34.

18. Ibid., 34.

19. "Statement of the Catholic Bishops of New Mexico," *Santa Fe Register*, March 12, 1948.

20. Ibid.

21. Transcript of Record, 43–51, 84–88 ("Affidavits of Service").

22. "Back Talk: Letters to the Editor," *Christian Herald* (April 1948): 88.

23. Letters of Joan Palmer and John Milleam, Ibid.

24. "Most Pupils Quit in Religious Row," n.p., February 4, 1953, NCWC Collection.

25. On public perceptions of sisters during the mid-twentieth century, see Sullivan, *Visual Habits*; Marian Ronan, "Danger and Longing: Roman Catholic Nuns in American Culture," *Religious Studies Review* 30.1 (January 2004): 13–21.

26. See for example *United States v. Board of Education for the School District of Philadelphia*, 911 F.2d 882 (3rd Cir., 1990); *Cooper v. Eugene School District*, 723 P.2d 298 (Ore. 1986).

27. "Secularism: Statement Issued November 14, 1947 by the Bishops of the United States and Signed in their Names by the Members of the Administrative Board, N.C.W.C.," pamphlet (Washington, DC: National Catholic Welfare Conference, 1947), 1.

28. For other examples, see Lowell, "Captive Schools: An American Tragedy."

29. Blanshard, *American Freedom*, 25–26.

30. Ibid., 89–90.

31. Ibid., 88.

32. For reflection that touches upon on the effects sisters' habits might have had on children, see Robert Orsi's chapter on "Material Religion" in *Between Heaven and Earth*. Orsi stresses the priority of the visual in children's classrooms, and describes a process of "corporalization of the sacred," which he argues was ongoing in Catholic ones. He defines this as "the practice of rendering the invisible visible by constituting it as an experience in a body . . . so that the experiencing body itself becomes the bearer of presence for oneself and for others" (Orsi, *Between Heaven and Earth*, 74, 86). Though Orsi does not pay particular attention to sisters' habits, or to legally contested classrooms, the sense of a Catholic worldview becoming incarnate in sisters' covered bodies, and transforming them into a religious presence to be absorbed by children, is useful. It helps to explain the deeply rooted worries shared among the habit's critics.

33. Blanshard, *American Freedom*, 88; Boettner, *Roman Catholicism*, 6.

34. Elizabeth Kuhns, *The Habit: A History of the Clothing of Catholic Nuns* (New York: Doubleday, 2003), 5.

35. Ibid., 175–182.

36. Ibid., 32–33.

37. Ibid., 98. For an extended treatment of this miraculous account and its reception within the Order, see Cordelia Warr, "Religious Habits and Visual Propaganda: The Vision of Blessed Reginald of Orléans," *Journal of Medieval History* 28, no. 1 (March 2002): 43–72.

38. Kuhns, *Habit*, 184.

39. Conway interview; Judis interview; "Peñasco," captioned photograph, n.d., Marywood Archives.

40. Judis interview.
41. Coburn and Smith, *Spirited Lives*, 2, 43.
42. *1917 Code*, 229–230 (Canon 596).
43. Blanshard, *American Freedom*, 88.
44. For historical and legal analysis of garb litigation, see Leonard A. Krug, "The Wearing of Religious Garb by Public School Teachers" (paper, University of Chicago Law School, 1960); E. Edmund Reutter, "Teacher's Religious Dress: A Century of Litigation," *West's Education Law Reporter* 70 (January 1992): 747; Virgil C. Blum, "Religious Liberty and the Religious Garb," *University of Chicago Law Review* 22, no. 4 (Summer 1955): 875; "Religious Garb in the Public Schools: A Study in Conflicting Liberties," *University of Chicago Law Review* 22, no. 4 (Summer 1955): 888; Holly M. Bastian, "Religious Garb Statutes and Title VII: An Uneasy Coexistence," *Georgetown Law Journal* (October 1991): 211.
45. Local disputes over garb began even earlier. See Coburn and Smith, *Spirited Lives*, 133–134. In New Mexico in 1892, the Albuquerque Board of Education ordered the removal of garb from classrooms in its district. The Sisters of Charity withdrew from classrooms as a result (Bacon, "Contributions of Catholic Orders," 12).
46. *Hysong v. Gallitzin Borough School District*, 164 Pa. 629 (1894).
47. Ibid., 55.
48. Ibid., 51.
49. Pa. Stat. Ann. Tit. 14 11–1112 (1982; originally enacted 1895). Qtd. in Bastian, "Religious Garb Statutes," 213.
50. *Commonwealth v. Herr*, 229 Pa. 132 (1910). Between the Pennsylvania court's two decisions, the Supreme Court of New York upheld a similar regulation prohibiting state teachers from wearing religious clothing in the classroom (*O'Connor v. Hendrick*, 184 NY 421 [1906]).
51. *Knowlton v. Baumhover*, 182 Iowa 691 (1918); *State Public School District No. 6 v. Taylor*, 122 Neb. 454 (1932); *Gerhardt v. Heid*, 66 ND 444 (1936); *Johnson v. Boyd* 217 Ind. 348 (1940); *Harfst v. Hoegen*, 349 Mo. 808 (1942); *City of New Haven v. Town of Torrington*, 132 Conn. 194 (1945).
52. These include *Knowlton v. Baumhover*; *State Public School District No. 6 v. Taylor*.
53. See for example *Gerhardt v. Heid*; *Johnson v. Boyd*.
54. "The State and Sectarian Education," *Research Bulletin of the National Education Association* 24, no. 34 (1946): 25, 36; "Comments: Church and State in American Education," *Illinois Law Review* 43 (1948–9): 383; "Religious Garb in the Public Schools."
55. *Gerhardt v. Heid*, 1.
56. *Gerhardt v. Heid*, 27–28.
57. Linda Grathwold, "The North Dakota Anti-Garb Law: Constitutional Conflict and Religious Strife," *Great Plains Quarterly* 13, no. 3 (Summer 1993): 189.
58. Ibid., 190.
59. Reverend C. A. Armstrong, qtd. in Ibid., 191.
60. The Committee for Separation circulated Frank Mead's article about the Dixon situation as a means of drumming up support for its own cause (Frank Mead, "Shadows Over Our Schools," copy distributed by North Dakota Committee on Separation of Church and State, Archdiocese Collections).
61. Grathwold, "North Dakota Anti-Garb Law," 189.
62. Ibid., 190.
63. Committee for Defense of Civil Rights (H. G. Nilles, Chairman), "Facts About Sisters Teaching in Public Schools in North Dakota" (Bismarck: The Committee for the Defense of Civil Rights, 1948), 7, 17. The committee reported printing 55,000 copies of this pamphlet (Ryan to Byrne, April 17, 1948, Archdiocese Archives). See also Committee for Defense of Civil Rights, "In Union There Is Strength/Let Us Avoid Division and Strife/Vote NO on the Anti-Garb Measure and Preserve Peace," pamphlet, n.d., Archdiocese Collections; Grathwold, "North Dakota Anti-Garb Law," 191–193.

64. Grathwold, "North Dakota Anti-Garb Law," 193.

65. Qtd. in Ibid.

66. Ibid., 194, 196; "North Dakota Nuns to Adopt Civilian Dress In Order to Teach Under New State Curb," *New York Times*, July 12, 1948; "60 Nuns Change Garb By North Dakota Law," *New York Times*, September 22, 1948.

67. "60 Nuns Change Garb."

68. See for example "Protestant Ministers in Public Schools," *America* 79, no. 3 (April 24, 1948): 47; "Underscorings," *America* 79, no. 15 (July 17, 1948): 341; "Ripples in North Dakota," *America* 79, no. 16 (July 24, 1948): 364; Margaret McEachem, "Nuns Carry on in North Dakota," *Catholic Digest* 13 (March 1949): 93–96.

69. Leo Dworschak to Byrne, April 12, 1948; Dworschak to Bradley, April 12, 1948; Ryan to Byrne, April 17, 1948; Ryan to Byrne, October 30, 1948, Archdiocese Collections.

70. Br. Cyprian Luke, FSC, personal interview, College of Santa Fe, August 12, 2005; "History of the College," website of the College of Santa Fe, http://www.csf.edu/about_csf/history (accessed March 5, 2008). In 1966, St. Michael's College was renamed the College of Santa Fe; in 2009 it became Santa Fe University of Art and Design.

71. Br. Benildus to Sister Superior at Aragon, March 10, 1948; Espelage to Byrne, March 30, 1948; Julian Rousseau to Benildus, March 15, 1948, Archdiocese Collections. Barker was assisted by his legal partner, H. J. Guthman.

72. William T. O'Sullivan to Byrne, April 3, 1948; Gino J. Matteucci to Byrne, April 5, 1948; Joseph L. Smith to Byrne, April 5, 1948; Eleanor Farina de Cola to Byrne, April 6, 1948; Joseph McNeany to Byrne, April 6, 1948; Maurice Sanchez to Byrne, April 10, 1948; W. Peter McAtee to Byrne, April 28, 1948, Archdiocese Collections.

73. Byrne to Maurice Sanchez, April 2, 1948, Archdiocese Collections.

74. W. Peter McAtee to Byrne, April 28, 1948; Angelo Fabrizio (Knights of Columbus, Albuquerque Fourth Degree) to Byrne, March 21, 1948; Byrne to Fabrizio, March 23, 1948, Archdiocese Collections.

75. Bradley to Frederick Hockwalt, December 31, 1947, NCWC Collection.

76. Qtd. in Ebersole, *Church Lobbying*, 47.

77. Ibid., 47–56; Lisa C. Moreno, "The National Catholic Welfare Conference and Catholic Americanism, 1919–1966" (Ph.D. diss., University of Maryland, 1999), 31.

78. Ebersole, *Church Lobbying*, 48. The administrative board of the NCWC comprised bishops elected by their peers, but the organization did not officially or unanimously represent the perspectives or positions of American bishops. As Lisa Moreno explains, the NCWC was more an advisory body than an official mouthpiece, and it often found itself at odds with elements of the American Church, particularly more conservative prelates and the heads of large, urban dioceses (Moreno, "Catholic Americanism," 32–34).

79. Fey, "Catholicism Comes to Middletown," 1411.

80. *Guiding Growth* was developed under the direct supervision of George Johnson, then director of the NCWC's Department of Education (Moreno, "Catholic Americanism," 131).

81. Ibid., 31.

82. Ibid., 171–176, 186–188; Ebersole, *Church Lobbying*, 134–135; 170–172. In its lobbying efforts the NCWC made a distinction between direct federal aid for parochial schools, which it was reluctant about, and government aid to support parochial students, which it supported. See Ebersole, *Church Lobbying*, 170–172; Moreno, "Catholic Americanism," 142, 175–176.

83. Ebersole, *Church Lobbying*, 51–53.

84. Ibid.

85. Moreno, "Catholic Americanism," 45; Jo Renée Formicola, "Catholic Jurisprudence on Education," *Everson Revisited*, eds. Jo Renée Formicola and Hubert Morken (Oxford: Rowman and Littlefield Publishers, 1997), 85. See Formicola for a discussion of the legal arguments that the NCWC, under the guidance of John Courtney Murray, offered in *Everson*.

86. Even as Fahy began work on *Zellers* during the summer of 1948, people in high places had their eyes on him. Fahy was compelled to withdraw from the case early in its appellate process when he received an appointment by President Harry Truman to sit on the Court of Appeals for the District of Columbia. He was eventually replaced on the *Zellers* legal team by ex-Connecticut Senator John A. Danaher.

87. "Charles Fahy: A Register of His Papers in the Library of Congress," prepared by Grover Batts (Washington: Manuscript Division, Library of Congress, 2004).

88. Eugene Butler to Howard Carroll, September 25, 1948, NCWC Collection.

89. Byrne to Bishops Metzger and Espelage, March 29, 1948; Espelage to Byrne, March 30, 1948, Archdiocese Collections; George Reed to Mr. Montavon, memorandum, May 12, 1948, NCWC Collection. According to one attorney at work on the case, Barker and Associates "had done very little to prepare our side of the case. The picture was far from a rosy one" (Butler to Carroll, September 25, 1948, NCWC Collection). See also Reed to Butler, October 9, 1948; Reed to Montavon, memorandum, May 13, 1948.

90. Archbishops John T. McNicholas and Howard Carroll to U.S. Bishops, June 30, 1948; Carroll to U.S. Bishops, March 25, 1949, NCWC Collection.

91. The seeds of this transformation had already taken root in the late 1940s, as Murray collaborated with the NCWC's legal department on responses to both *Everson* and *McCollum* (Archbishop John T. McNicholas to Father Wheeler, December 14, 1947, NCWC Collection).

92. *Who's Who in the P.O.A.U.?* (Huntington, IN: Our Sunday Visitor Press, 1951), 3–4.

93. On allegations of Oxnam's Communist affiliations, see Gaustad and Schmidt, *A Religious History of America*, 340.

94. *Who's Who in the P.O.A.U.?*, 21–34.

95. Ibid., 142.

96. Moreno, "Catholic Americanism," 189–191.

97. "Secularism: Statement Issued November 14, 1947 by the Bishops of the United States."

98. Ibid., 1, 4.

99. "The Christian in Action," excerpt (qtd. in "Catholic Bishops Hit Supreme Court," *The New York Times*, November 21, 1948: 1, 63).

100. James E. Harpster, "Religion, Education and the Law," *Marquette Law Review* 36 (1952–53): 26.

101. John Courtney Murray, "Is It Justice?: The School Question Today," *We Hold These Truths: Catholic Reflections on the American Proposition* (New York: Rowman and Littlefield Publishers, 1960), 150.

102. Ibid., 149.

103. Ibid., 151.

104. See Robert Nugent, "The Censoring of John Courtney Murray, Part I," *The Catholic World* 242.1444 (January/February 2008); Ibid., "The Censoring of John Courtney Murray, Part II," *The Catholic World* 242.1445 (March/April 2008).

105. Because reclaiming original intent was not a theological reflection upon Constitutional provisions, it never held the same potential for controversy that Murray's work had. When Murray began to publish his own ideas about church and state, he bypassed this historical approach, which he called "original legislative intent," as insufficient grounds for interpreting the First Amendment. In his essay "Is It Justice?" Murray acknowledges that this interpretive model has come to be equated—albeit erroneously—with the "official position of the Catholic Church in America." He argues that it is an insufficient approach primarily because it does not allow for the model of a living, dynamic constitution necessary for governance in a modern, pluralistic America (Murray, "Is It Justice?,"150).

106. Reed to Montavon, "Genesis of the First Amendment," memorandum, March 17, 1947; Reed to Montavon, "Genesis of the First Amendment," memorandum, October 10, 1947: 6, NCWC Collection. Although the NCWC did not file its own brief in *McCollum*, correspondences suggest that Reed was involved with an amicus curiae brief filed by the Illinois attorney general's office.

107. Reed, "Genesis," October 10, 1947: 3, 14.

108. Ibid., 17.

109. Ibid., 12.

110. NCWC Office of Information, "The Catholic Church in American Democracy," press release, January 26, 1948, NCWC Collection: 3–4. The historical argument presented by Reed and attorneys working on behalf of Catholic interests in the *McCollum* case did carry weight with one member of the Court—in his dissenting opinion, Justice Stanley Forman Reed quoted both James Madison and Thomas Jefferson, and argued that even Jefferson had not intended to exclude religious education from the university he founded. Referring to the Court's invocation of Jefferson's "wall" language, Reed concluded that "a rule of law should not be drawn from a figure of speech" (*McCollum v. Board of Education*, 247).

111. James O'Neill, *Religion and Education Under the Constitution* (New York: Harper and Brothers, 1949), 23.

112. Ibid., 153.

113. Leo Pfeffer, "Church and State: Something Less than Separation," *The University of Chicago Law Review* 19, no. 1 (Autumn 1951): 2–3.

114. Ibid.; James L. Burke "Catholics and the Supreme Court," *Thought* 24, no. 94 (September 1949): 397. See also Conrad Henry Moehlman, *The Wall of Separation Between Church and State* (Boston: Beacon Press, 1951).

115. Conrad Henry Moehlman, untitled review, *Church History* 18, no. 3 (September 1949): 194.

116. Thomas Woody, "Chiefly and Appeal to History," *The Journal of Higher Education* 21, no. 5 (May 1950): 274–275.

117. Charles O. Lerche, Jr., untitled review, *The William and Mary Quarterly* 7, no. 1 (January 1950): 152–153.

118. Moreno, "Catholic Americanism," 185, 195–196. This second book was eventually published as *Catholicism and American Freedom* (New York: Harper and Brothers, 1952).

119. Wilfred Parsons, SJ, *The First Freedom* (New York: McMullen Company, 1948).

120. Carroll to McNicholas, June 3, 1948, NCWC Collection.

121. Parsons, *First Freedom*, iii; Richard J. Purcell to Carroll, September 2, 1948; McManus to Carroll, memorandum, December 5, 1947, NCWC Collection. Purcell's earlier work included studies of Connecticut during the early republic, and of Irish immigrants to America. He has been praised as the "first Irish-American historian to try to put the study of Irish America on the scholarly map, as a valid subject of inquiry." See dedication to Purcell in J. J. Lee and Marion Casey, eds., *Making the Irish American* (New York: New York University Press, 2007), v–vii.

122. Frederick Hochwalt to Francis P. Keough, memorandum, April 18, 1950; John Tracy Ellis to McManus, March 6, 1950, NCWC Collection. Purcell died in 1950, and it is possible his health prohibited him from completing revisions that would have made his project more palatable to its critics.

123. John Tracy Ellis, "American Catholics and the Intellectual Life," *Thought* 30 (Autumn 1955): 351–388.

124. Carroll to Byrne, March 16, 1948, Archdiocese Collections.

125. Reed to Carroll, memorandum, April 5, 1948.

126. Reed to Montavon, memorandum, May 13, 1948: 4; McNicholas and Carroll to U.S. Bishops, June 30, 1948, NCWC Collection.

127. Reed to Byrne, May 12, 1948, Archdiocese Collections.

128. George E. Reed, *The McCollum Case and Your Child* (Washington: Legal Department, National Catholic Welfare Conference, n.d.).

129. Ibid., 9.

130. Ibid., 12–13. Reed expressed concern that *McCollum* might supplant not only *Everson*, but also *Pierce v. Society of Sisters*. On Catholic worry that parochial schools were under threat during this period, see also Clayton LeRoy McNearney, "The Roman Catholic Response to the Writings of Paul Blanshard" (Ph.D. diss., University of Iowa, 1970), 87.

131. Carroll to U.S. Bishops, March 16, 1948, NCWC Collection.

132. Sorauf, *Wall of Separation*, 178–196.

133. Ibid., 178.

134. One notable exception to the general Catholic absence of legal defenses of religious garb during this era came from Jesuit priest and Creighton University professor Virgil Blum. In a 1955 article published in the *University of Chicago Law Review*, Blum laid out his arguments for the permissibility of both sisters' vows and sisters' garb in public schools, under the Constitution's guarantees of religious liberty. His argument in support of sister's habits included three main claims: 1) that an individual has a "personal freedom" to choose her dress, and that this includes opting to follow either the fashion of her times, or the fashion of past times, 2) that a state must detect an "imminent danger" in order to prohibit a particular religious practice, and 3) that no such danger exists with habits, especially because they are statements of existence rather than didactic devices. As Blum explained, "to teach a student *that* something is, is fundamentally different from teaching the student *what* something is . . . it is one thing to know that a person is a Catholic; it is quite another to know the doctrinal truths and beliefs of that particular religious faith" (Blum, "Religious Liberty," 885). Later in life Blum went on to found the Catholic League for Religious and Civil Rights.

135. *Zellers v. Huff*, 49.

136. *Berghorn v. Reorganized School District*. See also Harold H. Punke, "Religious Issues in American Public Education," *Law and Contemporary Problems* 20 (1955): 158–161.

137. *Harfst v. Hoegen*, 22.

138. *Berghorn*, 30. Unlike the *Zellers* case before it, which invoked both federal and state constitutions, the Berghorn case was argued and decided strictly on the grounds of the Missouri state constitution.

139. The court cited the following: "All members of religious orders are subject to the Roman Pontiff as their superior to whom they owe obedience" (Canon 499, Qtd. in *Berghorn*, 23).

140. Ibid., 30.

141. Sorauf, *Wall of Separation*, 32.

142. *Rawlings v. Butler*, 6–7.

143. Butler to Bishop Walsh, April 9, 1954; Reed to Butler, memorandum, February 4, 1953, NCWC Collection.

144. Hochwalt to Superintendents of Diocesan Schools, March 17, 1948, NCWC Collection.

145. "Catholic Public Schools," survey, April 1948, NCWC Collection: 1. The eighty-three respondents represented approximately three quarters of the nations' dioceses; had all of the nation's dioceses responded the number of public–parochial schools reported would undoubtedly have been higher.

146. William Montavon, open memorandum, 16 July 1948, NCWC Collection.

147. Francis Keough to U.S. Bishops, memorandum, February 25, 1948, NCWC Collection.

148. Carroll to U.S. Archbishops, "'Catholic-Public' School Arrangement," memorandum, August 30, 1948, NCWC Collection: 6, 13.

149. Ibid., 16.

150. In addition to its work in New Mexico, Missouri, and Kentucky, the NCWC communicated about Catholic–public schools with Church officials in Indiana, Illinois, Wisconsin, Michigan, Colorado, Iowa, Texas, Idaho, Nebraska, South Dakota, Michigan, Minnesota, Massachusetts, Arkansas, New Hampshire, Ohio, Kansas, and probably other states as well. Many of these officials wrote to the NCWC requesting help with their situations (Miscellaneous correspondence, NCWC Collection).

151. See for example Reed to Butler, memorandum, October 10, 1950; Butler to Walsh, March 3, 1954, NCWC Collection.

152. National Catholic Welfare Conference News Service, September 15, 1952; National Catholic Welfare Conference News Service, August 25, 1952; Reed to Bishop John Tracy, June 6, 1952, NCWC Collection.

153. The Archdiocese of Dubuque reportedly included eleven sister-taught public schools and had much at stake in the status quo. National Catholic Welfare Conference News Service, December 25, 1950; Rev. A. A. Halbach to Hochwalt, December 20, 1950, NCWC Collection.

154. Department of Education, "Catholic Public Schools," memorandum, April 10, 1952, NCWC Collection.

155. "Employment of Nuns as Public School Teachers," memorandum, February 26, 1954, NCWC Collection.

156. Ibid. Most habits of the time included all of these prohibited objects.

Chapter 6

1. "Apparitions at Fatima Are Recounted in Tale About Blessed Virgin," *Santa Fe Register*, July 2, 1948.

2. Leslie Marmon Silko imagines the difficulties of one veteran who returns from the War to the Laguna Pueblo in her classic novel *Ceremony* (Leslie Marmon Silko, *Ceremony*, anniversary edition [New York: Penguin Books, 2006]).

3. Weigle, *Brothers of Light*, 110–111.

4. "Many Protests Raised Against Court Action About School Dispute," *Santa Fe Register*, March 26, 1948.

5. Ibid.

6. L. Hesch, "Requests Tolerance for Catholic Teachers," *Santa Fe New Mexican*, February 23, 1948; Mr. X., "Criticizes Mabry on Dixon Issue," *Santa Fe New Mexican*, March 9, 1948.

7. Edna Garcia interview.

8. Francisco Romero interview.

9. Zellers interview.

10. Lydia Zellers signed an affidavit stating that the original judge, the Honorable David W. Carmody, "cannot preside over said case with impartiality" (Transcript of Record, 81 ["Affidavit of Disqualification"]). This lack of partiality was deduced from the fact that Carmody was facing reelection in a district with a heavily Catholic population. See also George Reed to Howard Carroll, memorandum, May 26, 1948, NCWC Collection.

11. Transcript of Record, 83 ("Order Designating Judge"); "Judge Carmody is Disqualified in Religious Suit," *Santa Fe New Mexican*, May 14, 1948; "Portales Judge Hears Suit," *Santa Fe New Mexican*, n.d., Jones Papers.

12. Reed to Carroll, memorandum, May 26, 1948. The defendants pointed to existing law that included a procedure for hearing challenges to teachers who violated the state's school code. This was one of several motions to dismiss filed by different parties of the defense. See also "Dismissal of Suit Against Nuns Asked by Attorney General," *Santa Fe New Mexican*, April 30, 1948.

13. "Court Hears Pleas to End Dixon Suit," *Santa Fe New Mexican*, June 15, 1948.

14. "Judge Refuses to Dismiss Dixon Suit" *Santa Fe New Mexican*, n.d., Jones Papers; Transcript of Record, 105.

15. Dixon Free Schools Committee to Friends, n.d., Jones Papers.

16. Byrne to Religious, September 18, 1947, Archdiocese Collections.

17. Sr. Claire Marie to Byrne, September 18, 1947, Archdiocese Collections.

18. Barilla interview.

19. Conway interview.

20. Hofstetter, *Franciscan Sisters*, 116.

21. Br. B. Lewis to Byrne, September 22, 1947, Archdiocese Collections.

22. Bradley to Br. B. Lewis, September 24, 1947, Archdiocese Collections.

23. Ibid.

24. Br. B. Lewis to Byrne (with enclosed letter from Las Vegas school board), September 29, 1947; Sr. Cordia to Byrne (with enclosed letter from superintendent of schools, Sandoval

Co.), October 30, 1947; J. Abiguel Maes, Superintendent of Schools, Taos Co., open letter, December 1, 1947, Archdiocese Collections.

25. Br. B. Lewis to Byrne, September 29, 1947, Archdiocese Collections.
26. Judis interview.
27. Conway interview.
28. Sr. Rose of Lima to Bradley, n.d., Archdiocese Archives.
29. Sr. M. Seraphine to Moth. Euphrasia, February 8, 1948, Marywood Archives.
30. Mary Victor to Byrne, July 16, 1948, Archdiocese Collections.
31. Transcript of Testimony, 14 (pretrial hearing); Transcript of Record, 79 ("Motion for Extension of Time").
32. Sr. Claire Marie, Interrogatory, Marywood Archives: 2, 4, 5.
33. Ibid., 1.
34. Transcript of Testimony, 1830.
35. McNicholas and Carroll to U.S. Bishops, June 30, 1948, NCWC Collection.
36. "Answers to Interrogatories, Zellers v. Huff," n.d., NCWC Collection. Speaking privately to one another, NCWC attorneys expressed concern that completed interrogatories might be turned over to the Bureau of Internal Revenue. Several questions pressed sisters on their salaries. Sisters and other religious were exempted from paying income taxes based on the fact that they did not retain personal income from their employment (per their vows of poverty and obedience). Were they to stress this in their answers, however, the attorneys worried it would lend support to plaintiffs' argument that public funds were being paid not to individual teachers, but directly to the Church (Reed to Montavon, memorandum, May 13, 1948, NCWC Collection). Despite this concern, questions relating to sisters' salaries were ultimately dismissed by the court, which deemed the structure of sisters' payments—along with the nature of the vows that obliged them to that structure—irrelevant to the issue on hand—"whether or not sectarianism is being taught in public schools" (Transcript of Testimony, 24–26).
37. Sr. Claire Marie, Interrogatory, 4.
38. "Answers to Interrogatories."
39. Transcript of Testimony, 1835.
40. Ibid., 1841, 1845,
41. Ibid., 1843.
42. Transcript of Record, 93, 97 ("Motion").
43. Sr. Claire Marie, Interrogatory, 2.
44. Transcript of Testimony, 59.
45. Ibid., 58, 59.
46. Ibid., 17–53. The judge dismissed many questions as inadmissible. Questions concerning sisters' habits were preserved.
47. Ibid., 54; Transcript of Record, 152 ("Receipt for Interrogatories by Plaintiffs").
48. Ibid., 153–157.
49. Porfiero Romero interview, 1986.
50. Transcript of Testimony, 1573–1577 (testimony of Paul Stevens).
51. Sr. Pancratia to Bradley, March 7, 1948, Archdiocese Collections.
52. Thomas J. Lynch to William Federici, March 14, 1948; Federici to Lynch, March 18, 1948, Archdiocese Collections.
53. Elizabeth Barilla, group interview, January 13, 2006, Marywood Motherhouse, Grand Rapids, MI.
54. Porfiero Romero interview, 1986.
55. Transcript of Testimony, 1580, 1581 (testimony of Paul Stevens).
56. Conway interview.
57. Transcript of Testimony, 1593 (testimony of Paul Stevens).

58. McDonald to Moth. Euphrasia, March 7, 1948 (Qtd. in *Annals v. III, 1948–1960, pt. 1* [Grand Rapids: Sisters of St. Dominic Congregation of Our Lady of the Sacred Heart, n.d.], Marywood Archives: 94–95).

59. McDonald to Sisters, October 15, 1948, Marywood Archives, 3.

60. Ibid., 3–4.

61. Hofstetter, *Franciscan Sisters*, 116.

62. Ibid., 117.

63. Moth. Beninga to Byrne, June 4, 1948; Moth. Beninga to Byrne, July 14, 1948, Archdiocese Collections.

64. Byrne to Moth. Beninga, July 26, 1948, Archdiocese Collections; Hofstetter, *Franciscan Sisters*, 126.

65. Anonymous, memorandum, August 31, 1948, Archdiocese Collections.

66. According to the community's own history, the Dominicans in Abiquiu had an especially friendly relationship with the village's most famous resident, Georgia O'Keefe. Carmilla Mullay, OP, *A Place of Springs: A History of Dominican Sisters of St. Mary of the Springs, 1830–1970*, n.p., Marywood Archives: 278, 282, 283; "Dominican Sisters Coming to Teach First Six Parochial Grades in Dixon," *Santa Fe Register*, August 6, 1948.

67. Conway interview.

68. Ibid.

69. "Score of Witnesses Called in 'Dixon Case,'" *Santa Fe New Mexican*, September 25, 1948.

70. Ibid.

71. "Grades in Catechism Placed on Report Cards," *Santa Fe New Mexican*, October 4, 1948; "No Church-State Division: Decision Comes Quickly," *Santa Fe New Mexican*, October 8, 1948.

72. "Plaintiff's Counsel Rests in Dixon Case," *Santa Fe New Mexican*, October 6, 1948.

73. "Milne Testifies Albuquerque Rents Church Buildings," *Albuquerque Journal*, October 6, 1948.

74. Clifford Earle, "Fighting for Free Schools," *Presbyterian Life* (December 9, 1950): 11.

75. Moth. M. Victor to Sisters, October 25, 1948, Marywood Archives.

76. McDonald to Sisters, October 15, 1948, Marywood Archives: 1.

77. Ibid., 4.

78. Ibid., 4–5.

79. Ibid., 5.

80. Barilla interview.

81. Transcript of Testimony, 929, 930.

82. "Dixon Trial Recessed Until Next Monday," *Santa Fe New Mexican*, October 1, 1948; "Nun Says Children Want Religion," *Albuquerque Journal*, September 30, 1948.

83. Transcript of Testimony, 930.

84. Transcript of Testimony, 341.

85. The encounter between Jesus and Pontius Pilate occurs in all four canonical Gospels. It is narrated here in the Gospel of Matthew, from the English translation of the Latin vulgate: "And Jesus stood before the governor, and the governor asked him, saying: Art thou the king of the Jews? Jesus saith to him: Thou sayest it. And when he was accused by the chief priests and ancients, he answered nothing" (Matthew 27:11–12) (Holy Bible, *Douay Rheims Version* [Charlotte, NC: St. Benedict Press, 2009]).

86. Transcript of Testimony, 341.

87. Ibid., 345.

88. Ibid., 683–684.

89. Ibid., 684.

90. Ibid., 735–736.

91. Ibid., 736.

92. Ibid., 737.

93. Ibid., 1827–1828.
94. Ibid., 1826.
95. Ibid.
96. Ibid., 1829.
97. "Catholics Coming Out on Top in New Mexico Religious Garb Dispute," *Santa Fe Register*, October 15, 1948; Byrne to Carroll, March 12, 1949, Archdiocese Collections.
98. Fahy to Bradley, October 18, 1948; Bradley to Fahy, October 25, 1948, Archdiocese Collections.
99. Hensley found that in Abiqui, students were taught religion only by sisters not employed by the state, in church-owned buildings, before the beginning of the school day.
100. Tony Thein, "Dixon Ruling Bars 137 Catholic Teachers," *Santa Fe New Mexican*, n.d., Jones Papers.
101. Dixon Free Schools Committee to Friends, March 17, 1949, Jones Papers.
102. Thein, "Dixon Ruling."
103. Petition, October 20, 1948, Archdiocese Collections.
104. Petition signed by residents of Mora, March 28, 1949; Petition signed by residents of Guadalupita, March 30, 1949; Francis Aloys to Byrne, May 9, 1949; Residents of Cuba to State Board, March 28, 1949, Archdiocese Collections.
105. Bradley to Moth. M. Victor, March 13, 1949, copies to Rev. Moth. Edwarda (Nerinx, KY), Rev. Moth. Angelique (San Antonio), Rev. Moth. Alberta (Omaha), Rev. Moth. Reginalda (Denver), Rev. Moth. M. Leonida (Oldenburg, IN); Byrne to Moth. Baptista (Milwaukee), March 29, 1949, Archdiocese Collections.
106. Byrne to Keough, telegram, August 17, 1949, Archdiocese Collections. The only orders that responded to the archbishop's query with a willingness to send replacement teachers were the Sisters of Loretto, the Sisters of Divine Providence, and the Christian Brothers (Byrne to Reed, April 18, 1949, Archdiocese Collections).
107. Reed to Byrne, April 20, 1949, Archdiocese Collections.
108. Byrne to Keough, telegram.
109. Qtd. in *Annals*, 100.
110. Moth. M. Victor to Sisters, March 16, 1949 (cited in *Annals*, 103).
111. Byrne to Reed, April 28, 1949, Archdiocese Collections.
112. Moth. M. Victor to Sr. Joachim, Holy Saturday, 1949, Marywood Archives.
113. *Annals*, 107.
114. Ibid., 109. In 1942, the dioceses of Grand Rapids and Saginaw stipulated that religious communities operating in the diocese were required to pay lay teachers salaries if they could not provide enough sisters to fill teaching jobs in the diocese's schools. During the 1948–49 school year, the Grand Rapids Dominicans paid approximately $30,000 to lay teachers in Michigan (Ibid., 113–114).
115. Residents of Peñasco to Moth. Victor, August 5, 1949 (cited in Ibid., 109).
116. Qtd. in Ibid., 112. Mother Victor kept her word; a new group of Dominicans returned to open a parochial school in Peñasco in the fall of 1950.
117. Ibid.
118. Barilla interview.

Epilogue

1. "Catholics Say 'We've Won!' Despite Hensley Decision," n.p., Marywood Archives. See also "Ruling May Permit Church Dress," *Taos Star*, May 26, 1949.
2. Carroll to Byrne, March 19, 1949, NCWC Collection.
3. Reed to Butler, memorandum, n.d.; Byrne to McNicholas, April 22, 1949, NCWC Collection.
4. Reed to Carroll, memorandum, March 24, 1949, NCWC Collection.
5. Reed to Byrne, May 23, 1949, NCWC Collection.

6. Carroll to U.S. Bishops, March 25, 1949, NCWC Collection. The religious eventually retained John Watson of Santa Fe as local counsel for their cross-appeal. Charles Fahy initially signed on to work on the appeal from Washington, although his judicial appointment soon required him to step aside. The defense's appeal was jointly funded by the Knights of Columbus and the NCWC. See Byrne to Carroll, September 25, 1949, Archdiocese Collections; Byrne to Carroll, April 1, 1949; Carroll to Byrne, telegram, April 19, 1949, NCWC Collection.

7. Dixon Free Schools Committee to Friends, March 17, 1949, Jones Papers.

8. Art Morgan, "New Mexico School Kids Little Affected by Dixon Ruling," *Santa Fe New Mexican*, September 25, 1949.

9. Although the exact number of sisters teaching publicly at the beginning of the 1949 school year is uncertain, a year later William Bradley could identify twenty-nine sisters teaching publicly across six communities (Bradley to Reed, September 27, 1950, Archdiocese Collections).

10. "Protestants Will Appeal Dixon School Suit Ruling," *Santa Fe New Mexican*, September 20, 1949.

11. Dixon Free Schools Committee to Friends, September 26, 1949, Jones Papers. Upon learning of the plaintiffs' appeal, both attorneys for the religious and the attorney general's office (on behalf of the state board of education and budget auditor) filed cross-appeals.

12. Qtd. in *Zellers v. Huff*, 29. The resolution was passed on March 6, 1951. See also "Wearing of Religious Habits by Teachers in Public Schools Banned by New Mexico," *New York Times*, March 8, 1951.

13. Butler to Byrne, February 9, 1951, NCWC Collection; Byrne to Sisters Superior, March 26, 1951, Archdiocese Collections.

14. Both the NCWC in making its recommendation and the state board of education in passing its resolution hoped to create grounds on which the appeal might be dismissed. Attorneys for the religious used the board's resolution to later argue for the appeal's dismissal, contending that it along with the sisters' subsequent departure made the plaintiffs' questions moot (*Zellers v. Huff*, 29).

15. The prevailing policies regarding bus transportation continued in the wake of the supreme court's decision. A survey of parochial schools a few years after the decision found that students were still receiving textbooks from the state but were not permitted to ride to school on public buses (McGee, "Causes and Effects," 122).

16. "Well, We Got the Nuns Out!," cartoon, n.d., Marywood Archives. See also "School Daze," *Santa Fe Catholic Register*, July 16, 1948.

17. "Congregational History of the Sisters of Divine Providence," excerpt, private collection. In Dixon, parents demanded dismissal of the new principal J. E. Roybal, citing charges of obscene writing on walls and toilets and more serious charges of an attempted rape by students. Roybal was affiliated closely with Küppers, and supporters shot back that the accusations were unsubstantiated and politically motivated ("Stirred Dixonites Allege Schoolground Sex Antics," *Taos Star*, March 10, 1949; "Dixon School Embroglio Again Seethes as Group Charges Immorality Among Students, Inefficiency of Teachers; Authorities Are Cleared by Board," *Española Valley News* 12, no. 2).

18. *Miller v. Cooper*, 56 NM 355 (1952). See also "Two on Public School Staff Enjoined from Requiring Religious Services," NCWC News Service, September 19, 1949, NCWC Collection.

19. McGee, "Causes and Effects," 112–113, 120. For a complete account of educational situations in all communities affected by the lawsuit circa 1955, see Ibid., 110–125.

20. "Dixon Students Expected Here," n.p., n.d., Jones Papers; McGee, 115.

21. "The Consolidation of School Districts in the Southern Part of the County," *El Crepesculo*, n.d., Jones Papers; "Peñasco Rents School Unit from Church," *Santa Fe New Mexican*, August 3, 1949; McGee, 113.

22. McGee, "Causes and Effects," 125; "County Schools Hard-Hit by Decision in Dixon Controversy," n.p., March 3, 1949, Jones Papers.

23. McGee, "Causes and Effects," 121. This number trend is substantiated by figures from the *Official Catholic Directory*. According to the OCD, New Mexico had twenty parochial elementary schools in 1948 and forty-seven a decade later (*The Official Catholic Directory* (New York: P. J. Kenedy and Sons, 1948); *The Official Catholic Directory* [New York: P. J. Kenedy and Sons, 1959]).

24. Meyers, *The Education of Sisters*, 26.

25. Ibid., xxiii.

26. On the sister formation movement, see Mary L. Schneider, "American Sisters and the Roots of Change: the 1950s" (*U. S. Catholic Historian* 7.1 (Winter 1988)): 55–72; Marjorie Noterman Beane, *From Framework to Freedom: A History of the Sister Formation Conference* (Lanham, Maryland: University Press of America, 1993).

27. Schneider, "American Sisters," 65–66.

28. Ibid., 64.

29. "Dignitatis Humanae" ("Declaration on Religious Freedom"), December 7, 1965, *Documents of the Second Vatican Council*, Website of the Holy See, http://www.vatican.va/archive/hist_councils/ii_vatican_council/documents/vat-ii_decl_19651207_dignitatis-humanae_en.html (accessed July 6, 2011).

30. Pius XII counseled the First International Congress of Superiors General of Orders and Congregations of Women to "in things that are not essential make the adaptations counseled by reason and well-ordered charity" (qtd. in Kuhn, *The Habit*, 140). For a discussion of sisters' changing attitudes toward the habit at mid-century, see Kuhns, 139–160; Ann Plogsterth, "The Modernization of Roman Catholic Sisters' Habits in the United States in the 1950's and 1960's," *Dress* 1 (1975): 7–15.

31. "Perfectae Caritatis" ("Decree on the Adaptation and Renewal of Religious Life"), October 28, 1965, *Documents of the Second Vatican Council*, Website of the Holy See, http://www.vatican.va/archive/hist_councils/ii_vatican_council/documents/vat-ii_decree_19651028_perfectae-caritatis_en.html (accessed August 20, 2011).

32. On the reception of sisters' new clothing, both among women religious and lay Catholics, see Jean Reidy, CHM, "Nuns in Ordinary Clothes," *American Catholic History: A Documentary Reader*, eds. Mark Massa and Catherine Osborne (New York: New York University Press, 2008): 171–174.

33. In 2001 the groups again joined under the auspices of the United States Conference of Catholic Bishops.

34. Late in his career Reed helped prepare briefs of amicus curiae in several high-profile cases, including some dealing with limitations on abortion rights, and at least one dealing with obscenity censorship. See, for example, *Planned Parenthood of Missouri v. Danforth*, 428 U. S. 52 (1976); *Bellotti v. Baird*, 443 U. S. 622 (1979); *FCC v. Pacifica Foundation*, 438 U. S. 726 (1978).

35. *Engel v. Vitale*; *School District of Abington Township v. Schempp*.

36. For discussion of POAU's fracturing base of support during this era see Gordon, "'Free' Religion and 'Captive' Schools: Protestants, Catholics, and Education, 1945–1965," *DePaul Law Review* 56, no. 4 (Summer 2007), 1210–1219.

37. "LOI n° 2004–228 du 15 mars 2004 encadrant, en application du principe de laïcité, le port de signes ou de tenues manifestant une appartenance religieuse dans les écoles, collèges et lycées publics," *Legifrance: Le Service Public de la Diffusion du Droit*, http://www.legifrance.gouv.fr/WAspad/UnTexteDeJorf?numjo=MENX0400001L (accessed February 10, 2010). In an interesting turn of events, many French Muslim students have opted since the ban to attend Catholic schools, where religious clothing is permitted. According to a 2008 estimate, more than ten percent of Catholic school students in France are now Muslim (Katrin Bennhold, "French Muslims Find Haven in Catholic Schools," *New York Times*, September 30, 2008).

38. The newest ban makes an exception for mosques and other places of religious worship. Yasmine Ryan, "French Court Approves Veil Ban," *Aljazeera*, October 8, 2010, http://english. aljazeera.net/news/europe/2010/10/2010108113056514496.html (accessed November 7, 2010); Steven Erlanger, "Face Veil Issue in France Shifts to Parliament for Debate," *New York Times*, January 10, 2010.
39. The *niqāb* is a variation on the Islamic veil leaving visible only the wearer's eyes; it is often erroneously conflated by non-Muslims with the fully concealing Afghani *burqa*.
40. John R. Bowen, *Why the French Don't Like Headscarves* (Princeton: Princeton University Press, 2007): 4–5. On debates over the Muslim veil in France see also Joan Wallach Scott, *The Politics of the Veil* (Princeton: Princeton University Press, 2010).
41. Qtd. in Erlanger, "Burqa Furor Scrambles French Politics," *New York Times*, August 31, 2009.
42. Qtd. in Ibid.
43. "Belgian lawmakers vote to ban full-face veils in public," *The Washington Post*, April 30, 2010.
44. In his 2007 study John Bowen explains the difference between *laïcité*—the value that grounds France's public objections to religious clothing—and its rough American equivalents of secularism and church–state separation. Because under French Republican principles the social good takes unique precedence, the government reserves authority to negotiate (or grant distance to) organized religions in ways it believes will best achieve this good. Religious freedom in France is freedom *through* the state rather than freedom *from* the state. Unlike American church–state separation, French *laïcité* allows the government to actively support religion within a narrowly defined scope while categorically restricting other religious practices (Bowen, *Why the French*, 11–33).
45. U.S. Department of Education guidelines state that while "students ... have no Federal right to be exempted from religiously-neutral and generally applicable school dress rules . . ., schools may not single out religious attire in general, or attire of a particular religion, for prohibition or regulation." "Religious Expression in Public Schools" (revised May 1998), *Archived Information: U. S. Department of Education*, http://www2.ed.gov/ Speeches/08-1995/religion.html (accessed January 22, 2012). The right of students to wear headscarves was upheld in a 2004 settlement to a lawsuit brought by the Department of Justice against an Oklahoma school board that suspended a girl for wearing her headscarf to school (See "Muslim Student, Oklahoma District settle hijab lawsuit" [*The Associated Press*, May 20, 2004], *First Amendment Center*, http://www.firstamendment-center.org/muslim-student-oklahoma-district-settle-hijab-lawsuit [accessed January 22, 2012]. For a discussion of *Rajinder Singh Cheema, et. al. v. Harold V. Thompson, et al.*, a case involving Sikh children wearing the ceremonial kirpan to school, see Vinay Lal, "Sikh Kirpans in California Schools," *New Spiritual Homes: Religion and Asian Americans*, ed. David Yoo (Honolulu: University of Hawai'i Press, 1999). For other cases involving students' dress, see *Cheema v. Thompson*, 67 F.3d 883 (9th Cir. 1995); *Moshe Menora v. Illinois High School Association*, 683 F.3d 1030 (7th Cir. 1982).
46. Oregon repealed a similar garb law effective as of July 2011. William McCall, "Teachers Still Can't Wear Religious Clothing in 3 States," *USA Today*, September 2, 2009; Betsy Hammond, "Governor signs repeal on teachers' religious dress," April 1, 2010, *OregonLive.com* (website of *The Oregonian*), http://www.oregonlive.com/education/index.ssf/2010/04/ governor_signs_repeal_on_teach.html (accessed June 23, 2010).
47. *United States v. Board of Education for the School District of Philadelphia*. The plaintiff's suit claimed the garb statute was in conflict with Title VII of the 1964 Civil Rights Act, and therefore unenforceable. In reversing a lower court's decision in favor of the plaintiff, the Third Circuit relied upon the U.S. Supreme Court's summary dismissal of a similar case from Oregon (*Cooper v. Eugene School District*). The court concluded that the dismissal, "for want of a substantial federal question," affirmed the lower court's judgment in Cooper in all its particulars—including its determination that free exercise claims were without merit due to the state's compelling interest in maintaining religious neutrality.

48. On rethinking the civil religion model with an emphasis on the visual, see David Morgan, "Reconsidering Civil Religion: The Social Body of Belief," *The Immanent Frame*, January 15, 2010, http://blogs.ssrc.org/tif/2010/01/15/the-social-body-of-belief/ (accessed March 7, 2010). See also Morgan, *The Sacred* Gaze, 220–256.

49. McGee, "Causes and Effects," 113.

50. Delia Garcia interview.

51. Edna Garcia interview.

52. Francisco Romero interview.

53. James Yodice, "Two Churches End an Old Quarrel," *Albuquerque Journal*, May 24, 1999: A1; "Catholics, Presbyterians Mend Rift Dating to 1951," *Albuquerque Tribune*, May 25, 1999: A2.

54. Paul Logan, "Reconciliation Heals Wound," *Albuquerque Journal*, May 23, 1999: 1.

55. Qtd. in Yodice, "Two Churches."

BIBLIOGRAPHY

Archives and Collections

Americans United for Separation of Church and State Records, Public Policy Papers, Department of Rare Books and Special Collections, Princeton University Library (cited as AU Records).

Archives of the Grand Rapids Dominicans, Marywood Motherhouse, Grand Rapids, Michigan (cited as Marywood Archives).

Archives of the Sisters of Divine Providence, Our Lady of the Lake Convent, San Antonio, Texas.

Berghorn v. Reorganized School District No. 8. No. 43258. Legal documents, Missouri State Archives, Jefferson City, Missouri.

Dixon papers. Collections of the Archdiocese of Santa Fe, Santa Fe, New Mexico (cited as Archdiocese Collections).

Jones, Robert Papers. New Mexico State Records Center and Archives, Santa Fe, New Mexico (cited as Jones Papers).

Menaul Historical Library of the Southwest, Menaul School, Albuquerque, New Mexico (cited as Menaul Library).

National Catholic Welfare Conference/United States Catholic Conference Collection. American Catholic History Research Center and University Archives, Catholic University of America, Washington, DC (cited as NCWC Collection).

Palace of the Governors Photo Archives, The New Mexico History Museum. Santa Fe, New Mexico.

Zellers v. Huff. No. 5332. Legal documents on microfilm, Clerk's Office of the Supreme Court of New Mexico, Santa Fe, New Mexico (cited as *Zellers* Documents).

Interviews

Atencio, Margaret. Personal interview, July 19, 2010, Peñasco, New Mexico.

Barilla, Elizabeth, OP (formerly John Evangelist). Personal interview, January 12, 2006, Marywood Motherhouse, Grand Rapids, Michigan.

Barilla, Elizabeth, OP, Carmella Conway, OP and Sr. Donata Judis, OP. Group interview, January 13, 2006, Marywood Motherhouse, Grand Rapids, Michigan.

Conway, Carmella, OP. Personal interview, January 12, 2006, Marywood Motherhouse, Grand Rapids, Michigan.

Cordova, Anna. Personal interview, July 22, 2010, Dixon, New Mexico.

Garcia, Delia. Personal interview, July 22, 2010, Rio Lucio, New Mexico.

Garcia, Edna. Personal interview, July 21, 2010, Dixon, New Mexico.

Gomez, Alfredo. Personal interview, July 19, 2010, Dixon, New Mexico.

Jaramillo, Abelardo. Personal interview, July 20, 2010, Dixon, New Mexico.

Judis, Sr. Donata, OP. Personal interview, January 12, 2006, Marywood Motherhouse, Grand Rapids, Michigan.

Leyba, Lucille. Personal interview, July 22, 2010, Rio Lucio, New Mexico.

Luke, Br. Cyprian, FSC. Personal interview, August 12, 2005, College of Santa Fe, Santa Fe, New Mexico.

Romero, Ann Perpetua, OP. Videotaped interview, undated, Archives of the Grand Rapids Dominicans, Marywood Motherhouse, Grand Rapids, Michigan.

Romero, Francisco. Personal interview, July 20, 2010, Dixon, New Mexico.

Romero, Porfiero. Transcribed interview, 1974, Menaul Historical Library of the Southwest, Menaul School, Albuquerque, New Mexico.

———. Transcribed interview, 1986, Menaul Historical Library of the Southwest, Menaul School, Albuquerque, New Mexico.

Valdez, Ben. Personal interview, July 21, 2010. Dixon, New Mexico.

Zellers, Lydia. Transcribed interview, 1980. Lydia Zellers Information File, Menaul Historical Library of the Southwest, Menaul School, Albuquerque, New Mexico.

Newspapers and Periodicals

Albuquerque Journal
Albuquerque Tribune
Aljazeera
America
Baptist New Mexican
Catholic Digest
Christian Beacon
The Christian Century
Christian Herald
Christian Science Monitor
Church and State
The Churchman
The Converted Catholic Magazine
El Crepúsculo
Española Valley News
General Assembly Daily News
The Humanist
Junior Catholic Messenger
Liberty
The Nation
New Age
New York Times
The Oregonian
Presbyterian Life
Progressive World
Santa Fe New Mexican
Santa Fe (Catholic) Register
The Santa Fean Magazine
Scottish Rite Bulletin
Signs of the Times
Social Progress
Taos Star
Time
Treasure Chest of Fun and Fact
Truth Seeker
USA Today
Washington Post

Court Cases

Berghorn v. Reorganized School District No. 8. 364 Mo. 121 (1953).

Board of Education of the City of Cincinnati v. John D. Minor Et Al. 23 Ohio St. 211 (1872).

Cheema v. Thompson. 67 F.3d 883 (9th Cir. 1995).

Church of the Lukumi Babalu Ayei. City of Hialeah. 508 U.S. 520 (1993).

City of New Haven v. Town of Torrington. 132 Conn. 194 (1945).

Commonwealth v. Herr. 229 Pa. 132 (1910).

Cooper v. Eugene School District. 723 P.2d 298 (Ore. 1986).

Engel v. Vitale. 370 U.S. 421 (1962).

Everson v. Board of Education. 330 U.S 16 (1947).

Gerhardt v. Heid. 66 N.D. 444 (1936).

Harfst v. Hoegen. 349 Mo. 808 (1942).

Hysong v. Gallitzin Borough School District. 164 Pa. 629 (1894).

Johnson v. Boyd. 217 Ind. 348 (1940).

Knowlton v. Baumhover. 182 Iowa 691 (1918).

Kunz v. People of the State of New York. 340 U.S. 290 (1951).

Lemon v. Kurtzman. 403 U.S. 602 (1971).

McCollum v. Board of Education. 333 U.S. 203 (1948).

Miller v. Cooper. 56 N.M. 355 (1952).

Mississippi Employment Security Commission v. McGlothin. 556 So.2d 324 (Miss. 1990).

Moshe Menora v. Illinois High School Association. 683 F.3d 1030 (7th Cir. 1982).

O'Connor v. Hendrick. 184 NY 421 (1906).

Pierce v. Society of Sisters. 268 U.S. 510 (1925).

Rawlings v. Butler. 290 S. W.2d 801 (1956).

School District of Abington Township v. Schempp. 374 U.S. 203 (1963).

State Public School District No. 6 v. Taylor. 122 Neb. 454 (1932).

United States v. Board of Education for the School District of Philadelphia. 911 F.2d 882 (3rd Cir., 1990).

Wooley v. Spalding. 293 S.W.2d 563 (1956).

Zellers v. Huff. 55 N.M. 501 (1951).

Zorach v. Clauson. 343 U.S. 306 (1952).

Other Primary Sources

The 1917 or Pio-Benedictine Code of Canon Law. In English translation. Curator Edward N. Peters. San Francisco: Ignatius Press, 2001.

Archer, Glenn L., and Albert J. Menendez. *The Dream Lives On: The Story of Glenn L. Archer and Americans United.* Washington: Robert B. Luce, Inc., 1982.

Bacon, Frederick Mason. "Contributions of Catholic Religious Orders to Public Education in New Mexico Since the American Occupation." Master's thesis, University of New Mexico, 1947.

Beecher, Lyman. *A Plea for the West.* New York: Leavitt, Lord and Company, 1835.

Blanshard, Paul. *American Freedom and Catholic Power.* Boston: Beacon Press, 1949.

———. *American Freedom and Catholic Power.* Second edition. Boston: Beacon Press, 1958.

———. *Personal and Controversial.* Boston: Beacon Press, 1973.

———. *Religion and the Schools: The Great Controversy.* Boston: Beacon Press, 1963.

Blum, Virgil C. "Religious Liberty and the Religious Garb." *University of Chicago Law Review* 22, no. 4 (Summer 1955): 875–888.

Boettner, Loraine. *Roman Catholicism.* Philadelphia: The Presbyterian and Reformed Publishing Company, 1962.

"Bradfordsville—Ten Years Later." Pamphlet. Washington, DC: Protestants and Other Americans United, 1959.

Burke, James L. "Catholics and the Supreme Court." *Thought* 24, no. 94 (September 1949).

Captured. DVD. Private collection. Washington: Protestants and Others United for Separation of Church and State, 1959.

Charlotte, M., RSM, and Mary Synon, LLD. *These Our Are Freedoms. Book Seven. Catholic University of America's Faith and Freedom Series*. Washington, DC: Ginn and Co., 1944.

"Comments: Church and State in American Education." *Illinois Law Review* 43(1948–9): 374–388.

Committee for Defense of Civil Rights (H.G. Nilles, Chairman). "Facts About Sisters Teaching in Public Schools in North Dakota." Bismarck: The Committee for the Defense of Civil Rights, 1948.

Conroy, Helen. *Forgotten Women (In Convents)*. Second edition. New York: Agora Publishing Company, 1946.

Curriculum Development in the Elementary Schools in New Mexico. Issued by State Superintendent Charles L. Rose. Santa Fe: Santa Fe Publishing Company, 1944.

———. Second and revised edition. Issued by State Superintendent Charles L. Rose. Santa Fe: Santa Fe Publishing Company, 1947.

Dawson, Joseph. *Separate Church and State Now*. New York: Richard R. Smith, 1948.

———. *A Thousand Months to Remember*. Waco: Baylor University Press, 1964.

Dewey, John. *Freedom and Culture*. New York: G.P. Putnam's Sons, 1939.

"Dignitatis Humanae" ("Declaration on Religious Freedom"). December 7, 1965. Online Papal Archive of the Vatican. Website of the Holy See. http://www.vatican.va/archive/hist_councils/ ii_vatican_council/documents/vat-ii_decl_19651207_dignitatis-humanae_en.html (accessed July 6, 2011).

Dominican Sisters. *Curricular Studies: Practical Applications of the Principles of Catholic Education*. New York: Macmillan and Company, 1929.

Elizondo, Virgilio. *Spiritual Writings*. Maryknoll, NY: Orbis Books, 2010.

Ellis, John Tracy. "American Catholics and the Intellectual Life." *Thought* 30 (Autumn 1955): 351–388.

Espinosa, Aurelio. "New Mexico." *The Catholic Encyclopedia*, v. xi. New York: Robert Appleton Company, 1911. http://www.newadvent.org/cathen/11001a.htm (accessed April 13, 2008).

Fey, Harold E. "Catholicism Comes to Middletown." *Christian Century* 61, no. 49 (1944): 1410–1411.

———. *With Sovereign Reverence: The First Twenty-Five Years of Americans United*. Rockville, MD: Roger Williams Press, 1974.

Holy Bible, *Duoay Rheims Version*. Translation of Latin Vulgate. Charlotte, NC: St. Benedict Press, 2009.

Hook, Sidney. "Democracy and Education: Introduction." *The Authoritarian Attempt to Capture Education: Papers from the Second Conference on the Scientific Spirit and Democratic Faith*. New York: King's Crown Press, 1945.

Küppers, Peter. Unpublished memoir. Translated by Tomas Jaehn. Tomas Jaehn, private collection.

Lerche, Charles O., Jr. untitled review. *The William and Mary Quarterly* 7, no. 1 (January 1950): 152–153.

"LOI n° 2004–228 du 15 mars 2004 encadrant, en application du principe de laïcité, le port de signes ou de tenues manifestant une appartenance religieuse dans les écoles, collèges et lycées publics." Legifrance: Le Service Public de la Diffusion du Droit. http://www.legifrance.gouv. fr/WAspad/UnTexteDeJorf?numjo=MENX0400001L (accessed November 5, 2006).

Lowell, C. Stanley. "Captive Schools: An American Tragedy." Pamphlet. Washington, DC: Protestants and Other Americans United, 1959.

———. *Embattled Wall*. Washington: Americans United, 1966.

Luther, Martin. "The Pagan Servitude of the Church." *Martin Luther: Selections from His Writings*. Edited by John Dillenberger. Garden City, NY: Anchor Books, 1961.

Lynd, Robert, and Helen Merrell Lynd. *Middletown: A Study in Modern American Culture*. San Diego: Harcourt, Brace and Company, 1959.

McDonald, Maura, OP. "Contributions of the Dominican Sisters of Grand Rapids, Michigan to Education in New Mexico." Master's thesis, University of New Mexico, 1942.

McGee, Mary Clare, SBS. "The Causes and Effects of the 'Dixon Case.'" Master's thesis, Catholic University of America, 1955.

McGloughlin, Emmitt. *American Culture and Catholic Schools*. New York: L. Stuart Press, 1960.

McGreal, Mary Nona, OP. "The Role of a Teaching Sisterhood in American Education." Ph.D. dissertation, Catholic University of America, 1951.

Mead, Frank S. *On Our Own Doorstep*. New York: Friendship Press, 1948.

———. "Shadows Over Our Schools." *Christian Herald* 71, no. 2 (1948): 1–4.

———. "Shadows Over Our Schools." Pamphlet. Los Angeles, CA: Heritage Manor, 1958.

Meyers, Bertrande, DC. *The Education of Sisters: A Plan for Integrating the Religious, Social, Cultural and Professional Training of Sisters*. New York: Sheed and Ward, 1941.

Moehlman, Conrad Henry. Untitled review. *Church History* 18, no. 3 (September 1949): 194.

———. *The Wall of Separation Between Church and State*. Boston: Beacon Press, 1951.

Monk, Maria. *Awful Disclosures by Maria Monk of the Hotel Dieu Nunnery of Montreal*. New York: Francis F. Ripley, 1836.

Moyers, Robert Arthur. "A History of Education in New Mexico." Ph.D. dissertation, George Peabody College for Teachers, 1941.

Murray, John Courtney. "Is It Justice?" *We Hold These Truths*. New York: Rowman and Littlefield Publishers, 1960.

Nast, Thomas. *Miss Columbia's Public School*. New York: Francis B. Felt & Co., 1871.

New Mexico Historic Documents. Edited by Richard N. Ellis. Albuquerque: University of New Mexico Press, 1975.

O'Brien, John A. *Our New Friends*. Cathedral Basic edition (a revision of William S. Gray and May Hill Arbuthnot, *Our New Friends*). Chicago and New York City: Scott, Foresman and Co., 1942.

The Official Catholic Directory. New York: P.J. Kenedy and Sons, 1948.

The Official Catholic Directory. New York: P.J. Kenedy and Sons, 1959.

O'Neill, James. *Catholicism and American Freedom*. New York: Harper and Brothers, 1952.

———. *Religion and Education Under the Constitution*. New York: Harper and Brothers, 1949.

Pa. Stat. Ann. Tit. 14 11–1112 (1982; originally enacted 1895).

Parsons, Wilfred, SJ. *The First Freedom: Considerations of Church and State in the United States*. New York: McMullen Company, 1948.

"Perfectae caritatis" ("Decree on the Adaptation and Renewal of Religious Life"). October 28, 1965. *Online Papal Archive of the Vatican*. Website of the Holy See. http://www.vatican.va/archive/hist_councils/ii_vatican_council/documents/vat-ii_decree_19651028_perfectae-caritatis_en.html (accessed August 20, 2011).

Pfeffer, Leo. "Church and State: Something Less than Separation." *University of Chicago Law Review* 19 (Autumn 1951): 1–29.

Pfeffer, Leo. *Church, State and Freedom*. Boston: Beacon Press, 1953.

Pius XI. "Divini Illius Magistri." *Online Papal Archive of the Vatican*. Website of the Holy See. http://www.vatican.va/holy_father/pius_xi/encyclicals/documents/hf_p-xi_enc_31121929_divini-illius-magistri_en.html (accessed July 6, 2006).

Punke, Harold H. "Religious Issues in American Public Education." *Law and Contemporary Problems* 20 (1955): 158–161.

Reed, George E. *The McCollum Case and Your Child*. Washington: Legal Department, National Catholic Welfare Conference, n.d.

Reidy, Jean, C.H.M. "Nuns in Ordinary Clothes." *American Catholic History: A Documentary Reader*. Edited by Mark Massa and Catherine Osborne. New York: New York University Press, 2008.

"Religious Garb in the Public Schools: A Study in Conflicting Liberties." *University of Chicago Law Review* 22, no. 4 (Summer 1955): 888–895.

"Religious Expression in Public Schools" (revised May 1998). Archived Information: U.S. Department of Education. http://www2.ed.gov/Speeches/08-1995/religion.html (accessed January 22, 2012).

Sanchez, George. "The Education of Bilinguals in a State School System (1934)." *Education and the Mexican American*. Edited by Carlos E. Cortés. New York: Arno Press, 1974.

———. *Forgotten People*. Albuquerque: Calvin Horn Publisher, 1967.

"Secularism: Statement Issued November 14, 1947 by the Bishops of the United States and Signed in their Names by the Members of the Administrative Board, N.C.W.C." Pamphlet. Washington: National Catholic Welfare Conference, 1947.

Senter, Dorothy, and Florence Hawley. "The Grammar School as the Basic Acculturating Influence for Native New Mexicans." *Social Forces* 24, no. 4 (1946): 398–407.

Shields, Thomas. *Philosophy of Education*. Washington: Catholic Education Press, 1917.

Smith, Mary Joan, and Mary Nona McGreal, OP. *Guiding Growth in Christian Social Living: A Curriculum for the Elementary School*. Washington, DC: Catholic University of America Press, 1944.

Soran, M. Rose Theresa, OL. "Lorretine Educational History in New Mexico." Master's thesis, University of New Mexico, 1949.

"The State and Sectarian Education." *Research Bulletin of the National Education Association* 24, no. 34 (1946): 4–44.

Strong, Josiah. *Our Country*. Edited by Jurgen Herbst. Cambridge: Harvard University Press, 1963.

Toward Better Teaching of Soil and Water Conservation. University of New Mexico Publications in Education, no. 1. Albuquerque: University of New Mexico Press, 1947.

Who's Who in the P.O.A.U.? Huntington, IN: Our Sunday Visitor Press, 1951.

Woody, Thomas. "Chiefly and Appeal to History." *Journal of Higher Education* 21, no. 5 (May 1950): 274–275.

Secondary Sources

Anzaldua, Gloria. *Borderlands/La Frontera: The New Mestiza*. 3rd ed. San Francisco: Aunt Lute Books, 2003.

Atkins, Jane C. "Who Will Educate: The Schooling Question in Territorial New Mexico." Ph.D. dissertation, University of New Mexico, 1982.

Baca, Jacobo. "The Dixon Case, 1947–1951: The End of the Catholic Era in New Mexico Public Education." *La Crónica de Nuevo Mexico* 65 (July 2005): 3–7.

Bastian, Holly M. "Religious Garb Statutes and Title VII: An Uneasy Coexistence." *Georgetown Law Journal* 80 (October 1991): 211–232.

Beane, Marjorie Noterman. *From Framework to Freedom: A History of the Sister Formation Conference*. New York: University Press of America, 1993.

Beasley, Mary. "Pressure Group Persuasion: Protestants and Other Americans United for Separation of Church and State, 1947–1968." Ph.D. dissertation, Purdue University, 1970.

Billington, Ray Allen. *The Protestant Crusade, 1800–1860: A Study of the Origins of American Nativism*. New York: Macmillan, 1938.

Bourdieu, Pierre. *Outline of a Theory of Practice*. Translated by Richard Nice. Cambridge: Cambridge University Press, 1977.

Bowen, John R. *Why the French Don't Like Headscarves*. Princeton: Princeton University Press, 2007.

Bryce, Mary Charles, OSB. "Four Decades of Roman Catholic Innovators." *Enlightening the Next Generation: Catholics and Their Schools, 1830–1980*. Edited by F. Michael Perko. New York: Garland Publishing, Inc., 1988.

Buetow, Harold. *Of Singular Benefit: The Story of Catholic Education in the United States*. New York: The Macmillan Company, 1970.

Byrne, Patricia. "In the Parish But Not of It: Sisters." *Transforming Parish Ministry: The Changing Roles of Catholic Clergy, Laity, and Women Religious*. Edited by Jay P. Dolan, R. Scott Appleby, Patricia Byrne, and Debra Campbell. New York: Crossroad, 1990.

Casanova, Jose. *Public Religions in the Modern World*. Chicago: University of Chicago Press, 1994.

Casey, Shaun. *The Making of a Catholic President: Kennedy v. Nixon, 1960*. New York: Oxford University Press, 2009.

"Charles Fahy: A Register of His Papers in the Library of Congress." Prepared by Grover Batts. Washington: Manuscript Division, Library of Congress, 2004.

Coburn, Carol, and Martha Smith. *Spirited Lives: How Nuns Shaped Catholic Culture and American Life, 1836–1920*. Chapel Hill: University of North Carolina Press, 1999.

Coppa, Frank J. *Controversial Concordats: The Vatican's Relations with Napoleon, Mussolini, and Hitler.* Washington: The Catholic University of America Press, 1999.

Cotter, Elizabeth M. *The General Chapter in a Religious Institute.* Bern, Switzerland: Peter Lang, 2008.

Cover, Robert. "Nomos and Narrative." Forward. *Harvard Law Review* 97 (1983): 4–67.

Cross, Robert. *The Emergence of Liberal Catholicism in America.* Cambridge: Harvard University Press, 1958.

Cummings, Kathleen Sprows. *New Women of the Old Faith: Gender and American Catholicism in the Progressive Era.* Chapel Hill: University of North Carolina Press, 2009.

d'Agostino, Peter. *Rome in America: Transnational Catholic Ideology from the Risorgimento to Fascism.* Chapel Hill: The University of North Carolina Press, 2003.

DelFattore, Joan. *The Fourth R: Conflicts Over Religion in America's Public Schools.* New Haven: Yale University Press, 2004.

Deutsch, Sarah. *No Separate Refuge: Culture, Class and Gender on the Anglo-Hispanic Frontier, 1880–1940.* New York: Oxford University Press, 1987.

Dolan, Jay P. *The American Catholic Experience.* New York: Doubleday & Company, 1985.

Ebersole, Luke Eugene. *Church Lobbying in the Nation's Capital.* New York: Macmillan Company, 1951.

Everett, Diana. "Nativism, Catholicism and Public Education in New Mexico, 1870–1889." Master's thesis, Eastern New Mexico University, 1973.

———. "The Public School Debate in New Mexico, 1850–1891." *Journal of the Southwest* 26.2 (Summer 1984): 107–134.

Ewing, Rodney C. "Memorial of Arthur Montgomery, 1909–1999." *American Mineralogist* 85 (2000): 1848–1850.

Feldberg, Michael. *The Philadelphia Riots of 1844: A Study of Ethnic Conflict.* Westport, Connecticut: Greenwood Press, 1975.

Fessenden, Tracy. *Culture and Redemption: Religion, the Secular and American Literature.* Princeton: Princeton University Press, 2006.

Fitzgerald, Maureen. *Habits of Compassion: Irish Catholic Nuns and the Origins of New York's Welfare System, 1830–1920.* Urbana, IL: University of Illinois Press, 2006.

Formicola, Jo Renée. "Catholic Jurisprudence on Education." *Everson Revisited.* Edited by Jo Renée Formicola and Hubert Morken. Oxford: Rowman and Littlefield Publishers, 1997.

Franchot, Jenny. *Roads to Rome: The Antebellum Encounter with Catholicism.* Berkeley: University of California Press, 1994.

Gallegos, Bernardo P. *Literacy, Education and Society in New Mexico, 1693–1821.* Albuquerque: University of New Mexico Press, 1992.

Gaustad, Edwin, and Leigh Eric Schmidt. *The Religious History of America: The Heart of the American Story from the Colonial Times to Today.* Revised ed. New York: Harper One, 2004.

Geertz, Clifford. "Local Knowledge: Fact and Law in Comparative Perspective." *Local Knowledge: Further Essays in Interpretive Anthropology.* New York: Basic Books Inc., 1983.

Getz, Lynn Marie. *Schools of Their Own: The Education of Hispanos in New Mexico, 1850–1940.* Albuquerque: University of New Mexico Press, 1997.

Goen, C.C. "Baptists and Church-State Issues in the Twentieth Century." *American Baptist Quarterly* 6, no. 4 (1987): 226–253.

Gordon, Sarah Barringer. ""Free" Religion and "Captive" Schools: Protestants, Catholics, and Education, 1945–1965." *DePaul Law Review* 56, no. 4 (Summer 2007): 1177–1220.

———. *The Mormon Question: Polygamy and Constitutional Conflict in Nineteenth-Century America.* Chapel Hill: University of North Carolina Press, 2001.

———. *The Spirit of the Law: Religious Voices and the Constitution in Modern America.* Cambridge, MA: Harvard University Press, 2010.

Grathwold, Linda. "The North Dakota Anti-Garb Law: Constitutional Conflict and Religious Strife." *Great Plains Quarterly* 13, no. 3 (Summer 1993).

Griffith, R. Marie. *God's Daughters.* Berkeley: University of California Press, 1997.

Hall, David. "Introduction." *Lived Religion in America: Toward a History of Practice.* Princeton: Princeton University Press, 1997.

Hamburger, Philip. *Separation of Church and State*. Cambridge: Harvard University Press, 2002.

Higham, John. *Strangers in the Land: Patterns of American Nativism, 1860–1925*. New Brunswick, Rutgers University Press, 1955.

Hofstetter, M. Protasia, FMI. *The History of the Franciscan Sisters of Mary Immaculate in the United States of America, 1932–1992*. Amarillo: Miller National Corporation, 1992.

Horgan, Paul. *Lamy of Santa Fe*. Middletown, Conn.: Wesleyan University Press, 1975.

Hunter, James Davidson. *Culture Wars: The Struggle to Define America*. New York: Basic Books, 1991.

Hyer, Sally. *One House, One Voice, One Heart: Native American Education at the Santa Fe Indian School*. Santa Fe: Museum of New Mexico Press, 1990.

Jaehn, Tomas. "The Priest Who Made Schools Bloom in the Desert." *Seeds of Struggle/Harvest of Faith*. Edited by Thomas J. Steele, SJ, Paul Rhetts, and Barbe Awalt. Albuquerque: LPD Press, 1998.

Katz, E. "Patterns of Compliance with the Schempp Decision." *Journal of Public Law* 14 (1966): 396–408.

Key, David M. "Progressivism and Imperialism in the American Southwest, 1880–1912." Ph.D. dissertation, University of New Mexico, 2005.

Koehlinger, Amy. *The New Nuns: Racial Justice and Religious Reform in the 1960s*. Cambridge: Harvard University Press, 2007.

Krug, Leonard A. "The Wearing of Religious Garb by Public School Teachers." Paper. University of Chicago Law School, 1960.

Kuhns, Elizabeth. *The Habit: A History of the Clothing of Catholic Nuns*. New York: Doubleday, 2003.

Lal, Vinay. "Sikh Kirpans in California Schools." *New Spiritual Homes: Religion and Asian Americans*. Edited by David Yoo. Honolulu: University of Hawai'i Press, 1999.

"Land Grants." New Mexico Commission of Public Records State Records Center and Archives. http://www.nmcpr.state.nm.us/archives/land_grants.htm (accessed September 27, 2007).

Lannie, Vincent P. *Public Money and Parochial Education*. Cleveland: The Case Western Reserve University Press, 1968.

Larson, Robert W. *New Mexico's Quest for Statehood*. Albuquerque: University of New Mexico Press, 1968.

Lazerson, Marvin. "Understanding American Catholic Educational History." *Enlightening the Next Generation: Catholics and Their Schools, 1830–1980*. Edited by F. Michael Perko. New York: Garland Publishing, Inc., 1988.

Lee, J.J., and Marion Casey, ed. *Making the Irish American*. New York: New York University Press, 2007.

Mahmood, Saba. *Politics of Piety*. Princeton: Princeton University Press, 2005.

Manion, Patricia Jean. *Beyond Adobe Walls*. Independence, MO: Two Trails Publishing Press, 2001.

Marsden, George. *The Soul of the American University*. New York: Oxford University Press, 1996.

Martínez y Alire, Jerome J., JCL. "The Influence of the Roman Catholic Church in New Mexico under Mexican Administration, 1821–1848." *Seeds of Struggle, Harvest of Faith*. Edited by Thomas J. Steele, SJ, Paul Rhetts, and Barbe Awalt. Albuquerque: LPD Press, 1998.

Massa, Mark. *Anti-Catholicism in America: The Last Acceptable Prejudice*. New York: Crossroads, 2003.

Mazur, Eric Michael. *The Americanization of Religious Minorities*. Baltimore: Johns Hopkins University Press, 1999.

McGreevy, John. *Catholicism and American Freedom*. New York: W.W. Norton & Co., 2003.

———. *Parish Boundaries: the Catholic Encounter with Race in the Twentieth-Century Urban North*. Chicago: University of Chicago Press, 1996.

McKevitt, Gerald. *Brokers of Culture: Italian Jesuits in the American West, 1848–1919*. Stanford: Stanford University Press, 2007.

McNearney, Clayton LeRoy. "The Roman Catholic Response to the Writings of Paul Blanshard." Ph.D. dissertation, University of Iowa, 1970.

McNeil, Theresa. "Catholic Indian Schools of the Southwest Frontier: Curriculum and Management." *Southern California Quarterly*, 72, no. 4 (1990): 321–328.

Mondragón, John B., and Ernest S. Stapleton. *Public Education in New Mexico*. Albuquerque: University of New Mexico Press, 2005.

Montgomery, Charles H. *The Spanish Redemption: Heritage, Power and Loss on New Mexico's Upper Rio Grande*. Berkeley: University of California Press, 2002.

Moreno, Lisa C. "The National Catholic Welfare Conference and Catholic Americanism, 1919– 1966." PhD dissertation, University of Maryland, 1999.

Morgan, David. "Reconsidering Civil Religion: The Social Body of Belief." *The Immanent Frame*. January 15, 2010. http://blogs.ssrc.org/tif/2010/01/15/the-social-body-of-belief/ (accessed March 7, 2010).

Morgan, David. *The Sacred Gaze: Religious Visual Culture in Theory and Practice*. Berkeley: University of California Press, 2005.

Murphy, John F. "Professional Preparation of Catholic Teachers in the Nineteen Hundreds." *Enlightening the Next Generation: Catholics and Their Schools, 1830–1980*. Edited by F. Michael Perko. New York: Garland Publishing, Inc., 1988.

"Muslim Student, Oklahoma District Settle Hijab Lawsuit" (The Associated Press, May 20, 2004). First Amendment Center. http://www.firstamendmentcenter.org/muslim-student-oklahoma-district-settle-hijab-lawsuit (accessed January 22, 2012).

Nieto-Phillips, John M. *The Language of Blood: The Making of Spanish-American Identity in New Mexico, 1880s–1930s*. Albuquerque: University of New Mexico Press, 2004.

Nostrand, Richard. *The Hispano Homeland*. Norman: University of Oklahoma Press, 1992.

Nugent, Robert. "The Censoring of John Courtney Murray, Part I." *The Catholic World* 242.1444 (January/February 2008).

———. "The Censoring of John Courtney Murray, Part II." *The Catholic World* 242.1445 (March/April 2008).

Oates, Mary. "The Professional Preparation of Parochial School Teachers, 1870–1940." *Historical Journal of Massachusetts* 12, no. 1 (1984): 60–72.

Orsi, Robert A. "Material Children: Making God's Presence Real for Catholic Boys and Girls and for the Adults in Relation to Them." *Between Heaven and Earth: The Religious Worlds People Make and the Scholars Who Study Them*. Princeton: Princeton University Press, 2005.

———. "Snakes Alive: Resituating the Moral in the Study of Religion." *In Face of the facts: Moral Inquiry in American Scholarship*. Edited by Richard Wightman Fox and Robert B. Westbrook. New York: Cambridge University Press, 1998.

O'Toole, James. *The Faithful: A History of Catholics in America*. Cambridge: Harvard University Press, 2008.

Owens, M. Lilliana, SL. *Jesuit Beginnings in New Mexico, 1867–1882*. El Paso: Revista Católica Press, 1950.

Peters, Shawn Francis. *Judging Jehovah's Witnesses: Religious Persecution and the Dawn of the Rights Revolution*. Lawrence, Kans.: University Press of Kansas, 2000.

———. *The Yoder Case: Religious Freedom, Education and Parental Rights*. Lawrence, Kans.: University Press of Kansas, 2003.

Plogsterth, Ann. "The Modernization of Roman Catholic Sisters' Habits in the United States in the 1950's and 1960's." *Dress* 1 (1975): 7–15.

Quinonez, Lora Ann, and Mary Daniel Turner. *The Transformation of American Catholic Sisters*. Philadelphia: Temple University Press, 1993.

Rapagnani, Phyllis Burch. "A Tradition of Service: Roman Catholic Sisters in New Mexico." Master's thesis, University of New Mexico, 1988.

Reilly, Daniel F. *The School Controversy (1891–1893)*. Washington: The Catholic University of America Press, 1943.

Reutter, E. Edmund. "Teacher's Religious Dress: A Century of Litigation." *West's Education Law Reporter* 70 (January 1992): 747–761.

Reyhner, Jon, and Jeannne Eder. *American Indian Education.* Norman, Okla.: University of Oklahoma Press, 2004.

Romero, Juan. "Begetting the Mexican American: Padre Martinez and the 1847 Rebellion." *Seeds of Struggle, Harvest of Faith.* Edited by Thomas J. Steele, SJ, Paul Rhetts, and Barbe Awalt. Albuquerque: LPD Press, 1998.

Ronan, Marian. "Danger and Longing: Roman Catholic Nuns in American Culture." *Religious Studies Review* 30, no. 1 (January 2004): 13–21.

Rouse, Carolyn. *Engaged Surrender: African American Women and Islam.* Berkeley: University of California Press, 2004.

Russell, Hal. *Land of Enchantment: Memoirs of Marian Russell Along the Santa Fe Trail.* Edited by Garnet M. Brayer. Evanston, IL: The Branding Iron Press, 1954.

Schneider, Mary I., OSF. "American Sisters and the Roots of Change: the 1950s." *U.S. Catholic Historian* 7.1 (Winter 1988): 55–72.

Schwind, Mona, OP. *Period Pieces: An Account of the Grand Rapids Dominicans, 1853–1966.* Grand Rapids, Mich.: West Michigan Printing, 1991.

Scott, Joan Wallach. *The Politics of the Veil.* Princeton, NJ: Princeton University Press, 2010.

Silko, Leslie Marmon. *Ceremony.* Anniversary edition. New York: Penguin Books, 2006.

Smith, Anthony Burke. "America's Favorite Priest." *Catholics in the Movies.* Ed. Colleen McDannell. New York: Oxford University Press, 2007.

Smith, Christian, ed. *The Secular Revolution: Power, Interests and Conflict in the Secularization of American Public Life.* Berkeley: University of California Press, 2003.

Sorauf, Frank J. *The Wall of Separation: The Constitutional Politics of Church and State.* Princeton: Princeton University Press, 1976.

Sullivan, Rebecca. *Visual Habits: Nuns, Feminism, and American Postwar Popular Culture.* Toronto: University of Toronto Press, 2005.

Szasz, Margaret. *Education and the American Indian.* Albuquerque: University of New Mexico Press, 1974.

Torrez, Robert J. "New Mexico's Spanish and Mexican Land Grants." New Mexican Genealogical Society. http://www.nmgs.org/artlandgrnts.htm (accessed September 27, 2007).

Treviño, Roberto R. "Facing Jim Crow: Catholic Sisters and the 'Mexican Problem' in Texas." *Western Historical Quarterly* 34, no. 2 (2003).

Van Nuys, Frank. *Americanizing the West: Race, Immigrants and Citizenship, 1890–1930.* Lawrence, Kans.: University of Kansas Press, 2002.

Walch, Timothy. *Parish School: American Catholic Parochial Education from Colonial Times to the Present.* New York: Crossroad Publishing Company, 1996.

Walker, Randi Jones. "Protestantism in Modern New Mexico." *Religion in Modern New Mexico.* Edited by Ferenc Szasz and Richard Etulain. Albuquerque: University of New Mexico Press, 1997.

Warr, Cordelia. "Religious Habits and Visual Propaganda: The Vision of Blessed Reginald of Orléans." *Journal of Medieval History* 28, no. 1 (March 2002): 43–72.

Weber, David. *The Mexican Frontier, 1821–1846.* Albuquerque: University of New Mexico Press, 1982.

———. *The Spanish Frontier in North America.* New Haven: Yale University Press, 1992.

Weigle, Marta. *Brothers of Light, Brothers of Blood: The Penitentes of the Southwest.* Santa Fe: Ancient City Press, 1976.

———, ed. *Hispanic Villages of Northern New Mexico: A Reprint of the Volume II of the 1935 Tewa Basin Study.* Santa Fe: The Lightning Tree Press, 1975.

Welter, Barbara. "From Maria Monk to Paul Blanshard: A Century of Protestant Anti-Catholicism." *Uncivil Religion: Interreligious Hostility in America.* Eds. Robert Bellah and Frederick Greenspahn. New York: Crossroad Publishing, 1987.

Wiley, Tom. *Public Education in New Mexico*. Albuquerque: Division of Government Research, University of New Mexico, 1965.

Wright, Robert E., OMI. "How Many Are 'A Few'?: Catholic Clergy in Central and Northern New Mexico, 1780–1851." *Seeds of Struggle, Harvest of Faith*. Edited by Thomas J. Steele, SJ, Paul Rhetts, and Barbe Awalt. Albuquerque: LPD Press, 1998.

Yohn, Susan M. *A Contest of Faiths*. Ithaca: Cornell University Press, 1995.

INDEX